# TOO FEW WOMEN AT THE TOP

# TOO FEW WOMEN AT THE TOP

The Persistence of Inequality in Japan

**Kumiko Nemoto**

ILR PRESS

AN IMPRINT OF

CORNELL UNIVERSITY PRESS

ITHACA AND LONDON

First published 2016 by Cornell University Press

Printed in the United States of America

Library of Congress Cataloging-in-Publication Data

Names: Nemoto, Kumiko, 1970– author.
Title: Too few women at the top : the persistence of inequality in Japan / Kumiko Nemoto.
Description: Ithaca : ILR Press, an imprint of Cornell University Press, 2016. | Includes bibliographical references and index.
Identifiers: LCCN 2016010766 | ISBN 9781501702488 (cloth : alk. paper)
Subjects: LCSH: Sex discrimination in employment—Japan. | Sex role in the work environment—Japan. | Sex discrimination against women—Japan. | Women—Employment—Japan.
Classification: LCC HD6060.5.J3 N46 2016 | DDC 331.4/1330952—dc23
LC record available at http://lccn.loc.gov/2016010766

Cornell University Press strives to use environmentally responsible suppliers and materials to the fullest extent possible in the publishing of its books. Such materials include vegetable-based, low-VOC inks and acid-free papers that are recycled, totally chlorine-free, or partly composed of nonwood fibers. For further information, visit our website at www.cornellpress.cornell.edu.

Cloth printing              10   9   8   7   6   5   4   3   2   1

# Contents

# Acknowledgments

For this book, I interviewed a large number of people at five Japanese companies. I am grateful to the many people who helped to coordinate my interviews and also to those who took time to talk with me about their various experiences in the companies. I would like to thank all of those individuals who kindly and generously assisted me in my fieldwork.

The research I conducted for the book was supported by funding from many sources. I was able to spend 2010 to 2011 in Tokyo as a Japan Society for the Promotion of Science postdoctoral fellow at Hitotsubashi University. Colleagues and staff helped make my time in Tokyo productive. I would like to express my sincere thanks to the following faculty members at Hitotsubashi University—Tetsuro Kato, Kimiko Kimoto, Daiji Kawaguchi—for their warm support and valuable suggestions. I also received a Japan Center for Economic Research Grant in 2011. The Japan Studies Grant of the Association for Asian Studies enabled me to conduct research on court cases on sex discrimination in Japan. I thank the members of the Working Women's Network in Japan for providing me with many opportunities to attend lectures and various events regarding sex-discrimination court cases. I would like to thank Tak Ozaki and the excellent staff at the Social Science Research Council Abe Fellowship, who offered me helpful suggestions and an opportunity to speak at the Tokyo office. I am also grateful to those who extended opportunities for me to speak at Florida International University; Temple University, Japan Campus; and the University of California, Berkeley. Research funding from Western Kentucky University made possible my research trips from fall 2007 to spring 2014. In particular, I would like to thank Doug Smith, the chair of the Department of Sociology, for his generous support of this research and his offer of course reductions. I thank Vicki Armstrong, who took care of the countless receipts from the trips between Tokyo and Bowling Green. I also thank Kyoto University of Foreign Studies for its generous and kind support.

I express sincere thanks to my mentor, Christine Williams, for consistently taking time to provide inspiring suggestions and generous help to facilitate my research and writing. I have learned much from her critical and constructive comments on my work. I also thank Paula England, who took time to read some parts of this book early on and provided insightful and helpful comments. I am indebted to Heidi Gottfried for her kind reading of the entire manuscript and for offering constructive and important comments for the revisions. I am very grateful to my editor at ILR Press, Fran Benson, for her patience and encouragement. I thank the anonymous reviewer who took time to read the manuscript and provided me with important suggestions. In addition, Lynne Chapman and Sandra Spicher provided wonderful editorial assistance with the manuscript. I would also like to thank the following colleagues and friends for their warm help, encouragement, and insightful suggestions: Yoko Yamamoto, Sanae Ono, Hiroyuki Matsushita, Yoko Matsukawa, Miwako Mogi, Keiko Kaizuma, Matthew Marr, Naoko Komura, Susan Holloway, Ayumi Ito, Arthur Sakamoto, Karen Pyke, Tadayuki Murasato, Tatsuhiro Shimada, Naoko Shimada, and Makiko Nakayama.

Two tables in chapter 3 and some parts of chapter 6 previously appeared in my article "Long Work Hours and the Corporate Gender Divide in Japan" in *Gender, Work and Organization* 25 (2013) from John Wiley & Sons Ltd. Chapter 7 was previously published in substantially similar form as "Sexual Harassment and Gendered Organizational Culture in Japanese Firms" in *Gender and Sexuality in the Workplace* (Research in the Sociology of Work 20), 2010, Emerald Group Publishing Ltd. I acknowledge the permission granted by the publishers.

Finally, I would like to thank my mother for her love and support. Our chats over meals in Tokyo have always been a great source of enjoyment for me, and her humor, courage, and insights have given me a tremendous sense of support in my life.

# TOO FEW WOMEN
# AT THE TOP

# SEX SEGREGATION IN JAPANESE BUSINESS

The question of why Japan has only a small number of women with power and authority—and of how Japan might catch up with the United States and other Western countries in terms of social and economic status for employed women—is long overdue to be answered in the eyes of many feminist researchers and Japanese studies scholars.

Although the number of educated women in Japan has rapidly increased in the last few decades, there has been little change in women's economic status; this may further exacerbate the problems of the country's already declining birthrate and labor shortage, which may eventually lead to its economic decline. Foreign media have long reported on the plight of employed women in Japan and have often underscored the nation's need to modernize gender norms. Japan does appear to be progressing with the idea that the inclusion of women is vital for Japan's economic growth. Prime Minister Shinzō Abe stated in 2014 that women's social and economic advancement is necessary for the nation's future economic growth, as he urged the business and public sectors to increase the ratio of women managers and leaders to 30 percent by 2020. The Japanese business federation Keidanren, comprising over thirteen hundred companies, responded to the government by proclaiming that each firm should make voluntary efforts toward improving women's status to assure sustainable development of the Japanese economy.[1] Yet actual progress on overhauling sex-segregated employment and traditional workplace customs in Japan is slow. Why are there so few women in positions of authority and leadership in Japan? What prevents women from reaching the top?

Sex segregation is the major indicator of gender inequality in employment and work. Vertical segregation means that women are concentrated at the lower end of the employment hierarchy, and horizontal segregation refers to women's concentration in traditionally female jobs.[2] Mary Brinton has pointed out that Japan has higher levels of vertical sex segregation and slightly less occupational, or horizontal, sex segregation than the United States.[3] In particular, Japan has high vertical sex segregation in professional and managerial jobs, which is strongly shaped by an age hierarchy, a major characteristic of Japanese management.[4] Maria Charles and David Grusky agree that Japan's high level of vertical segregation is striking and that it is strongly correlated with age, yet they suggest that Japan may eventually catch up with the rest of the industrialized world in gender equality.[5] These scholars' studies also indicate that Japan's vertical sex segregation could be the result of Japanese companies' customs of lifelong employment, age-based promotions and pay, and related organizational and labor customs. Yet little systematic empirical research has been done on exactly how sex segregation in Japanese companies continues to be shaped by this set of employment customs.

In theory, modernization, democratization, and globalization have led to a gender equality imperative in most advanced countries, which have adopted egalitarian policies that promote the participation of women in the labor force in order to reconcile work and family life; the goal is to modify the male-breadwinner model and move closer to an egalitarian dual-earner model.[6] Thus, vertical sex segregation in most advanced countries is seen as having lost its legitimacy. Sex segregation has declined primarily because of (1) attitudinal changes toward gender roles, (2) an increase in female labor force participation, and (3) a decrease in the gender gap in educational attainment.[7] Legislation against explicit discrimination and more family-friendly policies have also contributed to the lessening of blatant discrimination. Charles and Grusky report that the idea that men are more competent or better suited than women to traditionally male jobs, such as professional management,[8] has increasingly withered in advanced countries.[9]

In general, the growth of women's education means a corresponding rise in women's value as human capital, career prospects, and earnings potential, thus pointing to an overall increase in women's economic autonomy and contribution to household earnings within a country.[10] Women with education are more likely to be better employed than those with less education in high- and middle-income countries.[11] Education (as a form of human capital) also makes women more attractive in the labor market and promotes their aspirations for economic independence. Paula England, Janet Gornick, and Emily F. Shafer write that "education inculcates gender-egalitarian attitudes; thus, highly educated women are expected to have higher employment levels for this ideological reason as well."[12] When the increased number of educated women promotes a corresponding increase in the skilled-labor supply and in egalitarian attitudes, it leads to decreased sex segregation.

Charles also points out that even though vertical sex segregation and blatant forms of sex discrimination have diminished in most advanced countries, and access to education and labor markets are more equalized in these countries, sex segregation in certain countries continues to be seen as legitimate.[13] Indeed, regardless of its modern institutions and the rise of women's education, gender inequality and vertical sex segregation have changed little in Japan. Japan has been the second-largest economy in the world for a long time, following the United States, but it remains one of the most gender-unequal countries. In 2013, Japan ranked 105th of 136 countries in the Global Gender Gap Report, in which the top countries are Scandinavian (Iceland, Finland, Norway, and Sweden). The United Kingdom ranked 18th and the United States, 23rd.[14] Japan's low ranking is attributable to its extremely small number of female lawmakers and business executives, evidence of high sex segregation in Japanese politics and in its economy.[15] Vertical sex segregation in the workplace, where few women hold positions of authority and most are concentrated on the lower rungs of the corporate ladder, remains the major characteristic of gender inequality in Japan. Only 10 percent of Japan's managers are women, far behind the United States and the United Kingdom, where women make up, respectively, 43 percent and 35 percent of managers.[16]

In terms of education, women's college enrollment rate in Japan soared from 12 percent in 1980 to 32 percent in 2000, and further to 46 percent in 2012.[17] However, the rate of women middle managers (*bucho*) has only increased from 1 percent in 1989 to 5 percent in 2011, while the rate of women managers at the lower level (*kakaricho*) increased from 5 percent in 1989 to only 15 percent in 2011. Because there has been relatively little increase in the number of women managers in Japanese companies despite the rapid increase in women's education, it is likely that further growth in women's education in Japan will not greatly affect the number of women managers.

The fact that there are few women in positions of authority—high vertical sex segregation—in Japan has often been explained as being a result of the country's institutional and ideological embrace of traditional gender norms. Belief in the male-breadwinner model continues to dominate the mindset of ordinary Japanese people, and family formation and government tax and pension policies have reinforced it. The typical Japanese family's welfare has long relied on its close connection with Japanese companies. A company's lifelong-employment system and its guarantee of economic security for a man, with the assumption that women will care for the family, have saved the government considerable welfare expenditure and propelled economic development in postwar Japan.[18] Past research on Japan has indicated that the ideology of gendered separate spheres has long provided justification for the corporate relegation of women to assistant positions in the workplace with limited opportunities; women have been expected to quit their jobs when they marry and thus were given mostly easy tasks and biased evaluations.[19] Others have pointed out that the workplace customs of lifelong employment and seniority pay and promotion in Japanese companies work against women, since the point of lifelong employment is that those who work longest are rewarded the most.[20] Business scholars have also pointed out Japanese management's exclusion of women and normalization of women's low status.[21] However, systematic studies have not yet been done on how each custom under the lifelong-employment system—including seniority pay and promotion, gender-based hiring, long working hours, and gender biases— hampers women's work prospects and, most important, leads to the high level of vertical sex segregation in Japan.

Women's marginal employment status has been the default in postwar Japan and has been at the nexus of Japan's institutional relations among the state, business and labor market, and family; thus, changing those things that have inhibited women's status will require changes in all of these other realms. When I argue that the low status of women has operated economically and ideologically as part of the Japanese protection-based employment system, I mean not only that part-time employed women and temporary women workers have enabled companies to save on labor costs,[22] but also that the logic of corporate cost saving has been inherent in the customs of hiring, pay, and promotion and has reinforced workplace stereotypes, which, therefore, continue to block women's chances to draw even with men. Reducing vertical sex segregation in Japanese companies will be difficult without changing this traditional logic by revitalizing the labor market, making rigorous use of performance-based pay and promotion over simple age-based seniority, and instituting affirmative action–type policies and gender-equality training. Without these changes, women in Japanese companies will likely continue to be relegated to low-paying jobs or simply expected to follow the patriarchal work pattern and face discrimination.

Gender inequality in Japan reminds us of Herbert J. Gans's popular sociological argument that poverty in America serves a latent function.[23] Gans argued that poverty does not wane because it serves the purposes of the affluent. He even provides a list of thirteen benefits to poverty in America. For example, the existence of poverty generates a labor pool that is willing to perform the dirty work that members of the affluent groups refuse to do. The poor also need assistance from psychiatrists, social workers, and police officers; thus, their presence generates a large number of jobs for these professionals.

They even consume expired food when it becomes available at cheaper prices. In an ideological sense, the poor also allow those in the middle class and the fortunate to feel better about themselves by reminding them of their Protestant work ethic and belief in individual achievement. Thus, they will remain where they are, at the bottom of society. According to Gans, poverty persists not just because it fulfills a number of functions but also because many of the alternatives to poverty would create dysfunction for the affluent and powerful members of society:

> Many of the functions served by the poor could be replaced if poverty were eliminated, but almost always at higher costs to others, particularly more affluent others. Consequently, a functional analysis must conclude that poverty persists not only because it fulfills a number of positive functions but also because many of the functional alternatives to poverty would be quite dysfunctional for the affluent members of society . . . social phenomena like poverty can be eliminated only when they become dysfunctional for the affluent or powerful, or when the powerless can obtain enough power to change society.[24]

Similarly, having women available as cheap labor at the bottom of the workplace heap has been functional not only for Japanese business, which can then save on labor costs, but also to the Japanese state, because having a caretaker at home has saved on welfare costs, secured men's employment, and contributed to Japan's economic development. There is little incentive to change women's status, similar to that of the poor in the United States, as long as the alternatives are expensive and dysfunctional to business management. The logic of the function of vertical sex segregation itself is nothing new. But just as the poor in the United States have been blamed for their status and their lack of power has been legitimized, women's low status has been tactfully legitimized in Japan. In this book I examine not so much how women's concentration at the bottom has been functional to the Japanese system but how Japanese companies' hiring, salary, and promotion practices and culture of misogyny have locked so many women out and allowed only a very small number of women, in the guise of honorary men, to go up the ladder.

Japan's corporate governance and management systems have also been driven and legitimized by the nation's determination to not only survive but thrive economically and its unstated goal of catching up with the West. Japan has long normalized the values of individual sacrifice, economic development and material wealth, and conformity to the state-led business system, and it has protected the economic security of men over that of women. It is not surprising, then, that Japan's business-state system (the core of Japanese capitalism) has normalized the dismissal of improvements to civil life in Japan, including the achievement of gender equality and family-work balance for its citizens.

In Japanese companies, gender bias is deeply embedded in the organizational customs associated with the system of lifelong employment—such as hiring, seniority pay and promotion, long working hours, and stereotyping—and correction of gender imbalance in these customs would require significant changes to employment and labor market practices in Japan. The case of Japanese companies shows that spontaneous desegregation of the employment systems in advanced countries, even when women are highly educated and some legal protections are included, is unlikely to occur. Even with the introduction of government-led interventions and the emulation of Western policies aimed at achieving gender equality, certain Japanese management customs are likely to continue to block egalitarian reforms in Japan. In my view changes to gender inequality must occur not just through understanding the institutionalized gender biases in traditional Japanese companies but also through active efforts to desegregate through employment and labor market reforms.

## Japan's Protection-Based Management and Coordinated Capitalism

The Japanese business system is characterized by its intimate institutional ties with the state. Japan's business-state ties have promoted the male-breadwinner regime. The ideology of the traditional division between the genders has permeated the culture and has been normalized in the realms of work, family, labor markets, and politics.

Japan's business system prioritizes the lifelong employment of male workers in order to sustain the family that is based on having a male breadwinner and to keep industrial relations stable and management insider oriented. Firms value individual workers' development of "in-firm" skills over skills that are not firm related, and there is little mobility and competition in the labor market. The term "Japanese management" usually refers to a set of customs, including lifelong employment and seniority-based pay and promotion policies, that guarantee an employee job security and family benefits. Workers do not change employers or companies but may change jobs inside a firm; this is what is referred to as the "internal labor market." An employee's long-term economic security is enabled by his company's intimate ties with and dependence on a large bank. The employer's reliance on bank financing enables the company to focus on long-term profits rather than short-term profits and competition. Under the lifelong-employment system, employers do not or cannot lay off workers even to save money, yet they may resort to offering early retirement to workers or terminating new hires, as well as hiring temporary staff. Lifelong employment is associated with the traditional male-breadwinner type of family, with the assumption of the man's lifelong devotion to the company and the woman's full responsibility for the family. Tax and pension policies in Japan have also explicitly favored male-breadwinner households. In contrast, US corporate governance and business management are based on competition and short-term profits, and their cost-saving strategies mostly rely on laying off employees. In addition, the custom of changing jobs and employers makes the US labor market diverse and competitive.

Scholars of the varieties of capitalism confirm that Japan's version differs dramatically from that of the United States. Japanese corporate governance practices are known as "coordinated market economies,"[25] or "coordinated capitalism,"[26] while those nations following the Anglo-Saxon model, such as the United States, are called "liberal market economies." Peter Hall and David Soskice divide developed countries into two groups depending on the countries' industrial relations, type of corporate governance, interfirm relations, employment relations, and the role of training and education in the labor market. They place Japan among the coordinated market economies along with countries such as Germany, Switzerland, the Netherlands, Belgium, Sweden, Norway, and Denmark.[27] Like these other coordinated market economies, Japan has a highly protective employment structure, a closed labor market, and close ties between business and the state. Japanese capitalism differs from that found in the United States and other liberal market countries in the high levels of complementarities in its business systems, especially firms' close ties with large banks that, through financial support, stabilize the firms' management and relations with other firms. This also enables lifelong employment for the employees of a firm, who, in return, are expected to show their gratitude in the form of devotion and loyalty to the company. Although in the United States and other liberal market economies shareholders pressure corporations to generate short-term profits, stakeholders such as financial institutions in Japan presumably focus on long-term goals, and this stakeholder protection enables firms to avoid market competition and pressures. In short, the close relationship in Japan among the state, the business sector, and the welfare system are different from such relationships in the United States. In the postwar decades, by providing economic security to employees and their families, Japanese firms have served as the central welfare agent and reduced the state's burden of welfare costs.

Workers in large Japanese companies rarely change employers because of the lifelong-employment system, so there is little mobility in the labor market. The lifelong-employment system serves to strengthen long-term group consciousness, as it rewards trustful relations among workers, insider-oriented decision making, and age-based promotions.[28] Bringing outsiders into a company would be considered a disruption to the hierarchy of the firm.[29] Lifelong employment saves the government from having to pay for unemployment insurance for laid-off workers; the government, in turn, offers the firms some advantages, including reduced competition.[30] But this system, while ensuring the economic security of male workers and their families, has been costly to firms because they cannot fire workers and must therefore seek other forms of corporate cost savings, such as paying low salaries to young workers and women, requesting that employees take early retirement, relocating workers, and mandating long work hours. Some argue that the lifelong-employment system should be abolished or limited to a smaller number of workers because of its inefficiency.

Lifelong employment is a complementary protective system (based on close corporate-government ties) that can enable firms to avoid economic risks and uncertainties in the market and maintain stable corporate and industrial relations.[31] However, the system's emphasis on insider networks, workers' minimal mobility in the labor market, and the lack of individual competition for promotions and pay increases, which are solely based on workers' ages, lower worker motivation and reduce business and organizational innovation while keeping authority and control on the side of management.[32] Japan's coordinated system has been criticized as having hampered economic growth as well as business innovation and individual creativity.[33] Despite these claims, however, the relationships that business has with the government and banks—and those between business and labor—have changed little. Regardless of criticism of their methods, Japan's system of business management and the Japanese labor market have undertaken few changes, simply because substantial transformations would be costly and would potentially destabilize the close relations among businesses, the state, industry, and employees. Steven Vogel explains that the major actors in Japanese capitalism, including the firms, banks, and unions, rely on such institutions and traditions as lifetime employment, main bank relations, and interfirm networks to reduce their transaction costs, and firms will not abandon their customary relations with the other actors under a system of coordinated capitalism unless they can count on obtaining greater efficiencies that outweigh the costs of sacrificing the current benefits.[34] It can be difficult to change only one part of the system without disturbing the equilibrium of the entire system. Masahiko Aoki writes:

> The presence of institutional complementarities certainly means that it is difficult to change only one piece of a coherent arrangement. But if shifts . . . become significant enough to cause substantial strategic adaptations by the agents in some domain, then overall institutional

arrangements may become subject to a test because of complementary relationships across the domains. . . . Institutional complementarities thus never imply that existing institutional arrangements are frozen nor remain inertial. It implies that the process of change is initially conditioned by existing complementary relationships and cannot be arbitrarily designed and enforced by law.[35]

Even though Aoki indicates that the system of Japanese business customs as a critical part of the Japanese business-state complementary system is not likely to change rapidly, he also adds that some companies are modifying traditional management customs and that institutional equilibrium among corporations, labor, and the state has also been slowly shifting and rebalancing. Yet it is likely that desegregation, or reducing the gender imbalance that exists under Japanese management, will be difficult precisely because sex segregation has been functional as a cost saver to business and the government in Japan.

The question asked by many business scholars who research Japanese companies is whether Japanese coordinated capitalism is ever likely to evolve into US-type liberal market capitalism. Vogel writes that "Japan has not adopted the US liberal market model because the Japanese did not want to adopt it," and the overall benefits of Japan's current reforms have been unclear.[36] Meanwhile, Japanese companies remain reluctant to lay off workers, but those companies with high foreign ownership are likely to try downsizing.[37] George Olcott's study of several Japanese firms' organizational changes shows the persistence of traditional Japanese management in Japanese companies, even under the strong influence of foreign shareholders.[38] Although foreign ownership of Japanese companies is increasing, foreign firms in Japan may find it difficult to fully put into practice their home country's management model since managers and shareholders must adapt themselves to the local context.[39] Scholars who produced earlier studies have shared the view that even though some Japanese firms may increasingly incorporate hybrid elements of Western management Japan is unlikely ever to approximate the type of liberal market-based corporate management and employment system seen in the United States.[40] Some critics point out that Japan's brand of capitalism has veered off the evolutionary path and is not adaptive to global changes.[41] Yet most current researchers agree that Japan's institutional complementarities and the equilibrium among Japanese employees, corporate management, the state, the labor market, and the family will continue to be sustained by several factors. These include vested interests (including existing lifelong-employed corporate and government workers);[42] an entrenched business culture that values trust, loyalty, and consensual decision making;[43] an aversion to the US-type market-driven economy and concern about social inequality;[44] and the traditional value placed on conformity over individual freedom and creativity.[45] What these business scholars have not adequately addressed is that such a model of protection-based corporate governance and codependent capitalism also makes women's low status in Japanese companies very slow to change.

## The Latent Function of Gender Inequality in Japanese Business

Takeshi Inagami and D. Hugh Whittaker describe Japanese firms as "community firms," with a culture based on employees' strong "we-consciousness" and an exchange of loyalty for security, and point out that gender discrimination and male dominance are central to this culture, with women in Japanese firms mostly treated as "quasi-members . . . or non members."[46] In a comparison of Japan's business-state system with those of Sweden and the United States, Sven Steinmo argues that the pervasiveness of gender discrimination in Japanese business will eventually harm the Japanese economy by making the labor market still more rigid, causing reductions to Japan's labor force and further lessening women's incentive for reproduction.[47] But there remains the question of how exactly the exclusion of and discrimination against women in Japanese companies operates in Japanese management customs. Why is vertical sex segregation inevitable under these customs? What is the logic of gender in each custom that is particularly disadvantageous to women?

Seniority pay and promotions coupled with provision of household benefits—the system that exists under the current Japanese management structure—generates a gender gap that in turn acts against women workers' long-term upward mobility in their careers. Under the current system, workers must stay with a company for many years to receive promotion to management, which usually does not occur until the employee is in his or her late thirties. This system of waiting until the late thirties or later for promotion makes it difficult for many women workers to incorporate reproduction and family life into their plans. Thus, young women are incentivized to choose the caretaker path over that of career advancement. The lack of mobility in the labor market also restricts women's ability to go up the career ladder.

Some companies continue to use career-track hiring, in which women are explicitly relegated to assistant-level jobs with low pay and little chance of promotion. Even when companies do not use career-track hiring, they still hire far more men than women and simultaneously hire a large number of educated women as temporary workers for assistant positions. As long as Japanese companies retain lifelong-employment spots exclusively for men and simultaneously protect middle management and senior men with age-based salary increases, they have an incentive to cut costs by continuing these gender-biased hiring practices.

By committing to lifelong employment, Japanese companies have provided a social safety net to families in lieu of having it provided by the Japanese state.[48] Because companies do not fire workers, they have to search elsewhere for cost reductions, and their options are limited. Under the lifelong-employment system, firms can use traditional workforce reduction strategies such as *shukko* (secondment, or temporary transfer to a related firm) and *tenseki* (permanent transfer to a related firm),[49] or they can force early retirement on some senior workers. But Japanese companies lay off far fewer workers than US companies such as IBM or AT&T.[50] Japanese firms introduced some liberalization reforms in the 1990s and started hiring young male and female temporary workers in order to save labor costs. But the firms' reforms resulted in a dichotomization of the labor force between young workers (often women) with no economic security and senior workers with economic security and generous benefits.[51] This division of workers continued to be a popular cost-saving method for many Japanese firms in the 2000s.[52] This partial liberalization is not adequate, however, to cover the cost of having lifelong workers, especially when a company's revenues are falling. Mari Miura points out that Japanese companies' strong employment protection has been maintained through this use of a large number of cheap part-time and temporary female workers.[53]

Furthermore, the custom of long working hours, which is another central cost-saving method of Japanese management, reifies the male work norm and bolsters sex segregation by rewarding only those women who emulate this style. The culture of long working hours can incorporate women only as long as they successfully follow the pattern of prioritizing their work over their personal and family lives. Thus, the overwork norm reinforces the dilemma facing women workers, who often conclude they have only two options in their careers: they either emulate the male work norm or opt out.

Finally, it will be many years before the number of women managers in Japanese companies reaches parity with that of men, as there is so little mobility in the labor market under lifelong employment and opportunity is mostly based on seniority. Women workers' absence in high-level management in Japanese companies reinforces traditional gender stereotypes and makes it difficult to reduce gender essentialism and misogyny in the workplace.

## Gendered Management Customs in Japan

Past studies have revealed that women's low status is embedded in the organizational customs of Japanese companies. A few scholars have pointed out the link between Japan's employment system and gender-discriminatory practices. For example, Brinton and others have pointed out that lifelong employment and seniority pay are disadvantageous to women workers who might wish to start families;[54] they preferentially reward men who work for long years without interruption.[55] The same customs reinforce gender stereotypes that depict women as being incapable of lifelong devotion and sacrifice for their companies,[56] even though these same companies offer them only assistant-level jobs because of the likelihood that they will quit when they marry and have children.

A few ethnographic studies of Japanese companies have revealed the nexus between the employment system and marginalization of women workers. For example, Yuko Ogasawara's ethnographic study of a large bank in the 1980s and Karen Shire's interviews with employees of financial and automobile manufacturing firms in the 1990s demonstrated that the hiring track for women relegates them to marginal positions with lower pay and few promotion chances and that women have traditionally been expected to quit their jobs when they marry.[57] Shire found that women workers "were evaluated on their grooming and temperament, while men were evaluated on decision making and analytical style, and how they expressed opinions."[58] Ogasawara's work illustrated Japanese women's unique combination of resistance to and conformity with male authority. The women workers in her study served their Japanese companies as "cheap and docile labor" while simultaneously resisting the corporate hierarchy by explicitly taking authority lightly and "hid[ing] critical, observant eyes underneath their demure attitudes and feminine smiles."[59]

Kimiko Kimoto's study of general merchandise supermarkets and department stores disclosed how the Japanese management system negatively affects women's ambition.[60] She observed that many women workers are given "boredom-inducing jobs" or assistant-level work and express low ambition to climb the managerial ladder, especially if it requires extremely long work-hour commitment. Alice Lam's book about a large department store demonstrates that the gender division, wherein the women sell and the men manage, is embedded in both male and female mentalities and normalized in organizational culture.[61] Lam points out that the uniqueness of Japanese management lies in its normalization, justification, and maintenance of sex discrimination in ordinary customs.[62] Heidi Gottfried's study of temporary-help agencies found that the companies' hiring of women temporary workers included screening based on gendered traits such as age, appearance, tone of voice, and posture, especially because "women's ornamental appearance becomes an important qualification for attracting the male gaze."[63] In her article, she reported that women were mostly relegated to being men's assistants and judged according to traditional male views of attractiveness. She found that the relationship between regular full-time male workers and temporary female workers represented a typical gender regime. She concluded that "organizations select workers on the basis of an aesthetic code that predisposes the preference for female embodiment of temporary work and privilege attributes linked to masculinity and the heterosexual family man."[64] Japanese managers apparently have long subscribed to gender essentialism, heteronormative behaviors, and have normalized sex segregation in given tasks, responsibilities, and opportunities. These organizationally embedded and normalized gender biases and discriminatory customs have been legitimized by the male-protection-based employment system in Japan's coordinated capitalist society.

Strong employment protection in a business may even exacerbate employers' gender biases and workplace vertical segregation. Margarita Estevez-Abe argues that the degree of sex segregation in capitalist countries is shaped by their different corporate skill regimes: countries with coordinated market economies, which institutionally support firm-specific skills and emphasize workers' long-term economic security, have higher levels of organizational vertical segregation than countries with liberal market economies, where credential-based skills, such as those obtained through education, are more highly valued.[65] She argues that in countries with coordinated market economies employers' long-term commitment to their workers along with strong job protections and the high costs associated with hiring and firing workers institutionally legitimizes a negative bias against female workers, given that women are likely to interrupt their careers for childbearing, while liberal market countries carry fewer biases because they rely heavily on gender-neutral characteristics in hiring, such as educational diplomas and vocational certifications. According to Estevez-Abe, a reduction in vertical segregation in coordinated market countries may require a reduction in workers' overall employment protections.[66]

I shall revisit the above arguments and examine the direct and causal links between the business and management practices of Japanese companies and the consequences of vertical sex segregation. In the 1980s, and even in the early 1990s, there were very few women managers or working mothers in Japanese companies. Only 15 percent of women attended four-year colleges, and 20 percent of women attended two-year colleges in the late 1980s. But the gender gap in education has been rapidly narrowing. Furthermore, because of decreasing pressure to marry at a young age, there are increasingly high numbers of educated employed women in various positions and at a variety of levels in large Japanese firms. Also, because of the government's promotion of married women's continuing presence in the workplace and lenient parental leave, working mothers are increasingly visible in the workplace. However, corporate customs and culture continue to shape a high level of vertical sex segregation and constrain women's upward mobility.

Until the early 1990s, the age norm played an important role in women's decision to marry, with both families and employers pressuring women to marry by their late twenties, and many women quitting their jobs when they married.[67] But marital age has become highly variable in Japan because of the "younger generation's departure from adherence to the strong age-at-marriage norm of their parents' generation."[68] The decline of the marital age norm and the marital norm itself, combined with the rapid rise in women's education and employment and a deregulated labor market that is increasing the number and types of positions women workers are hired into, have changed the way that many women are conducting their working lives. Thus, it is critical to question Japan's structural and institutional sex segregation, especially its slowness to change as it relates to organizational and management customs. I believe that what it will take to implement desegregation is more than just increasing the number of women employers and women managers, who may simply be seen as ornaments by other workers. Japanese companies need women with power and authority, but this will require some serious structural and organizational changes accompanied by changes in beliefs and practices common to Japanese corporate governance and capitalism. Incorporating women workers into the current Japanese management system as equals with men will also be costly unless Japan transforms the lifelong-employment system and related customs. Taking gender equality seriously in Japanese firms will require increased awareness of the responsibility of traditional Japanese management for the low status of women in Japan.

## Democratic Values in Japan

It has been assumed by many that gender equality would progress along with Japan's modernization. However, because gender inequality has been a critical part of institutional equilibrium in Japan, addressing it requires great changes to the Japanese system. In addition, Japan's slow pace in the reduction of sex segregation and gender inequality may be partly due to Japanese capitalism's strong adherence to nondemocratic "survival" values, driven by the business community and the state, rather than by more rational and individualistic values.

Ronald Inglehart and Christian Welzel argue that gender egalitarianism is a critical component of democracy and human advancement and an emancipatory force in modern nations that shapes the development of the autonomous self.[69] If the rise of gender egalitarianism is connected to the rise of values relating to democracy and individual autonomy, can we explain Japan's slow progress in terms of the absence of these values? According to Inglehart, Pippa Norris, and Welzel, a country's economic development leads to an increase in democratic values and thus to greater gender equality.[70] Measuring societies' values on two dimensions—traditional values vs. secular-rational values and survival values vs. self-expression values—they explain that societies with the strongest traditional values strongly emphasize the importance of parent-child ties, deference to authority, family values, and nationalism, while societies leaning toward secular-rational values have preferences centered on individual difference, independence, and freedom. Societies that are all about survival also place the highest value on materialism and hard work while having little tolerance for difference and diversity. Inglehart, Norris, and Welzel argue that as economic development progresses there should be a shift from survival values toward self-expression values and that this should also lead the society to adopt gender equality, since daily work in modern knowledge-based societies requires individual judgment and innovation rather than following routines dictated from above, and thus an individual's self-expression becomes indispensable.[71] Democratization is a complex process that a society's religious heritage, work structure, and level of economic development all influence.[72] Japan is economically developed, but traditional Japanese values emphasize family and group conformity and a catch-up-with-the-West type of survival imperative, which enforces homogeneity, a hierarchy-dominated corporate culture, and a business-state coordinated system.

According to this theory of democracy and gender equality, the rise of such an economy leads to increasing emphasis on self-expressive values and then to the development of democracy (not the other way around). The rise of material, intellectual, and social autonomy leads to people's aversion to hierarchy and authority and their preference for freedom and equality.[73] The rise of liberal democracy is a key to the progress of gender equality in a country, and the rise of liberal democracy occurs when there are shifts in traditional values and the development of a public consciousness opposed to traditional authority, collectivism, and conformity. The continuing dominance in Japan of rigid hierarchical systems and conformity in business management suggests that Japan is much closer to authoritarian countries than to Western democratic countries. If Japan's capitalism revolves around traditional nondemocratic values, it is not surprising that gender inequality, which is also a critical element of Japanese capitalism, has not been reduced substantially.

Japan's system of capitalism is understood as being entirely different from the liberal, individualistic capitalism of the United States. Some argue that Japan's social values—especially the values of conformity and the hierarchy based on age, gender, and education—inhibit the evolution of Japanese society, individual creativity, and innovation.[74] Conversely, some scholars argue that the values of conformity and hierarchy in Japan are simply characteristic of a different democratic style and that Japan is a solidly democratic country that just happens to be different from Western democracies.[75]

Gøsta Esping-Andersen famously described three state regime types: (1) the social democratic model, exemplified by the Scandinavian countries with their strong emphasis on the role of the state in guaranteeing gender equality, social rights, and household welfare; (2) the conservative welfare model, in which families rely on the male breadwinner and men's long-term employment; and (3) the liberal state, with its strong emphasis on individualism and the market.[76] Japan belongs to the second type, in which women's job status is low and their equality is also suppressed by traditional family values and roles. Andersen argues that Japan's welfare system is shaped by the dominance of these old-fashioned values, which reflect the country's Confucianism-oriented, age-based hierarchical system. In Andersen's model, Confucianism in Japan is like Catholicism in Europe, which has blocked gender equality and women's independence in countries such as Italy and Spain.[77] Mary Alice Haddad likewise points out that Confucianism values group orientation and the social order.[78] Regardless of such different bases of democracy, Haddad explains, Japan's younger generation has been becoming more democratic than previous generations, and political institutions have also become more democratic than before.

Others disagree with the claim that Japan's emphasis on group values and hierarchy derive from Confucianism, especially considering that Asian countries are characterized by diverse cultural values and beliefs (even though all are influenced by Confucianism).[79] Thomas Rohlen is one of these; he posits that parenting and socialization are the major factors contributing to Japanese acceptance of order and hierarchical authority.[80] Others argue that group conformity might stem largely from Japan's modernization and industrialization after World War II.[81] Group conformity was indeed the driving force behind the development of Japanese companies and thus the country's economic growth after the war.

Decision making is also based on group conformity in Japanese organizations, but it has been criticized as the source of organizational inertia in these firms. Group conformity usually is institutionalized along the lines of a gendered and age-based hierarchy. Because such value systems are reinforced by salaries, which are also based on age and gender, the pay system may need to be uncoupled from cultural values before democratization of the decision-making process can occur.

Japan's civil society has been state led to a great degree in its modernization process; the state is considered a worthy object of subordination or sacrifice.[82]

Andrew Barshay cites the regulation scholar Toshio Yamada's words—"One cannot understand postwar Japan without looking at corporations"—and reframes Japan's civil society in terms of Kiyoaki Hirata's concept of Japan as "the enterprise state" in which worker relations with both the firm and the state are based on intense conformity and exploitation, characterized by a lack of autonomy or fairness.[83] Referring to Tetsuro Kato and Hirata, Barshay argues that the frequency of workers' deaths by overwork, or *karoshi*, demonstrates their subordination to their firms, and that this brutal exploitation of workers has been an entrenched part of state-led corporate development.[84] Turning to the Japanese thinker Yoshihiko Uchida, Barshay further writes:

> In modern times, Japan had gone from "semi-feudal" to "supermodern" through the agency of war, reconstruction, and growth, but without the full realization of civil society. Would Uchida have found in the decadence of the postwar system a chance for a fundamental redefinition of Japan's civil society? Or would he have thought that in the name of globalization, civil society was again being sacrificed to the gods of capital? On the one hand, while severe competition eroded profits, technological innovation also created new possibilities for their realization by reducing "socially necessary labor time." In this situation, some workers could find themselves with less (or shared) work but increased "time sovereignty" and the chance for enhanced participation in civic life as the collective narcissism of the enterprise gave way to a more mature and diversified perspective. Alternatively, in a society that has tended to equate the status of "human being" (*ningen*) with enterprise membership, greater unemployment would surely bring pervasive anomie or worse, while those who retain their identity as corporate employees might find themselves subject to still greater demands for unrewarded labor.[85]

Japan's economic development and modernization did not entail democratic practices and beliefs in the Western sense; instead, Japan, in building its democracy, mandated the subordination of labor to the state and the company. Here, the "survival" of the nation-state was seen as the mission of companies and individual workers alike. This "survival" value also legitimizes the existence of a gender hierarchy and the division of labor. In this context, Japan's survival as a first-rate modern country was seen to require group-led conformity under Japan's system of coordinated capitalism, and the values of equality, diversity, and individualism would have to wait. Japan's deficiency in individual autonomy—and its lack of importance to Japan's democracy—has been pointed out by the political scientist Maruyama Masao, who posits that it was a major cause of wartime fascism in the country.[86]

The dominant concepts of conformity and hierarchy in Japanese management do not incorporate the value of equality. It would require great effort to replace the virtue of self-sacrifice with the Western notion of "work-life balance" in Japanese companies. The "survival" value of Japanese capitalism has not been reduced or replaced by the "self-expressive," and management and labor markets continue to operate accordingly. Sex segregation in Japanese companies should be examined in the context of Japan's adherence to survival- and conformity-based management. Women workers' aspirations, as well as their opportunities for upward mobility and economic independence, have been suppressed by the dominant state-driven economic-development regime and tailored to fit gendered separate-sphere values. If gender egalitarianism is a critical component of democracy and human advancement,[87] desegregation in Japanese firms will thus require value shifts in existing management. The Japanese government might expect a state-led gender policy copied from the West to bring about gender egalitarianism in Japan, but it is not a matter of one policy; rather, change must reverberate through the entire system of Japanese capitalism. Steinmo points out the problem with Japan's traditional "survival" or "catch up with the West" attitudes: "Japan is unlikely to successfully adapt if it continues to simply import policies from abroad. Its leaders should instead consider both how to adapt new ideas to the system's strengths and weaknesses, as well as consider what kind of country they would like to build."[88] Under enterprise-led economic development, gender egalitarianism, individualism, and a flexible labor market have not been fully developed. The labor market and employment structure in Japan, based on age, gender, and education, must become responsive to and reward individual aspirations.

In the United States, gender egalitarianism has progressed partly as a result of liberal individualism. Paula England explains educated middle-class American women's aspiring to do traditionally male jobs and a narrowing gender gap in these jobs in terms of America's valuation of liberal individualism and a belief in self-expressiveness and equal opportunity.[89] American women strive to seek their "true selves" and attain greater upward mobility than was possible for their mothers. For individual belief in self-fulfillment to translate into high-ranking jobs, though, the labor market must guarantee certain levels of equal opportunity. In Japan such envisioning of a "true self" may not be so difficult on an individual level, but navigating personal desire and realizing that true self in the rigid labor market and sex-segregated Japanese companies is very difficult. As long as the labor market and employment structure lack the flexibility to adjust to such developments, gender inequality in Japan is unlikely to change.

Finally, when we compare past changes in women's status in the United States with those in Japan, the role of effective laws and courts with the authority to reprimand companies for discrimination cannot be ignored. Japanese gender laws are known to be ineffective, with the state lacking the ability to impose sanctions and penalties on companies that flout the rules. The laws also are biased toward Japanese companies, and the Japanese courts follow a set of highly bureaucratic and conformity-driven norms, making them unwilling to set legal precedents and positioning them as highly conservative as concerns gender equality.[90] Japan has not therefore seen the passage of laws helpful to the emergence of gender egalitarianism, whereas in the United States, the Civil Rights Act of 1964, the guidelines of the Equal Employment Opportunity Commission (EEOC), and various decisions of the Supreme Court—applied within firms by corporate and legal professionals such as attorneys, personnel professionals, human resources specialists, and consultants—have made huge contributions to developing gender-parity measures and grievance procedures.[91] Also, the discourses of capitalism and democracy, in which the values of fairness and efficiency overlap, have pushed the US business and legal climates toward greater gender equality. If a legal system that can push for and materialize democratic values is necessary for desegregation and egalitarianism, Japan may have to take a different approach.

## Organizational Analysis

I base this book about sex segregation in Japanese firms on feminist studies written from the gendered-organizational perspective, which allows more context-specific analysis of gendered customs and practices than other organizational approaches. By using the gendered-organizational perspective, I situate sex segregation and unequal power dynamics in certain customs within the concrete contexts of Japanese firms. Organizational analysis allows us to discover how sex segregation has been reinforced informally through hierarchies, hiring practices, gender biases, and worker relations.

Traditionally, sex segregation has been explained from two differing viewpoints: a demand-side perspective that emphasizes such things as employers' statistical discrimination against women workers and a supply-side perspective that sees the gender gap as mostly resulting from women's choices (being less committed to or invested in their jobs as compared to men due to their domestic responsibilities or different socialization paths and preferences).[92] In the labor economy, the human-capital theory emphasizes women's lack of investment in education or their choice of occupations that require fewer skills and less engagement as a result of their spending more time outside of work.[93] Furthermore, even with increasing corporate and governmental intervention and the entrance of more educated women into the labor market, sex segregation persists because of unchanging workplace practices. The organizational culture retains gender biases and stereotypes that are embedded in workplace customs. Traditional explanations of sex segregation, however, do little to help us understand the mechanisms and processes by which sex segregation is reinforced at the organizational level.[94]

## Gendered Organizations

Feminist scholars have argued that the logic of organizations entails gender and that gender equality is unattainable without organizational changes in gendered customs and practices.[95] Studies of gendered organizations shed light on the context-specific analysis of organizations—including the operation of gendered beliefs, ideologies, and dominant patterns of behavior that are unique to certain workplaces and occupations—and their impacts on workers' relationships and identities, aspirations, and career paths. These studies examine the "mechanisms that produce inequality at work" as "inequalities of gender, race, class and sexuality [that] are deeply entrenched in workplace cultures, interactions, and even the identities of workers."[96]

Studies of gendered organizations often examine the ideologies of gender at multiple levels of the organizational structure. Joan Acker suggests that we examine the operation of gender-divisive ideologies in five aspects of organizations: (1) the division of labor, (2) the construction of symbols, (3) interactions among workers, (4) individual identity, and (5) organizational logic and assumptions that often shape the hierarchy of the organization.[97] An organization often legitimizes the ideology of separate spheres by recreating "the gendered divide between paid work and unpaid family reproductive work, consigning the latter, and women, to a subordinated and devalued position as practice and belief put the demands of the work organization first over the demands of the rest of life."[98] By normalizing separate-sphere beliefs, the organization also legitimizes its "nonresponsibility" for "human survival and reproduction," thus marginalizing reproductive and caring activities that are tied mostly to women's work.[99]

Studies of gendered organizations often employ the concept of "masculinity" to illuminate workers' dominant gendered behaviors that have been constructed in the workplace. A variety of masculine customs and practices in the workplace—such as aggressiveness, competitiveness, autocracy, and market- or profit-driven behavior—have been postulated as common factors that deprive women of power,[100] but, importantly, men's and women's beliefs about and practice of masculinities in the workplace differ depending on the structural position of women and their degree of power and authority.[101] It is well known that most Japanese companies have been shaped by the separate-sphere ideology and traditional masculinity and femininity. Also, examining Japanese firms' practices and beliefs illuminates how the organizational structures, customs, and hierarchies that have reinforced sex segregation remain central to Japan's institutional regimes.

Dana Britton offers an important critique of studies of gendered organizations, arguing that "the meaning of labeling an organization, an occupation, a policy, or a practice as gendered is still theoretically and empirically unclear."[102] Britton and Laura Logan, however, write that even though studies of gendered organizations offer few theoretical generalities, their context-specific approach adds "complexities" to the field, and they maintain that such complexities "increase our knowledge of the processes whereby organizations become gendered."[103] Gendered-organizational perspectives are useful for assessing various types of work and professional mechanisms of gender. For example, Christine Williams, Chandra Muller, and Kristine Kilanski write that basic organizational logic has been transformed over the past few decades because, under the so-called new economy, "work is increasingly characterized by job insecurity, teamwork, career maps, and networking," yet the processes by which the work is organized continue to have gendered impacts and consequences.[104]

I employ the gendered-organizations approach in this book because it offers the opportunity for an in-depth and contextualized analysis of the organizational practices and beliefs that have reinforced vertical sex segregation in five Japanese companies. Looking at multiple aspects of organizational customs and structures is effective when internal and external corporate changes occur—such as the rapid rise of educated women in the workforce and the implementation of corporate policies regarding gender equality—yet organizational inertia remains unchanged.

In US research, the gendered-organizational approach also takes into account context-specific diversity and equality programs. Even in the United States, which is far more desegregated than Japan, further progress in uprooting sex segregation has been slow, and many organizations have failed to change or even question gendered customs and beliefs.[105] Robin Ely, Herminia Ibarra, and Deborah Kolb point out that existing organizational remedial programs tend to locate the problem only in women.[106] Ely and Debra Meyerson argue that organizations have employed three types of interventions: (1) the "fix women" approach, (2) the "value femininity" approach, and (3) the "create equal opportunity" approach. In the "fix women" approach, a firm tries to eliminate gender inequality by changing women and training women to perform on a par with men.[107] This approach, which mostly encourages women to assimilate to the existing organizational norm, blames women as the source of the problem and leaves the organization's male standard unchallenged. Whereas the second approach, "value femininity," encourages workers to value traditional femininity and gender differences, this does little more than reinforce women's appropriateness and the gendered power imbalance. The third approach, "create equal opportunity," aims to remove structural gender barriers primarily through formal policy-based changes such as affirmative action programs, formal mentoring, and work-family programs. Although policy-based interventions have greatly contributed to the decline of some barriers, Ely and Meyerson argue that they are not sufficient because they do not challenge the beliefs and norms that legitimize the gender imbalance. They suggest the necessity of putting in place more context-specific interventions against unequal informal practices in addition to formal policies concerning work rules, labor rules, labor contracts, managerial directives, job descriptions, performance-appraisal systems, and distribution of work responsibilities, including the information people receive regarding advancement in the organization and tacit criteria for competence or fitting in.[108] Corporate culture plays an essential role in the likelihood of firms' implementing effective organizational strategies and diversity programs.[109] Thus, it is not enough to have some type of formal gender policy in place; in addition, workers' views of organizational culture and workplace accommodation of formal changes in gender policy need to be examined.

## Gender Bias

Knowledge of gender biases and stereotypes is important in understanding sex segregation. Gender biases, often institutionalized, stem from differing motives on the part of employers and managers. They often derive from organizational inertia or an employer's reluctance to implement changes in old customs. Barbara Reskin and Debra McBrier argue that organizational inertia maintains employers' sex-based ascription or gender-essentialist biases because of employers' aversion to paying the extra selection costs associated with filling jobs with women or even creating new formal structures.[110] To most hiring managers, who prefer to choose persons who resemble themselves, it can feel like a risk to place women over men. Organizational inertia is often "built around cognitive, interactional and institutional processes" that can reinforce the gendered division of labor in the form of recruitment, evaluation, hiring, and retention of employees.[111] At the same time, any rapid or forceful attempts to change old customs may be met with complaints that exhibit gender bias and prejudice. In the Japanese companies I researched for this book, women with power have been historically few, and recent increases in the number of women managers in these companies have been met with mixed emotions by existing workers and viewed through the lens of traditional gender stereotypes.

Gender bias also derives from a strong belief in male primacy. Research shows that "there is little direct evidence that men are more productive workers than women," and it also indicates that it is not clear that men are less stable employees, even though women "as a group" might have more interrupted careers.[112] England argues that employers mistakenly underestimate group average productivity and use gender stereotypes, and she refers to this as "error discrimination."[113] Donald Tomaskovic-Devey and Sheryl Skaggs argue that the productivity of individual workers is shaped and constrained by their existing roles, which are assigned according to the organization's division of labor and that the gender gap in productivity is thus more likely to derive from the unequal structure of the gender division than from individual traits.[114] With little reason other than prejudice, employers commonly place higher trust in men than in women. Traditional male domination in upper-level positions intensifies the decision makers' gender biases.[115] When uncertainty is involved in managerial work, employers and decision makers tend to show gender bias in their inferences about a candidate's ability to perform at a high level.[116] Previous research provides evidence to refute the common employer bias that women workers are less committed to their jobs than men. In their research in Britain and the United States, Elizabeth Gorman and Julie Kmec found that "women have to try harder than men at work, across a wide variety of jobs," as "employers impose higher performance standards on women than on men, even when men and women hold the same jobs."[117] As a result, women may experience greater job stress, exhaustion, and burnout, and this indicates that, even as explicit discrimination becomes less common, the mechanisms of job experiences and rewards remain highly gendered.[118]

In Japanese companies, with their custom of lifelong employment, statistical discrimination has been commonly employed to justify hiring men and women for different positions. Using statistical discrimination, employers have avoided hiring and promoting women because of their perception that they are more likely to resign from their jobs or be more intermittent in terms of job productivity. Male supremacy has been a major assumption of Japanese management because of men's higher likelihood of lifelong commitment.

Gender bias also promotes in-group preferences, which leads to the exclusion of women from male bonds. It is known that male decision makers are more likely than female decision makers to prefer male candidates for hiring and promotion.[119] Studies have found that powerful groups constantly seek to institutionalize their privileges,[120] so employers tend to place men ahead of women in labor queues for the most desirable jobs.[121] Homophily is often maintained as a result of workers' and clients', as well as employers', in-group preferences. Networking is an outcome of in-group preferences and thus is an aspect of the gender-based reciprocal business system. In a study of one thousand financial network members, it was demonstrated that even when women break into male circles workers may rank network members along gendered lines.[122]

By the same token, it may work in women's favor when there are a high number of women with authority; they may be motivated to help other women or prefer to interact with others who are similar to them.[123] Purcell, MacArthur, and Samblanet argue that past research has shown that "institutionalizing, and legitimizing, female leadership increases equality (e.g., greater influence and pay for women), and placing men and women in the same positions may lessen inequality over time."[124] In highly male-dominated environments, such as Japanese companies, the recruiting of women or women entering male-only circles may take considerable effort unless top management intentionally generates such paths for women workers or increases the number of women with authority who are powerful enough to change male-only customs in their companies.

## The Importance of Women with Power

The impact of women with power and authority on desegregation is a critical question for organizational theorists. Studies suggest that the presence of more women in managerial positions relates to a reduction in segregation.[125] For example, it is known that women's representation in managerial jobs, especially in high-level leadership positions, reduces the wage gap between women and men.[126] Regarding workplace programs, executives are more likely to adopt diversity programs when they have higher proportions of white women in management who push for these programs.[127]

According to Kevin Stainback and Soyoung Kwon, when women are present in leadership positions, it helps female subordinates in the following three ways: (1) in-group preference in hiring, promotion, and wage-setting decisions; (2) increased access to career-enhancing social networks and mentoring opportunities; and (3) reduced gender stereotypes and increased women's representation in higher level positions.[128] In their empirical study of South Korean organizations, Stainback and Kwon found that organizations with a higher percentage of women in managerial jobs tend to have lower observed levels of sex segregation.[129]

Japanese companies exhibit an extreme form of vertical sex segregation, as they are severely lacking in women leaders. This is not just the case in the business world; the overall society suffers from an absence of women with power and authority. The effect of this absence of women with power on subordinate workers has not been well investigated. Past studies in the United States and Europe, however, have addressed the negative consequences of a lack of women leaders in organizations. One good example is Ely's comparative study of male-dominated law firms and gender-integrated law firms in the United States.[130] She found that the women in male-dominated law firms had far more negative views about their career prospects, other female workers, and their self-images than the women in gender-integrated law firms. Women workers' views of their jobs, their careers, and themselves in male-dominated law firms are often shaped by men's views of what they want from the women. According to Ely, women in male-dominated firms in which few women with power are present perceive that playing two roles is critical to their success: the masculine role and the seductress/sex object role—"roles defined by men's preferences."[131] She notes that women workers in these firms express stronger gender stereotypes, a sense of less competence and satisfaction, and lower expectations for promotion than women in gender-integrated law firms. Women workers in Japanese firms may be in circumstances similar to those in the male-dominated firms in Ely's study, perhaps subscribing to a high level of gender bias themselves and feeling pessimistic about their advancement and future job prospects. In organizations with few senior women or women with power, those few can turn into "queen bees" and becoming complicit with the privileged group of men, denying the firm's sexism, turning a blind eye to women's disadvantaged position, and maybe even mistreating younger women.[132] Although some authors point out that such an image of senior women can be highly male biased or sexist, the appearance of queen bees is well known as an organizational symptom of male dominance. Because there have been few female managers in most Japanese companies, it is not surprising that tensions among women workers reflect misogyny or competition and hierarchy among women.

Beyond the lack of women leaders, the problems in Japanese companies extend to the way the government and companies have superficially increased the numbers of women rapidly over the last few years without addressing structural and organizational problems. This causes workers and managers to question whether those women are as qualified as the men holding the same positions. Such concerns and criticisms about Japan's government-led desegregation may also increase criticism of new women managers in Japanese companies.

## Overview of the Book

The following chapters investigate the logic of gender and organizational processes in which sex segregation and gender inequality emerge in the customs of hiring, pay, and promotion; the practice of long working hours; workplace gender stereotypes; gendered consequences of overtime work; and sexual harassment.

Chapter 2 locates the absence of women in high positions in Japanese companies in the context of Japan's coordinated capitalism by looking at state-business-labor relations, corporate governance, the family-and-welfare regime, and Japanese laws and courts. Focusing on the economic decline and intensified global competition in the 1990s, I explain how Japan's postwar default settings in the realms of corporate governance, the labor market, the family regime, and the legal system have changed to some degree, and recast gender inequality in light of these changes. Little change in the custom of lifelong employment, however, and a lack of mobility in the labor market continue to sustain the traditional gender division in Japan's capitalist system. The Japanese government now promotes women's employment and the reconciliation of family with work, yet it continues to embrace the male-breadwinner family-welfare regime as opposed to an egalitarian vision of family and welfare policies. Meanwhile, Japanese companies have started supporting gender equality as a goal of corporate social responsibility, but the country's limited labor laws as well as the lack of penalties or fines of the Equal Employment Opportunity Law (EEOL) make the nation's firms ineffectual in eradicating discriminatory customs and practices.

I look at the legal systems in Japan and the United States and ask why vertical sex segregation remains entrenched in Japan regardless of the enforcement of gender equal laws, such as the Equal Employment Opportunity Law and ratification of the UN Convention on the Elimination of All Forms of Discrimination against Women (CEDAW) by Japan. I comparatively discuss sex-discrimination court cases in Japan and in the United States, with a focus on how the US legal system has played a critical role in addressing and reducing employers' discriminatory practices in America, while in Japan, the laws and courts still tend to side with the Japanese business community and state.

Chapter 3 explains my methodology and the background characteristics of each firm (five companies: three financial firms and two cosmetics firms) in which I conducted interviews, including information on the management, ownership, and circumstances of women's status and employment. The five companies initiated reforms with regard to women's employment in the early 2000s in response to two large forces: the implementation of Japanese governmental guidelines on improving women's employment and the global business imperative relating to gender equality. I discuss the five firms' reforms regarding women's employment and assess interviewees' responses with a focus on recent changes, including increased hiring of career-track women, the promotion of women managers, the provision of training programs that target women candidates for management, the abolition or modification of track hiring, and the provision of lenient parental leave. I also note the increase in foreign ownership of Japanese companies and its impact on gender equality. Even though there may be some correlation between the high level of foreign ownership and distinct reforms in terms of the integration of women, the reforms did not seem to strikingly diminish gender inequality in the firms I looked at. Compared to the three financial firms, the two cosmetics firms had a larger number of women workers and working mothers, and their turnover rate was low, yet they had few women at the top, just like in the financial firms. The two financial companies continued to use career-track hiring, making use of a large number of temporary women, which is a classic cost-saving method used by Japanese companies.

Chapter 4 explains how major Japanese management and employment practices—seniority pay and promotion, track hiring, and household benefits—work against women's upward mobility and reify sex segregation in Japanese companies. I compare the salaries and benefits of men and women in similar age groups in the five companies, and explain the current Japanese employment system, which is based on seniority pay, track hiring, and household benefits and is highly gender biased. Within the career-track system, firms can hire women as career-track, contract, or temporary workers. The current system legitimizes women's cheap labor and provides low motivation for upward mobility. I also discuss how such a gender-divisive hiring and pay structure has generated tensions among women workers and how it has contributed to their low aspirations.

Chapter 5 examines how men and women workers in Japanese companies participate in the re-creation of and/or navigation of gender biases and stereotypes. Male managers legitimized statistical discrimination and gender biases based on the ideology of separate spheres. Also, male managers' "hero" narratives—consisting of men's homosocial bonds, business networks, and willingness to sacrifice their money and time for the firm—support the ideology of male superiority. Some male workers I interviewed saw women as being inferior to men and incapable of doing some of the tasks that are mostly done by men. I look at why some young women workers in the cosmetics firms, in which the number of low-level women managers has been rapidly increasing, expressed strong negativity about women managers. Young women delegitimized the women managers and their authority while at the same time legitimizing male managers, following an erotic and amicable heteronormative script. Finally, using the notion of queen bees, I examine the women middle managers' expressed negativity about and detachment from younger women in the workplace. Men and women workers alike rely on gender stereotypes of women as inferior to men, and these misogynistic views of women are reinforced by the absence of female authority in the male-dominated workplace.

Chapter 6 shows how the culture of long working hours continues to reinforce vertical segregation in the workplace through three processes: remasculinization of management; young women's as well as non-career-track women's low aspirations and their view of the difficulty of balancing work and family; and working mothers' disadvantages relating to men's lack of involvement at home. The custom of long working hours can incorporate women as long as they successfully emulate men's overwork norm by prioritizing their work over their personal and family life. Long working hours polarize women's choices because the ideology of separate spheres places most family responsibility on the woman. I also look at how the custom of overwork in Japanese companies may lead to men's loss of personal health and family time. Even though engaging in long working hours has been a traditional custom of Japanese companies, it can also lower the likelihood of new hires and reduce worker productivity.

Chapter 7 examines women workers' different interpretations and experiences of workplace sexual behaviors and interactions. I explain the processes by which workplace sexual interactions, including harmful behaviors, are normalized and tolerated. I discuss three types of sexual workplace interactions in Japanese firms that are described and interpreted very differently by women workers because of their differing contexts and argue that women's interpretations of sexual behaviors can vary from enjoyable to harmful, depending on the organizational context.

In the concluding chapter I reflect on important changes and future reforms that Japan needs to work on if it wishes to reduce sex segregation, not only at the organizational level, but also in management structures, the labor market, and the overall employment picture.

# THE JAPANESE WAY OF CHANGE

Recasting Institutional Coordination,
Sustaining Gender Inequality

Before I discuss sex segregation in the five Japanese companies in the next chapter, I will contextualize in this chapter the absence of women in management in Japanese companies in terms of the characteristics of Japan's system of coordinated capitalism. By coordinated capitalism, I mean the institutional dependencies among the Japanese state, the business and labor market, the family, and the legal system that have upheld and protected the primary goal of Japan's postwar economic development and modernization. Japan's "catch-up" or survival-based business system has melded these institutions together for the national goal of economic advancement and has also forged a traditional gendered regime, which, with lifelong employment, continues to constrain the labor mobility and employment choices, as well as the creativity, of the individual in Japanese society. With the economic decline and intensified global competition of the 1990s, Japan was forced to make some adjustments in its postwar default settings in terms of corporate governance, the labor market, the family regime, and the nation's laws, but the brand of Western liberalism it adopted did not truly diversify social and economic values or the labor market, particularly not with regard to gender. Japan employed liberalism only in the sense of cutting labor costs.

Masahiko Aoki explains that the concept of the "lost decade" (the 1990s) captured the minds of many people because the beliefs that had once been taken for granted in Japan shifted rapidly.[1] During this decade, Japan lost the postwar optimism tied to its economic prosperity, and it also lost the ability to sustain its institutional coordination. The partial reforms instituted by the government saved corporate costs but also destabilized employment, and they did not invigorate the existing business and employment system. The problems of sex segregation and gender inequality are tied to Japan's inability and unwillingness to transform its survival-based postwar employment customs and values. But there were some important institutional changes in the 1990s, and this chapter will review the extent of their impacts on sex segregation in the employment system in Japan.

In the 1990s, there was increasing foreign investment, Japan's major banks lost power over Japanese companies, and the traditional Japanese employment system came under close scrutiny from Western shareholders. There was a rise in neoliberal ideology and the introduction of liberalization reforms, such as the institution of performance pay and promotion and the increased hiring of irregular employees. The end result of these changes, however, was an increase in the number of economically insecure temporary employees and the ultimate protection of the vested interests of the lifelong-employment system.

Japan's postwar model of the male-breadwinner family and the associated welfare regime have accommodated women's employment since the 1990s. Prior to this era, the Japanese state's striving for postwar economic growth explicitly encouraged the male-breadwinner type of family formation, supporting men's role as sole earners and women's responsibility for the home. But increasing concerns about the declining birth rate led the Japanese government to begin promoting women's employment (as in Western countries, but with less of a focus on egalitarianism).

Various legal and policy changes were introduced in the 1990s in Japan. As a response to international pressure that was brought to bear because Japan was perceived as making little progress in women's employment, the nation passed a series of gender-equality laws in the 1990s. Japanese corporations even expressed their willingness to continue to push for increasing women's employment as a gesture of compliance with the Western business norm, but they still opposed any forceful policies in this area. So, even though the number of educated women workers has been rapidly increasing, Japanese companies, the Japanese family, and the Japanese courts have done little to adapt coordinated capitalism to better accommodate the needs of women.

Japanese court cases can be compared with US court decisions on sex discrimination in order to understand how Japanese laws and court rulings on sex discrimination challenged the existing corporate gender regime and whether they effectively addressed gender inequality in Japanese society. Japanese courts, unlike US courts, remain unwilling to change gender-unequal customs and challenge Japanese companies' "discretion" or authority with regard to these customs.

# Japan's Coordinated Capitalism

## Lifelong Employment

As Mari Miura writes, Japanese management is based on a tradeoff between strong employment protection and extensive managerial discretion and control of labor conditions.[2] Japanese firms' management has long been characterized by lifelong employment, low interfirm mobility, seniority-based wages and promotions, and firm-specific training.[3] Lifelong employment became the dominant pattern of employment in the 1950s, yet it is hardly universal as it applies to only one-fifth of the working population in Japan.[4] The lifelong-employment system with seniority-based promotions and wage increases was "contingent on high economic growth and a youthful labor force" and reflected the particular historical conditions in postwar Japan, such as a shortage of skilled labor, a surplus of unskilled labor, rapid technological change, and the absence of a strong craft union tradition.[5] Lifelong employment was the primary method used to sustain Japan in its attempt to "catch up" with Western development.

Labor mobility is highly restricted in Japan, which eliminates unpredictability and cuts labor costs for employers. Most Japanese companies hire fresh college graduates, who start job hunting a year or more before their starting date. A student is expected to enter a firm immediately on graduation and, typically, to stay with that firm until retirement in order to develop long years of firm-specific skills. Employers in firms might view negatively a gap of a few years between college graduation date and starting work. Because long years of cultivation of firm-specific skills for a company is very important, and graduating from college on time is a component of human capital, "individual failure or indecisiveness cannot be compensated for by further human capital investment later in the life cycle."[6] The importance of age as human capital in Japanese firms has changed little over the last three decades. Because a person is expected to stay in one company for life, a middle-aged hire is rare. And, due to the strong emphasis on firm-specific skills, a fair method to evaluate performance, ability, and skills or creativity or talent is not really available. Job mobility in Japan continues to be among the lowest in OECD (Organization for Economic Cooperation and Development) countries.[7] As a result, organizational inertia is a chronic problem in Japan, and business innovation is extremely difficult.

Education and age are the factors that determine the organizational hierarchy in Japanese firms. Promising workers, often the ones who graduated from elite colleges, are given greater opportunities for job rotation and on-the-job training.[8] As Mary Brinton notes, three factors that were present in Japanese firms in the 1980s—the competitive educational system, an age-based hierarchy, and a firm's internal labor market—remain intact today and continue to determine workers' human capital.[9]

Regarding the age-based hierarchy, Ronald Dore says that Japan's seniority system is similar to "European bureaucratic pay structures for teachers, police, civil servants and so on."[10] Workers' evaluations, promotions, and wages are all based on seniority, and their wages increase steeply in their thirties and forties.[11] Because the seniority system rewards workers' long years of accumulated work experience and devotion to one company, it "creates a very poor fit between Japanese women's life-cycle patterns and managerial occupations."[12] Japanese companies have a very limited number of senior women because most of them, in the past, left their companies when they married or when they had children.

A Japanese firm traditionally is "run by its elders, who are primarily concerned with the reputation and future prosperity of the firm and the welfare of its members."[13] It also is characterized by the values of conscience, loyalty, and devotion. Dore also compares the Japanese firm to the British army or diplomatic corps, in which individuals are expected to demonstrate the "soldier's sense of regimental loyalty,"[14] as well as "robust consciences and levels of personal trust."[15] The traditional age-based hierarchy and "good behavior" are exalted over job performance, achievement, and competency. In other words, Japanese companies have not developed methods to differentiate among and evaluate individual workers based on educational credentials, work experiences, language abilities, and other skills that are not firm specific .

Overtime work is central to Japanese management, as it is the major corporate cost-saving method employed when firing workers is not an option. Employers basically avoid having to make new hires by simply increasing the work hours of their existing employees. Whereas lifelong employment provides workers with the promise of job security, in return workers are expected to provide long-term "flexible" hours of labor to the firm. The lifelong-employment system is thus characterized by "flexicurity," based on "a balance between security of tenure and flexibility of working conditions."[16] Regular workers (those who are permanently employed) are expected to work long hours with little family or personal time; to accept low wages in the early stages of their careers; to agree to rotations across different divisions and branch offices; and to face the possibility of early retirement or transfer to different divisions or smaller branches of their parental firm.[17]

Since the 1990s and Japan's economic decline, a few Japanese companies have superficially adopted Western management techniques, including laying off workers, hiring a large number of temporary staff, and basing evaluation and promotion on performance. These typically have led to the destabilization of employment but did nothing to fundamentally change lifelong employment or increase labor mobility and equal opportunity.

## Corporate Governance and Liberalization in the 1990s

Japan's lifelong-employment system has been firmly interlocked with large Japanese banks and financial firms, which are at the heart of the country's system of "coordinated capitalism" (or "institutional complementarities").[18] In contrast with Western firms, Japanese firms are known to aim for long-term profits and productivity rather than short-term profits, with large banks stabilizing them through long-term financing. A firm's tight relationships with one main bank and other financial and trading firms maintains the security of lifelong employment within the organization. Whereas Anglo-American firms employ a shareholder system and aim at maximizing shareholder value and investment profit, Japanese firms' governance, a so-called stakeholder or cross-shareholding system, is centered on a main bank or large financial or trading group offering protection from the threat of a takeover and the stress of short-term market pressures.[19] The board of directors in a Japanese firm, usually dominated by insiders, ensures that management and employees hold shared views and interests.[20]

> Cross-shareholding may safeguard top management focus on long-term business strategy, but also act as a precondition for vesting insider control and preventing strategic change of Japanese firms. . . . Lifetime employment and seniority wages contribute to investment in firm-specific skills, but potentially hinder or delay needed restructuring. The insider-dominated board structure and managerial career patterns assure the continuity of business policies and long-term view, but also favour business conservatism and empire building.[21]

Thus, Japanese companies' custom of lifelong employment coupled with bank financing reifies internal control by management and legitimizes employee conformity.

Major banks make an implicit promise to rescue failing firms by providing additional loans, refinancing existing debt, guaranteeing firms' other debts, and assigning bank members to act as firm managers and directors. The Japanese government also provides an incentive to banks for rescuing potentially profitable firms through institutional rents.[22] Jennifer Amyx notes that the main-bank system helped stabilize industry throughout the high-growth period in Japan.[23] The finance ministry had implicitly guaranteed the banks' long-term lending relationships with the companies.[24] Officials from the main banks commonly served as the investing companies' vice presidents or in positions on their boards of directors, serving not just as lenders but also as shareholders.[25] This bank-centered stakeholder (shareholding) system builds on the value of insider (cross-shareholders and employees) consensus and a cooperative business strategy, and it leads to a tendency on the part of firms toward "vesting insider control and preventing strategic change."[26]

In the 1990s, a variant of reforms based on liberalism was introduced into the Japanese system, mostly as a way to save labor costs, even though it left untouched the basics of community-oriented management. A series of banking crises weakened Japan's banks when they sold large portions of firm shares;[27] the larger firms lessened their ties with the banks while the smaller firms continued borrowing from them.[28] This prompted Japanese firms to turn from the major banks to the capital markets for financing. Foreign direct investments and foreign ownership of firms rapidly increased in the 1990s. In 2005, foreign investors, almost all from the United States or Europe,[29] owned 23.7 percent of stocks listed on the Tokyo stock exchange, a large increase from the 14.1 percent they owned in 1999 and the 6 percent they owned in 1992.[30]

The increase in foreign ownership of Japanese firms put a strong psychological pressure on Japanese managers, as foreigners asked Japanese management to make various changes in their traditional customs, even as the Japanese banks and other financial investors in the firms remained silent.[31] This pressure inevitably prompted Japanese firms to depart from their traditional insider-oriented style of management and adopt Anglo-American business customs, as management had to take into account much more short-term shareholder values and profits, the firms' downsizing, and the divestiture of assets.[32] The Western shareholder system values reduction of excess employment, divestment of less profitable businesses, and matching wages to productivity.[33] Nonetheless, it is not clear to what extent the increase in foreign investment is likely to change the lifelong-employment practices and traditional conservative business culture of Japan. Even though Japanese companies are increasingly likely to implement cost cutting in order to ensure their profits and even their survival, it is not clear how Japan can invigorate the existing employment and management system, which is based solely on firm-specific skills, without mobilizing the labor market.

For Japanese firms, the traditional method of downsizing or reducing labor costs has been an employment adjustment that includes a freeze on hiring new graduates, the offer of voluntary early retirement, transfers of employees to other firms, and internal reallocation rather than laying off existing regular workers. Some argue that outsiders on a board of directors are more likely to resort to methods such as layoffs or voluntary retirement, whereas insiders are more disposed to protect incumbent employees by decreasing new hires.[34] However, others report that the relationship between foreign ownership and firms' radical departure from traditional lifelong employment is not so straightforward.[35] The successful operation of foreign firms requires an extensive adjustment between the global company and the host country in employment and management practices. Past research on automotive companies has found that institutional differences between Western countries, such as the United States or United Kingdom, and Japan have made the home country's transfer of the production and management system to the Western country difficult (unless the parent company and the host country share similar institutional characteristics in their management and employment systems).[36] According to this research, local employees may not conform to, and may even actively resist, the foreign company's implementation of home-grown organizational and employment customs, and such worker resistance could negatively influence the foreign firms' profits and productivity. Further studies will be necessary to determine how Western firms in Japan could effectively implement their home customs of hiring, firing, and evaluation in Japanese branches, particularly because there is so little mobility in the Japanese labor market and individual skills are not evaluated adequately as they are not firm specific. Japanese companies are likely to further destabilize the overall employment picture and decrease employee protection without revitalizing the labor market.

## Liberal Reforms and Increasing Temporary Hires

In addition to the banking crises and increases in foreign ownership, international pressure for liberalization or deregulation of the Japanese labor market also contributed to Japanese firms' incentive to adopt some aspects of the Western management style. Karen Shire points out:

> Among the international organizations, the OECD is a strong proponent of American style flexible labor market policies. . . . Among the major OECD recommendations for Japan are the deregulation of temporary work and the improvement of the availability of firm external training and skill certification to enhance labor market mobility. . . . Japan scored among the group of highly regulated labor markets, on a par with Germany.[37]

Many firms have introduced small shifts from a seniority-based wage system to a so-called performance- or productivity-based system, and increased their numbers of temporary and contract workers rather than laying off existing regular employees. However, some have pointed out that Japan's shift from seniority-based to productivity-based pay was superficial. Kimiko Kimoto wrote that even though the idea of productivity-based evaluation became widespread quickly in Japan in the 1990s and was touted in the media, the actual changes made by companies were limited. She continued:

> The idea of a productivity-based system has some ideological impact as it has rejected traditional Japanese management, which has always been characterized by loyal devotion and commitment to one's company, and it emphasized individual responsibility (which was lacking in traditional management) . . . The workers' loyalty to the firm may have been weakened by the ideological emphasis on self-responsibility. Their employment security may also have been weakened. But their long-term employment practices have not changed. Middle-aged and older men continue to work long hours and show great devotion to their company.[38]

Indeed, in a study of over a thousand firms in Japan,[39] less than 20 percent stated that they value employees' productivity over their years of service and age in their evaluation system. Japanese firms continue to hire new college graduates and only occasionally fire midcareer workers; thus, any change to the internal labor market is only tentative.[40]

Steven Vogel points out that Japan's so-called performance-based wage system is a "cover for wage restraint. . . . [The Japanese firms] reduced the base wage and increased the performance-based component, but on average they did not pay out performance bonuses sufficient to offset the lower base. In practice, most firms maintained relatively modest discrepancies in wages among a particular cohort."[41]

Japan's performance-based wages are characterized by a very small gap between those who accomplish the most and those who do the minimum. It is essentially unchanged from seniority pay in terms of how it rewards individual workers, but it saves firms money and grants them greater authority than the traditional pay system.

Prior to the 1990s, in order to sustain core male workers' lifelong employment and seniority-based wages, Japanese firms would hire a large number of part-time workers, offer voluntary early retirement, and institute hiring freezes if they needed an "employment adjustment."[42] In the 1990s, however, Japanese firms expanded their hiring of irregular workers, such as temporary workers, as their major means of cost savings. (There have been three reforms to the Japanese temporary help law—in 1990, 1994, and 1996—and one major revision—in 1999.)[43] As a result of this increase in the use of irregular workers, the gender gap in the labor market further increased. A large number of the temporary workers were women, and they served as a buffer that protected lifelong-employed male workers; this arrangement further deprived women of access to regular or lifelong employment.[44] In this way, Japanese firms kept the lifelong-employment system and the security of their core regular workers untouched, thus preserving an internal labor market, reducing the cost of irregular workers, and deepening the division between lifelong regular workers and irregular workers.[45]

From 1992 to 2001, the regular employment rate for women decreased from 62 percent to 52 percent, and by 2010 it was down to 46 percent. During the same period, the regular employment rate for men shifted from 91 percent (in 1992) to 88 percent (in 2001) to 81 percent (in 2010).[46] The disparity between regular and irregular workers reinforced a labor market that already exhibited deep gender divisions, and regular women workers performing clerical jobs were increasingly replaced with temporary workers.

> Clerical work has been the largest area of temporary dispatched work in Japan. Despite the extension of allowable occupations for temporary work to technical and professional occupations with the 1990 and 1996 reforms, a steady decline in the proportion of all dispatched workers in these occupations continued. In 1997 70% of all dispatched workers were in clerical roles, and 11.7%, the second largest proportion, in professional and technical work. Two-thirds of all temporary dispatched workers are women. Further, women are over-represented in the less skilled areas of temporary work (e.g. 92% of clerical work), while men dominate the only clearly skilled occupational grouping: professional and technical workers.[47]

Under deregulation and liberalization in the 1990s, a large number of women were relegated to irregular or temporary worker positions, thus further reinforcing gender inequality and safeguarding Japan's male-breadwinner welfare regime. Women were further pushed to the periphery of the Japanese labor market, with little opportunity to advance, despite having the same education as men.[48] Heidi Gottfried points out that under global pressure to liberalize Japan enacted contradictory reforms to deregulate temporary women workers, thus cementing their low status and wages. During the same period, it also engaged in a series of reforms for gender equality, such as revisions to the Equal Employment Opportunity Law and the Basic Law for a Gender-Equal Society.[49] Chizuko Ueno agrees that "neo-liberalist reform had double-edged effects";[50] while the vested rights of privileged employees became visible, less privileged women workers were pushed further into marginal statuses, while those women who were already privileged, such as female regular employees and managers, ended up benefitting.[51] Ueno argues, therefore, that the neoliberal reforms of the 1990s established contradictory dichotomized career paths and economic statuses for educated women in the Japanese labor market.

## Vested Interests and Inertia

In the 1990s, the major banks' loss of financial and managerial power over the companies in Japan, the increased foreign investment and ownership of Japanese firms, and a surge in neoliberal ideology and liberalization pressure all contributed to the disruption of the traditional Japanese employment system by introducing Japanese firms to the Western paradigm of shareholder governance, individual performance tied to pay and promotion, and an expansion in the hiring of irregular employees. However, the central structure of the lifelong-employment system in Japanese firms has not changed as a result of the changes during this period, even though labor mobility has somewhat increased, mostly through further dichotomization of employees into regular workers and irregular workers.[52]

The many core male workers who already had secure jobs before the changes started in the 1990s were largely exempt from the threat of layoffs, and their existence continued to sustain the traditional management style and organizational culture of Japanese firms. Lifelong employment, which, to this day, retains support in the Japanese business community,[53] continued to "preserve job security for incumbent core workers" and to "squeeze out older and younger workers from the benefits of permanent tenure," as well as to intensify the flexicurity dynamic of the lifelong-employment system.[54] This Japanese version of "liberalism" has proven to be an exploitative form, designed to save existing lifelong employees and preserve coordinated capitalism, in which employees' individual skills and diverse backgrounds are valued much less than conformity and devotion to the firm.

Dore suggests that the Japanese stakeholder system remains intact because top managers are nearly all home-grown products of a system that prizes lifetime commitment to the firm, and there has been little change in the bureaucratic internal-promotion system.[55] Japanese companies continue to value firm-specific skills and the internal labor market.

The excessive protection of some regular workers is also a result of Japanese laws that have prohibited their adverse treatment.[56] Men's lifelong employment is intact within a continuing gendered welfare regime in which the male core workers enjoy good pay and benefits to support themselves and their wives and children, whereas a large number of equally qualified young women work in temporary jobs. Kazuo Yamaguchi and Yoshio Higuchi argue that the Japanese management system remains deeply embedded in this breadwinner-based welfare regime in which Japanese firms base salaries not only on male workers but also on their wives and children, as if hiring the worker's entire family.[57] The middle-aged men whose wives do not work outside the home usually oppose changing this long-standing employment system—and they have enormous power in their firms, in government, and in labor unions.[58]

Edward Lincoln has pointed out that the existing lifelong employees have a major vested interest in preventing change in these employment customs:

> Consider that the senior management of all major firms comprises lifetime employees who have worked their way up through the system. Surely they would prefer to maintain the system in which they prospered, and until or unless major changes in the financial system yield a set of shareholders, bond holders or lenders who put them under extreme pressure to change management behavior, there is no reason to expect them to advocate real change.[59]

Aoki sees Japanese corporate governance and management as on track for diversification as a result of the increasing presence of foreign shareholders.[60] However, as I noted, the increase in foreign shareholders does not automatically mean there will be changes in Japanese management. Implementing Western management principles and practices inside Japanese companies can be very difficult because of the deeply institutionalized practices in the Japanese business context.[61] Rather than expecting Japan to absorb more tenets of Western management, some believe that Japan's system of capitalism, however constrained, has already gone through a highly selective but nonetheless real adaptation to and hybridization of aspects of the Western system.[62] Furthermore, Japan's system of coordinated capitalism "is inimical to quick institutional adjustment, with concomitant costs in terms of economic performance."[63] Thus, without considerable economic and political pressure, Japan is not likely to change any further.

Others, however, see fundamental change as vital to Japan, simply because the existing undemocratic and nonliberal management system is ultimately not rewarding either to management or to workers. Sven Steinmo writes:

> The Japanese economic model was based on a system of deference to authority and the widespread confidence that those in power would use their authority for the long-term interest of the whole. . . . Partly because Japan lacks a strong state and partly because the liberal attitudes . . . about individual freedom have never been key to the system, the liberalizing reforms that have been instituted were insufficient to transform the systems as a whole. . . . If Japan did not want to be left in the dustbin of history, it too had to embrace the future and allow individualism to blossom. . . . A system in which management and workers stayed with the same companies their entire lives and salary and promotion was based almost exclusively on seniority and hierarchy, would necessarily

undermine innovation and the development of entrepreneurial spirit that would be required in the globalized world economy.[64]

Many have opined that Japanese management is centered on conformity and control rather than on individual creativity. Lifelong employment is also not entirely about economic security but about group values—loyalty, commitment, and trust—that senior members of the Japanese business community continue to see as vital to the Japanese economy.[65] Their nostalgic and nationalistic sentiments toward these values, coupled with an aversion to the US-type market economy, are to blame for the low rate of change in Japanese companies.

Japanese capitalism also remains firmly embedded in a system that values traditional insider networks and bonds, and that promotes the "inertia of cultural reproduction and the continuing dominance of a communitarian managerial ethic of benevolent responsibility."[66] In addition, as a result of the surge in the hiring of irregular female workers after deregulation, Japanese firms retain a sex-segregated labor force: core lifelong-employed middle-aged males, who insist on traditional insider-based management culture, and young irregular workers, who serve the former group as assistants. When we look at Japanese firms' culture, it is not difficult to see that many of the factors that make change difficult also hinder women's access to the insider-only community.

## The Postwar Male-Breadwinner Employment Regime

The family in Japan is another institution that was integral to the operation of coordinated capitalism in the postwar period of economic development. During this period, the expectation was that women's main place would be at home with the family, though their cheap part-time labor also supplemented economic development. Women fulfilling the caretaker role at home cut postwar Japan's welfare spending, and their part-time flexible labor outside the home cut firms' labor costs. Thus, the Japanese state promoted women as caretakers and assistants who served the head of the household and not as individual earners in the national economy.

In the 1970s, the Japanese state, seeking a flexible solution to rising labor costs, continued to turn to women as part-time workers and full-time unpaid caretakers of children and the elderly.[67] These women served, in effect, as shock absorbers for the labor market. Through its tax and pension policies, the state explicitly promoted this scenario of women fully devoting themselves to the caretaker role or working only part time. Even in 2012, a wife whose earnings were below 1.03 million yen ($10,300) did not have to pay income tax at all, as she qualified for a dependent-spouse income tax break.[68] In addition to this tax break, many

Japanese firms have provided married male employees with a "spousal benefit" for their employed wives if the wives earn less than 1.03 million yen.[69] Under the national pension plan and employer-based pension plans, a wife who earns less than 1.30 million yen ($13,000) annually has not had to pay for any type of pension plan but has been entitled to receive a pension as a dependent of her employed husband. The economic incentive for women to devote themselves entirely to their families was even further strengthened in the 1980s. Before pension reform took place, a married woman in Japan, whether she had a job or not, had to pay into the national pension plan for herself and stood to lose her right to receive a pension if she divorced. After the reforms in 1985, married women were given the right to receive their full pension whether or not they divorced. (They are paid by the taxpayers.) Little support has been given to single-mother households during this same period (though Japan did start, in 1965, offering a lenient survivor's pension to a wife whose husband had died).[70] The continued existence of the exemption for the social security fee for married women demonstrates Japan's explicit privileging of the household based on the male-breadwinner over other types of households, incentivizing women to take part-time or low-paying jobs.[71] Thus, it structurally encourages sex segregation in the labor market and the continuance of the traditional organizational hierarchy.

By making women take care of the elderly and children, and requiring corporations to pay for married couples' insurance, pensions, and living benefits, Japan's male-breadwinner welfare policy has saved the state a considerable sum of money and helped rein in a huge government budget deficit.[72] The system also has had a great impact on women. Marriage became a major means for women to attain economic security in the 1980s, because the male-breadwinner welfare policy made it difficult for unmarried women to be economically independent without falling into poverty.[73] The ideology of the "good wife and wise mother" became a national slogan in Japan's modernization. The "three-year-old myth," the idea that a mother should stay home to take care of her children until they turned three years old, also reinforced women's place within the domestic sphere.

The number of salaryman/housewife couples in Japan increased from 5 million in 1955 to 11 million in the 1980s.[74] Since the 1980s, the position of "housewife" has been widely viewed as a desirable status rather than as a sign of a woman's inability to be independent or as an indication of her lack of employment skills and opportunities. But the Japanese feminist Sakiko Shiota, referring to Ann Oakley's description of housewives as the privileged class who manage to escape poverty and prove their social status by attaching themselves to husbands, strongly criticizes this glamorized notion of housewives, arguing that it has promoted women's economic dependency on their husbands to the detriment of their own financial security and dignity—both of which men normally attain from their own jobs.[75]

The housewife in Japan has been provided security by both the Japanese state and her husband, especially because wives traditionally manage their husbands' entire income.[76] Shiota argues that the dual protection the housewife receives comes at the expense of tax money and writes that the wife's not working beyond the amount of tax exemption is a choice made by the married couple; the husband receives her domestic service, and thus her husband, or she herself, should pay for the pension and tax from their total income.[77] While this situation has begun to be publicly criticized, these pension and tax policies persist and continue to benefit men, especially those who earn high incomes. For example, in 2011, receiving a wife's pension exemption was more common among high-income earners in Japan; about 70 percent of those who did not pay the wife's pension were married couples in which the man's income was over 9 million yen ($90,000).[78] Under the welfare policy that has promoted women's low income and economic dependency on their husbands, a large number of married women have tended to quit their jobs after giving birth and later reenter the labor market as part-time workers. Mari Osawa notes that compared to those of the other OECD countries, poverty rates among the male-breadwinner households were only slightly lower than among the households in which all household members worked (dual-earner, single, or single parent).[79]

In the postwar period, Japanese companies relied heavily on the male-breadwinner model of families and the gendered structure of the welfare regime. By the 1990s, the state had enacted the Part-Time Labour Law, further reinforcing these gender-specific policies and making it easy for women to enter part-time work.[80] Even when the birthrate further declined in the 1990s, the Japanese government continued to redefine women's dual roles as workers and mothers. Heidi Gottfried and Nagisa Hayashi-Kato have criticized Japan's series of measures to counter the low birthrate, including the Angel Prelude Plan:

> This policy links a pro-natalist campaign to the health and wealth of the nation: The health of the nation depends on the women increasing their fertility in order to reproduce the future workforce and to care for elderly parents at home, whereas the wealth of the nation depends on women's own labour force participation as part-time workers.... Non-standard employment among women was part of an overall strategy to maintain the pro-growth economic regime, which had the consequence of accentuating gender differentiated labour markets.[81]

In contrast with that of the 1980s, the Japanese government in the late 1990s expressed support for women's roles as paid domestic workers and family caretakers and put in place a national care system for the elderly, which was intended to reduce the burden on women.

Osawa argues that it was around 1996, with new national incentives to enhance the economy and reduce women's household burden, that the traditional male-breadwinner model started to be questioned in Japan.[82] The administration of Prime Minister Ryutaro Hashimoto put in place a gender-equality office and then enacted the 1997 revision of the EEOL. Osawa writes that a series of policy changes in the late 1990s demonstrated much improved government support of employed women.[83] Japanese feminists have also mentioned some fortuitous factors between 1996 and 1998 that prompted the Japanese government's gender-equal initiatives regarding women's employment, such as the Liberal Democratic Party's having been forced into an alliance with the progressive parties—New Party Sakigake, led by Akiko Domoto, and the Social Democratic Party, led by Takako Doi (both women).[84] In 2001, Prime Minister Junichiro Koizumi appointed five female cabinet members and was proud of his administration being aligned with the slogan "gender-equal society."[85] Also, in 1999, the Basic Law for a Gender-Equal Society was passed, which promised comprehensive measures to promote gender equality, women's advancement in various fields of society, and an increase in women leaders. However, critics have expressed concern that the Basic Law for a Gender-Equal Society was largely symbolic,[86] and that "the Council for Gender Equality within the Prime Minister's Office . . . is primarily an advisory and liaison body with no administrative power."[87]

From the late 1990s to the 2000s, however, the Japanese male-breadwinner welfare system remained largely unchanged. Concerned about the declining birthrate, Japan initiated a series of life-work balance policies beginning in the 1990s, and such policies also helped legitimize the discourse of gender equality in Japan.[88] Japan's gender-policy reforms purported to be about women's balancing work and family, but they were not clearly enough defined as being about gender egalitarianism. In short, Japan's postwar welfare regime and division between the genders has been modified but not entirely replaced with an egalitarian model. Even though the Japanese state claims to fully support women's employment and balancing work with caretaker obligations, the state has ultimately done little regarding gender equality.

Glenda Roberts points out, however, that the birthrate drop caused the Japanese government to create a legal infrastructure that takes into account the principle of gender equality, including a series of "family-friendly" policies.[89] Yet, even though the government-issued guidelines for family-friendly firms have been helpful for women workers, the legislation is only for "administrative guidance" and lacks enforceability.[90] Roberts maintains that even though work-life balance policies allow some women working full-time to keep their jobs, their benefits do not extend to men, as they are not considered to be the main caretakers of the family,[91] nor do the policies cover part-time or irregular women workers. Roberts questions why these policies "do not apply to these workers, [which] leads one to wonder whose balance 'family-friendly' policies aim at keeping."[92] Since Japan's major policy change on women's employment is not about gender equality in employment or family, it is not surprising that the majority of irregular women workers receive no benefit from any of the policies relating to women's employment.

In 2009, about 42 percent of employees in Japan were women.[93] Yet the number of women who work in irregular jobs (part-time, temporary, or contract workers) surged from 32 percent in 1985 to 53 percent in 2009.[94] Men in irregular types of employment went from 7 percent in 1985 to 18 percent in 2009. It is notable that the once stable status of male breadwinner has been slowly declining because of men's declining wages and the destabilization of lifelong jobs, yet women's employment status has not filled the gap because it has not improved much. The postwar notion of the "housewife" continues to enjoy some popularity among unmarried Japanese women, even though many now see it as an economically unrealistic option. In 2010, only about 20 percent of unmarried women and 10 percent of unmarried men viewed the housewife model as the most ideal way of managing a family, and 35 percent of unmarried women and 40 percent of unmarried men also thought that women should be reemployed after raising children to a certain age. Nonetheless, the fact that the full-time homemaker continues to earn more cultural respect in Japan than in the United States needs to be understood in the context of Japan's postwar welfare regime,[95] whose persistence is reinforced by the state and business regime as well as by national ideology.

## Highly Educated Women and Vertical Sex Segregation

I now address the increase in the number of educated women in Japan and examine how this trend relates to continuing sex segregation in the Japanese company. Educated employed women increasingly continue to work, regardless of whether they are married or have children, yet the number of women in positions of power and authority remains low.

"Vertical segregation" refers to women's concentration in clerical and low-level management positions;[96] vertical sex segregation is a major cause of gender inequality in Japanese companies.[97] It has been pointed out that Japan shows higher levels of sex segregation than the United States in all of the following areas: managerial, professional and technical, and service-sector work.[98]

Women managers are still rare in Japan. In 2010 women made up only 13.7 percent of all subsection chiefs (*kakaricho*), 7.0 percent of section chiefs (*kacho*), and 4.2 percent of department heads (*bucho*) or general managers (table 2.1). These do indicate large increases from the numbers seen in 1989, however, when women made up only 4.6 percent of subsection chiefs, 2 percent of section chiefs, and 1.3 percent of department heads.[99]

Even with the increases from 1989 to 2010, Japan is still far behind the United States and the United Kingdom, where women constitute 43 percent and 35 percent, respectively, of managers (table 2.2).[100]

Japanese firms have viewed the problem of the lack of female managers as unsurprising, especially when workers' promotions rely heavily on years of service; until very recently, a large number of women quit their jobs on marriage

**TABLE 2.1**   Percentage of women managers in Japan, 1989–2012

| MI | 1989 | 1995 | 2000 | 2005 | 2010 | 2012 |
|---|---|---|---|---|---|---|
| Subsection chiefs (*kakaricho*) | 4.6 | 7.3 | 8.1 | 10.4 | 13.7 | 14.4 |
| Section chiefs (*kacho*) | 2 | 2.8 | 4 | 5.1 | 7 | 7.9 |
| Department heads (*bucho*) | 1.3 | 1.3 | 2.2 | 2.8 | 4.2 | 4.9 |

*Source:* Based data in Gender Equality Bureau Cabinet Office, "White Paper on Gender Equal Society, 2013."

**TABLE 2.2**   Percentage of women administrators and managers in twelve countries

| COUNTRY | PERCENT |
|---|---|
| Philippines | 52.7 |
| United States | 43.0 |
| France | 38.7 |
| Australia | 36.7 |
| United Kingdom | 35.7 |
| Norway | 34.4 |
| Singapore | 34.3 |
| Sweden | 31.2 |
| Germany | 29.9 |
| Malaysia | 25.0 |
| Japan | 11.1 |
| South Korea | 9.4 |

*Source:* Based on fig. 1 in Gender Equality Bureau Cabinet Office, "Toward Active Participation of Women as the Core of Growth Strategies, White Paper on Gender Equality, 2013."

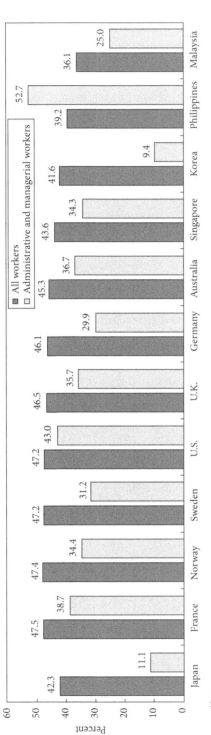

**FIGURE 2.1** Women among administrative/managerial workers.

Notes:
1. Based on the "Labour Force Survey (Basic Tabulation)" by the Ministry of Internal Affairs and Communications (2012) and "Databook of International Labour Statistics 2012" by Japan Institute for Labour Policy and Training.
2. 2012 data are used for Japan, 2008 data for Australia, and 2010 data for other countries.
3. For the purpose of "Labour Force Survey" by the Ministry of Internal Affairs and Communications, "Administrative and Managerial Workers" include company officers, company management staff, and management government officials among workers. Definition of administrative and managerial workers varies across countries.
4. "Labour Force Survey" by the Ministry of Internal Affairs and Communications uses the population assumed on the basis of the fixed population according to 2010 census (new reference) as the base of calculation.

*Source:* Gender Equality Bureau Cabinet Office, "Toward Active Participation of Women as the Core of Growth Strategies, White Paper on Gender Equality, 2013."

or childbirth and thus were unlikely to accrue many years of service. In 2006, about 46 percent of large companies (those with more than 5,000 employees) responded to a question about having few female managers by stating that few women had the necessary knowledge, experience, and judgment to fill such positions; about 52 percent of those said that, although there were women workers with the potential to be managers, they needed to stay long enough to be promoted. About 37 percent reported that women quit before they became qualified to be managers (table 2.3).[101] These responses suggest that women's continual employment in one firm is the best solution to increasing the number of women managers in Japanese firms.

Previous researchers have pointed out that the track-hiring system has deprived women of equal opportunity.[102] The track-hiring system relegates a large number of women to "non-career-track" positions that involve clerical assistant-level work and "area-career-track" positions that are similar to career-track positions but with no obligation to relocate. Neither non-career-track workers nor area-career-track workers are given the same benefits and promotion opportunities as career-track workers. Almost all men with a college education are hired as career-track workers, in contrast with the handful of women with the same education who are hired in these positions. In about 120 firms in Japan, women made up only about 22 percent of all the career-track workers who were hired in 2014 (table 2.4). (It should be noted that this figure is a large increase from the roughly 9% in 2009.)[103]

The track-hiring system was still common among large firms in the financial industry in 2006 (tables 2.5 and 2.6); about 49 percent and 47 percent of large companies (those with over 5,000 employees) were using it in 2010 and 2012.

**TABLE 2.3**  Employers' responses (by percent) to the question Why are there few female managers? (companies with more than 5,000 employees) in 2006

| RESPONSE | PERCENT |
|---|---|
| Few women have the necessary knowledge, experience, and judgment to fill such positions. | 46 |
| Although there are women with the potential to be managers, they need to stay long enough to be promoted. | 52 |
| Women quit before they became qualified to be managers. | 37 |
| Management positions require relocation, which women can't do | 9 |
| Management positions require overwork and night work. | 9 |
| Women are responsible for housework and thus cannot do management jobs. | 3 |
| Women cannot do difficult management jobs. | 2 |
| Women themselves do not want to do management jobs. | 14 |
| Other | 15 |

*Source:* Based on Ministry of Health, Labour and Welfare, "Basic Survey on Women's Employment, 2007.

**TABLE 2.4**   Women hired in career-track positions, 2009–14

|                              | 2009 | 2010 | 2011 | 2012 | 2013 | 2014 |
|------------------------------|------|------|------|------|------|------|
| Percentage of women hired    | 9.2  | 11.5 | 11.6 | 18.8 | 19.1 | 22.2 |

*Source:* Based on Ministry of Health, Labour and Welfare, "Career Track Hiring, 2015."

**TABLE 2.5**   Japanese companies with career-track hiring, 2006–12 (percentage by size)

| YEAR | ALL COMPANIES | 5,000 OR MORE EMPLOYEES | 1,000–4,999 | 300–399 | 100–299 | 30–99 |
|------|---------------|-------------------------|-------------|---------|---------|-------|
| 2006 | 11.1          | 55                      | 43.6        | 30      | 17      | 6.3   |
| 2010 | 11.6          | 49.2                    | 45.9        | 26.1    | 16.4    | 8.6   |
| 2012 | 11.2          | 46.8                    | 44.5        | 31.7    | 17.5    | 7.5   |

*Source:* Based on Ministry of Health, Labour and Welfare, "Data on Career-Track Hiring and Positive Action, 2013," fig. 1, p. 2.

**TABLE 2.6**   Japanese companies using career-track hiring, 2006 and 2008 (percentage per industry)

| INDUSTRY         | 2006 | 2008 |
|------------------|------|------|
| Service          | 10   | 8.8  |
| Mining           | 9.6  | 7.9  |
| Construction     | 10.1 | 10.6 |
| Manufacturing    | 10.4 | 11.5 |
| Utilities        | 13.6 | 13.7 |
| Communications   | 12.9 | 9.9  |
| Finance/insurance | 42.8 | 34.4 |
| Real estate      | 20.6 | 17.6 |
| Medical/welfare  | 8.3  | 4.7  |
| Education        | 21   | 19.1 |
| Transportation   | 7.2  | 9.6  |
| Wholesale/sales  | 15   | 13.7 |

*Source:* Based on Ministry of Health, Labour and Welfare, "Data on Career-Track Hiring and Positive Action, 2013," fig. 2, p. 3.

The percentage using it among all firms was about 12 percent, with 34 percent of financial and insurance companies of all sizes using it in 2008 (table 2.6).[104] From 2006 to 2008, the overall rate of those using the career-track hiring system in each industry seems to have declined, yet the percentage in the financial and insurance industries remained high.

The track-hiring system has been posited as the major source of discrimination and marginalization of women workers in Japanese companies. One study revealed that non-career-track women in a securities firm in Japan were treated differently by managers, who provided performance assessments of them based on their grooming and temperament, while men were evaluated on decision making and analytical style and the ways in which they expressed their opinions.[105] The track-hiring system creates "gender queues,"[106] and women workers in non-career-track positions are explicitly marginalized because they are expected to quit when they marry.[107] These women workers also seem to accept their marginality. In Yuko Ogasawara's ethnographic study of a bank from the 1980s non-career-track women workers were seen as "less wedded to the company; they regard authority lightly," and also as accepting of short-term careers, boredom in their assigned jobs, lack of opportunity, and the expectation that they would quit when they married.[108] In her bank study, the women clerical workers saw other women as competitors in the race for marriage, because those who did not quit were labeled as social failures.[109]

Past studies have found that the majority of women workers are commonly relegated to assistant positions, and the assumption that they would eventually quit their jobs to take care of family has been deeply embedded in Japanese companies. But informal discrimination against women workers in Japanese firms is not limited to the track-hiring system. Because Japanese firms typically lack job descriptions and set responsibilities, the evaluation of job performance is often about "the person rather than the person's job performance."[110] Also, women are not given the same tasks and training as men.[111] In some cases, men "are thrown into men-only teams and shoulder all the responsibility for the workplace as though they were the elite troops of a reserved army," while women are assigned duties that do not challenge them or give them a sense of participation; thus, "a sense of boredom and futility haunts women."[112] Such explicitly segregated paths deprive women workers of their aspirations and steer them to the marriage exit,[113] and when they do exit, this only confirms the stereotypical view that women lack ambition and will choose marriage over careers.[114] In addition, in many companies, women have difficulty finding managerial jobs attractive because no female role model is available.[115]

In many of these past studies, however, gender inequality reflected a gender gap in education. In Kimiko Kimoto's study of retail firms and general merchandise stores, college graduates made up only 8 percent of the women in the workplace at the time of the interviews; the author argued that Japanese firms' explicit relegation of women to assistant status reflected educational differences between men and women. This gender gap in education has, however, rapidly diminished. The percentage of women attending four-year colleges or universities soared from 15 to 45 percent between 1990 and 2010, while the percentage of men increased from 33 to 56 percent (table 2.7).[116] Accordingly, from 1985 to 2012, the proportion of newly hired women workers who were college graduates

**TABLE 2.7**   Four-year-college enrollment in Japan by gender, 1986–2012 (percentage)

|  | 1986 | 1990 | 1991 | 1996 | 2001 | 2006 | 2010 | 2012 |
|---|---|---|---|---|---|---|---|---|
| Women | 13 | 15 | 16 | 25 | 33 | 39 | 45 | 46 |
| Men | 34 | 33 | 35 | 42 | 47 | 52 | 56 | 56 |
| Two-year college enrollment (women only) | 21 | 22 | 23 | 24 | 16 | 12 | 11 | 10 |

*Source:* Gender Equality Bureau Cabinet Office, "White Paper on Gender Equal Society, 2013."

**TABLE 2.8**   Percentage of newly hired women and men who were college graduates, 1985–2014

|  | 1985 | 1990 | 2000 | 2005 | 2010 | 2012 | 2014 |
|---|---|---|---|---|---|---|---|
| Women | 12.7 | 14.9 | 36.1 | 49.3 | 57.8 | 60.1 | 62.8 |
| Men | 41.1 | 40.2 | 54.3 | 57.7 | 61.9 | 61.9 | 63.1 |

*Source:* Ministry of Health, Labour and Welfare, "Current Situation on Employed Women, 2013."

increased from around 13 percent to about 60 percent of the total, which closely approximated the percentage of men who were college graduates (table 2.8).[117]

Leonard Schoppa calls the increase in highly educated, highly motivated young women, and the strides they have made in employment, a "gender revolution" in Japan.[118] Ueno points out, however, that the increase in highly educated and career-track women workers occurred simultaneously with another change—the expansion of the use of temporary women workers—and calls the two trends "the double-edged effects of neoliberalism."[119] Still, in combination with the nation's rapid population decline and the egalitarian imperative, this increase in highly educated women could further erode the preeminence of the male-breadwinner model of work and family in Japan.[120]

Interestingly, whereas it was common until the late 1990s for women workers to quit their jobs when they married, none of the unmarried workers whom I interviewed for this book reported workplace pressure to marry and quit, and all reported that, by 2007, it was an outdated norm. With the increasing trend toward late marriage (or no marriage at all) and the growing number of highly educated women, it has quickly become uncommon for women workers to "retire upon marriage" in Japan. In fact, highly educated young women increasingly prioritize work over marriage.[121] Schoppa writes, "Young Japanese women today are very different" in their high aspirations for their jobs, their higher education achievements, and their lack of interest in being full-time housewives.[122] From 1987 to 1997, among eighteen- to thirty-four-year-old unmarried women, those who mentioned the role of full-time housewife as an ideal fell from 34 percent to about 20 percent, and this pattern remained the same in 2010.[123] Also, in the same study, the proportion of those women who wanted to continue to work and have a family at the same time increased from 19 percent in 1987 to 36 percent in 2010.

Furthermore, the rate of regular employed women leaving the workplace on the birth of a child has been decreasing.[124] A study of over 1,000 women between the ages of thirty and forty-four, which measured the women's continual employment from 2005 to 2011 regardless of education, confirmed that the number of women staying in their jobs is increasing.[125] The same study pointed out that highly educated and professional women, in particular, increasingly continued in their jobs by taking parental leave.[126] Over 60 percent of women who were regular employees in urban areas before 1998 quit their jobs when they had children, but only about 30 percent of them quit after 2005, while over 60 percent took parental leave and continued in their jobs.[127] Even among the women who were not regular workers, the rate of quitting after giving birth, while higher than among those who were regular employees, largely decreased after 2005.[128] In a study of about 3,900 women in 2009, 46 percent quit their jobs when they married and 30 percent quit when they had a child.[129] In other words, it is likely that women's continual employment may further increase in Japanese companies in the future, considering that close to 90 percent of women take parental leave in large Japanese firms.[130]

It is too soon to conclude, however, that women workers quitting their jobs is becoming obsolete. The number of women who quit their jobs when they have a child is still seen as a major reason for the absence of female managers in Japanese firms. In 2001, 67 percent of full-time employed and part-time employed women quit their jobs.[131] Ueno states, "Even today, in 2000, nearly 70 percent of women workers leave their jobs on marriage and childbirth, and this figure has remained the same in the last two decades. The major reason for this is because women in their reproductive age have been already thrown into the flex labor market with no job security."[132] In other words, women workers, especially those with meager opportunities for career advancement, continue to see marriage as a viable exit. That is, women with fewer opportunities may continue to quit their jobs on marriage, while those who obtain career-track positions as regular workers may continue to work. This may mean that the cultural norm of the "marriage exit" will not become entirely obsolete unless women stop seeing marriage as providing the best solution to their marginal economic or employment status.

## Sex Segregation and the Legal System

In the 1990s, Japan's laws and policies with regard to gender equality improved as a result of international pressure. The Equal Employment Opportunity Law and other Japanese laws remain weak, however, in the face of sex segregation.

I will question why adoption of such laws has not led to significant changes in the gender customs and authority structures in Japanese companies. Then I look at recent sex discrimination court cases in Japan, comparing the weak approach of the Japanese court system with the dynamic role that US courts have played during the same period as the agents of social change.

## The Equal Employment Opportunity Law

Since the world conference of the International Women's Year was convened by the United Nations in Mexico City in 1975, the UN has become a hub of the international women's movement, with a strong emphasis on the development of human rights or "women's social rights."[133] The UN Convention on the Elimination of All Forms of Discrimination Against Women (CEDAW), which was adopted in 1979, recommended that states follow its principles and commit to undertaking a series of measures to improve discrimination against women in all forms. Bina Agarwal claims that the women's movement and collective pressure could mobilize the public, international aid agencies, and local bureaucracies and increase their bargaining power in the fight for the betterment of women's conditions.[134] Japan's women's movement consists of far smaller and less formal grassroots coalitions than those in the United States, yet they constantly appeal to international organizations to pressure the Japanese government regarding Japan's slow progress in improving the status of employed women.

CEDAW encourages "state parties to take all appropriate measures to resist the traditional cultural norm which disadvantages women and stereotypical assignment of sole or major responsibility for childcare to women."[135] Japanese feminists agree that the emergence of an international "gender equality regime" has greatly encouraged the mobilization of women to fight for effective initiatives to improve employment inequality and has increased the power of women's groups' to pressure the Japanese government.[136]

Women's groups in Japan have strongly requested that the Japanese government follow the CEDAW's report and ratify the optional protocol so that Japanese individuals can directly appeal to the CEDAW to investigate a violation of the convention. But the Japanese government has not ratified this optional protocol, explaining that it conflicts with Japan's judicial system and legislative policy. The CEDAW does not have the power to punish the country for a violation of or the failure to follow the convention. The United States has not even ratified the convention because of congressional suspicion of and aversion to international treaties, and Japan may resort to the same tactics. Thus, the CEDAW seems to be limited in its influence on future social and legal reforms in Japan.

Japan ratified the convention in 1985. As Joyce Gelb noted, "Japan's decision to participate formally with respect to the newly developing international norms related to gender equality seems to have been at least partially due to a desire to be considered a 'modern' nation, worthy of prestige and acceptance."[137] She points out that women's groups have been effective in using CEDAW to embarrass and pressure the Japanese government to demonstrate that it is meeting international human rights standards, yet its efficacy still remains limited.[138]

After the Japanese government signed on to CEDAW in 1980 and ratified it in 1985, it enacted the Equal Employment Opportunity Law in 1986 in order to comply with the UN treaty. While CEDAW defined discrimination against women and provided ratifying countries with legal and policy advice regarding revision of existing policies or enactment of measures for the advancement of gender equality,[139] the EEOL did not prohibit discrimination with regard to recruitment, hiring, assignments, and promotions; it only required employers to make a good faith effort in these areas.[140] After passage of the law, Japanese companies started hiring a small number of "career-track" or "managerial-track" women workers in order to demonstrate their compliance with the idea of gender equality.[141]

The 1997 revision of the EEOL changed employers' "duty to endeavor not to discriminate" to outright prohibition of discrimination in recruiting and hiring, promotion, training, and job assignments.[142] But far from improving the law, the 1997 revision abolished the protective provisions that restricted women from performing overtime and late-night work;[143] this, coupled with the liberalization of temporary employment, further exacerbated poor working conditions for a large number of temporary women workers.[144]

There were other changes in the 1997 revision. First, it included a definition of sexual harassment as a type of gender discrimination. It required employers to explain their policies to their employees, to implement schemes to deal with complaints, and to counsel sexual harassment victims.[145] Also, the 1997 revision granted an employee the right to force an employer into mediation, which would be overseen by the Ministry of Health, Labour and Welfare.[146] It also introduced to firms the option of using "positive action" or "affirmative action," and provided some consulting-related services by the government. However, the 1997 revision did not include effective enforcement; it mentioned offering administrative guidance, but only with the "empty threat" of publication of the names of noncomplying employers. (The ministry had not published the names of any violators as of 2013.)[147] Finally, the revision did not address "indirect discrimination," which "involves employer practices or requirements that are facially neutral but result in disadvantageous treatment that affects a group of people disproportionately."[148] The revision never touched on the major problematic practices that Japanese feminist and women's groups have claimed as typical of "indirect discrimination," such as the differential treatment of women and men because of the two-track hiring system and the division between regular workers and irregular or temporary workers who often perform the same jobs.

The 2007 revision of the law included the prohibition of particular types of indirect discrimination, such as (1) using height and weight requirements in recruitment and hiring; (2) requiring a managerial-track applicant to accept a transfer to anywhere in Japan; and (3) requiring candidates for promotion to have been previously transferred to other places. Employers who do have such requirements must justify their use rationally.[149] The 2007 revision also extended the prohibition of discrimination based on sex into the areas of demotion, change in job type or employment status, encouragement of retirement, mandatory retirement age, dismissal, and renewal of a labor contract.[150] It also prohibited employers from engaging in disadvantageous treatment, such as terminating a woman's employment during pregnancy or within a year after giving birth, or terminating her for taking child-care leave.[151]

Regardless of the expansion of employer behaviors that are deemed discriminatory, the 2007 revision had no effective enforcement mechanism, nor did it mandate positive action.[152] It did not provide incentives for employers who follow the law, such as tax breaks or additional funding,[153] nor did it prescribe punitive measures, such as heavy fines or criminal sanctions, for companies that demonstrate a pattern of sex discrimination.[154] And the 2007 revision still lacks a broader definition of, and prohibition of, indirect discrimination, which would include wage and promotion discrimination based on the two-track system. Overall, the 2007 revision to the Equal Employment Opportunity Law is seen as being ineffective, unlike Title VII of the Civil Rights Act in the United States, because it does not prohibit the major customs associated with gender inequality, such as the track-hiring system; in fact, "the courts see the EEOL as merely a statement of policy that illustrates the current social trends."[155]

In 1999, another important law, the Basic Law for a Gender-Equal Society, was passed, promising comprehensive measures to promote gender equality and women's advancement in various parts of society, as well as an increase in the number of women leaders and managers.[156] The cabinet approved a second plan in 2005, including the goal to expand women's participation in policy decision-making processes and to increase the number of women occupying leadership positions to at least 30 percent by 2020.[157] However, because the law lacked the power to enforce any type of gender-equal policy and thus to change the current gender structure, it has been criticized as being merely a "symbolic source for improving equality."[158]

In the 1990s, serious national concern about population decline and the shrinking future labor force in Japan led policymakers to improve parental leave for workers. The Child Care Leave Law, first passed in 1991, was revised as the Child Care and Family Care Leave Law in 1995. Under 2004 revisions to the law, workers are entitled to a one-year leave that can be extended to up to one-and-a-half years, and the leave is available to both sexes.[159] Workers can be paid up to 40 percent of previous earnings from employment insurance during continued leave, and the employee who has a child younger than elementary school age can take five unpaid leave days and can request a limit on overtime work as well as an exemption from night work.[160] Depending on the size of the company, the child-care leaves that private firms offer vary in availability and length,[161] with public or government-related institutions offering the longest parental leave (three years). In 2013, Prime Minister Abe announced that the leave is to be extended from one to three years.[162] The Japanese business federation, Keidanren, consisting of over thirteen hundred Japanese firms, has expressed general support for an increase in child-care facilities and an enhancement of work-life balance.[163] It is important to note that, in 2007, 90 percent of the working women who gave birth in Japan in the previous year took child-care leave, while only 1.6 percent of working men whose spouses gave birth in the previous year did.[164]

The 2007 EEOL also addresses the government's support for and encouragement of firms' use of positive action, although it neither mandates that companies adopt it nor imposes any type of penalty against firms that never use it. In a survey of about 4,000 companies, about 75 percent of firms with over 5,000 employees used positive action in 2010, while about 50 percent of firms that had between 1,000 and 5,000 employees used it in the same year.[165] Larger firms, then, are far more likely to implement positive action than smaller firms.

Japan has been quite energetic in implementing the EEOL and its revisions, with their lenient parental leave, during the last twenty years. However, the EEOL does little to truly alter Japanese business customs or to pressure the authority structures or upset the vested interests of Japanese companies. The weak Japanese laws are one of the reasons why vertical sex segregation remains much more entrenched in Japan than in other similarly developed countries. I will examine several court cases that demonstrate the pattern of Japanese courts' customary conformity to the wishes of the business community.

## The Courts and Sex Discrimination

Japanese courts are known to be favorable to corporations, and sex discrimination cases have not been an exception to this. It should be noted, however, that the verdicts of some past lawsuits in Japan, when international authorities such as a large global company or the United Nations intervened, have been overturned in favor of plaintiffs.[166]

The Japanese Constitution, in article 14, prohibits discrimination based on race, creed, sex, social status, or family origin in political, economic, or social relations.[167] However, the courts have traditionally argued that the article is not applicable to the private sector; thus, its protection has been weak and limited in the realm of employment-related sex discrimination. Even when judges have found sex discrimination in wages or promotion to be a violation of article 14—and thereby unconstitutional—they have also said that laws were not broken because the defendant did not violate article 90 of the Civil Code or the Labour Standards Law; in these cases they then dismissed the plaintiff's claim of sex-based discrimination. The Labour Standards Law mandates equal treatment of men and women with regard to wages; however, employers can pay different wages to men and women who perform the same tasks when they are able to justify the difference with respect to some factor "other than the employee's gender or gender stereotypes."[168] Japan's Labour Standards Law is also very limited, since it does not prohibit gender-based discrimination with regard to hiring, firing, or promotion, or in other employment-related situations.[169]

In addition to article 14 and the Labour Standards Law, Japanese courts have used a principle based on article 90 of the Civil Code, the "public order doctrine," to nullify any juristic act that is contrary to "public order and good morals." The Japanese courts have regarded some sex discrimination–related employment practices as a violation of public order and morals. Regardless of the implementation of the EEOL, Japanese courts continue to rely on article 90 because the EEOL has no legal enforcement mechanism itself. In many old cases filed in the 1960s, 1970s, and 1980s, Japanese companies were challenged by the courts or lost cases for their discriminatory treatment of women based on beliefs such as (1) female workers are inferior to male workers; (2) women workers are good at simple tasks but not suitable for more responsible jobs; (3) men are the breadwinners and women are the caretakers; and (4) women are meant to be mothers and are less efficient workers than men.[170]

From the 1960s to the 1980s, discrimination was argued in many cases in which Japanese companies forced women to retire on marriage, the birth of a child, or pregnancy, because of the violation of public order based on article 90.[171] From the late 1960s to the early 1970s, the courts ruled in many cases that different retirement ages for men and women workers constituted discrimination, as such policies violate public order. In the 1969 Tokyu-Kikan Kogyo Company case, the Tokyo District Court found that the firm's retirement age of thirty for women workers, which differed from the men's retirement age of fifty-five, was irrational and violated public order. In 1971, in Matsuro v. Mitsui Shipbuilding Corporation, the employer required that all women retire on marriage with one year extension of work and no extension on childbirth. The Osaka District Court claimed that this was a case of sex-based discrimination that goes against public order.[172] However, the Tokyo District Court in 1986 articulated that, while unreasonable sex discrimination in wages and mandatory retirement violates public order, an employer's failure to grant equal opportunity in recruitment and hiring does not violate public order.[173]

Japanese courts are known to be reluctant to condemn companies' discriminatory practices with respect to initial hiring and promotion, and they have been lenient about employers' "freedom of choice" in these areas.[174] They have rarely found sex discrimination in wages under the Labour Standards Law. In 2009, the Tokyo District Court ruled that female clerical workers at Showa Shell Co., compared to male clerical workers with the same educational qualifications, were discriminated against in their wages; therefore, the court found that Showa had violated article 4 of the Labour Standards Law. The court ordered Showa Shell to pay a consolation fee and court costs to twelve female workers, but it did not ask the firm to pay the actual costs that resulted from the sex discrimination because of the difficulty of calculating these costs under the lifelong-employment system. Furthermore, the court added that the employer should have freedom in its evaluation and promotion decisions and should base them on its own judgments under the long-term employment system; thus, the employer's treatment of the plaintiffs remained within its rights.[175] Yasuko Yunoki, one of the plaintiffs, wrote that the court, by emphasizing the employer's freedom to promote under the lifelong-employment system, had made the employees' right to be protected against wage discrimination, defined under the Labour Standards Law, meaningless.[176]

It has been common for the Japanese courts to rule that large firms' double-track hiring is *not* a violation of article 90 of the Civil Code, because the firms implemented career-track hiring and promotion prior to the implementation of the 1997 EEOL revision. They have claimed, therefore, that any discriminatory treatment of women as a result of track hiring that occurred before the 1997 EEOL is not illegal. It is notable that "the Court focused only on two-track systems that companies apply discriminatorily and as a cover for discrimination, not on two-track employment systems in general."[177] In a series of sex-discrimination lawsuits, the courts often dismissed the plaintiffs' requests that the courts consider firms' treatment of women a violation of Japan's treaty under CEDAW because the treaty does not have retroactive effects.[178] In 2001, the Osaka District Court claimed that the hiring gap between men and women at Sumitomo Chemical, which reflected the social norm of gender roles around 1960, was not a violation of article 90. The court recognized that the company had assigned an exam to employees on a subject that did not relate to their jobs and also found that women had a low rate of career-track change. However, it also claimed that such a pattern did not necessarily relate to sex discrimination. Because the firm had long had a track-changing exam, the court claimed that it had provided opportunities for women workers to change their career track and that it was the individual responsibility of each woman to use them to change her track.[179] However, because women employees in general had not been offered the same level of skills training as men, they might not pass the exams when given the chance to take them.[180] For example, in the case of Nomura Securities, only six of the 1,532 qualified women changed their career tracks.[181] Companies may say they hire only men for career-track positions and mostly women for non-career-track positions because career-track workers may be transferred anywhere inside of Japan and most women are not willing to relocate; since non-career-track workers are never transferred, these positions are deemed more appropriate for women, and thus the differing treatment is justified.[182]

There are a couple of cases in which international lobbying resulted in a favorable outcome for the plaintiffs. In a 2000 case, Sumitomo Electric Industries, which placed all men hired with a high school diploma throughout Japan on the management track and all women with a high school diploma in assistant-level clerical jobs, was found by the Osaka District Court to have engaged in sex discrimination under article 14 of the Japanese Constitution. It was noted that the company had treated men and women differently in the areas of hiring, training, transfers, promotions, meeting participation, and business travel. However, the court referred to the firm's freedom to engage in economic activity (even though its hiring customs prior to the EEOL went against the Japanese Constitution) and asserted that the employer's gender-unequal treatment was not a violation of public order (under article 90 of the Civil Code) but rather was a reflection of social norms in the 1960s, long before the enactment of the 1986 EEOL.[183] Miyoko Tsujimura argues that the court's dismissal of the case, on the grounds of its not being a violation of article 90 of the Civil Code, deprives the Japanese Constitution of its authority, despite the court's claim that the firm's practice was discriminatory and a violation of the constitution. She adds that, since the social norm in the 1960s itself violated the Japanese Constitution, it should not be used as a standard of measurement to validate customs from that era; if the court found the firm's hiring and promotion under the track system prior to the EEOL to be in violation of article 14, it should also have found that it was contrary to public order under article 90 of the Civil Code.[184] The court stressed, however, that article 14 of the Japanese Constitution cannot apply to private individuals and that the Labour Standards Law does not therefore apply to sex discrimination in hiring. Furthermore, the court asserted that the 1986 EEOL had only promoted firms' efforts to improve gender equality and that it was the 1997 revision of the EEOL that for the first time prohibited sex discrimination in employment opportunities and treatment of men and women; therefore, only the firm's practices after the 1997 revision could be claimed as discriminatory. The Osaka District Court dismissed the plaintiff's claim in 2000. Japanese women's groups reported the unjustness of the ruling to the UN, and CEDAW, in 2003, recommended that the Japanese government work toward gender equality in the labor market, eliminate the gender wage gap, and enhance awareness of the sex discrimination inherent in such practices as track hiring.[185] In a 2000 case, Sumitomo Electric Industries, the Osaka High Court overturned the initial ruling, finding that the employer practiced sex discrimination, and ordered a settlement favorable to the plaintiffs, mentioning gender equality as a universal value and noting that continuation of past discriminatory customs reverses progress.[186]

The Nomura Securities Case clearly demonstrates the effectiveness of international pressure on Japanese companies. Thirteen female employees of Nomura Securities initially filed a suit against the firm because of track hiring in which women were relegated to non-career-track jobs and discriminated against in pay and promotions. In 2002, the Tokyo District Court ordered Nomura Securities to pay compensation to the twelve women plaintiffs only for the damages that took place *after* the enactment of the 1997 EEOL revision. The Tokyo Court decided that track hiring before the 1997 EEOL revision was not discriminatory.

The plaintiffs in the Nomura Securities case then filed complaints with the International Labor Organization, claiming that the company's use of the track system was a violation of ILO Convention No. 100, which resulted in the organization requesting that the government take necessary measures. But, more important, the Sweden-based investment-rating company Global Ethical Standard Investment Service blacklisted Nomura Holdings (the parent company of Nomura Securities) for sex discrimination and stated that they should not receive investments.[187] In order to prove its compliance with international business practices, Nomura Securities put ethics rules in place and settled with the plaintiffs who had sued the firm for its discriminatory track system. International business pressure such as that enacted by this Swedish investment service proved to be far more effective than indirect pressure on the Japanese government, Japanese companies, or even international courts. The case of the Swedish agency's blacklisting tells us that Japan might be willing to comply with gender equality only when not doing so might damage their names and reputations, and hurt profits. In 2004, the Tokyo High Court ordered a settlement, which resulted in a favorable payment and promotions for some of the women.

Distinct wage discrimination was found in the next case I describe. In 1995, six women workers claimed that a wage gap based on the double-track system was sex discrimination and filed a lawsuit against Kanematsu Corporation. Initially, in 2003, the Tokyo District Court dismissed the plaintiffs' claim that the double-track system kept wages lower for non-career-track women than for men who did the same work, because the double-track system violates neither the Labor Standards Law nor article 90 of the Civil Code, even though it is unconstitutional. The court said that the company had introduced a new system to change one's career track if one wished and that this system was rational; thus, the firm's wage system did not violate public order under article 90.[188]

The Tokyo High Court, however, overturned this 2003 decision after the plaintiffs submitted detailed documents that showed that there was little difference in the value of the work that men and women employees did yet these women were paid lower salaries and given fewer promotions.[189] The court held that the wage gap based on the track system, in which a fifty-five-year-old woman could not earn more than a twenty-seven-year-old man, violated the Labor Standards Law as well as article 90, and thus the employer's treatment of the women had been illegal.[190] In 2009, the Supreme Court upheld this Tokyo High Court ruling, fourteen years after the original case. Mitsuko Miyaji, a lawyer who is an expert on sex-discrimination lawsuits, pointed out that the Kanematsu ruling had, for the first time, recognized sex discrimination in wages that occurred prior to the enactment of the 1997 EEOL revision.[191]

In another case, in 2005, the Osaka District Court claimed that not all track hiring and promotion can be exempt from violation of article 90 of the Civil Code. It ruled that women workers who had the same ability to conduct their work as men were discriminated against at Sumitomo Metal, that this should be dealt with separately from the track-hiring system, and thus it violated article 90 of the Civil Code.[192]

In Japan, neither double-track hiring nor sex-discriminatory pay practices have yet been seen as illegal unless there has been detailed evidence that the pay, promotion, or hiring practices were explicitly discriminatory based on sex. Still, the last couple of cases have shown apparent progress, with the courts moving away from rigidly deciding that the career-track division is not evidence of sex discrimination because it reflects the social order of the 1960s prior to the 1997 EEOL. What has made these courts' decisions strikingly different from the rulings in other cases is the effect of direct pressure from international authorities such as multinational corporations.

Also, the courts have shown a willingness to consider the quality and value of work assigned to male and female employees in these cases based on documentation. The court in the Kanematsu case examined the quality and value of the jobs that were assigned to the male and female workers and compared each with their wages.[193] Five out of five women employees at Kanematsu did the same work or more work than men in terms of knowledge, skills, responsibilities, assigned roles, emergency responses, and expected outcomes and work environments,[194] but they were paid about half to 60 percent of the men's wages.[195]

Women's groups such as the Working Women's Network in Japan have continually reported to CEDAW and ILO that the lack of the principle of "equal pay for work of equal value" is an obstacle to fair resolution of sex-discrimination court cases in Japan. They have requested that the Japanese government comply with CEDAW and with ILO Convention No. 100 and include the principle of equal pay for equal work in the Labor Standards Law. Given the impact of the Swedish agency's response in the case of Nomura Securities, relying on external pressure may continue to be the best way to address the injustice of discrimination and Japan's reluctance to reduce it. CEDAW and women's groups have also suggested stated that the "equal pay for work of equal value" principle should be applied to irregular workers such as temporary and part-time workers, who often perform the same types of jobs as regular workers yet do not receive the same wages and benefits. Whereas the 2007 EEOL does not consider companies' use of career-track hiring to be discrimination because career-track paths represent different types of jobs, women's groups and scholars have claimed that career-track hiring is a form of "indirect discrimination" and, as such, must be explicitly banned in the next revision of the EEOL.

Regardless of article 14 of the Japanese Constitution, the Labour Standards Law and the 2007 EEOL are currently limited in their ability to remedy the track-based hiring, promotion, and wage system. The custom of gender-divided tracks is still deemed an integral part of the employment system of many firms, and the courts are reluctant to deal with it without clear evidence that male and female employees have been assigned the same jobs. The most recent court cases, such as those involving Kanematsu or Sumitomo Metal, have demonstrated that the courts may investigate the actual gaps between men and women workers even when they do not deal with the track-based system itself. But the track system can be deemed a form of institutional discrimination, given that it offers different payment and promotion opportunities to men and women who have exactly the same qualifications and education. Several decades ago, the system might have been more justifiable than it is now because in those days the differences in pay and promotion overlapped somewhat with educational differences between men and women. Yet now that employed women's educational qualifications, as well as their ambitions, approximate those of men, we need to question why Japanese companies continue to adhere to the custom.

In addition to Japanese courts' reluctance to penalize Japanese companies and employers without the intervention of international bodies, the most recent court case reminds us that the Japanese court system has also been very conservative in its support of Japan's labor and employment system. In 2008, a woman who worked for nearly thirty years at Chugoku Electric Power Inc. filed a sex-discrimination lawsuit against the company. The plaintiff claimed that the majority of male workers received a promotion to chief by their late thirties—over 90 percent of all men were promoted to chief, compared to only 25 percent of women—and that even a man twelve years her junior had received the promotion ahead of her; the plaintiff had remained in the lowest rank of employees for the entire thirty years she had worked for the company. The plaintiff was also required to assist male workers by engaging in traditionally gendered jobs such as cleaning tables and bathrooms for men who stayed at the facility.[196] Hiroshima District Court in 2011 dismissed the plaintiff's claim of sex discrimination, stating that the seemingly gendered treatment she experienced was an outcome of her job performance. It argued that nothing is wrong with individual differences in the pace of promotions and that they depend on performance evaluations. In particular, considering that prior to 1999 women were prohibited from working past midnight (and were thus negatively evaluated for their inability to work overnight), and also that most women in the company were not interested in promotions and left their jobs on marriage and childbirth, it was reasonable that some women might have received lower evaluations than men.[197] The plaintiff appealed, but the Hiroshima High Court in 2013 dismissed the case saying that the company's promotion system is neither sex divided nor discriminatory and that the plaintiff apparently did not deserve promotion as she was negatively evaluated as being self-centered, rigid in adhering to her own views, and lacking teamwork ability.[198] The court insisted, even though the plaintiff pointed out a gender division in promotions, that the difference in promotion and pay was not necessarily gender based. Both court decisions apparently regarded the employer's evaluations of the plaintiff as objective and correct, thus siding with traditional gender stereotypes exhibited by the employer and legitimizing the company's practice of sex segregation. Regarding the court's blaming the plaintiff, the plaintiff's attorney Mitsuko Miyaji noted that the court decision never questioned the Japanese companies' taken-for-granted traditional *mura-ishiki* (small-village mentality) and the excessive value placed on teamwork; thus, the court supports old-fashioned Japanese *mura* values even when as the plaintiff claimed such values themselves may be the problem.[199]

Also, according to Miyaji, the wording of the court's decision in this case was strikingly similar to language appearing in the Japanese Supreme Court judges' informal discussion memo,[200] which had been created by the General Secretariat of the Supreme Court and unofficially circulated among judges.[201] This memo explicitly stated that the court had ruled that Japanese employers have considerable freedom in management and personnel affairs and that it should be rare for cases to go against this custom.[202] There is also a section on the gender gap in promotion. The document goes on to state that even when there is a promotion gap between men and women who started their careers in the same year (such as a ratio of eighty men to twenty women being promoted), this pattern itself does not prove discrimination.[203] Given that there is great similarity between this memo and the wording of the decision in the Chugoku Electric Power Inc. case, it is possible that the judge in the case might have simply followed the guidance in this memo in dismissing it. In fact, it is extremely common for Japanese judges to refer to such memos, called *saibankan kyougi*, which are informal and circulated among local judges.

The plaintiff appealed to the Supreme Court in 2013 and claimed that indirect discrimination is prohibited by CEDAW as well as by article 14 of the Japanese Constitution, and that the case ought to be reconsidered under those laws. In March 2015, the Japanese Supreme Court dismissed the case, claiming that it found no reason to reconsider the plaintiff's appeal of the 2013 decision. Miyaji explained that the Supreme Court did not accept the plaintiff's appeal because the case concerned Japanese companies' discretion with regard to employee promotions and other management matters and that the Supreme Court must obey the wishes of the Japanese government and Japanese business.[204] Considering that the company is one of the largest Japanese electronics firms and the local government is the largest stockholder in the company, it is easy to speculate that the goal of the decision is to protect the company for the sake of Japan's national and business interests.

As long as the Japanese courts continue to explicitly protect Japanese companies' "freedom" in personnel affairs, including discrimination against women, little progress against sex discrimination is likely. The courts, along with Japanese companies and the government, have been critical actors in Japan's system of coordinated capitalism. J. Mark Ramseyer and Eric Rasmusen argue that the General Secretariat of the Supreme Court and Japanese courts (judges) have obeyed the dictates of the Liberal Democratic Party.[205] Former Supreme Court judge Hiroshi Segi, in a 2014 book, calls the Japanese court system a group of slaves or a prison camp, subordinated to the General Secretariat of the Supreme Court and concerned only with clearing cases bureaucratically.[206] Segi argues that the Japanese courts cannot do much in terms of civil liberties, not only because they follow the lead of politicians and lawmakers, but also because they prioritize conforming to the General

Secretariat of the Supreme Court and previous cases above all else.[207] If subordination is at the core of Japanese institutional coordination (with the courts subordinate to the General Secretariat of the Supreme Court and the General Secretariat controlled by the government), it is easy to see sex segregation as just another form of institutionally legitimized subordination in Japan's system of coordinated capitalism. This suggests that changing sex segregation in Japanese companies will not be possible unless the system of institutional coordination is interrupted.

In the United States, class actions have greatly influenced corporate perceptions of race- and gender-based discrimination, playing important roles in large employers' implementation of antidiscriminatory policies regarding hiring and promotions. Simply because of the large amounts of money and the large number of plaintiffs involved in each case, class actions against discrimination can do fatal damage to firms. The strong desire to avoid such damage has provided an incentive for companies to do rigorous research on discriminatory practices and to institute antidiscriminatory training in the workplace. Frank Dobbin and Erin Kelly's study of how several landmark US Supreme Court decisions on sexual harassment shaped corporate and professionals' behavior shows that companies' personnel experts and human resource workers (who are largely women) have played a vital role in preparing grievance procedures and preventative measures and training.[208]

Class actions not only change corporate policies, they also have an impact on public perceptions of gender inequality in the workplace. The 1970 AT & T case, the first that resulted in a settlement in the millions of dollars, involved 15,000 women and minority workers.[209] The Equal Employment Opportunity Commission filed the suit against A T & T for discriminatory hiring and promotion practices. A T & T was ordered to pay $38 million in unpaid wages and required to reveal annual improvements in its hiring and promotion practices for the next six years. Similarly, when the EEOC sued Mitsubishi Motor Manufacturing America on behalf of 300 women for repeated sexual harassment, including touching and groping, the firm agreed, in 1998, to pay out $34 million and to revise its sexual harassment policies and grievance procedures with mandatory employee training.[210] In 2010, several women brokers sued Merrill Lynch, owned by Bank of America, for sex discrimination. Women financial advisers alleged discrimination in pay, client accounts and referrals, and professional support that results in men holding cumulative advantages over women. The lawsuit resulted in a $39 million settlement for about 4,800 women financial advisers and trainees, and it also required Merrill Lynch to hire consultants on team practices.[211]

The social and cultural impacts of class actions often go beyond a company's finances. Morgan Stanley paid $54 million to settle a sex-discrimination suit in

2004. Even though more than 300 women were paid in the settlement, $12 million went to one bond seller who was denied a promotion because of her gender, excluded from men's client meetings at strip clubs, and fired for being hostile to her supervisor who had received promotion over the plaintiff.[212] After this and similar Wall Street cases of discrimination, several aspects of corporate culture, in particular business meetings routinely held in strip clubs, drew public attention as potentially discriminatory behavior. Many companies in the United States have now implemented policies to avoid behavior that excludes certain employees.[213]

The US jury system also allows citizen participation in court decisions. In 2010, a New York jury ordered one of the nation's largest pharmaceutical companies, Novartis, to pay $250 million in punitive damages for sex discrimination in pay and promotions and a hostile workplace; 5,600 women were party to the class action. The company's old boys' club was notorious, and allegations included inequity in pay and promotions, a rape by a doctor, and discrimination after pregnancy.[214] In 2014, a federal jury in California ordered AutoZone to pay a former employee for discriminatory treatment related to her pregnancy, including employers' rude behavior to her and her firing. Punitive damages amounting to $186 million were ordered to be paid to her. In this case, the punitive damages far exceeded the plaintiff's actual loss and were intended to penalize the company. Such punitive damages are not permitted in the Japanese system; the policy against them is strict.[215] Few countries in the world use the jury system in civil cases, and this practice exemplifies a participatory type of democracy. Japan introduced the jury system in criminal courts in 2009 but not in civil cases.

Class actions, the use of juries in civil cases, and the awarding of punitive damages have served as effective tools for addressing employers' discriminatory practices in the United States. The threat of lawsuits forces companies to change corporate culture and customs and implement appropriate training, and it also increases the sense of urgency for making such changes. Such urgency regarding corporate change is rare in Japan. Mechanisms that might make Japanese companies more accountable, including the risk of punitive damages, should be the subject of further discussion.

## Gender Equality and Global Business Trends

The legal, governmental, and corporate changes that have taken place from the late 1990s to the present in Japan have caused some destabilization of traditional gender norms in Japanese employment, the welfare system, and family life. However, the legal, governmental, and corporate changes regarding gender equality in Japan did not derive from civil demands, public protests, or social movements as they did in the United States. The Japanese governmental effort is largely the outcome of international pressure and Japan's desire to comply with Western business norms. Corporate policies designed to promote gender equality have resulted from Japanese firms' conformity to global standards of corporate social responsibility and corporate accountability.

In the 1980s and 1990s, the Japanese business community explicitly opposed the legalization of parental leave by insisting on the traditional role of mothers and the difficulty of finding substitute workers to fill in for women who take leave.[216] Even as late as 2002, the business community continued to express its concerns regarding the burdens on business of a parental leave policy, and insisted that firms' efforts be voluntary.[217] It also opposed revising the EEOL regarding sex discrimination in hiring, firing, and retirement, and disapproved of administrative interventions or sanctions against firms for violations, insisting that solutions could be explored under the initial version of the EEOL and that there was no need for a revision of the law.[218] The Japanese business associations (both Keidanren and Nikkeiren) also opposed mandating sexual-harassment prevention in the workplace, a measure that was to be included in the 1997 revision of the EEOL.[219]

With the emergence of the global discourse on corporate social responsibility in the early 2000s, the Japanese business community changed its stance of outright opposition to one of rhetorical support. It started publicly advertising its efforts to incorporate female employees as an aspect of corporate goals and responsibilities, following global standards. The United Nations launched the Global Compact in 2000, which addressed four areas of concern—human rights, labor, the environment, and anticorruption—in which firms had a "voluntary" or "self-regulatory" responsibility to meet certain ethical standards.[220] However, even in the global context, corporate social responsibility has "often [been] characterized by piecemeal and fragmented reforms and window dressing,"[221] and the gap between rhetoric and actual policy has been criticized for remaining so wide; in addition, companies' actual reporting and disclosure has been fraught with problems.[222] Furthermore, the discourse on corporate social responsibility in civil society has close ties with neoliberalism and market forces in having generated competition within industries and businesses that deal with corporate social responsibility, such as consulting.[223] Finally, and most important, "many campaigning organisations—in their quest for media coverage and political visibility—encouraged the rise of corporate social responsibility, yet in so doing diminished the scope for state regulation and, more recently, opened up tensions within civil society over whether or not to engage further with corporations over CSR [corporate social responsibility]."[224]

In 2003, the Japan Association of Corporate Executives (Keizai Doyukai) discussed the importance of utilizing excellent workers regardless of sex, age,

education, nationality, or employment type, as well as the importance of ensuring a family-friendly environment and a diverse and flexible employment system;
the Ministry of Health, Labour and Welfare also referred to the enhancement of
women's employment as an aspect of corporate social responsibility.[225] In 2005,
regarding the Basic Law for a Gender-Equal Society and the goals of gender equality, Nihon Keidanren claimed that worker-employer cooperation is desirable and
criticized the government for ignoring industrial efforts and overlooking firms'
workplace customs.[226] The Japanese business community, however, still contends
that it will follow the laws only when needed and that their interpretation and
application depends on the particular situation in each firm.[227] As some point
out, until gender equality becomes more associated with corporate profits, it will
not be publicly accepted as a subject for business discourse in Japan.[228]

Stephanie Assmann argues that laws such as the EEOL are not seen as a threat
by the business community but rather a reminder to Japanese companies about
their responsibility to increase gender equality and diversity in management.[229]
Leon Wolff similarly points out that neither the government nor other public
institutions in Japan have the authority to monitor sexual-harassment prevention and complaints, even though sexual harassment is covered in the EEOL;
with only private monitoring of civil rights in Japan, public policy on gender is
invisible.[230] Even though important laws on gender equality have been passed
and a corporate campaign to enhance women's employment has been widespread since the late 1990s, it is critical to note that gender equality–related laws
in Japan remain limited and that there has been an absence of public discussion
and a dearth of education on the subject. And the business community in Japan
continues to indicate its opposition to any forced changes in corporate customs
in regard to gender egalitarianism.

Jennifer Chan-Tiberghien reminds us of the "Japan problem" by citing Dutch
scholar Karel van Wolferen that Japan has been criticized for its sluggish and
weak policy change because of the power relations among the bureaucracy, the
Liberal Democratic Party, and business interest groups.[231] But Japan may not
be an exception in its weak governmental initiatives to change existing social
inequality. Even in the United States, where women's employment status is much
higher than in Japan, Frank Dobbin writes that "while the civil rights movement
spurred John F. Kennedy's affirmative action order in 1961 and the Civil Rights
Act of 1964, activists played little role in deciding what compliance would look
like. . . . While activists went on to influence public policy, they no more designed
corporate compliance than did civil rights activists. . . . Judges rarely did more
than give the nod to programs already popular among leading firms. . . . Congress
rarely did more than allow innovations to stand."[232] He argues that it was not
"America's weak state" but rather the corporate personnel experts who created

regulatory regimes internal to firms: by "defining how firms could comply with the law, they also defined what was illegal."[233] It was these personnel experts who enabled the "paradigm shift" that made fairness and equality the norm. Dobbin concludes, "So judges looked to leading employers when asked how firms should comply with fair empowerment laws. Employers frequently defended themselves by arguing that they had copied the best practices of their peers. . . . Big companies hired consultants to offer sexual harassment training in the 1990s, and the EEOC endorsed that approach."[234]

However, things seem to be far different in Japan with its capitalism that is short of embracing democratic values. Dobbin, pointing out Americans' equation of capitalism with democracy, reveals that many American corporate personnel experts believe that "true equality of opportunity would achieve both fairness and efficiency." Such strong public feelings about fairness and the ideal of democracy are clearly absent in Japan. While the strong belief in individual success and prosperity has been the driving force behind America's capitalism, what has driven Japan's postwar development is the state-led modernization imperative. Japan's emphasis on firm-centered collectivism and group orientation at the cost of the individual conflicts with the idea of individual equality and gender equality. Moreover, even though the "weak" US state may have driven "private sector activism in the protection of citizen's rights,"[235] there was a civil rights movement that called for Congress to outlaw discrimination in employment, education, and housing and public accommodation, and federal contractors were required to pay the same wages to and provide equal opportunities to men and women. Japan lacks such social, cultural, and legal foundations to motivate corporate initiatives that would implement workplace equality, while public and legal support to drive equality to the forefront are absent in Japan.

At the end of the 1990s, the Basic Law for a Gender-Equal Society triggered a backlash in Japan, unleashing strong conservative and nationalistic sentiment. Conservatives argued against the revision of the Civil Code to introduce the option of married women keeping their own surnames, claiming such a change might lead to the collapse of the family. The Japanese Society for History Textbook Reform and other conservative groups claimed that gender equality in Japan would cause the demise of the traditional family, rampant radical sex education, and the decline of citizens' sense of devotion to the Japanese state.[236] The backlash against the Basic Law for a Gender-Equal Society was centered on public fear and anxiety over the equation of gender equality with a rejection of traditional femininity and masculinity in Japan. Japanese feminists saw this reaction as resulting from a public lack of understanding of individual rights and dignity. Yayo Okano writes:

> Even after sixty years of democracy, the Japanese do not have a shared
> sense of what equality under the law is, and the ideas that are written in
> the law. Japanese politicians may not know the meanings of them either.
> Many men and women who are involved in the backlash were obsessed
> with the fear that their individual dignity will be rejected by the Basic
> Law for a Gender-Equal Society . . . such fear may come from their lack
> of sense that they, as men and women, did choose how they live their
> lives and they are responsible for how they live.[237]

The Basic Law for a Gender-Equal Society "is at least an important symbolic
source for improving equality under the emergent public gender regime in
Japan."[238] Yet there is also concern that the law appears to be a "spur-of-the-
moment response, lacking the concept of human rights, and process of guaranteeing individual dignity and decision-making ability, regarding gender."[239] But
it is not just this particular law that lacks the concept of equality; Japanese society has lacked opportunities, both in the public arena and in higher education,
to contemplate the concepts of individual equality and human rights in depth.
Thus, it is hard to imagine that Japan will follow the United States in implementing similar equality policies. Lacking legal enforcement, sanctions, and a belief
system respectful of individual equality, Japanese corporations may just be making a temporary and symbolic gesture toward compliance.

In this chapter we looked at the shifting shape of Japan's coordinated capitalism, with a specific focus on the structural changes in corporate governance,
the employment and management system, the traditional gender-based family
regime, and Japanese laws. Throughout the 1990s, even though many Japanese
companies started incorporating limited liberalism into their business management by hiring large numbers of temporary workers and superficially employing
performance-based pay and promotion, they continued to maintain traditional
management customs based on the ideology of separate spheres, in which women
workers are polarized into two groups: a small group of managers and a large
group who remain at the bottom of the ladder as temporary workers. There has
been little mobility in the labor market because the lifelong-employment structure requires workers' lifelong devotion and promotes firm-specific skills over
non-firm-specific skills.

The postwar male-breadwinner family regime partially departed from the traditional housewife model by incorporating women's continual employment, but
it has not evolved further into an egalitarian or dual-earner model. The woman
in the typical Japanese family remains reliant on her husband's income because
of her economic dependence and lack of power in the labor market. This makes

it difficult for the Japanese family to shift to the gender-egalitarian and dual-income family norm seen in Western countries. While the declining birthrate has led the Japanese government to increasingly promote women's employment, the persistence of a separate-sphere gender ideology and customs in Japanese companies, the labor market, and the Japanese family continue to block women from gaining economic status equal to that of men.

The number of educated women has rapidly increased, but vertical sex segregation in Japanese companies remains persistent. Although the past custom of young women quitting their jobs to devote themselves to the family as caretakers is declining, women still remain concentrated on the bottom rungs of the ladder. Japan's corporate culture and customs need further investigation since they negatively influence women's upward mobility.

In addition, the Japanese courts continue to lack authority in this area, as they can impose few useful penalties on employers and persist in protecting Japanese state-business interests and blocking corporations from shifting toward desegregation in the labor market. As a result of the global profusion of gender-equality imperatives and international pressure during the last three decades, Japan implemented and revised the Equal Employment Opportunity Law and the Basic Law for a Gender-Equal Society. However, Japan's ratification of CEDAW and implementation of EEOL have done little to bring changes to Japanese companies' sex-segregated management customs and labor market structure.

The Japanese courts, except when international organizations have intervened, have continued to protect Japanese employers' "discretion" and "freedom" in the areas of promotion, pay, and hiring, acting as if they are a loyal servant to the Japanese state and business community. In this chapter we looked at various sex-discrimination cases in Japan, contrasting their outcomes with those of similar US cases. The cultural values of equality, fairness, competition, and corporate responsibility have been addressed and often questioned in the US legal system, which has caused the courts to become an active agent of social change, while Japanese courts have continued to lack the ability to question existing social values and change the unequal customs of Japanese companies, prioritizing their conformity to the interests of the state and business community. That Japanese laws and courts care less about discrimination, injustice, and equality than they do about their own obedience to authority makes explicit why the status and rights of Japanese women have not truly improved since the 1980s.

In the next chapters, I shift my focus to examining the interview data and sex-segregated customs in the workplaces of five large Japanese companies. First I will discuss my methodology and the background characteristics in terms of management and women's employment status in these organizations.

# SEX SEGREGATION IN FIVE JAPANESE COMPANIES

After discussing the design of the original research I conducted for this book I will share detailed information on the historical and social background of the five Japanese companies I studied. Japanese corporate customs are known to be highly homogeneous,[1] yet the five firms' reforms with regard to women's employment varied significantly, with the differences relating to factors such as each company's history, management, and ownership. I also comparatively highlight the responses of some of the employees to the reforms in women's employment.

As I have discussed, Japan's corporate and governmental reforms to increase the number of women employees and managers started around the same time that the number of foreign shareholders in Japanese businesses was increasing (in the late 1990s and early 2000s). Simultaneous with this, the system of Japanese lifelong employment started to change, with companies adopting some Western liberal practices. It was also a time when corporate social responsibility was becoming a global business norm and when the Japanese government started emphasizing women's return to work after childbirth. This chapter illuminates how these global and local factors interacted with Japanese companies' initiatives to increase the number of employed women and women managers. A few workers I talked to pointed out that their companies started increasing female managers and retaining married women and workers who were mothers in accord with Japanese governmental guidelines on promoting women's employment and/or compliance with the global imperative of gender equality. Regardless of the universal pressures for these reforms, the companies' approaches varied, and some firms were a long way from attaining gender equality.

The male workers I talked with (and some women, too, though not as many) commonly expressed some level of skepticism, indifference, or opposition to the reforms to increase women workers and managers. Men's negativity was pronounced in Japanese financial companies, which have a large number of non-career-track women as assistants and few female managers. Mothers and women in low managerial positions were fairly visible in the cosmetics companies, by contrast; that there are more women employed in cosmetics firms does not mean that management is less sex segregated than in financial firms.

## Methodology of the Case Studies

There are two types of sociocultural pressure that have shaped companies' reforms of women's employment: first, conforming with the government's push to increase women managers was viewed as a necessity by many managers; and second, companies did not want to be seen as lagging behind international management standards and did not want to risk dissatisfying foreign owners. Administrators who favored conformity to the Japanese government's demands focused on the desirability of winning governmental recognition, such as family-friendly or gender-equality awards. Other companies emphasized the increasing influence of foreign ownership as well as expansion of global subsidiaries of their companies; they saw an increase in women employees, both in general and as managers, as important in meeting global standards of management.

Desegregation policies and reform methods (mostly through affirmative/positive action or top-down promotions and hiring) were similar among all the companies, in that the firms promoted more women workers to management and generally increased the hiring of women across the board. Only one company that I studied altered the customs of traditional Japanese management in order to implement gender egalitarianism; this bank eliminated career-track hiring entirely and adopted midcareer hiring in addition to offering "pure" lifelong employment. The other companies did not touch the traditional system of lifelong employment in reforming women's employment. Many men and women workers whom I talked with were skeptical that changing firms' hiring policies would result in significant desegregation in the workplace. They saw their firms' reforms as no more than temporary interventions or superficial gestures of conformity.

# Design

I used the in-depth interview method, which enables a researcher to highlight complex social processes and structures of gender. I conducted sixty-four in-depth interviews in 2007 with a diverse group of workers in Tokyo who were employed at three financial companies and two cosmetics companies (table 3.1; company names are pseudonyms). However, access to interviewees and even the selection of the firms was mostly beyond my control. I contacted university

**TABLE 3.1** Summary of interview results at five large companies regarding women in management, 2007

| COMPANY CHARACTERISTICS | FINANCIAL COMPANIES | | | COSMETICS COMPANIES | |
|---|---|---|---|---|---|
| | DAIGO LIFE INSURANCE | SHIJO ASSET MANAGEMENT | MIKADO BANK | HANAKAGE COSMETICS | TAKANE COSMETICS |
| Sales turnover | $25 billion | $10 billion | $60 billion | $120 billion | $60 billion |
| Number of workers | 9,000 | 900 | 2,000 | 6,000 | 15,000 |
| Number of workplaces in Japan | 80 | 3 | 31 | 16 | 19 |
| Number of female workers interviewed | 8 | 8 | 5 | 9 | 9 |
| Number of male workers interviewed | 6 | 4 | 4 | 5 | 6 |
| Female managers in 2007 (%) | 7 | Less than 2 | 20 | 6 | 14 |
| Female managers in 2013 (%) | 16 | n/a | 26 | 11 | 26 |
| The ratio of employees (male: female) | 1:1 | 7:3 | 1:1 | 1:1 | 1:1.5 |
| Hiring divisions | Career-track/area-career-track/non-career-track | Career-track/area-career-track | Abolished in early 2000 | No | No |
| Female board members in 2014 (N) | 0 | 1 | 1 | 1 | 3 |
| Foreign board members in 2014 (N) | 0 | 0 | 3 | 0 | 1 |

*Note:* Company names are pseudonyms.

faculty and alumni at a few Tokyo universities, informing them of my research plan involving cosmetics firms and financial firms and was thereby introduced to my initial contacts in each company. I was only able to gain access to the employees of the five firms through managers to whom I was introduced by the informants. Therefore, I could not determine the number of people interviewed, nor could I control for their ages or job titles. I employed snowball sampling when I could, but the managers I talked to sometimes found the respondents for me. My goal was to interview a large number of respondents with different job titles in order to collect diverse voices regarding gender disparity.

I focused on large Japanese companies and their reforms with regard to gender equality; my belief was that they had changed little since the 1980s in terms of women's status. These companies are also the largest employers of highly educated women in Japan; thus, their policies matter greatly to such women. I chose five companies in two industries that are distinctly different, both in terms of the sex composition of career-track workers and in terms of public image. The two cosmetics companies employed a much higher number of career-track women workers than did the financial companies, and the cosmetics companies did not use double-track hiring. The cosmetics industry is also seen as one of the most "woman friendly" in Japan, whereas the image of financial companies is traditional and highly patriarchal. One of the two cosmetics companies where I conducted interviews had consistently ranked at the top of the Most Woman-Friendly Companies in Japan list. I expected this company to be truly more woman friendly than the others. However, I found that female upper managers were scarce in all the firms. All had high numbers of temporary workers, mostly women. This large group of employees received no benefit from the companies' reforms to aid women. These firms also maintained the central practices of Japanese management. In other words, they had more similarities than differences with regard to male-dominated organizational customs and practices.

I interviewed thirty-nine women and twenty-five men (table 3.2). All the men were career-track workers. Twenty-nine of the women were career-track workers, nine were non-career-track workers, and one was a contract worker. Of the twenty-five men, twenty were married; sixteen had stay-at-home wives, and three had a wife who worked only part-time, while only one man's wife worked full-time. Of the thirty-nine women I interviewed, sixteen were married. Of the twenty-one women who worked in financial firms, three had children, while of the eighteen women who worked in cosmetics firms, six had children. The average age of the women was thirty-four, and the average age of the men was thirty-nine.

I personally conducted all the interviews in Japanese, mostly in coffee shops or offices. The office door was closed so that other workers did not hear the interviews. I recorded the interviews and transcribed them for analysis, then

**TABLE 3.2** Status characteristics of men and women interviewed in five large companies, 2007

| | NO. (%) OF MEN AND WOMEN INTERVIEWED | |
|---|---|---|
| CHARACTERISTICS | WOMEN (n = 39) | MEN (n = 25) |
| **1. Employment** | | |
| status Career-track worker | 29 (74) | 25 (100) |
| Non-career-track worker | 9 (23) | 0 |
| Contract worker | 1 (3) | 0 |
| **2. Age** | | |
| 20–29 | 12 (31) | 2 (8) |
| 30–39 | 20 (51) | 11 (44) |
| 40–49 | 6 (15) | 11 (44) |
| 50–59 | 1 (3) | 1 (4) |
| **3. Marital status** | | |
| Single | 23 (59) | 5 (20) |
| Married | 16 (41) | 20 (80) |
| Married with stay-at-home spouse | | 16 (64) |
| **4. Education** | | |
| High school graduate | 0 | 0 |
| Two-year college graduate | 6 (15) | 0 |
| College graduate | 29 (75) | 22 (88) |
| Graduate degree | 4 (10) | 3 (12) |

*Note:* "N" = number of people.

*Source:* Based on my table previously published in *Gender, Work and Organization* 20, no. 5 (September 2013) © 2012 John Wiley & Sons Ltd.

translated them into English. Each interview lasted from one to three hours. I used pseudonyms for the companies and for the individuals. The interviews were semistructured. Using Joan Acker's concept of the "gendered organization structure" as a guideline,[2] I asked each individual about workplace culture and individual experiences, including training, career prospects, workplace interactions, work hours, and work-life balance.

The foreign ownership rate was about 40 percent in four of the companies (for two of them, the 40% ownership refers to their parent companies), while one firm, Mikado Bank, was over 50 percent owned by foreign companies. As I discuss below, the level of foreign ownership is not the best indicator of whether a firm is moving toward a more Western style of management or more egalitarian policies with regard to women's employment. All four firms' approach to management and reforms to women's employment were similar and were grounded in Japanese management customs, regardless of their high levels of foreign ownership.

Daigo Life Insurance Company has about 42,000 employees and over 30,000 sales employees across Japan. The company has long used career-track hiring, and non-career-track women are able to change to the career track—usually after several years of work experience, a certain number of months of insurance sales experience, the successful completion of exams, and managers' recommendations. Until very recently, the company had an internal policy of forcing women to resign when they married. Women now constitute 7 percent of managers. The firm offers up to three years of parental leave with one month paid. A worker can reduce work time by one hour a day until the child reaches the age of three.

Shijo Asset Management has about 900 employees and belongs to the large Shijo Financial Group, which employs over 10,000 workers across Japan. About 70 percent of its employees are men. The company uses career-track hiring, even though it recently changed the name of "non-career-track" to "regional track" so that all women would officially be called "career-track" workers. Many workers described this change as superficial, because salary, benefits, and promotions remain highly differentiated based on the traditional gender division. Non-career-track women are able to change to career-track positions. Shijo offers up to two years of parental leave. A worker can reduce work time by up to two hours a day until a child reaches the age of nine. At Shijo, women constitute about 2 percent of managers.

Mikado Bank has about 2,300 employees, half of whom are women. It offers up to two years of parental leave. The bank abolished career-track hiring in the early 2000s after an American company took over the firm. Women make up 20 percent of managers.

Hanakage Cosmetics has about 11,000 employees. There is no division between career-track and non-career-track employees. Women constituted about 6 percent of managers in 2005. The firm offers one year of parental leave. Until the child is three years old, workers can reduce daily work time by up to two hours.

Takane Cosmetics has about 10,000 employees in total and 7,000 sales specialists (mostly women) across Japan. Almost all the college-educated women Takane hires are brought in as career-track workers. Women make up about 14 percent of managers. Takane offers up to five years of parental leave. Workers can reduce work time by up to two hours per day until the child reaches nine years old.

The sample I used is too small to make a thorough generalization about all Japanese firms, but it provides critical insights into the organizational processes by which working long hours influences existing gender inequality in Japanese firms. I oversampled women so that I could focus on their experiences. Whereas I asked the same questions of both women and men, the men sometimes responded curtly or did not give detailed responses, especially to questions regarding such matters as sexual harassment and parental leave. In order to make men feel comfortable during the interviews, I sometimes shifted the topic away from work-related gender inequality to the subject of time spent with a man's wife and children at home. My being a female Japanese researcher certainly made female respondents more comfortable in talking with me than male subjects.

## Foreign Ownership and Women's Status

Corporate reforms regarding women's employment in Japanese companies started as part of an effort by Japan not to be left behind in the era of globalization. Changing the gender imbalance has been prompted by Japanese companies' concerns about international pressures on Japanese business and the increasing number of foreign shareholders that these companies are beholden to. However, as I noted previously, a high rate of foreign ownership does not necessarily correlate with greater reforms in the area of gender equality, nor does it equate with the conversion of traditional Japanese customs to the Western style of management.

Since the 1990s, traditional Japanese management has incorporated a few elements of the liberal market model. Masahiko Aoki has pointed out that there has been destabilization of the main-bank system, coupled with a slow but irreversible "evolution" of Japanese firms into organizations with market-driven management.[3] He sorted Japanese companies into three types: traditional Japanese management-based corporations (J-firm type) and two hybrid-type corporations, one (type 1) that has a high number of foreign shareholders and one (type 2) that has more performance-based hiring and promotion, even though it may have traditional bank-based financing and a board dominated by insiders.[4] Traditional Japanese J-firm type corporations rely on main-bank financing with low levels of foreign ownership and continue to base their hiring on the systems of lifelong employment and seniority pay. Type 1 hybrid companies are characterized by high levels of foreign investment and rely on corporate bonds rather than commercial banks for their financing, while their employment and promotion systems have partially incorporated individual meritocracy. Type 2 hybrid companies, among which are many high-tech and information technology firms, are similar to the J-firm type in bank financing and intercorporate ownership but are characterized by low levels of lifelong employment.[5] J-firm type companies make up 55 percent of Japanese firms, and type 1 and type 2 hybrids make up about 10 percent of the country's firms.[6] Aoki's model explains the close links between a company with a high number of foreign shareholders and its use of market-oriented management. Indeed, some companies with strong foreign investment may be very interested in converting, or even pressured to covert, to the Western style of management, which exhibits far more gender egalitarianism. Overall, however, Japan's willingness to evolve toward market-oriented management seems to be limited—and so is gender desegregation in its companies.

The increasing prevalence of foreign ownership may be a promising sign for Japanese firms' accommodation to US-type management and organizational practices. In fact, some scholars have noted that foreign companies in Japan have offered better career paths and opportunities to Japanese women than have traditional Japanese companies.[7] Current studies of foreign ownership and Japanese management, however, show that a positive correlation is not obvious. George Olcott in *Conflict and Change* reports that the impact of increased foreign ownership on traditional Japanese management practices has been limited. He argues that even when companies with high levels of US ownership, such as Shinsei Bank, make a few changes to management practices—such as increasing midcareer hires, destabilizing the promise of lifelong employment, and instituting a performance-based bonus system—they still differ dramatically from US companies in terms of market-type management. Olcott explains that few changes may occur to a host country's management, regardless of the high level of foreign ownership and the involvement of these owners, because of institutional duality and differences in organizational structure, employment systems, and the levels of skills and hierarchies in different national contexts.[8] Thus, Olcott warns that globalization does not mean the instant occurrence of convergence: "The greater the institutionalized distance that multinationals travel, the more carefully they need to consider the ways in which they adapt to local conditions."[9] Such difficulties regarding change, Olcott and Nick Oliver argue, are especially pronounced in the sphere of women's employment in Japanese firms. Olcott and Oliver observed some increase in female managers but very little attitudinal shift among employees in companies with increased levels of foreign ownership.[10]

In the five companies I studied, there seems to be some correlation between the level of foreign ownership and management's desegregation reforms. Unlike other Japanese firms, Mikado Bank, which is under US management, abolished the notorious career-track hiring system and integrated all of its women workers with its career-track workers. In another departure from most Japanese firms, the bank also increased the hiring of women, both in midcareer and as new hires. Mikado Bank has the highest foreign ownership (57%), with Hanakage Cosmetics at about 49 percent and Takane Cosmetics at about 35 percent. The parent groups of both Shijo Asset Management and Daigo Life Insurance have foreign ownership of about 44 percent and 47 percent, respectively. Of the five companies, Mikado Bank has the highest percentage of women in management (even though the total remains below 30%). Both Shijo Asset Management and Daigo Life Insurance have less than 2 percent female managers, and Hanakage has only about 7 percent. The presence of foreign ownership may suggest the amount of pressure a company's management feels about globalization. However, these five companies have largely retained traditional employment systems and have mostly engaged in top-down affirmative action reforms, in which they have tried to enhance women's status only within the traditional management and employment framework. (The exception is Mikado Bank, which has used midcareer hiring and slightly relaxed lifelong employment.) Because sex segregation is shaped by the logic and customs of the Japanese employment system, the "adding women" approach without accompanying changes in the existing employment and promotion system will accomplish little, as I discuss in more detail in the next chapter .

# The Five Companies

## Mikado Bank: Moderate Liberal Reform

Several major Japanese banks went into bankruptcy and lost power and influence in the financial meltdown of the 1990s. These banks, which greatly contributed to the country's postwar economic growth, were said to have been bankrupted because of Japan's high degree of regulation and rigidity, the government's slow response to crises, and their lack of transparent internal management.[11] The bad loans made by Japanese banks as of 2000 amounted to 30 trillion yen, and the loss in GDP as a result of the banking crisis was said to be almost 12 percent in 1999.[12] In addition to the shock of the real estate bubble bursting in the 1980s, deregulation had banks shifting loans from large companies to small, often unknown, firms, which frequently resulted in default.[13] Mikado Bank was one large bank weakened by massive amounts of bad loans in real estate–related businesses. In the late 1990s, several members of Mikado Bank's top management were arrested, and two Mikado Bank managers committed suicide when their deceptive practices, intended to hide the bad loans, were uncovered.

Mikado Bank was sold in 2000 to a US private equity firm, and its top managers were replaced by foreigners. This drew great public attention when it occurred because Mikado Bank was a traditional and highly regulated Japanese bank, known to have intimate ties with the Japanese state. Today, US corporations such as JPMorgan Chase continue to be among the major stockholders in Mikado Bank. When I conducted my interviews in 2007, the management of Mikado Bank was dominated by foreigners, but later, due to financial losses, foreign board members were let go and replaced by a predominantly Japanese team. When I talked with the company's workers in 2007, top foreign managers were hired from large US banks and were provided with typical US compensation—well over one million dollars a year—which is at least five times higher than the salary of a Japanese middle or upper manager in the same bank. Some men and women I interviewed talked about the high salaries and benefits of foreign managers and their lifestyles, with maids and nannies, as symbolic of the defeat of Japan's community-like and economically egalitarian firms by the American system that is built on unequal employee salaries.

On its takeover of the bank in 2000, the new management apparently faced complaints and resistance from the old Japanese management. As a result, the foreign managers shed Japanese workers who were over fifty by offering voluntary but lucrative early retirement packages in an attempt to avoid disruptions and resistance from these senior workers. The current board members of the bank are mostly Japanese. The workers I talked to in their twenties and thirties mentioned that ambitious cohorts are free to leave the firm for better-paying jobs, as is the case with American companies. Yet, even though ambitious employees have this option, lifelong employment in Mikado Bank is still the norm. The bank's mid-career workers, especially those who worked there under Japanese ownership in the 1980s and 1990s, tend to plan on working there until they retire. Overall, the bank seems to be a hybrid, an uneven mix of Japanese and US management customs.

Makiko, a thirty-nine-year-old female assistant general manager in investment banking, said that the firm was divided into two groups in the early 2000s: those who supported the US style of management and those who insisted on the old Japanese approach. A large number of those who disagreed with the US style of management, many of whom were in their fifties, resigned from the firm.

> Now we have half Japanese and half foreigners in this bank. I speak English since I grew up in the United States. I think I am now far more valued by the current management than in the past. . . . Some Japanese men would constantly accuse me of "becoming a green-eye" or acting too much like the American staff by sending out my personal e-mails to other workers. I said to them, "If you complain about the new manage-ment and me, why don't you just buy all the company's stock first? This is an organization, and I have to follow its rules, whether US or Japa-nese." . . . It was bad. . . . When the new managers ordered something, many Japanese men would sabotage it. They would just ignore it, not doing what they were told. They would say, "That's not what a Japanese bank would do!" Now, even though many senior Japanese men don't want to follow the American management, they never say anything to the top but are just polite and quiet.

Some English-speaking educated women apparently have benefited more from American management than from the traditional Japanese management, and they also praised the American style as more globally promising and gender egalitarian than Japanese management. Makiko expressed the opinion that she gains more respect from other workers and does a better job under American management than under the Japanese management because of her English-speaking ability, which allows her to communicate well with managers, and also because of her appreciation of clear top-down Western-style governance. She said, "I like the current management better than the Japanese one. The orders and decisions mostly come from the top, clear and straightforward. There was really no governance when we worked under the Japanese management. You couldn't tell sometimes who was in charge of this firm!"

The new top management consists of many Americans and some Europeans. After they were put in charge, they started hiring a large number of workers from other foreign financial firms. They also started hiring midcareer Japanese workers with US educational credentials and overseas job experience. Instead of implementing American management and employment systems, however, the bank kept most of its traditional customs, such as providing workers with spousal, family, and housing benefits and hiring a large number of new college graduates yearly. This may have been simply because of the difficulty of translating an American management style into a Japan business context.[14] The top management might have been concerned about the workers' resistance to the firm's overly large or overly American makeup and its system of individualist or performance-based rewards. Because the previously Japanese-owned Mikado Bank was a large lender in Japan, it is likely that it still continues to serve many Japanese companies as their main bank or major lender; thus, it may want to keep its Japanese corporate identity rather than entirely promoting itself as an "American" bank. It may also have some other Japanese financial firms as stockholders, and it may have many Japanese board members. Thus, regardless of the explicit American buyout, no one I talked with saw the bank as an entirely American firm.

I noticed that although the bank offers lifelong employment and workers' benefits, some younger workers' salaries and benefits (at least among those I talked with) are less than the amounts I heard about from workers in the other two financial firms. Japan's system of lifelong employment allows workers to have decent salaries and benefits in exchange for their lifelong labor in the firm; thus, if the firm does not expect a worker to remain there for his or her entire life, the firm no longer has any incentive to pay a decent salary and benefits. It is not surprising, therefore, that Mikado Bank pays younger workers less than other Japanese financial companies.

Although many expected that the US-centered management would impose liberal market reforms on Mikado Bank, and that the communitarian group-oriented customs of Japanese firms would be discontinued, in reality the central characteristics of hiring, promotion, and long-term security have been retained by the bank. As for women's employment and family policies, I did not find any of them particularly American or Western, with the exception of nullification of track hiring for women and the headhunting of midcareer American MBAs, both women and men, by the company. The human resources staff also mentioned the firm's effort to increase women managers and employees, which was started in an effort to comply with the Japanese government. But overall, the relatively limited changes may have been because the bank was large and had many Japanese clients and institutional ties and networks; thus, management might have decided not to stray too far from the corporate customs of other Japanese banks.

As previously mentioned, the new management at Mikado did make one very significant change: it abolished the two-track hiring system and integrated all workers, both male and female, into the career track as equals. Mika, a forty-four-year-old female manager in human recourses, told me that the previous Japanese management had invested little in women workers, who were primarily non career track at that time because most women quit work on marriage. In fact, the bank had an official policy regarding marriage: one partner, either the man or the woman, must quit the bank when marrying another worker within the bank. It was usually the woman who quit. For women at that time to change their track from non career track to career track, they had to take in-firm exams, which Mika described as "very hard to pass." She said, however, that the custom of women workers in large firms quitting their jobs when they marry has become obsolete. After removing the hiring tracks, the bank said that about 20 percent of its managers were female at the time of my interviews. (The number increased to 26% in 2013.)

Mikado Bank started a "*jyosei katsuyō*" (utilizing women) program in 2003. The female manager in the human resource office said, "In 2003, our company promoted women over men because of the recommendation from the Ministry of Health, Labour and Welfare. We promoted women to higher titles. For the first year, the men complained quite a bit. . . . We continued positive action for two or three years. We still don't have any female board members." The workers I interviewed at this bank seemed to see their bank's policies on hiring and promoting women workers as part of the American or global business norm and as a method to grow profits rather than as a matter of individual equality or human rights. Workers attributed the increasing numbers of women to the intensification of competition and Japan's conformity to global business practices. Some male workers noted that hiring a large number of women is good for public relations. Other men commented that promoting women's employment and status could be a remedy to the problem of Japan's declining population. A forty-two-year-old male manager at Mikado said, "We should know that men workers are no longer sufficient to keep Japan's labor force competitive with other countries." He emphasized that a top-down order is necessary to change Japanese companies and that American management in the reforming of Mikado Bank is necessary. He said, "This firm has hired a number of excellent women who have worked in large US securities firms and consulting firms. . . . I don't mind female bosses at all. As the presence of more women increases competition among workers, some men complain, 'Why do only women get promoted?' They think it is reverse discrimination. But nothing in this country will progress without some top-down enforcement of the change."

After the takeover by the new management of Mikado Bank, a small number of female managers were given reasonable promotions and pay; a large number of non-career-track women workers were laid off; and those former non-career-track workers who stayed in the firm were integrated into career-track jobs. However, much of the division between the career-track and non-career-track women workers remained even after the track hiring system was abolished, partly because of confusion on the part of the non-career-track women about what was expected of them, as well as pressure to conform to the previous norms. The workers I interviewed reported that the non-career-track women who were hired under Japanese management in the 1980s and 1990s "continue to do the assistant work no one wants to do."

Under the new US management, the hierarchy among women workers at Mikado Bank changed. The highest-paid, best-treated, most quickly promoted women were those who had MBA degrees and had worked for US or other Western firms; the next in the hierarchy were the career-track women hired under the previous Japanese management. The previously non-career-track women continued to be paid the least and were informally expected to do the assistant jobs other workers refused to do, even though they were called career track. This polarization among women in Mikado Bank continues to exist but is suppressed.

Some workers in the bank also mentioned that they missed the community-like characteristics of traditional Japanese firms, which apparently disappeared after US management took over. There were no regular drinking events, either. A couple of male workers I interviewed mentioned that the workplace was becoming highly individualistic under US management. A forty-two-year-old assistant general manager said: "In the old days under Japanese management, all the Japanese did extra work for others without complaining about it. Now, nobody wants to help anybody. I think the firm should evaluate highly those who do extra work for others." It will be interesting to see individualism, performance-based evaluations, and the culture of competitiveness increasingly integrated into the

Japanese workplace, and Mikado Bank may offer a good case study, but this is beyond the scope of this book.

Mikado Bank is an example of a place where the gender-equality initiative took hold within the context of foreign ownership or the liberalization of Japanese corporate governance. The firm also changed some tenets of traditional Japanese management, such as lifelong employment, and started to hire mid-career workers. The bank's new management abolished career-track hiring and increased new hires of women to levels almost equal to those of men. The workers I interviewed saw reform of women's status and rising gender-equal opportunities as logical and necessary steps along the path of globalization, especially under US management.

Visible workplace changes, such as the presence of many foreign upper managers, a decrease in senior Japanese male workers, and an increase in workers having MBAs, may encourage workers to view a firm's increased hiring and promoting of women as just another necessary change in an increasingly globalized world. Even with these changes, however, Mikado Bank remains sex segregated. Several workers at the bank mentioned that the firm's increased hiring of women workers has been limited to sections such as retail, a traditionally feminized area of the bank. Also, even though career-track hiring was abolished, a large number of previously non-career-track women continue to do assistant-level jobs. Furthermore, the absence of women in positions of power continues to sustain workers' gender biases. The segregation of men and women is reinforced in a less visible and more informal way. Finally, many of the women managers I talked to noted that neither growth in the number of women managers nor in the number of career-track women is yet large enough to threaten men's power at Mikado Bank. Foreign ownership and management, then, have not yet led to dramatic desegregation. As far as new hires go, Mikado Bank also expressed commitment to gender-equal or even female-dominated hiring. This sounds promising, but it takes many years under the systems of lifelong employment and seniority promotion before these new hires can become managers.

## Daigo Life Insurance: Few Changes

Daigo Life Insurance has retained most of its traditional Japanese customs. It is one of the largest life insurance companies in Japan in terms of assets, and it has been under the control of a major *keiretsu* or group of interlocked companies since the early twentieth century. Multiple companies under the major *keiretsu* groups are codependent on the main bank and share each other's stock. As with other companies under the control of major Japanese *keiretsu*, the firm is highly traditional. The woman workers I talked with described the company as almost like a totalitarian society or medieval feudalist community. At Mikado Bank, I ran into many foreign workers; busy-looking workers rushed around the floors, and lively coffee shops were located inside the building; I saw none of this at Daigo Life Insurance. All of the offices—and in fact the entire building—were very quiet with no sounds of people walking or talking. Yet all the workers I talked with were relaxed and smiling, though extremely polite and formal. I wondered about the oppressive silence, which was not just my observation but which was mentioned by some of the women I interviewed. Was it the air of paternalism and authoritarianism that made the workplace extremely quiet? Were the workers and managers I met calm and relaxed because the company offers them high levels of lifetime economic security? Or, as in other large traditional Japanese firms, was the quiet simply indicative of employees' conformity to order and authority?

A few people I talked with mentioned a past policy of the firm that mandated that women resign on marriage as an example of the firm's highly traditional attitude toward women workers. Some remembered married women who were forced to quit by their bosses. In fact, twelve women workers sued the company in 1995 for being forced to quit their jobs or for being discriminated against in term of promotions when they continued to work. One of the twelve plaintiffs described being asked by her boss to resign when she became pregnant; she was transferred to a floor with no phones or female restrooms so that she had to repeatedly climb stairs to deal with clients on the phone and also to use the restroom. The employer insisted that the quality and amount of work done by married women generally lessens, but in 2002 the court ruled this claim irrational and ordered the employer to pay $900,000 to the plaintiffs. This lawsuit indicates that Daigo Life Insurance had normalized authoritarian and patriarchal customs.

Daigo Life Insurance has over 30,000 female insurance agents in over one thousand local offices in Japan. In 2011 the company was sued again, this time by a woman who was in charge of a local office on account of her male boss's "power harassment," or constant bullying and harassing remarks. The plaintiff said her boss would blame her for the office's low sales numbers or force her to lie about her sales; his treatment led to her severe clinical depression and ultimately her resignation. The court ruled that the firm was responsible, and it eventually paid about $400,000 to the woman in compensation.

In 2005, Daigo Life Insurance started a gender-equality program that included increasing the firm's hiring of female career-track workers and promoting women into middle management. The company's reform committee for women's employment was tasked with decreasing the high turnover of career-track women, married women, and mothers. The firm designated government guidelines and awards as goals to reach. It also discussed the increasing importance of compliance with a global standard resulting from globalization of financial markets. Therefore, the firm, like many other financial firms, has tightened its business compliance. Women's employment appears to be one of the areas in which the firm wants to improve. But, as a long-time *keiretsu* member with mostly Japan-focused management, the company generally still exhibits more concern about its Japanese reputation than its global standing.

Increasing the number of female managers and career-track workers is a serious concern for the company. In 1994 the firm hired, for the first time, a total of fifteen career-track women among over a hundred new hires, and from 1995 to 2005 it hired between four and seven women annually, compared to over a hundred new male hires. In 2006, Daigo increased the annual number of hires of career-track women workers to thirteen, and in 2007, it further increased the hires to thirty-seven, then hired close to ninety women in 2009. But a thirty-five-year-old section manager of its human resources office told me that, as with many Japanese firms, Daigo Life Insurance has a long history of difficulty in retaining career-track women, as most of them quit after a few years.

Because the company has long valued the traditional Japanese brand of patriarchal culture, long work hours, and educational elitism, its unconventional promotion of women to management positions and its hiring of larger numbers of women for career-track positions were often seen as unwelcome by many male workers I talked to. The reform committee for women's employment was seen as isolated from the rest of the section; thus, it could be viewed as a temporary display of the company's interest in promoting an image of gender equality. "Ms. Saito is really having a hard time in managing the firm's new policy to activate women's hiring, retention, and promotion because no one is really supporting her or interested in the policy, either," said a twenty-nine-year-old male worker.

Some workers were concerned about the rapid increase in young career-track women in the firm. Three female managers in the firm expressed reservations about the young workers, arguing that they often take advantage of the firm's long parental leave and leave the workplace without doing adequate jobs. They mentioned that some young working mothers are disrespectful of the values of teamwork, devotion, and obligation, and that increasing the hiring and promotion of career-track women can harm the workplace. A thirty-five-year-old female section manager in the human resources office said: "It is important that working mothers take parental leave. But I get frequent complaints from other workers that some of them leave too early without doing much work. . . . You are paid money, so why don't you do more? . . . The workplace atmosphere gets really bad because of those who leave early." Apparently, there is a gap between how the women managers work and how young career-track workers work. I will discuss the generation gap between managerial-level women workers and young women workers in the section on gender bias.

Until a few years before I conducted the interviews, the firm did not have any workers who were mothers because they were all forced to quit on marriage and childbirth. The firm apparently has faced some challenges in coordinating and accommodating mothers' or future mothers' requests, because the workplace culture at Daigo Life Insurance is such that combining work and the caretaker role continues to be seen as difficult for women.

Negativity has also been expressed by some in regard to promoting women because it is seen as unfair because of women's supposed lack of qualifications and work experience. A thirty-seven-year-old male middle manager said: "The company really pushes women to get promotions, entirely in opposition with the past (the firm used to force women to quit when they married). But I believe in meritocracy. It is entirely useless to put some token woman in management who doesn't know anything about the job. I am not sure where the firm wants to go with such a policy. . . . I know a lot of men are wary of it and feel very constrained by the policy." Such expressions of negativity also shape young workers' views of female managers. A twenty-six-year-old non-career-track woman said, ambivalently, "I hear many men complain about the firm's positive action. They say it is unfair that the company pushes women into higher positions." She herself is not interested in a career-track job and tacitly indicated her support of this senior men's view of positive action.

A few men at Daigo Life Insurance questioned not so much women's lack of qualifications as their lack of adequate training and experience compared to those of male workers. A twenty-nine-year-old man referred to this gap between male workers and female workers in the areas of training, experience, and qualifications when he said, "The women workers need to be trained well by the company." What he, and others, mean by training includes not just formal and professional work but also such informal experience as networking and team building inside and outside the firm.

Another difficulty is tension among women workers. One forty-two-year-old male general manager felt it was too much work to accommodate women workers' various requests, which depended on their job status and sometimes their marital or parental status, especially since the firm, like many other firms, categorizes women workers based on whether they are regular workers or temporary workers, and whether they are career-track, area-track, or non-career-track workers. This categorization of female workers makes desegregation, gender equality, and female solidarity almost impossible in Japanese companies. The increase in career-track women has not made it easier for managers to negotiate tensions among women employees. At Daigo Life Insurance, until recently, there were very few career-track women, no working mothers, and a large number of non-career-track women. There also existed an extremely clear division of labor between men (as workers) and women (as assistants). The rapid increase in career-track women coupled with the small increase in women managers has started to destabilize the taken-for-granted norms and has generated tensions not only among women but also between women and men in the workplace. I will discuss this in more detail in chapter 4.

Similar to the male employees at the other four firms where I conducted interviews, the men at Daigo Life Insurance were not particularly enthusiastic about the firm's efforts to increase the number of female managers and career-track workers. Some men (and women) believe the increasing number of women harms the atmosphere and decreases productivity. A large number of men and a considerable number of women persist in seeing the traditional division of workers—men as the core workers and women as assistants—as desirable. Concerns about the firm's explicit positive action seem to be strong in Daigo Life Insurance because the company has greatly valued its patriarchal workplace culture and masculine work norms. Along the same lines, the company has placed a high value on many of the tenets of traditional Japanese management, including lifelong employment, seniority, career-track hiring, and an age- and education-based hierarchy. The number of women managers and career-track workers is small, while there are more non-career-track women than ever before doing cost-saving labor. Though the company has started to hire more career-track women, the number is significantly smaller than the number of new men hired. As I have repeated throughout this book, career-track hiring and hiring large numbers of temporary women workers allows only a small number of elite women the opportunity for upward mobility while reinforcing sex segregation. Basically, the firm has reiterated the same strategy that it did in the 1980s when the Equal Employment Opportunity Law required that companies prove their efforts to equalize the workplace. Overall, Daigo Life Insurance has changed little in terms of its sex-segregated customs.

## Shijo Asset Management: Limited Adjustment

Shijo Asset Management operates as a part of the large Japanese *keiretsu* group known as Shijo Investment Group, which in 2008 expanded its financial business in the United States, Europe, and Asia. Shijo Investment Group consists of banks, securities companies, and real estate businesses in Japan, the United States, Europe, and Asia. Over 40 percent of the group's stockholders are foreigners, yet it is among the most highly traditional large Japanese groups with many intrafirm networks. Many Japanese banks have had close ties with the Shijo group for various types of joint business ventures, as well as being the group's major lenders. The group's securities firm originally started business as a bank and spun off at the beginning of the twentieth century. In late 2008, the group took over some Lehman Brothers' branches in Asia and Europe. Although it has acquired a more international flavor since the takeover, Shijo Asset Management is still known as a typical Japanese firm with strong ties to the government and large Japanese banks.

In the late 1990s, the board members of Shijo Securities and a few members of the Japanese Ministry of Finance were arrested for bribery and corruption. Shijo Securities had been famous for having a highly militant workplace culture and hypermasculine employee customs. It was well known in Japan that male workers in Shijo Securities were trained to compete ruthlessly to win clients and aim for the highest sales. In 2013, a former employee of the firm sued his boss for "power harassment" after being asked to sell his car and write a letter of resignation when his sales did not reach his assigned quota. The Tokyo district court ruled in favor of the employee, ordering the firm to pay the cost of damages.

While Shijo Securities is a large firm with over 10,000 employees, Shijo Asset Management has only about 900 workers. A few upper managers at Shijo Asset Management transferred from Shijo Securities, and employees at Shijo Asset Management felt they needed to get used to the culture of the parent firm, even though Shijo Asset Management does not share the hypermasculine workplace culture of Shijo Securities. The workers I talked with at Shijo Asset Management described the firm as not as masculine or militant as Shijo Securities, but they did note that the firms are similar in that women are invisible in both, and they also pointed out that traditional Japanese management customs, including career-track hiring and lifelong employment, are dominant in both firms.

According to a manager in the human resources office of Shijo Asset Management, the company cut back on new hires after the global financial crisis in 2008. Following its takeover of a large American bank after the Lehman Brothers collapse, the firm started hiring Japanese workers who had graduated from US colleges. The manager was careful to mention that the firm now hires 50 percent men and 50 percent women, as if this were clear evidence of corporate gender equality. Among the most recent crop of twenty newly hired college graduates, ten were US-educated Japanese, mostly female, and the rest were Japanese educated in Japan, mostly male. The human resources manager emphasized that the firm follows the global business imperative, which goes beyond the issue of gender equality in Japan. She said: "You know, since we hired people globally after acquisition of the US bank, we don't specifically focus on gender or women anymore. We emphasize 'diversity' because we now have such a diverse group of workers. We care, not just about workers' gender, but also about nationality, race, etc."

Shijo Asset Management engages in career-track hiring, and it has a large number of area-career-track women workers whose chances of promotion are very limited. At the time of the interviews, the firm had over 100 career-track women workers and 150 area-career-track women workers out of their 900 employees. Thus, in its gender reforms, Shijo Asset Management continues to use the traditional tactic of providing gender-equal opportunities to only a small female elite and using the remainder of its female employees as cheap labor. Shijo Investment Group is eager to present itself as a global capital company; thus, it highlights its high level of corporate social responsibility. Yet the firm adheres to the tenets of traditional Japanese management. One exception is that Shijo Asset Management started hiring midcareer workers from other financial institutions, so one-third of its workforce comes from other companies. However, employees mentioned that those who lead the race for promotion are the ones who entered Shijo Asset Management as new college graduates.

Women make up fewer than 2 percent of managers in the firm. The male managers I interviewed were mostly indifferent to women's employment status in the company. Four of the male middle managers I interviewed indirectly avoided my question about the firm's increasing utilization of women workers by claiming that most women they know are non-career-track workers from the 1980s and 1990s who are assistants to men, selling securities to individual clients in store windows.

A forty-year-old male manager in charge of a product section that had about twenty-five workers said, "I don't think men and women are equal," and "I really don't think the company wants more women." He expressed his dislike of working with women, arguing that they are more short-sighted, emotional, and irrational than men, and noted that he did not want to deal with the tensions among women workers in different employment categories. The men in their forties I interviewed did not hesitate to express gender stereotypes—a situation not helped by the absence of women with power in the firm who could show such images to be myths. These men simply had never worked with high-powered women. In their minds, they still saw most women workers as assistants.

All eight of the women workers I interviewed in the Shijo firm described it as highly male dominated. Four reported direct and indirect experiences that they considered discriminatory, in the forms of derogatory comments about women by employees or clients, women earning lower salaries than men of similar status, and the relegation of women to lower job positions.

The women managers were invisible in the firm. At a highly male-dominated workplace like Shijo, women tend to blame themselves for their lack of visibility.

A female human resource manager said she herself was pushed into management because of affirmative action and that the absence of women managers was due to women workers' overall lack of ambition and aspirations rather than to inadequate changes in the firm's structure and customs. The women expressed a sense of resignation every time I asked questions about the firm's reforms with regard to women's employment. There is a contradiction, clearly, between Shijo Asset Management's claims of globalization and its adherence to a traditional male-centered style of management and the continued use of women as cheap labor.

## Takane and Hanakage: Visible Working Mothers

Takane and Hanakage are the largest Japanese cosmetics firms. They both ranked in the top ten of the world's largest beauty companies in 2008; US- and European-owned companies dominated the top thirty.[15] Takane started as a pharmaceutical store in Tokyo at the end of the nineteenth century, and Hanakage started around the same time as a general store, also in Tokyo, selling soaps and imported stationery. When Japan began striving to catch up with the West, both Takane and Hanakage sold their brands as "aspirational symbols of modernity."[16] The companies have had great success in making Western beauty available in a Japanese context, selling such products as skin whiteners. Even though the Japanese or Asian emulation of Western white women through skin whitening is often seen as a cultural sign of racism, it also has aspects of resistance and creativity, with the skin-whitening products representing a "reassertion of traditional beauty aesthetics and a rejection of Western fashions."[17] Takane has successfully done business in China since the 1980s, and one-third of its revenue now comes from outside Japan.[18] Hanakage first introduced shampoo products (the name of the shampoo was Modern) in the 1920s;[19] the company has been more successful in the area of toiletry products similar to those sold by Procter & Gamble than Takane, which focuses more on cosmetics. Hanakage also has successful ties with China, and both Takane and Hanakage earn four-fifths of their revenue elsewhere in Asia and the Pacific.[20]

The cases of Takane and Hanakage are slightly different from those of the financial companies, because neither company uses career-track hiring, both already employ many women and mothers, and their reforms to women's status and employment have not targeted hiring more women career-track workers or offering more lenient leave to working parents. In fact, Takane started its own reforms to increase the number of women in management and retain working mothers in the 1990s, a decade earlier than other Japanese companies. Takane is known as a "woman-friendly" company and often ranks as one of the most gender-equal companies in Japan, largely because of the fast-paced increase in its number of women managers. Hanakage also advocated woman-friendly programs and extensive parental leave in the 1990s.

When I interviewed the employees of Takane in 2007, women made up 14 percent of total management, but by 2013 the number had increased to 25 percent. The company's performance has been unstable—the president resigned in 2013 due to its poor performance—but the number of female managers keeps increasing. A woman from the Ministry of Health, Labour and Welfare joined the company as a board member on her retirement (a common practice that results from intimate corporate-government ties in Japan). Takane also has an American female board member who moved from Procter & Gamble. The female management rate is likely to reach the current administration's goal of 30 percent by 2020. Also, the women's turnover rate is low—in other words, there are not many women who quit after marriage or childbirth. Takane has its own child-care facility, which the employees can use. The growing rate of women managers as well as the low turnover rate of married women and mothers at Takane are quite distinctive among Japanese companies.

However, a few things still belie the promise of gender equality. First, Takane has about 12,000 regular female workers, but it also has 9,000 temporary or irregular female workers (among all its related companies). This is a great example of the polarization of women workers. Among regular Takane employees who work inside Japan, men number 3,500; in contrast, Hanakage has about 6,000 regular female employees and 1,500 temporary or irregular female workers (in all of the group's related companies). But 75 percent of Takane's leaders and managers are still men; close to 800 out of 3,500 reach leadership positions, while only 270 out of 12,000 women attain such positions. And, in 2013, while 1,500 female workers took parental leave, only five male workers took it. In other words, there is a clearly gendered division of labor and a male-dominant management culture, regardless of the company's glossy woman-friendly image. When I interviewed men and women in their forties and older, I noticed a tension between men and women workers, which I did not sense among the men and women in their twenties. In fact, the female upper manager I talked with left the firm a couple of years after our interview in which she had told me about the difficult reforms and slow change in Takane's male-dominated environment.

At Takane, female managers were about 5 percent of the total in 1997, and this increased five times in fifteen years. In other words, the company was the same as more traditional Japanese companies. Hiroko, a fifty-six-year-old assistant general manager in the human resources office at Takane, explained several changes the firm made in the 2000s: "In 2002, the firm finally stopped paying spousal and family benefits only to male workers. . . . This company had mostly non-career-track women workers in the past, and . . . the firm started hiring only career-track workers from 2007 or 2008 and integrated all female workers into the career track (transferrable type workers and local area workers)." Whereas many women at Takane continue their jobs after childbirth, normally taking a year or longer of parental leave, until recently they were given the lowest grade on their evaluations for doing so. Hiroko explained:

> It took two or three years to change the evaluation system. . . . When women took parental leave, their evaluations would go down. . . . When we promote workers, we look at their evaluations from the past three years. It is a big part of our decision. If you get D, the lowest grade, even once, your total evaluation from the three years goes down. Thus, men's evaluations would be better than any of the workers who were mothers. The men were therefore promoted simply because they never had a D in their evaluations. Now, if a woman takes parental leave, she will not be given any grade during that period, just a blank, so it won't influence the total evaluation negatively.

She emphasized that reform of the most woman-friendly company in Japan took off only after 2002.

During our interview she raised her voice when she said, "In this firm, workers who have anything to do with gender equality are not welcome at all!" Clearly she has had a hard time with the top managers' reluctance to change their views on women's employment; however, she also criticized women workers who not only don't want to change but who don't even see their lack of power as a problem. She said that many women simply do not believe in the necessity of a gender-equality program and do not grasp that women's promotions would never occur without affirmative action. She expressed her frustration and resentment several times during the interview.

> We tried positive action at Takane from 2000 until 2005. A great number of men complained about the training the women were given and questioned why only women got these privileges. . . . The women do not believe that they are promoted because of positive action. They don't like this. They believe that they are simply excellent. But, in reality, they can't be managers. They don't seem to know that. . . . When I suggest some changes to the men in the meetings, all the men understand the idea of gender equality in their heads and agree with me about providing women with training and workshops that specifically target them. But then, when I ask them to recommend female managers for promotion, they say no, they don't have a single woman to recommend for a managerial position.

She continued, "These men blocked all the changes I proposed. They are just too old to think about changing the system." Her boss moved her to a different section, and he and his coworkers immediately terminated the gender-equality program. She worked for the department of corporate social responsibility for a while, but the top managers, who continue to dismiss her initiatives, downsized the corporate social responsibility department until it became just "the CSR room." Hiroko described herself as being unwelcome in the firm, and one male manager I talked with agreed with this assessment. A middle manager in his forties, he said that management did not care about what Hiroko did and described her as an isolated activist.

As I will discuss in chapters 4, 5, and 6, Takane does much better than other Japanese companies in terms of its numerical increase in women managers. However, regardless of very recent improvements in its hiring, promotion, and evaluation systems, Takane retains a highly male-dominated management structure similar to that of many other Japanese firms. Some of the recent changes in Takane, such as hiring a new president from outside the firm and shedding over 1,000 employees through early retirement incentives in 2005, seem to indicate the firm's slight shift from traditional Japanese management. This may suggest that desegregation or gender egalitarianism in employment and management do not go along with traditional Japanese management customs. If a Japanese firm cannot cut costs by using women's cheap labor, it has to find other ways to save, and Takane's management might find that laying off highly paid male managers who are over forty is a more rational and efficient way to keep the company going than continuing to protect these senior men through traditional management customs.

Even though Hanakage has a lower percentage of female managers than Takane, it employs a good number of women and mothers, and its turnover rate is low, similar to Takane's. Hanakage is well known for having a long-work-hour culture. As I discuss in a later chapter 6, the case of Hanakage, according to my interviews with its employees, shows that the combination of a long-work-hour culture with seniority promotion and pay, typical of traditional Japanese management, makes it extremely difficult for women workers to manage both job and family. Those who get ahead must first endure long years of service based on age and long daily work hours, a situation that has lowered women's aspirations and made it difficult for them to plan families. The case of Hanakage shows that some customs of Japanese management hamper women's upward mobility. The combination of daily long working hours and a long wait before promotion clearly contributes to women leaving their jobs and the low percentage of women in management. Overall, workers at Takane and Hanakage viewed the workplace as accommodating mothers very well, but with that one exception the cosmetic companies are no more gender equal than the three financial firms in terms of vertical sex segregation.

The cosmetics companies' retention of women and mothers merits further in-depth discussion and analysis, however, especially considering the extremely high number of women in Japanese companies who used to resign when they married or gave birth. The presence of a good number of working mothers and the low turnover rate of women workers in the two cosmetics companies are clearly to the result of the firms' lenient child-care policies and flexible work-hour arrange-ments for working parents (even though those who use the policy are mostly women). The companies' lack of customs that encourage or even force women to resign on marriage and childbirth also serves to promote a less discriminatory atmosphere than in the other companies. Also, seniority-based promotion with less competition may make it easier for women to keep their jobs. Even though I argue that seniority promotion works against (1) women's aspirations, (2) their upward mobility, and (3) reproductive planning, the age-based seniority system does offer women a degree of financial security and some ability to move up. In fact, because of seniority promotion at Takane, about 80 percent of the firm's employees attain their first three promotions and a decent salary (about $70,000) by the age of thirty, even though an employee has to wait until forty before being promoted to management. In addition, both cosmetics firms seem to respond to working mothers' requests, such as asking for more flexible working hours and transfers to less demanding sections, and such an atmosphere makes women want to stay with these companies.

However, enhancing working mothers' desire to continue with the com-pany does not mean women have a high chance of promotion to management. In fact, the Japanese customs of long working hours and seniority promotion makes it difficult, overall, for women to combine upward career mobility and family formation, as I will discuss in chapter 6. The lenient child-care policies and good economic security promised by the seniority-promotion and lifelong-employment systems in Japanese firms could successfully increase the number of women and mothers working in nonmanagement positions, but management will likely continue to be dominated by men. Women may enjoy prominence on the lower rungs of the corporate hierarchy, but they may stay there. Thus, the increase in working women and mothers, and even the rapidly increasing female management rate at Takane, does not necessarily indicate a decrease in vertical sex segregation.

The ratio of female to male managers has been increasing more quickly at Mikado Bank and Takane than at the other firms where I conducted interviews. At Mikado Bank, the termination of the gender-based custom of career-track hiring, the integration of the non-career-track women into career-track positions, and the midcareer hiring of those who have American educational credentials and overseas job experience have transmitted a message to employees that the firm is willing to change its traditional management customs. That the bank is run by American management might have made these reforms easier than they would have been in the other companies. Even though the bank continues to retain lifelong employment and many other traditional customs of Japanese firms, the management also uses performance-based pay combined with traditional seniority, and its employees are free to leave the firm for better jobs and pay. Unlike the typical traditional Japanese bank, Mikado Bank seems to offer larger bonuses and earlier promotions to those who perform better than others. (It may be the case that it has a lower base salary than other similar Japanese banks to curb its labor costs and pay more to those who demonstrate the best performance.) As for its women workers, the bank was not able to resolve the negative consequences of its previous career-track hiring, since those who had previously worked as non-career-track women or assistants informally continued to do assistant-level work and were thus segregated into the bottom jobs.

The bank's hiring of workers with different backgrounds and its use of midcareer hiring might have increased the pool of women qualified for management. However, as I discuss in chapter 5, some workers at Mikado Bank pointed out that women managers tend to have titles in name only, which are superficial and have nothing to do with management. Making someone a manager in name only is a traditional custom in Japanese firms that is used to make the workplace harmonious and to reduce competition among workers. This tactic seems to be commonly used by companies that want to increase the number of women managers. The bank still lacks women at the top levels of management (as I discuss in chapters 5 and 6).

At both Hanakage and Takane, few women quit their jobs when they had children. Yet these firms are dominated by men in upper management, with women concentrated at the lower levels. At Takane, the number of low-level female managers has increased quickly in the last ten years. Many of my interview subjects agreed that women workers rarely leave the workplace after marriage or childbirth because of the firm's lenient parental leave. Unlike Mikado Bank, Takane has relied on the traditional Japanese corporate practices of lifelong employment and seniority promotion. Because lifelong employment and age-based promotions offer a high level of economic security to workers, women who plan to balance their jobs with family life may find it an attractive place to work. However, lifelong employment may also work against women's career development. The low turnover of the married women workers and the increasing number of women in low or even middle-level management does not mean that there are more women in the higher positions.

Shijo Asset Management and Daigo Life Insurance are both part of traditional Japanese *keiretsu* groups and have low percentages of females in management. Both men and women managers expressed negativity about the firms' increasing the number of women managers and workers. They described the firms' egalitarian reforms as being merely a corporate gesture, done for the sake of the Japanese government. Though both firms have increased their hiring of career-track women workers, they also continue to hire a large number of non-career-track women and temporary female workers. These companies are continuing to use most women as cheap labor.

In the next chapter, I discuss how the Japanese traditions of seniority pay and promotion and career-track hiring tend to work against women and their career prospects. I also discuss the ways in which career-track hiring and temp hiring lowers women's aspirations and increases their negativity.

# WOMEN AS CHEAP LABOR

Salaries, Promotions, Ghettos, and the
Culture of Woman Blaming

In this chapter I examine the processes supporting vertical sex segregation in
Japanese management practices and the labor market. I also look at the larger
picture of Japanese business and labor relations, in which women's low status
has been a critical factor. Major Japanese management practices—seniority pay
and promotion, track hiring, and household benefits—work against women's
upward mobility and reify sex segregation in Japanese companies. In its logic,
Japanese management is distinctly different from Western management; in Japanese management, both seniority pay and track hiring discourage women's
continual employment and promotion to upper positions, and thus Japanese
companies can use women as a major source of cheap labor. By comparing
the salaries and benefits of the men and women I interviewed in similar age
groups, the ways in which companies use women workers as a labor cost saver
are revealed. Traditional companies continue to pay household benefits mostly to
men, a tendency that shapes the large gender gap in wages. Because of their lack
of mobility in the labor market and the exclusive emphasis in many companies
on in-firm skills, women who are already in low positions have little opportunity
to obtain better jobs outside of their firms. The prevalence since the early 2000s
in Japan of American-style "performance-based pay" has been exaggerated, and
its superficial use in many companies alongside the much more common use of
seniority pay is a problem.

Vicki Smith has pointed out that while some women have been able to enter
the realm of managerial and administrative work, many other women remain in
part-time and temporary work ghettos and that this pattern of gender inequality

might be an inevitable result of the corporate hierarchy of the postindustrial workplace.[1] Japanese management has a long history of using a large number of marginalized women workers, and the companies I studied hired and sorted women with similar educational background into various marginal positions, while proclaiming their commitment to desegregation. Career-track hiring lowers women workers' motivation and aspirations and reifies status differences among women. Women have typically been arranged in the hierarchy with temp women, often looked down on and pitied, at the bottom. As a result, women's relations to other women are a common source of workplace tensions. Women employed as assistants are bullied as a result of their being relegated to positions with no power and little possibility of upward mobility.

# Why Women Are Paid Less Than Men

Three major customs of Japanese management have very different impacts on women and men: seniority pay, career-track hiring, and household benefits. Japan's system of seniority pay is said to be a poor fit for the typical Japanese woman,[2] yet there has been little examination of how it continues to suppress and work against women's upward mobility. These three unique customs have counteracted efforts at desegregation and perpetuate the low pay and low status of women in Japanese companies. Also, the lack of mobility in the labor market in Japan disables women's mobility and solidifies their low status.

## How Promotion and Seniority Pay Work

Before I discuss how seniority pay and promotion work against women, I will briefly explain the general steps in the process of promotion and how they relate to pay in the Japanese companies I researched. The five firms I studied followed more or less similar pay and promotion schemes based on age, except for Mikado Bank in regard to its foreign managers and Takane in regard to its foreign board members. The major characteristic of this promotional path is the number of years required before becoming a middle manager: about fifteen years after beginning to work for the company. Promotions take place every three or four years after an employee's starting date, and major promotions, to management, occur in the late thirties or early forties. For example, at Daigo Life Insurance, it takes about fifteen to twenty years to become a middle manager. Staff members (*syokuin*) may move to senior staff (*syunin*) after about four years. Senior staff may be promoted to subsection chief (*fuku-sanji*) in ten years, and then they may be promoted to manager (*sanji*) after fifteen to twenty years. Only a very few middle managers will ever be promoted to departmental heads (*bucho*) or, beyond that, to the board. Regarding salary, the amount increases steeply for employees in their late thirties or early forties. At Daigo Life Insurance, a twenty-four-year-old career-track woman reported her income as $45,000 annually, but the annual salary rises to between $90,000 and $100,000 at forty. One thirty-seven-year-old male subsection chief reported a salary of about $90,000 annually, while a thirty-eight-year-old woman general manager earned about $130,000 per year. (This gap can probably be explained by the woman being a middle manager with a higher rank than the male subsection chief.)

At Takane, workers in their early twenties are paid about $35,000, and this is said to go up to $45,000 after three years. By the age of thirty most workers reach level three, which pays about $70,000 per year. However, two-thirds of employees are not promoted further. An employee may become a *kacho*, or manager, no earlier than forty, with a salary of $90,000, and a deputy manager by fifty, earning $110,000. By fifty-five, an employee might attain a general manager position, which pays $130,000. In my interviews at Takane Cosmetics, a twenty-seven-year-old female career-track worker reported her annual salary as about $48,000, while a thirty-eight-year-old female career-track worker earned about $70,000. This is slightly less than the $78,000 that a thirty-nine-year-old man in the firm earned. A forty-six-year-old male manager at Takane earned about $110,000, and a forty-nine-year-old female manager earned $120,000. Because the two people in their forties whom I interviewed were both managers and had much higher salaries than the rest of the workers at Takane, it is clear that long years of service and being in management positions clearly boosted workers' salaries.

Hanakage has a similar custom of seniority pay and promotion. New hires start at $50,000, and the salary increases to $60,000 by the late twenties. If a worker becomes a leader in his or her midthirties, the salary rises to $75,000. Manager level is reached around forty with pay of $90,000 to $100,000, and general manager by the age of fifty with a salary of $120,000. In my interviews at Hanakage Cosmetics, a twenty-eight-year-old woman earned about $55,000, while a thirty-seven-year-old manager reported his income as about $90,000; another male worker, this one thirty-nine but with no management title, reported a salary of $70,000. Other men and women who were over forty in this firm reported similar incomes.

At Mikado Bank, there are four different titles below the board member position: staff member (*tanto*); manager (*dairi*); deputy manager (*jicho*); and general manager (*bucho*). Each position also has two or three ranks within it, with different salaries depending mostly on years of service. All the workers I interviewed at Mikado Bank who were in their late thirties or early forties held the title of *jicho* or deputy manager. Mikado Bank, despite US ownership, has retained some major Japanese customs, such as lifelong employment and seniority pay. The workers at the bank had divided views about this situation. Some saw the firm as emphasizing individual performance over seniority, while others, mostly in their thirties and forties, viewed management as basing evaluations and pay on seniority rather than on individual performance. However, a younger worker there did not see lifelong employment as the norm at the firm. He indicated that those with ambition and opportunities leave the bank: "When I look at about fifty workers who started their jobs in the same year, who each served about ten years at this firm, I see about twenty-five men who have already left the firm. Then, only five out of twenty-five are a bit above staff positions and they are probably aiming at *dairi*. Another five stay at the level of senior staff. But the remaining fifteen have no title and continue in positions with no titles." Overall, Japanese companies employ similar promotion and pay systems. Under the Japanese seniority system, a worker can reach low management in his or her early thirties, but promotion to middle manager occurs in the forties.

## How Seniority Pay and Promotion Sideline Women

Mary Brinton has pointed out that the levels of sex segregation increase with age in Japanese companies;[3] similarly, the number of women decreases higher up on the promotion ladder. In the past, there were few women in the middle and upper management levels of Japanese companies, largely because women quit their jobs when they married or had children. More attention should be paid to the pay and promotion system itself as gender biased and explicitly working against women rising in their careers. The rule of seniority pay in Japan is that workers' major raises and promotions occur after they have given about fifteen to twenty years of service to the company. Promotion to management based on seniority, then, requires workers to perform at a high level and prove their commitment between the ages of thirty and forty, when most women are getting married and having children.[4] This system makes it difficult for many women to manage their family planning and thus puts them at a disadvantage. Many women may not pursue promotions or may simply quit their jobs before they receive a major promotion, and the company will save on labor costs. This seniority system, then, lower women's aspirations and encourages them to make compromises in climbing the career ladder. Thus, it legitimizes gender-unequal pay and promotion. Needless to say, this custom also makes men's ability to spend time as caretakers of the family difficult.

The lifelong employment system in Japan, however, promises long-term economic security to women, and thus it promotes woman's continuous employment after marriage and childbirth, especially when there is lenient parental leave. If women are not interested in ascending the promotion ladder, lifelong employment can still guarantee their lifetime economic security; this can be a fine arrangement for working mothers. In such cases, women who are mothers may be concentrated on the lower rungs of the ladder, and the company will thus save money. Yet I argue that this system discourages highly motivated women from pursuing advancement. Those who are very competent and ambitious will suffer because they not only get few rewards for their achievements at the early stages of their careers but they have to keep going for fifteen or twenty years until their employer offers them their first promotion, and they will have to coordinate their family lives accordingly. Thus, Japanese lifelong employment and seniority pay promotes traditional gender dynamics and the division of labor in the workplace.

In my interviews, women in their twenties particularly expressed concern about the seniority system. Women's concerns about seniority pay and promotion were similar across the companies, and even at a young age, their aspirations seem already to have been lowered. A twenty-seven-year-old area-career-track worker at Daigo Life Insurance said, "I cannot imagine myself being successful in this company . . . the firm is dictated by seniority. The women may go up when they get old. . . . I mean, women can speak up only after they get old! . . . I want to have a child, too. But I feel like you can't do anything until you get into your fifties and sixties. It is hard to envision what I would be doing when I get that old in this company." A twenty-nine-year-old female worker at Hanakage Cosmetics commented about the difficult decision women have to make with regard to family and career prospects, and indicated that their hardships are increased by gender inequality in the workplace: "A promotion is entirely based on seniority. So nothing will happen until one reaches one's forties. All of us get promoted pretty much at the same time. . . . When we approach the age of forty, we work hard. If you are a woman, you work extremely hard to get promoted with little time for family and children. There are some women who get promoted after their forties. But all of them have always had their parents take care of their children." As the age of promotion in the seniority system coincides with the upper limits of women's reproductive years, women must find a way to put extra effort into work and family if they want both by their late thirties or early forties.

A thirty-seven-year-old female manager at Shijo Asset Management said, "Since things are determined by age in Japanese companies, people who want to be rewarded for individual achievement cannot get that. They go to foreign firms for better recognition and better pay." Better pay and better recognition in the early stages makes career development and family formation much easier for most women. The absence of these rewards in the Japanese seniority system apparently lowers women's aspirations and their desire to stay in Japanese firms.

Again, if women want to settle for minimal promotions with job security and a good salary, lifelong employment can be rewarding as it guarantees economic security. Many working mothers at Takane and Hanakage are among those who are satisfied with this situation; they earn decent salaries, even though very few of them hold management positions. But the characteristics of the seniority system work against many women's career plans and success in their actual career paths, and thus cause them to stay on the lowest rungs of the career ladder. Furthermore, since there is little labor mobility, the women have little opportunity to change their jobs unless they take part-time or temp jobs that have far less economic security and stability than their regular jobs provide.

## How Career-Track Hiring and Temp Hiring Reduce Labor Costs

Hiring women as cheap labor has been a central cost-saving method of traditional Japanese management. The custom continues to be the largest cause of vertical sex segregation in many Japanese companies. Despite career-track hiring being criticized as discriminatory against women, it continues to save firms money and is often praised as a perfect solution for working mothers to balance their family life with work. Some companies, such as Daigo Life Insurance and Shijo Asset Management, removed the label "non-career-track" from these positions while still relegating women to lower-paying positions than the men. Under the current custom in some companies, while men are employed in an unnamed (though clearly career-track) category, women are sorted into an array of subcategories, ranging from career-track workers to non-career-track workers, area-career workers, temporary or contract workers, and part-time workers. Such multiple-track hiring continues to reify sex segregation and the gendered pay gap while allowing firms to save on labor costs. Even though many Japanese firms now claim their hiring and promotion practices are gender equal, they still use a great number of temporary workers who are mostly women, and these temp workers receive none of the benefits that the businesses offer. And their salaries are typically less than one-fourth of men's salaries. Thus, the Japanese business community can claim that it is promoting gender equality and soliciting women's employment while being silent about its use of hundreds of temp women. These temp women sometimes have better educational backgrounds and more work experience than the regular workers, but they are very rarely promoted to be regular employees.

In my study of the five firms, I learned that Daigo Life Insurance and Shijo Asset Management continue to use the track-hiring system. Regardless of their emphasis on reform of women's employment, these companies did not find any

contradictions in sorting newly hired women with education and skills similar
to those of new male hires into very different positions with regard to pay and
promotions. At both firms, the number of career-track women is far lower than
the number of non-career-track women, almost to the point where there will be
no way to equalize the numbers in the near future.

At Shijo Asset Management, among about 900 regular workers, there are
about 100 career-track women workers and 150 area-career-track women workers. Daigo Life Insurance started hiring career-track women in 1994 (hiring only
two that year). From 1995 to 2005, they hired only four to seven women each year,
in contrast to the 150 to 160 men they hired annually. In 2006, they increased the
number of career-track women hired annually to thirteen, further increasing it
to thirty-seven in 2007, and hired close to ninety in 2009. It is estimated that
Daigo Life Insurance today has a total of about 200 career-track women workers,
which is only about 2 percent of all workers. Meanwhile, they have about one
to two thousand temporary workers, mostly women. Daigo Life Insurance just
recently generated another category, called *yuki ippanshoku*; this is a two-year
limited non-career-track position. In the sections I have learned about at Daigo
Life Insurance, there were a far larger number of non-career-track women and
temporary staff women than career-track women. One of the sections in human
resources, which has a relatively high number of women compared to the other
sections, has a total of thirty-five workers. Among all the women workers in this
section, only two are career-track workers and another two are area-career-track
workers. About eight are non-career-track workers, and five are part-time or contract workers.

Career-track hiring has been a major labor cost-saving method for Japanese
companies, and many continue to use it. Even worse, many companies are now
employing a large number of temporary women workers whose salary is far
lower than that of the non-career-track workers. Japanese firms can hire two to
four (or even more) women for the same amount paid to one man. At Shijo Asset
Management, two career-track women workers (one a thirty-seven year old in
marketing, and the other a thirty-eight year old in corporate communications)
told me that their annual salaries, including bonuses, total about $110,000.[5] The
amounts are pretty similar to those of men of a similar age. For example, the salary of a thirty-three-year-old male worker in the communications department
was about $100,000. Meanwhile, in the same firm, a thirty-one-year-old area-
career-track woman in sales (a graduate of a two-year college) was paid about
$50,000, and a thirty-year-old dispatched worker (also a graduate of a two-year
college) was paid about $30,000 per year. The comparison of several individu-
als' salaries by themselves shows that area-career-track workers and dispatched
workers at Shijo Asset Management are paid less than half or even a third of the

salary of career-track workers. (I do not have detailed data on how the firm's seniority pay scale and extra family benefits influence annual salaries.) Also, while a thirty-three-year-old man in the same firm was paid about $100,000, a thirty-four-year-old area-career-track woman was paid about $80,000. Even though area-career-track workers are described as being at the same level as career-track workers, their salaries are clearly lower than those of regular career-track workers of a similar age.

At Daigo Life Insurance, a thirty-five-year-old woman career-track worker in human resources and a thirty-seven-year-old man in investments were paid similarly, about $100,000 a year. Another thirty-eight-year-old career-track woman who was a manager in human development was paid about $130,000 annually, a salary similar to that of a man in his early forties, who earned about $120,000. The woman had achieved high sales goals for many years as a local branch manager based near Tokyo, and her long years of sales competency probably led to her somewhat higher salary.

Also at Daigo Life Insurance, a thirty-six-year-old non-career-track female worker with a two-year college degree was paid about $26,000 a year, which is about one-fourth of what a thirty-five-year-old career-track woman earned. While one twenty-nine-year-old male worker in human resources was paid $85,000, a thirty-year-old non-career-track woman with a college degree was paid less than half that, or only $35,000. Comparing two women of similar ages—a twenty-four-year-old career-track woman with a college degree who earned about $45,000 and a twenty-six-year-old non-career-track woman with a college degree who reported $30,000 as her annual salary—shows that the gap between the two tracks seems to be increasing.

At Mikado Bank, even though the career-track custom was abolished in the early 2000s and all the women there are categorized as career-track workers, those women who used to be non-career-track workers are still paid less than half of what the career-track women are paid. The workers, in fact, are divided both in their salaries and in their allocated tasks. A thirty-four-year-old woman who was hired as a non-career-track worker was paid about $60,000, which is exactly the same as the annual salary of a twenty-four-year-old man. A forty-four-year-old woman who was previously hired as a non-career-track worker earned about $80,000, which is less than half of the $200,000 paid to a thirty-eight-year-old man.

In the context of the American workplace, Alexandra Kalev uses the concept of the "glass cage" to refer to the type of job segregation in which women and racial minorities are concentrated in the lower levels and in marginal jobs, and in which their capabilities and aspirations are also negatively stereotyped.[6] Career-track hiring in Japan might be similar to the "glass cage," since individuals in non-career-track positions are highly thwarted and suppressed in their upward mobility and in their ability to obtain equal pay. Even though Kalev's research indicates that women and racial minorities may reach the managerial level after collaborative and interactive trainings, Japan's non-career- track positions offer few options for moving out of the cage. The caged women are also doomed to stay in their low positions because there is little mobility in the Japanese labor market except for those working in temp positions.

## How Household Benefits Widen the Gender Pay Gap

Housing support and family benefits also reinforce the gender wage gap. Men receive more benefits than do women workers. Because women can be non-career-track workers or temps with no benefits, married men, more often than women, claim head-of-household status and thus receive spousal and family benefits. Benefits for the career-track employee usually include housing, health insurance, a pension, and allowances for family members. If you are a non-career-track worker, housing and allowances are not included. If you are a temporary worker, no benefits are included. Even if you are a career-track worker, there seem to be informal rules about who gets paid, and how much, which mostly benefit the men in middle and upper management.

Among my interviewees, most married men had wives who did not work outside the home; these men received some type of family benefits. Many women workers I interviewed, however, did not receive spousal or family benefits, either because they lived with their parents or their husbands or simply because they were not qualified, as they were non-career-track workers. The custom of family benefits exacerbates the gender pay gap and privileges the male-breadwinner type of household over other types.

All five firms that I studied provided career-track workers (but not area-career-track workers) with housing benefits and family benefits, even though the amounts and periods of payment varied depending on the firm and on workers' marital status. At Daigo Life Insurance, the unmarried career-track workers are paid about $1,000 per month for their housing costs for as long as they are employed, or they may choose to live in a firm-owned apartment for a monthly rent of $100. Married workers are encouraged to live in company-owned family apartments for low rents until they retire, but they do often purchase their own houses or apartments, with the firm making them a loan to cover their mortgages.

At Shijo Asset Management, the amount of housing benefit and the period to be covered differed among career-track workers; as an example, one married man was offered $900 per month. Mikado Bank paid about $600 for the first four years to unmarried workers and $450 after the fifth year. Takane paid unmarried workers about $750 and married workers $900 for the first seven years of their employment. At Hanakage, unmarried workers could live in the firm-owned dormitory for about $100 per month. Otherwise, the unmarried received about $270 per month. Those who were married and owned a home were given $600, but the amount was reduced after the worker reached the age of forty. These firms also, in general, offered over $4,000 annually for spousal benefits and about $400 apiece for children or other family members, often for as many as five individuals, including the spouse.

Most workers whom I interviewed believed that they were receiving the same amount of benefits as others; however, even for those hired as career-track workers, the amounts differed. It is likely that some companies in Japan continue to privilege married men over single women, as has long been the custom, and to provide far better benefits to the former than the latter. One woman at Shijo Asset Management said, angrily, "I don't know how the system of payment works in this company." Mina, a thirty-eight-year-old single female career-track worker previously employed by a US securities firm and a French bank in Japan, had moved to Shijo Asset Management two years before my interview. Even though she was hired as a career-track worker, the firm did not pay her any housing support. Whereas most Japanese firms usually let employees take out loans at a better interest rate when they purchase a house, she was told by the firm that she was disqualified because she had only worked for the firm for two years. It was not clear how many years of service would qualify a worker to receive the firm's loan. One of her male colleagues said that she was disqualified because she was older than twenty-five, which, he said, might be the age limit for qualifying for housing and loan support. But Mina knew some career-track women in the firm who were under twenty-five and were also offered no benefits. She speculated that she was discriminated against because she was a woman and not a fresh college graduate like so many male workers there. Regardless, it is important to note that none of these rules and policies regarding benefits were explained to the workers.

Interestingly, no man whom I interviewed had had similar problems. Mina compared her case to that of her male colleague: "This is typical discrimination. There is this guy in my section whose wife works full time as a manager with no children. The company pays most of his rent. I can't believe it. I pay for everything by myself."

Indeed, Ryo, a forty-year-old worker at Shijo Asset Management, moved from another large securities firm two years prior to the interviews (much like Mina). He received a monthly housing allowance of about $2,000. The only difference between Mina and Ryo was that he was a middle-level manager, one rank higher than her, and his salary was also higher than hers. But this does not explain why the firm did not pay her any housing support while fully covering Ryo's housing. While Mina believed her lack of a housing benefit was because she was hired midcareer from the French firm rather than being hired fresh from college, another male worker whom I interviewed who had also moved from a different firm did receive housing benefits. (Satoshi, a thirty-three-year-old married worker at Shijo Asset Management, moved from a Japanese insurance firm a few years earlier; he received monthly housing support of about $900.)

Mina also wondered if she was not paid housing support simply because she was unmarried. But it is the married women who often do not receive benefits, because their spouses often earn more than they do. While we cannot conclude that the firm's failure to pay housing support to Mina and some other career-track women while paying it to men who were similar to Mina in work tenure, age, and rank is sex discrimination, it is certainly worth further investigation. Are career-track women treated the same as career-track men? Neither Japanese firms nor the government seem to be monitoring this.

It seems that the more sex segregated a company is (in terms of such things as the female management rate and use of the hiring track), the more it pays for housing support and family benefits for workers (who are mostly men). The firms' protection of married men's financial security seems to go hand in hand with their differential treatment of women workers as a cost-saving measure. Ironically, cutting the heavy family and housing benefits they pay to married men could, of course, save the firms considerable money as well.

## Women's Lack of Upward Mobility in the Labor Market

In a mobile and competitive labor market such as that in the United States, employees strive to acquire a variety of non-firm-specific skills, including higher educational credentials, professional training, and work experience, in addition to acquiring in-firm skills and taking advantage of firm resources. Employers in a mobile labor market evaluate their employees based on both in-firm and non-firm-specific skills and on performance. When the labor market is mobile and competitive, potential for upward mobility as a good worker is assessed on the basis of various factors, and not exclusively on in-firm skills. Since, in a mobile labor market, a person is free to move to another workplace to take a better job, the worker is also responsible for cultivating attractive skills and expertise. The hiring of midcareer workers with advanced skills and varied work experiences also makes an organization and workplace alive, innovative, and competitive, and helps to prevent inertia.

By contrast, Japan's lifelong-employment system has encouraged employees to devote themselves to cultivating only firm-specific skills and to devote those skills exclusively to one company for their entire lives. Employees are not expected to change companies to achieve upward mobility nor are they, regardless of weak performance, fired. As long as the labor market is immobile, a firm's management can maintain strong control over its workers, and workers are less motivated to develop themselves. Management is also under little pressure to change its traditional customs and implement innovative reforms.

Other than dedication and conformity to the employer, what exactly are the so-called firm-specific skills in Japanese companies? At least at the beginning of a worker's career, it can include formal education and age. Within a Japanese company, upward mobility is influenced by age and educational background, even when they have little to do with a worker's later performance or attained skills. In the United States, age and education might also be important factors in hiring, but employees need to prove they can actually complete tasks successfully in their area of specialty, which can also be marketable and contribute to upward mobility. In Japan, no outside-firm skills or professional skills matter for upward mobility within the firm. An exclusive emphasis on the age-based hierarchy along with a lack of labor mobility makes the power of management strong, increases employee conformity, and makes the workplace authoritarian.

The lack of mobility in the labor market and the extreme emphasis on in-firm skills makes it difficult for women who are already in low positions to move up to better jobs. Japanese companies' emphasis on age and on a four-year college education (university brand ranking) causes workers to be ranked based on these elements. Women may be relegated to non-career positions regardless of their elite college graduate status, though some women with backgrounds at elite universities may be able to leave the segregated path. However, unlike in the United States where women may be highly competent and possessing abundant non-firm skills, most of the women in Japanese companies won't be able to ascend in the corporate hierarchy in Japan.

## Age-Based Hierarchy and Education

Seniority pay and promotion in Japanese companies are based on age when starting employment. An age-based hierarchy can make deference and respect among workers the norm.[7] The age-based system in Japanese companies is designed to lower the incentive for shirking and to strengthen the group orientation of the business, while furthering each individual's identity within the firm.[8] However, when age is the major determinant of promotions and pay increases, it can easily lower worker motivation; workers in this situation learn to accept the absence of explicit competition and the importance of group consciousness and patriarchal conformity typical of highly traditional Japanese firms.

At Daigo Life Insurance, Alisa, a twenty-seven-year-old area-career-track worker, described her workplace as having an atmosphere like that of a totalitarian country because lower-level workers are expected to demonstrate absolute subordination to senior management. "Things go on pretty much based on seniority," she said. "I can't really say anything against even a *kacho*-level (middle-level) manager." Emphasizing the manager-subordinate distinction, she compared the interactions between top managers and regular workers to premodern rituals: "It is really like a feudalist society. When we greet the top management or board members, we stand in line and bow really deep as if we are paying our respects and showing our total submission to the daimyo lord or the emperor. We are like the vassals for feudal lords." The highly patriarchal hierarchy of the firm, where only a few women work—and those mostly as assistants— greatly alienates many of the ambitious career-track women, who find few women with power to mentor them and who quickly learn that their education and ambition won't be valued as much as the years they have worked for the company.

In addition to sustaining management's control and authority over decision making, an age-based system of pay and promotions also lowers individual aspirations, competition, and creativity. The emphasis on conformity can also lead to an excess concentration of power in a small group of insiders. With no pressure on them to address their faults, Japanese companies have little incentive to change the hierarchical system.

Education, and especially the prestige attached to certain universities, influences the upward mobility of workers within large Japanese companies. The name of a person's alma mater or graduate school may prove to be a critical negotiating piece for women trying to break into top management. Almost all the women middle managers I interviewed in financial companies graduated from elite universities; such an education can actually trump gender in many Japanese companies. Some of these women managers expressed the belief that they might have received preferential treatment over some male workers because they graduated from the top national universities; they are also among the few career-track women who graduated from top universities in their workplaces. By preferential treatment they meant faster promotions, no transfers to local branches, and access to larger numbers of clients. At the point of hiring, the name of a worker's alma mater represents the cultural and familial capital that enabled him or her to pass a series of school entrance exams.[9] University prestige can also predict success in the corporate race in Japanese firms because of alumni networks. Japanese universities actively maintain university-corporation ties.[10] Alumni ties and alumni-student ties are so strong that alumni may informally assist in the firms' recruitment of college graduates.[11] A worker's alumni ties or possession of the right college brand could continue to influence his or her internal network and the promotion path throughout an entire career. (A few men and women I interviewed mentioned the existence of "old boy" connections within and outside their firms, though none of them suggested that such ties directly shape internal decisions regarding promotion or salaries.) At Daigo Life Insurance, of the six midlevel managers I interviewed, three graduated from top national universities and two others graduated from top private universities. However, as shown by the growing number of graduates from American MBA programs and four-year colleges (who are seen to possess superb competitive human capital) at Mikado Bank and Shijo Asset Management, Japanese companies may further increase the hiring of non-Japanese graduates, which will add diversity to the labor market. But educational credentials, with an emphasis on the names of the universities, will continue to influence upward mobility in Japanese firms, especially for women. The rate of women who graduate from elite universities in Japan is still smaller than that of men, but if the gender imbalance among graduates of top institutions such as the University of Tokyo declines, it could be a great step toward desegregation and the reduction of gender bias among Japanese companies. Still, as long as Japanese companies continue to base hiring and salary decisions on factors such as age and university brand, organizational rigidity and inertia due to decreased worker aspirations (especially among women) and increasing labor costs may remain problems.

## Performance-Based Pay and Associated Problems

What will be the effect on sex segregation and women's status in Japanese companies if performance-based pay rather than seniority becomes the norm? The answer depends on other labor and management conditions, such as labor mobility and the quality of performance-based evaluations.

Even though traditional Japanese management has been tenacious and the seniority system continues to regulate the scale of pay and promotion in the five companies I looked at, there has been a subtle shift in the seniority system toward performance-based pay and promotion. Such changes are more pronounced at Mikado Bank than at the other four companies, which all seem to follow the more traditional and straightforward seniority system. Some young workers have welcomed the introduction of performance-based pay and complained to me that the changes are too weak, while others expressed concern that weakening of the seniority system will result in increasing uncertainty about employee promotions and pay.

Contrary to the popular view that US ownership has converted Japanese companies to an "American" performance-based pay system, the changes at Mikado Bank have not been as thorough as they might have been. Eiji, a thirty-eight-year-old deputy manager at Mikado Bank, raised his voice when he said, "Performance-based pay? It is such a lie, and that is not what is going on here." The bank apparently maintains the traditional customs of lifelong employment and seniority as its major framework. However, the firm seemed to adjust some of the workers' bonuses so as to reflect each worker's performance and achievement (however those are defined). Eiji said that his salary was higher than the average other workers of his age received:

> I generated about a $15 million profit for this bank just by myself last year. For such a contribution, I feel my salary is way too low. Well, they pay me annually about $200,000: a $100,000 base salary and a $100,000 bonus. Normally, people of my age get paid bonuses of, at most, about $40,000 to $50,000 by the seniority scale, in addition to the $100,000 base salary. . . . Even when I get promoted to *bucho* (general manager), the salary won't be that different. When I am promoted to board member, the salary will go up steeply, to $1 million.

Eiji's salary is indeed slightly higher than that of other workers his age, such as the forty-two-year-old male deputy manager of the strategic development section whom I interviewed, whose annual salary was about $180,000. I also talked to a woman who had worked at the bank longer than Eiji. She had the same title as Eiji, deputy manager. By seniority, she should have been ahead of him in title and salary. But he was the section chief, and she was his subordinate. This illustrates that workers' pay and promotions do not exactly correspond to their years of service or seniority.

While many in their twenties and thirties whom I talked with, like Eiji, expressed strong support for performance-based pay over seniority pay, the senior men, who had followed the seniority custom a long time, strongly resented and resisted the firm's deviation from it. Eiji had been assigned as a board member to Mikado's subsidiary trust bank and was dispatched there for a couple of years. He was the only worker who was in his thirties, and all of his subordinates were older than him. He said his presence as a board member made the older men resent him.

> The men's jealousy was terrible. I was thirty-eight years old, and all the subordinates were much older. They were talking about suing the

firm for assigning me to the board. They were just so jealous of me. They would write a ten-page memo about what a terrible worker I was and circulate it to the other workers in the firm. . . . I just ignored it. I did not pressure them to act differently or accuse them of doing that, either. . . . I was calm and just explained to them some of my interpretation of why the company's management assigned a young guy like me to the board. I told them that I understood if they did not agree with my management. They became quiet after that. No one said anything.

The US management chose Eiji as a board member over senior Japanese men who did not like the American style of management, and their disapproval of Eiji reflected their negativity toward the leadership.

Changes to seniority also generated concerns among other men. Take a company such as Hanakage, where a forty-one-year-old man, Shigeo, was opposed to the firm's departure from the traditional system. He raised his voice as he described his meager chance of getting promoted due to the large number of cohorts:

When I was hired in 1991, they hired about five hundred new graduates a year. Then, later in the 1990s, for a few years, they didn't hire anyone because of the economic recession. They never laid off anyone, either. . . . So there are too many workers who are in their forties, of my age and generation. That means that a lot of us won't be able to rise in the hierarchy and will have to remain nonmanager workers until we retire.

Since the seniority system does not function well when an excessive number of workers are the same age, firms need to be selective and introduce performance-based evaluation on at least a partial basis. In his comments, Shigeo exaggerated the unsuitability of performance-based pay and promotion for Japanese firms: "The seniority system of the firm is gone! But I know the top managers of this company feel performance-based pay and promotion doesn't fit this company because it depresses the workers' motivation and aspirations. It doesn't work in Japan! . . . In [internet technology firm] Fujitsu, the productivity-based system did not work well. Honda still maintains Japanese-style management." Even though Shigeo says that performance-based pay may lower workers' motivation, my interviews found just the opposite to be true: seniority pay and promotions seem to lower the motivation and aspirations of many women and men. But what Shigeo points out is correct in that performance-based evaluation in Japanese companies, with everything else remaining the same, may greatly depress worker motivation and aspirations while further increasing management power over its employees.

According to Vogel, performance-based pay in Japan is a "camouflage for wage restraint," which keeps "the pay disparities within a narrow range."[12] Thus, the overall average wage of individual workers is likely to be lower than in the past. Also, because the pay gap in compensation between those who accomplish the most and those who did nothing is not large, it is hard to imagine that this so-called performance-based pay is at all similar to the pay system in the United States. Thus, it will also do little to enhance worker motivation. In short, Japan's performance-based pay is largely the same as seniority-based pay; it gives more authority and power to the firms without rewarding individual achievement.

Because midcareer hires are uncommon in Japan, and those who want to change employers often don't have the opportunity to do so, and because performance-based evaluations tend to be based only on in-firm skills and are often biased and subjective, management does not have to worry about workers' leaving a firm and can force its subjective in-firm evaluation on its employees, who therefore have little choice other than to cultivate in-firm skills. Therefore, the shift to performance-based pay and promotion can easily lead to management justification of exploitative working conditions.

The Japanese version of performance-based pay might potentially help some women ascend to management faster than in the current seniority-based promotion system, and thus the number of women in management may increase. However, when management continues to "cage" low-paid women through career-track hiring and temp hiring, many women will remain stuck. The combination of little mobility in the labor market and in-firm biased performance-based evaluations may further polarize the women who ascend the ladder and those who remain at the bottom.

In any case, in my interviews, many workers at Hanakage described the firm as continuing to rely on seniority. A thirty-nine-year-old manager, Takao, asserted that changes to the promotion and pay system had been small: "In the past, all of us got promoted at the same time, but that doesn't happen anymore. When I see others who have the same years of service, I see some of them are not even promoted to manager yet. But our salaries are not that different, anyway. . . . I have some subordinates who are in their fifties. So, there is some change." He insists that seniority continues to play a central role in determining salary and promotions. However, even small changes in the seniority system apparently threaten men's economic security, a privilege long taken for granted. Older men in particular, who see seniority as a norm of the employment system, are unlikely to welcome the firm's rewarding younger employees' competency and achievement.

Not surprisingly, my interviews found that young women and men expressed a strong preference for performance-based pay over seniority pay. They explained that seniority pay lowers workers' motivation and aspirations. Young workers pointed out that the traditional seniority system in Japanese firms privileges only the senior men, regardless of the younger workers' competency and workload. A few women at Takane mentioned that the introduction of performance-based evaluations was necessary to make sure that qualified workers are promoted to management, since incompetent workers were often promoted in the past based solely on age.

Japanese firms' seniority pay becomes extremely costly when there are too many workers of the same age whose lifelong employment needs to be sustained at the expense of other nonregular workers at the same company (who are often women). But some still oppose the introduction of performance pay because "how a firm evaluates us gets increasingly unclear." They say Japanese firms' lack of a clear and objective scale of measurement, or even a clear definition of "performance" or "achievement," could make performance-based pay problematic. Others argue that performance-based promotion is itself an excuse to cut business costs. Implementing performance-based pay in Japan is one of the tactics used by Japanese firms to save on costs, since it allows them to cut base wages and only apply a small-scale difference to bonuses. It is not surprising, then, that performance-based pay often lowers workers' motivation and further increases management control in Japan.

Indeed, as I have discussed, the Japanese style of performance-based pay and promotion has serious flaws, as it reflects a mostly a narrow range of in-firm skills and as performance-based pay without a mobile and competitive labor market can increase management control over employees and may not solve the problem of sex segregation. Japanese management can exploit its application of Western performance-based pay and promotion by increasing its authority to subordinate and even fire employees. Japan should work to increase labor market mobility and introduce evaluation standards that reflect global, not local, business conduct. These changes could lower sex segregation if the performance-based evaluations reflected larger business and industry needs and led to the enhancement of workers' aspirations and mobility rather than reinforcing existing customs and in-firm skills. Why? Because increasing workers' skills allows them to bargain for better salaries and jobs. Labor mobility would enable workers to move from one company to another, and the use of performance-based rather than seniority promotions would give women more control over their career prospects, promotion timing, and family planning. A competitive labor market and performance-based pay are not panaceas, as we can see that sex segregation and discrimination are still embedded in the United States. But these would be important first steps in Japan.

Regarding cost savings, if Japanese firms intend to keep the lifelong-employment system in a slow-growing economy, they may have to implement further schemes to cut labor costs. Explicitly using women as their major cost-saving method must be stopped, as it increases sex segregation and hampers women's upward mobility. Other cost-saving options include lowering base wages and cutting benefits of existing and new workers. However, whether Japanese firms that are increasingly exposed to global competition can afford to sustain a model from the past and, if so, what types of cost cutting can best help them do this, needs further investigation.

The use of sharp-scale performance-based pay, similar to that used in the United States, and increasing the mobility of the labor market are possible options. Some argue strongly that performance-based pay may increase pay inequality among workers and banish the economic egalitarianism that Japanese firms have long valued. But, again, this so-called economic egalitarianism has only applied to senior men, with many companies taking advantage of cheap female labor and legitimizing economic inequity among women in order to reward these older male employees. Changing the pay and promotion system, and modifying lifelong employment, could also alter the workplace culture of firms in positive ways. The Japanese business community needs to engage in real, fundamental reforms rather than just importing partial ideas from Western management.

# The Problem of Women Serving as Cost Savers

Hiring women as cheap labor has been a central cost-saving method of traditional Japanese management; having them work as assistants to men has served to entrench Japan's postwar family-work welfare regime. This remains the major cause of vertical sex segregation in some Japanese companies. Career-track hiring is notorious, typical of Japan's sex-discriminatory employment practices, but it continues to exist and is even praised as a perfect solution for working mothers to balance their family life with work (even though many of those non-career-track workers are not mothers). Regardless of desegregation reforms, some companies continue to sort women into several different employment statuses as a means of saving money. Under this system, while men are employed under an unnamed category (assumed to be a career-track position), women with similar or the same educational background can be hired either as career-track workers, non-career-track workers, area-career-track workers, temporary or contract workers, or part-time workers. Management's negative stereotypes of women and traditional views of the gender division, along with a desire to save labor costs, continues to block women's equal opportunities for pay and promotion. Career-track hiring and temp hiring lower women's aspirations, heighten women's mutual negativity, waste women's skills, and normalize the inequality and the hierarchy in the workplace.

## Non-Career-Track Women and Depressed Aspirations

Many firms continue to hire a small number of career-track women and a larger number of women for non-career-track positions, often regardless of the similar educational backgrounds of the candidates. For example, at Daigo Life Insurance, most career-track men and women graduated from top universities, and most of the area-career-track women and non-career-track women whom I interviewed also graduated from the same good schools.

At both Daigo Life Insurance and Shijo Asset Management, divisions between the career-track workers and other types of workers are demarcated, not just in terms of salary and promotion but also the workers' perceptions of each other, even though the differences in actual job duties are sometimes unclear beyond the career-track worker's longer hours and possible future relocation to a remote branch. Career-track women reign at the top of the hierarchy of the women workers. They are few in number at both companies; thus, they can gain respect from men and even obtain special treatment, such as faster promotions and no transfers to branches outside Tokyo. Alisa, a twenty-seven-year-old, was hired as an area-career-track worker about a year prior to our interview. Alisa speculated that regardless of her elite college degree, the firm relegated her to an area-career-track position because she was not a fresh college graduate. She found little difference between what she did as an area-career-track worker and what career-track workers do. She expressed some resentment that she was not a career-track worker: "I am a chief of the section, so I am higher than many workers in rank, but I am still seen as being lower than most career-track workers. For example, I usually receive e-mails about news only after career-track workers are informed." It bothers her that she continues to be denied access to some information that is available only to the career-track workers and that her e-mail address, in the firm's e-mail list, always appears after those of the younger career-track women who have, as yet, no job titles. She said, "Only career-track women can gain respect from workers, but not non-career-track women."

Women sometimes apply for non-career-track jobs in order to avoid the long working hours that are often required of career-track workers. But they also work as area-career-track workers because they might have no other option or because the career-track positions are limited to new graduates of elite colleges. A twenty-seven-year-old area-career-track worker at Shijo Asset Management who had moved from a large pharmaceutical company thought that she had been deceived about her hiring as an area-career-track worker.

> At all stages of the interviews, this company never told me that I would be hired only as an area-career-track worker. In the last interview, they finally told me that they would hire me as an area-career-track worker. I couldn't believe it. Those hiring people in this firm are just so traditional. I can tell that they see me as just a girl who had already changed jobs two times after I graduated from college, and I should just appreciate the fact that I was given a job in a large, well-known firm like this one, even if it is not a career-track job.

Her starting salary, which includes few benefits, is lower than that of the career-track workers, and she wishes to change to the career-track as soon as she can.

When it began to reform its women's employment practices, Shijo Asset Management changed the names of its hiring tracks and now refers to both career-track and area-career-track positions as "career track." (Many interview subjects corrected my equation of the term "area-career-track workers" with the term "non-career-track workers," since they are not the same thing.) Thus, on paper, there are no non-career-track women and no career-track hiring in this company. However, area-career-track workers' lower pay and lack of promotion opportunities remain the same as in the traditional career-track system.

At Daigo Life Insurance, to change one's track from non-career track to area-career track requires a minimum of six years' work and excellent evaluations. One woman told me that it took her ten years to change tracks. The indirect message to women workers is that firms want most women to stay in low-paying positions, as no man would take such jobs. Reforms are needed to make the change from the non-career track to the career track easier.

An aversion to long working hours often leads women to apply for non-career-track jobs. However, women usually find such jobs, sometimes explicitly at the assistant level, unrewarding and humiliating. Akiko, a thirty-year-old temporary contract (*haken*) worker at Shijo Asset Management, had worked for the firm for over a year. When I interviewed her, she was about to marry and quit her job. She stressed that she would never work as a dispatch worker, and it was obvious that job dissatisfaction led to her desire to quit. The firm never considered that she had previously worked for a larger securities firm as a stockbroker. At Shijo Asset Management, she was given only an assistant-level job, which she described as a waste of her time. She was paid no benefits, not even transportation fees. Her comments reflect her view of working in financial firms in general.

> In my previous firm, I was selling securities to individual clients. I have now worked one year and three months at Shijo Asset Management as a dispatched worker. Pouring tea and pushing the elevator buttons are always the woman's job here. . . . I sometimes had to pour tea twenty times a day. If I do more than ten times, it takes too much time and I can't do my work. . . . But they think it is my job. . . . Many men would just dump all the assistant work onto me, and I know that's what I am supposed to do. . . . One man would come tell me to copy a one-page paper for him. Just one page. I couldn't believe it. He sits much closer to the copy machine than I do. . . . I noticed that the dispatch women workers who wish to do the same type of jobs as the career-track and non-career-track workers eventually quit this job because they are never given decent jobs. . . . There is no bonus compensation and no transportation. The salary is very low. . . . I will never work as a *haken* in the future.

The lack of a formal system that can evaluate a woman's previous professional experience and nonfirm skills seems to make it easier for management to relegate most women to assistant-level jobs.

Once a woman is hired in an assistant position, it seems rare for her to be motivated to try for a better job. A twenty-seven-year-old non-career-track worker at Daigo Life Insurance who graduated from a top university said that even though she wants to do more difficult and responsible work as a career-track worker, she does not want to work long hours every day, until nine or ten at night, like the career-track workers do. "I should accept the fact that I am hired as a non-career-track worker," she said. "I want to do more challenging work. But if I was given such work, I would complain because I am paid such a low salary." In other words, she would do the higher quality work only if she were better paid.

A twenty-six-year-old non-career-track woman, who also graduated from a top university, expressed great dissatisfaction because she was relegated to being the assistant to a senior man. In her remarks she focused on her boss, a fifty-eight-year-old manager: "Non-career-track women are just assistants in this company. . . . The boss I worked for asked me to do all the secretarial work. He wanted me to get prescriptions from the doctor. . . . I had to make all his phone calls for him. He used me as a substitute for his wife. He got mad if I didn't do what he said. I had to do my real work after doing all that extra work for him." She viewed her unofficial "wife" role as an extra duty she had to fulfill in addition to her assigned work. When I asked why she decided to work as a non-career-track worker regardless of her prestigious university graduate background, she said she did not want to work too much. At her previous job, she had seen many coworkers overwork themselves to the point of illness. It was an intentional decision, then, for her to work as a non-career-track worker.

Rosabeth Kanter's famous notion of "depressed aspirations" works well to explain the attitudes of non-career-track workers and temporary workers in Japanese firms; these workers typically express low aspirations when they anticipate their limited opportunities for upward mobility.[13] A promise of status and power enhancement, however, can breed competitiveness, though this might only apply to career-track workers.[14] Relegating women to positions with few resources and opportunities can hurt their productivity as well as their motivation and aspirations. It could be one cause of the high turnover rate among women in low positions.

The difference in employment types among women reinforces the existing sex segregation in Japanese firms. The small number of career-track women might not care about the gendered hierarchy of employment, since they share with men basically the same job and salary. Some career-track and even area-career-track women feel they are privileged because they have a lifelong career in a good firm and they are in far better positions than non-career-track or dispatched workers. A few women I interviewed said that they view the gender divisions and hierarchy as something they cannot change—rather, they make the best of the situation. For example, a thirty-eight-year-old area-career-track woman at Shijo Asset Management said, "I don't care much if this firm hires more women or not. . . . The men are the ones who compete for better pay and promotions. The women workers are harmless to them. I like the fact that the men protect the organization. I like to be protected. I just want to do whatever I want to do in a safe and protected environment." It seems that the male-dominated workplace and her being in an area-track position do not concern her or make her care about gender inequality. She sees finding an individualistic accommodation rather than seeking some structural and collective solution as better for her in a highly gender-unequal workplace. The relegation of many women to lower positions seems to deprive some women of critical views of unequal employment customs and pay scales, to mold their sense of resignation along the lines of ideas of traditional femininity, and to promote an attitude of pursuing personal satisfaction over workplace equity.

Some have argued that because women in Japanese companies generally lack the high aspirations held by men and prefer to work fewer hours and focus more on their families, the career-track hiring system meets both the demands of the companies, which want to cut labor costs, and of women, who want to work fewer hours. This sounds to me like a rationalization, and in my interviews I found many women in their twenties and early thirties who would prefer to move to career-track positions. (This is especially true at Shijo Asset Management, where the working hours are the same for career-track and area-career-track workers.)

## Lunch Hour and Dress Codes as Status Indicators

In Japan more than in the United States, a person's uniform often demarcates class and occupational and employment status. Status divisions between career-track women and area-career-track women are far more pronounced at Daigo Life Insurance than at other places; one area in which these divisions are seen is in workers' dress codes. The career-track women wear formal suits, while non-career-track workers wear casual clothes. Temporary women workers at the front desk wear a two-piece type of uniform. These temporary receptionists usually put on a lot of makeup and give the impression that they are like models or cover girls for the company. With their hyperfeminine appearance, they would not look like office workers without wearing the company uniform. The non-career-track workers' not wearing formal suits may be just an informal norm, but all the women I talked with followed this norm and did not breach the rules. Alisa, who is an area-career-track worker, said she consciously wears formal suits every day "because I don't like to be seen as a non-career-track worker." Only the career-track women are expected to always wear formal suits; the non-career track women being in casual fashions explicitly sends the signal to everybody that non-career-track workers are informal and are assistants to those who wear professional suits.

Another area in which differences are apparent is lunch customs. Both career-track men and career-track women eat lunch in the firm's cafeteria, even though they do not eat together there. Non-career-track workers bring their lunch or buy it outside and eat in their offices, but they do not go to the cafeteria. Also, with regard to the length of lunchtime, "career-track workers don't take a full hour break, but non-career-track workers do take a full hour," said Alisa, who, as an area-career-track worker, often follows the customs of career-track workers. The career-track workers are expected to spend only fifteen minutes in the cafeteria because of the firm's emphasis on the "virtue" of work. It seems that how long they spend in eating lunch and where they eat lunch are critical indicators of the extent to which they are bound to the firm. Career-track workers show their total conformity and full subordination to the company by eating in the company's cafeteria and spending as little time as possible doing so.

In all the firms where I interviewed, workers described men and women going to lunch separately as common. One worker at Mikado Bank said the gender division at lunch reflects the past customs of Japanese firms, in which most men were career-track workers with busier work schedules than the women workers, who were mostly non-career-track workers who held assistant jobs. A thirty-four-year-old female worker at Mikado Bank did say that "some highly ambitious young women go to lunch only with men" and that these mostly younger women, because they want to network with men, were attempting to break the custom of segregation. But the workers overall did not question this segregated lunch culture, a custom that may also show the continuing gender order as it relates to actual tasks and to workers' status. Except for workers in career-track positions, blocked opportunities and paths are hard to unblock.

## Hierarchical Tensions among Women Workers

In the three financial firms where track hiring exists, women workers, unlike men, are often placed in a hierarchy depending on their position—career-track, non-career-track, or temporary work—regardless of a lack of difference in work experience and education. Workers at the higher levels look down on the lower-level women or feel bad for them because they have no financial security.

The men and women at Shijo Asset Management point out that regular workers often behave dismissively toward contract women workers. A forty-year-old male middle manager said, "I had many dispatched women workers in my section. I was the leader of the team, and they did great jobs, but people praised only me, not them." He continued:

> People in our company discriminate against dispatched temporary workers. So they don't stay here long. They quit their jobs quickly. Some women often draw a line between themselves [regular workers] and temporary workers, and say things like, "I am a regular worker, and you are not." It is very difficult to manage the tensions among women. The company also used to make a notation such as "temporary staff" at the end of a temporary worker's name, but they stopped doing that recently.

Regular women differentiating themselves from lower-status women is not uncommon in a male-dominated workplace. In a workplace where there are few women with authority, and in which the mobility of the lower-status group is limited, it is likely that members of the lower-status group will engage in self-enhancing strategies that undermine solidarity within their group.[15] In addition to the problem of the lack of women leaders and role models in such a system, women in the hierarchy may see one another as subjects to feel sorry for, look down on, or to feel envy toward, rather than as coworkers with some shared goals.

Several women at Shijo Asset Management made comments to me about feeling sorry for the dispatched women workers for their lack of financial security, which regular workers have; in their opinion, these temporary workers need to find husbands. A forty-three-year-old female middle manager said, "I know that there are several of those who remain in a dispatched position who still have not married. People are worried about them." A thirty-year-old dispatched worker in Shijo Asset Management herself said: "It is horrible to see some senior women in their forties still working as dispatched workers. There is a woman who is single and thirty-eight years old and still in a dispatched position. She was just laid off by the company. Everybody says that she should marry as soon as possible." At Shijo Asset Management, the lowest-ranked women workers are often the focus of not only concern and pity but also blame for not having the same economic security as regular employees. They are almost automatically assumed to be not as capable as the regular men and women workers. They also become the target of frequent gossip.

Though the dispatched workers at Shijo Asset Management were given mostly assistant jobs, the dispatched and temporary contract workers at Daigo Life Insurance did work similar to that of regular workers, making the division between regular and irregular workers less clear. A thirty-year-old non-career-track woman said, "Dispatched workers sometimes do overwork like we do. . . . One time, when the general manager (*kacho*) was handing out bonus stubs to each worker in our section, one woman who did not work long hours raised her voice in front of everybody, saying, 'We dispatched workers are not paid those bonuses! We do exactly the same work as those who are given bonuses!' Nobody said anything." Even though the inequality among women workers causes tensions, no one whom I interviewed seemed to see it as a serious issue of inequity. Instead, most workers saw such divisions among highly educated women as a sort of fatal hierarchy that shapes a person's future and even their individual sense of worth. Many of them addressed the conflicts and tensions among women workers but tended to blame them on the problems of individual workers.

According to Vicki Smith's study of temporary workers in the American context,[16] temps in the United States are often integrated into the organization and sometimes have authority and greater skills than permanent workers rather than being marginalized and segregated in overt ways, though this further obfuscates structural inequality, since they are paid lower wages than the permanent workers and have little mobility to go up the corporate ladder. Still, Smith found that the temporary workers, in pursuing permanent positions and refusing to be defined by others as marginal, often "engage in strict self-discipline that well serve[s] a production system based on individual initiative, decision making, and responsibility."[17] They also saw themselves more as permanent workers and distanced themselves from negative stereotypes of temporary workers (having weak work ethics, lacking commitment, being lazy, and being deviant).[18] The American temporary workers' resistance and "successful" assimilation into the permanent workforce contrasts sharply with the views of the Japanese workers I interviewed, who often saw temporary workers negatively, as marginal and the source of women's problems in the workplace.

One forty-two-year-old general manager said it takes him considerable work to accommodate his women workers' different requests. He referred first to the tension in his section between workers who are mothers and those who are not. Then he commented on the tensions among women because of their different employment statuses. In the corporate finance section that he runs, six out of nine workers are women. He meets with both men and women, individually, every three months in order to ask about their goals, achievements, and levels of satisfaction. He said, with a sigh, "The men do not quit their jobs, so we don't have to worry about them at all. The men are much easier to work with." He added:

> Dispatched women workers don't get along with each other. They are concerned about who will quit next. Their tension affects the workplace atmosphere, and I think the firm needs to reduce the number of temp hires. . . . The old non-career-track women and the workers who are mothers—they don't get along with each other. . . . One young career-track woman tries to get along with the men and the non-career-track women, but she is just putting too much effort into keeping a good relationship with both groups. I just had to move this worker to a different section so that she could focus on her job. . . . Women's relationships are very difficult.

The manager viewed the tensions among the women workers as harmful to the other workers in the same section but did not take the view that such tensions were caused by the firm's unequal hiring structure. Hiring the women at different levels, with large gaps in their pay and benefits regardless of their educational backgrounds, job experience, and the similarity of their tasks, is what generates this tension. But the problems that arise are attributed to general stereotypes or to irrational conflicts among the women workers themselves.

It is obvious that Japanese employers make it difficult for women to bring their collective voices together to protest structural inequalities. Female workers in Japan do not seem to communicate with other workers within their own firms or in other firms regarding their resentment and frustration about the status gap between career-track and non-career-track positions. And this causes the women to be divided and fragmented, reifying the tension and negativity in the workplace.

## Bullying and Discouraged Ambitions

Even though I did not hear that bullying was particularly common in the five companies, several women did report incidents of women fighting and being bullied. One area-career-track woman talked about bullying as resulting from the insecurity among non-career-track workers. This may illustrate why low-level women workers, deprived of opportunities and subjected to strong gender beliefs, promote heteronormative competition regarding who among the workers is the most traditionally feminine.

In general, bullying by women is not uncommon, as women constitute over half of all bullies, and female bullies choose females as targets about 90 percent of the time.[19] Women often rely on "relational"—manipulative or covert—aggression to dominate others, since such aggression does not violate traditional gender norms.[20] Relational aggression involves (1) socially aggressive behaviors such as gossiping, social exclusion, social isolation, and stealing friends or romantic partners; and (2) relationally aggressive behaviors such as not talking to someone, not socializing with someone, deliberately ignoring someone, and threatening to withdraw emotional support or friendship.[21] A few female and male workers whom I interviewed did mention that they had experienced or observed these types of indirect aggression, particularly female exclusion or women ignoring other women. A couple of male managers mentioned that women's fights in the Japanese workplace are often more emotionally expressive, and thus more visible and potentially harmful, than conflicts among male workers.

In the 1980s, the competition among non-career-track women in Japan to marry so that they could exit the workplace was commonly reported;[22] however, I did not find any evidence of this in my interviews with current women workers. This is because the marriage age norm has changed in the decades since the 1980s.[23] Marriage is no longer seen as the ultimate goal for many women, as it was in the past. In addition, a large number of non-career-track women workers have been replaced by temporary workers. But the femininity competition continues, influenced by women's lack of opportunities and sense of powerlessness.

A thirty-one-year-old area-track woman worker at Shijo Asset Management explained that the non-career-track women in her previous workplace, a securities firm, would gossip about her, force her to go to lunch with them, or ignore and exclude her.

> There were a couple of different groups among non-career-track workers on the floor. They were very hierarchical and strongly bonded. They always gossiped, like in elementary school, about their coworkers, mostly about the women's appearances, their manners, money, and their husbands. . . . People would ignore me or speak behind my back.

> I think it was because I got along with the male workers. . . . I had to go
> to lunch every day with the women even though I had little money. One
> woman would often accuse me, asking why I had to work there when
> I was married. She said I didn't need to work. It was usually elderly
> women.

In the financial firms, it seems that senior women's ignoring one another and
gossiping were more common in the past when more non-career-track women
were in the workplace. As some have pointed out, the system of seniority may
have contributed to these women's rude behaviors aimed at younger women. The
women workers in these firms are segregated and bonded based on their ages,
level of education, marital status, and so on, and when other women violate the
hierarchy or group expectations by displaying masculinity or allying with men,
this may disturb the older women.[24] Some women workers might be hostile to
women whom they view as deviating from the normalized femininity of which
the elder women approve. When very few women in the workplace were married,
being married may have been enough to make a woman seem like a legitimate
target.

Because women have few outlets in which to channel their ambition in the
workplace, they may resort to interpersonal femininity contests from which they
can gain a sense of self-worth. Past studies have noted non-career track women's
depressed aspirations and sense of "boredom" and "futility" in their positions
as assistants.[25] Offering women better opportunities for advancement and more
training, and stimulating professional ambition through the presence of more
high-powered female role models in management, may be the best scheme for
lessening or transforming their resentment.

Robin Ely found that women in male-dominated law firms, compared to
women in gender-integrated law firms, "characterized more of their relationships with women peers as competitive in ways that inhibited their ability to
work together." Also, women in male-dominated firms "often focused on feelings
of envy and jealousy."[26] Ely argues that "limited access to senior positions may
foster these kinds of competitive experiences" and that women in more gender-
integrated firms seem to channel their competitive feelings more productively.[27]
Thus, women's bullying, or even just negative competition with other women,
may be one more harmful result of organizational sex segregation.

The seniority system in Japanese companies is likely to lower women's aspirations,
as it conflicts with their career plans and career paths. Seniority pay and promotion are likely to discourage highly motivated women from attempting to ascend
the career ladder in these companies. At the same time, lifelong employment

guarantees the employed women economic security. In other words, the current seniority norm can hurt young women with high motivation and aspirations and discourage women's upward mobility, yet it can also increase the number of women who continue to work. Companies, through track hiring or the hiring of temp women, pay the non-career-track and temp woman far less than men of the same age (sometimes less than one-fourth as much), and this continues to save labor costs.

Japan's lack of labor mobility and its reliance on age- and education-based hires make women's upward mobility highly constrained. Currently, Japanese companies are making limited use of performance-based pay, but this system continues to emphasize employees' in-firm skills, based as it is on the assumption of lifelong employment and sex-segregated customs. Because few employees will leave their company for a better job, the company's management has exclusive control over the employees' labor conditions. Because existing Japanese management and labor practices and customs are unlikely to change, the distinct sex segregation in Japanese businesses will likely continue. If Japanese companies' use of performance-based pay and promotion is more widely and substantially implemented, this could increase the number of women in management; however, the large number of women who are "caged" in non-career-track positions, which are different from management track positions, may not benefit from these changes.

Of course, I do not argue that the seniority system is the sole reason for the sex segregation that exists in Japanese companies. Gender bias and discrimination, which are separate issues, may have as much or more to do with women's concentration on the lower rungs of the hierarchy. Kazuo Yamaguchi studied about ten thousand employees of 1,677 companies in Japan and found that only about 20 percent of women with over thirty years of service had achieved middle-management status, while the same percentage of men had become middle managers after eleven to fifteen years of experience.[28] Even considering educational backgrounds, men were promoted faster than women in many Japanese companies, and Yamaguchi attributes this gender gap to "premodern" customs of Japanese firms or traditional gender beliefs and biases. Without question, seniority promotion does operate against women, and with further gender bias added to it, the chance of women actually becoming managers remains slim.

Even though some critics argue that employers' use of track hiring could prove to be an effective solution both for the companies, which want to save on labor costs, and the women, who want to spend more time with their families, I found that most women in non-career-track positions are not married nor do they have children yet they are still relegated to assistant positions from the start, not necessarily based on their qualifications. Hiring women as temporary or contract workers also legitimizes sex segregation and women's negativity toward other women. Due to the large pay and promotion gaps among women workers, differences in employment status will lead to class divisions among them. Such gendered hiring cements sex segregation in Japanese companies, and the lack of mobility in the labor market further lessens the likelihood that women will be able to move up or into better jobs.

In the next chapter I will examine the four patterns of gender bias and stereotypes that are commonly observed in the five companies I studied.

# PRODUCTION AND NAVIGATION OF GENDER BIAS

Heroic Masculinity, Female Misogyny,
and Queen Bees

In the previous chapter we saw how Japanese companies' central customs of lifelong employment and seniority pay with promotion work against efforts to reduce sex segregation and hamper women's chances to go up the corporate ladder to positions of power. Performance-based rather than seniority-based salaries and promotions would not only increase worker motivation and encourage a reasonable level of competition while reducing excess labor costs, they would also make women's career plans and work-life balance far easier.

I now want to shift our focus from salaries and promotions to the patterns of gender stereotyping that have been specific to the Japanese business system. I will examine how men and women workers in Japanese companies participate in and navigate existing gender biases and stereotypes, and how the narratives and images of hegemonic masculinity and traditional femininity play out in workers' perceptions of other workers. Because the gender stereotypes and biases that have emerged among Japanese men and women workers are historically and institutionally specific to Japan's business customs, I will start with an overview of hegemonic masculinity and the development of corporate masculinity before looking at the narratives and images of masculinity from which gender biases, belief in the ideology of male supremacy, and misogynistic perceptions emerge. Of the five Japanese companies under review, the financial firms have fewer women managers than do the two cosmetics companies. In the financial firms, the ideal worker is hypermasculine in behavior, with aggressive sales and negotiation skills, while men often view women workers only as assistants or helpers. In the cosmetics firms, regardless of the increase in numbers of low-level women managers, young women's negativity toward older women was a major concern.

Taking into account the above firm-based differences, four patterns of gender bias and stereotyping can be seen in the five companies. Male managers have an aversion to women workers and they normalize male supremacy in the financial firms. The ideal and most trusted worker is a man, one who will willingly sacrifice himself for the job and successfully navigate the workplace networks. Women are seen as lacking in such abilities and unwilling to engage in these behaviors. Female misogyny and queen bees describe women's aversion to other women of different ages and in different positions of power. Young women workers in "women-friendly" firms explicitly express their aversion to managerial women while willingly supporting their male superiors; they view male managers as more reliable than women. The young women's work relationships are shaped by the erotic and amicable heteronormative script in which young women paired with paternal male managers struggle with pathetic female managers, who, as authority figures, are delegitimized. Female managers, or "queen bees," in turn express their detachment from young women, whom they see as lacking in competency. Overall, I argue that both men and women workers express high levels of misogynistic and gender-divisive perceptions of their fellow workers, and that these patterns of gender bias clearly mirror the Japanese companies' male-protection management approach and business customs.

## Hegemonic Masculinity in Postwar Japan

In the post–World War II period, Japan attained rapid economic development through strong state guidance and constant bureaucratic intervention designed to protect its industries and businesses. Responding to the state and business imperatives of economic development, individual men and women devoted themselves to the breadwinner and caretaker roles, in their separate spheres. The ideology of working hard for Japan's economic development was instilled and normalized in the separate gendered spheres. Throughout the postwar period, men's devotion to their jobs and fulfillment of the breadwinner obligation has been regarded as at the core of Japanese manhood. Male corporate workers were deemed to be "workers vested with the soul of capital,"[1] and being a "human being" was equated with enterprise membership; thus, a male worker's subjectivity was associated with the heroic sacrifice of himself to the job/company, which sometimes led to the tragedy of death by overwork.[2] A man's full devotion and subjection to his company in exchange for a lifetime of economic security was emphasized as virtuous masculine behavior. Being a corporate worker meant that a man was not expected to be an individual or autonomous worker but instead would belong to the enterprise state. Even though such exploitative business practices were criticized and challenged,[3] the institutional and organizational systems in Japan continue to hold such masculinity as the dominant model. Also, the model of willingly sacrificing manhood is a gendered reference point and the norm by which women too are judged, and that they are expected to emulate.

Change at the individual or organizational level is not adequate to transform gender biases and help end sex segregation in Japanese companies, because the concept of ideal manhood has long been institutionally promoted in Japan's development and modernization. Hegemonic masculinity represents the institutional and organizational characteristics and performances, including behaviors, symbols, and signs of "ascendancy," that an individual man attempts to achieve in various social and cultural contexts.[4] It signifies the man's power and authority over other men and also sustains men's collective dominance over women. Hegemonic masculinity and the privileges it provides can denote social, cultural, economic, and political success for men. They accomplish and display their power and dominance through their speech, fashion, physical appearance, activities, and relations with others.[5] At the individual level, attitudes and behaviors such as being tough, aggressive, and competitive; masking one's emotions; and achieving success and financial stability are manifested by men in order to attain positions of power. Masculinity in business settings is often revealed in such traits as aggression and competitiveness and being goal driven.[6] In decision-making managerial settings, a "tough-minded approach to problems" and prioritizing "task accomplishments" over personal and emotional considerations are considered necessary.[7] Being authoritarian and paternalistic are the critical traits of management masculinity.[8] Men may also collectively mobilize and display "masculine superiority" and draw boundaries that women cannot cross in corporate settings.[9] At the same time, women in business contexts are expected to display and engage in "emphasized femininity," to comply with gender inequality, accommodate men's desires and interests, and accept men's power.[10] Women are expected to engage in "fragility in mating scenes, compliance with men's desire for titillation and ego-stroking in office relationships, [and] acceptance of marriage and childcare as a response to labor-market discrimination against women."[11] Thus, a workplace atmosphere is created in which individual workers conform to, emulate, and resist the existing models of femininity and masculinity.

In post–World War II Japan, corporate manhood, as represented by the image of the salaryman with lifetime economic security, paired with the femininity represented by the housewife, served to sustain the system of hegemonic masculinity.[12] With the decline of the Japanese economy in the 1990s and the resulting institutional destabilization, the concept of manhood in Japan has become somewhat diversified or fragmented, largely because of the surge in the number of men who do not obtain lifelong economic security or cannot fulfill the traditional provider role. Yet, even though the average Japanese man's income has declined, the salaryman, or corporate worker, remains the dominant image of manhood. James Roberson and Nobue Suzuki point out that manhood and masculinity are the product of institutions, and that the salaryman in Japan is the embodiment of the Japanese capitalist employee, state taxpayer, and family provider.[13] The salaryman has been "the embodiment, real and ideal, of the ideological model of masculine superiority and success which other men are assumed to aspire to," especially in his level of economic security, which many working-class men do not attain.[14]

Manhood in Japan continues to be bound by traditional gender obligations. Breadwinner masculinity serves as the norm whereby a man judges other men, and men's exclusive focus on their jobs constrains their other activities.[15] Many men still believe that the gendered separate spheres are beneficial to individuals and to society as a whole.[16] Even when they feel little fulfillment either in their work or family life, they are pressured not to deviate from their traditional gender obligations.[17] Alcohol consumption leading to intoxication is a popular method of sustaining and solidifying manhood in the workplace; drinking allows men to transgress rigid social norms and roles while maintaining their community membership.[18] Younger Japanese men increasingly reject the traditional breadwinner model of manhood by engaging in leisure-oriented or appearance-driven (fashion or body-centered) "herbivore masculinity," and some even distance themselves from traditional marriage.[19] But such alternative versions of manhood are far from democratizing Japan or transforming its traditional gender ideology.

The Japanese housewife, lacking in social and economic independence, has been the institutional marker of emphasized femininity in Japan.[20] The cultural dominance of housewife femininity in Japan even extends to the workplace, where it is manifested in the roles of caretaker, helper, and assistant. The gender ideology is so strong in Japan that workplace sex segregation is often seen as the consequence of men and women's essential differences. Robin LeBlanc found that some Japanese men explain the absence of female politicians in Japan by saying that women simply lack the ability to form the necessary political networks and solidarities, and that they also do not develop the sense of mutual obligation and interpersonal warmth that men do.[21] Such an essentialized view, based on male supremacy, revealed itself in my interviews with male workers.

Using women as low-paid assistants and thereby lowering corporate costs has long been at the heart of Japanese corporate management. The custom has legitimized the ideology of male supremacy, misogyny, and compulsory heterosexuality in the workplace. Moreover, a long absence of women leaders and women in positions of authority has reinforced the myth of male supremacy and promoted workers' distrust of women workers' ascendancy.

The image of powerless and incompetent female workers that results from having too few female authority figures can negatively affect younger women workers' identities and career prospects as well as their perceptions of other workers.[22] Rosabeth Kanter argues that if there are few women in positions of power relative to powerful men, those men will incorporate women only in stereotypical ways, thereby forcing the small number of women in management to conform to the masculine organizational culture.[23] The absence of women leaders also legitimizes workers' use of sex as a salient category and gender stereotyping as a relevant tool to judge and evaluate workers.[24] Kanter says the number of men and women with power needs to be balanced in order to reduce gender bias, discrimination, and gender-based perceptions of workers.

Both the men and women I talked with in Japanese companies continue to see women workers as limited, costly, and burdensome to their workplaces. Not only men, but also women, were suspicious of females who achieve professional success and exhibit skill and potential. As long as Japan's corporate management continues to normalize and justify sex segregation, it will continue to subscribe to the model of male supremacy in which all workers view women only as permanent subordinates and assistants.

## Gender Bias and Constrained Femininity

Japanese companies' vertical sex segregation is reinforced by workers' and management's perceptions of gender. In both financial and cosmetics firms, male managers continue to view women workers as inferior to men and relegate them to stereotypical assistant roles. This is mostly because of the Japanese companies' continuing devotion to male-breadwinner and separate-sphere gender ideology, which have sustained the Japanese welfare regime. Because of the corporate, cultural, and social emphasis on the woman's place being in the home, Japanese employers' statistical discrimination has become normalized to such a degree that women workers are perceived as less productive than men because of the likelihood that they will interrupt their careers because of their caretaker roles.

The absence of women managers makes it even more difficult for men to change their traditional perceptions of gender and to overcome their distrust of women workers, whom they don't view as equally competent. Eiji, a thirty-eight-year-old deputy general manager in the investment banking section at Mikado

Bank, commented explicitly that he does not see many female managers in the workplace who possess real organizational power because many of them have been given the job title but no subordinates to manage. According to Eiji, the increase in women managers has occurred mostly among the lowest management positions, and many of these hires are not related to the actual management of the firm. He said: "Those who really manage people and those who have just the title of 'manager' are different. Although the number of women who have a title above *kakaricho* [the lowest manager] may be increasing, they usually have no subordinates. They just have titles. One woman in my section just got promoted to manager, *bucho dairi*. She has the title but possesses no management authority. She has nothing to do with management." As was common in many financial companies in Japan, the previous Japanese management at Mikado Bank clung to the conventional expectation that women would leave their jobs on marrying. Thus, the instant association of "woman" with "family caretaker" remains strong, especially among the middle-aged men in these companies. During our interview, Eiji tried to justify his gender beliefs by explaining them from the perspective of statistical discrimination (the idea that employers do not want to hire women as they may leave their jobs when they have a child): "I support the idea of gender equality, but I don't understand the logic that women should be paid the same as men when they don't do the same work as men." He continued:

> Women workers take maternity and parental leave . . . if, say, a woman works only from ten to four, we suffer from it. This person goes home at four when we are still dealing with clients and need something by tomorrow. So, as long as she goes home at four, we can't ask her to do important jobs. If she is a non-career-track worker and we pay her about $30,000 per year, we can still incorporate her. But if we pay $100,000 per year, as a career-track worker, it is a waste of money even to hire her. Therefore, it is better to invest in a man than in a woman. . . . But a single woman is as useful as a man. Single women have the same chances to get promoted as men.

This over-generalized view of women as costly would seem to represent classic stereotypes among employers, who traditionally justify the hiring of women workers as assistants in much this way. That is, women's careers are interrupted by family responsibilities, so the best scenario is for a firm to hire most women as assistants who can be paid less than half of what men are paid. Even though Eiji assumes that only a woman would leave work at four to take care of her child, what would a firm do if a man did this? Would the firm cut his wages or relegate him to an assistant-level job? The rigid classification of women as more costly needs to be reassessed from different perspectives if the rigidly gender-divided work and family customs in Japan are ever going to change.

Eiji insisted that women's place is at home, not work: "It is not that workers who are mothers are disrespected in Japan. They get tremendous respect at home from their kids and their husbands. The system just doesn't pay for the work of these women. Such a contradiction should be resolved at the welfare level or by the government, not by corporate management. The corporations should not be responsible for it." As Acker has discussed, the concept of the company not being responsible for the family is typical of the old corporate logic.[25] But Japanese companies, unlike companies in the United States, form part of Japan's welfare system and are therefore responsible for the gendered labor of the family sphere. Japanese firms have long been explicitly "responsible" for the man, who has traditionally been the sole breadwinner of the family. The postwar Japanese state made Japanese companies responsible for the shape of the family. The family sphere and the woman's devotion to it have been constructed as part of the corporate welfare regime. If, as Eiji insisted, firms should not be responsible for women's reproduction because corporations are not in charge of workers' welfare, what should be questioned is the liability of the Japanese state and the companies who have maintained a system of male primacy and female inferiority.

In the financial companies I looked at, in which the number of women managers has barely increased over two decades, gendered beliefs popularly held in the 1980s and 1990s have rarely been challenged until early 2000. Eiji, like many other men of his generation, seemed to be a firm believer in gendered separate spheres, an idea that continues to legitimize essentialist gendered images. He did not hesitate to express his view that men are better workers than women.

Some men said that firms are forced to hire more women than men mostly because men are in short supply and women workers are cheaper. Ryo, a forty-year-old male general manager at Shijo Asset Management, said, "I think the firm wants men, but men are in high demand so they have to hire women." Ryo wished that there were more male workers simply because he believes that men are more competent than women and women are not willing to take the management jobs or simply lack ambition:

> I don't think men and women are equal. . . . I have always worked with women. When I was in the previous securities firm, many women there never wanted work with too much responsibility. They would say, "I am not paid for such work." Many of them were very immature. . . . I mean, women are sensitive and speedy, and men cannot be like that. Men are slow, but they have larger perspectives and better networks. Women, in general, have narrower perspectives. They have a

hard time listening to what others say. Men and women have different thinking patterns and perspectives. . . . I am not saying that women should just do assistant work . . . but, maybe, they should do what they like after marriage.

He did not hesitate to apply his negative views of these assistant workers to all women, at least partly because he has not worked with women having a higher status and greater power than he does. This attitude is not uncommon among male middle managers, and their gender biases continue to go unchallenged largely because they have never dealt with women with authority. Under the lifelong-employment system in Japan, in which it takes over ten years to become a low-level manager and no managers come from other companies, the chance of a woman worker becoming a manager is far slimmer than it is for a man. This is because the number of initial hires of women is low, and, at least in the past, a large number of Japanese women quit their jobs after marriage and child-birth. (This is not the case for men.) The Japanese business system, with lifelong employment and seniority promotion, and with discriminatory hiring practices such as double- and triple-track hiring, never really enables many women to attain the level of manager.

Men's distrust of women workers and view of women as inferior to men remain strong regardless of many firms' recent efforts to promote women to management. Even in the cosmetics firms, where more women are workers and managers than in the financial firms, some men criticized women for a lack of professionalism or professional training and job experience, conflating these problems with women's essential gender characteristics. At Hanakage, Shigeo, a forty-one-year-old man and one of two males in a group of ten workers in a sec-tion doing household research, expressed his frustration with women workers, raising his voice: "The meetings are not really meetings. They are just women chitchatting. I cannot participate in such meetings. I cannot say anything in the meetings. . . . I think their presentations and discussion of the research are too subjective and emotional. They don't pay attention to others' feedback and per-spectives at all. . . . I think men and women's communication styles and their views are just different." He complained that women workers in his section lacked skills in the areas of discussion and presentation. His perception that women lack professionalism may be due more to these particular women's lack of experience and training rather than to some innate difference. In such cases, the company's employee-training program needs to be reexamined. Also, working in a female-dominated section may threaten Shigeo's identity as a traditional male worker, and he may have been asserting his view of male supremacy to defend himself against the feminization of the workplace.

In some Japanese firms, some categories of women workers have not been given adequate training, as women were so long relegated to being assistants and excluded from training opportunities. Women who are left out of training and not encouraged to obtain higher skills may lack not only competitive skills but also confidence. Eiji at Mikado Bank pointed out generational differences among women: "Younger women than my generation work competitively. But most women in an older generation than me [early forties or older] still act like passive assistants. They don't assert their views, don't ask me questions, and don't consult with me as much as I expect them to. They seem to be afraid of doing things based on their own decisions and just wait to be told what they should do. If I ask questions, they just say things that are safe to say." His comments show the clear generational differences among women workers. Even though firms must provide adequate training and promotion opportunities to women workers at every level to break workers' perpetuation of gender stereotypes of women as mere assistants, how to raise the aspirations and skills of the older generation of women, who were entirely relegated to assistant jobs, is a critical question. Yet, blaming age or generational differences for gender inequality is falsely shortsighted.

A twenty-four-year-old career-track woman who works for Daigo Life Insurance maintained that the perception of women belonging in secondary positions is still pervasive among men in their twenties: "The number of career-track women is increasing, so men's perception of women is changing. . . . But still, men are so concerned about the hierarchy and they hate seeing women earn more than men. Even men in their twenties say all the time that they want to marry a woman who will be a housewife. I think they were just raised by such a mother, so they don't know any other models." She expressed annoyance regarding these traditional perceptions of women but offered no suggestions for how and when such views might change. Some women just accept such limited views on the part of men and tacitly play along, playing up their femininity. Kanter argued that men categorize women by picturing them in stereotypical roles; this "role encapsulation" includes such categories as mother, seductress, pet, and iron maiden.[26] Similarly, Joan Williams explains that women themselves seem to need to "willingly" express themselves through these traditional feminine roles: "Women can succeed only by stepping into one of a limited number of conventionally feminine roles: the princess, who aligns with but does not threaten the dominance of a powerful man; the mother, who seeks to ensure everyone else's welfare; the cheerleader, who applauds male achievements; the efficient queen, who cheerfully accepts the ministerial tasks; the daughter, who looks up to the men around her."[27] Rather than revising gender customs, which will require high levels of organizational and institutional reform, male workers continue to rely on the old customs that constrain women, folding them into these traditional roles.

Even senior women managers and career-track women in financial firms said that when they were new or low in seniority, they had to "prove" that they were actually women. So they did all the typical assistant tasks, including tea pouring and cleaning of workers' desks, so as not to "stick out" from the large number of non-career-track women. Maki, a deputy manager at Mikado Bank, said, "The bank hired me on the condition that I get along with the non-career-track women." Misa, a twenty-four-year-old at Daigo Life Insurance, said, "The male workers held a departmental meeting to discuss if I should do tea pouring or not, because they had never worked with a career-track woman before. They decided I should do tea pouring because I am the youngest." The workers were constantly reminded of a "woman's place"—in other words, that they should act as willing caretakers or "wives" who can "get along with" other women. In combination with the seniority system, traditional gender ideology in Japan mandates that a young woman worker, regardless of her talent and skills, should demonstrate subservient femininity as a wife and daughter.

Young women workers are expected to serve men as assistants not only in the financial firms but also in the cosmetics firms. Young female employees of the cosmetics companies claimed that they did extra secretarial work for the senior men. Rie, a twenty-six-year-old worker at Takane, managed a department head's schedule, answered all the phones for her section, and did extra research for a department head. "Men are not asked to do such things," she insisted. Misa, a twenty-four-year-old career-track worker at Daigo Life Insurance, reported that she was often asked to sit next to male workers or managers at after-work drinking meetings because "[the men] want me to listen to them." Although attending drinking events was important for her new career, she believed she was wasting her time and felt uneasy about her career prospects. "I feel like I am a hostess in a club. . . . I have to constantly say, 'Wow, that is great' or 'I understand' and nod at whatever they say," she asserted. An organizational culture that sees young women as men's assistants—or that expects women to be caretakers, mothers, or sex objects—can influence women workers' self-confidence and productivity negatively, both because they must spend extra time doing assistant-level tasks and because they feel they are valued for their caring and serving rather than for their competence.

Linda McDowell, citing Luce Irigaray and Joan Riviere, points out the fatal damage that women's performance of femininity does in a male-dominated workplace. McDowell explains:

In a provocative paper a provocative paper, originally published in 1929 but recently influential again, Joan Riviere (1986) documented the implications for women who took on a masculine identity in order to compete in the professions, She suggested that women who take on a masculine identity may also put on 'a mask of womanliness' or masquerade in a feminine guise in order to 'avert anxiety and the retribution feared from men' (35). And here we see the echoes of the male bankers who were at ease neither with masculine women nor with feminine women. In Riviere's case notes, which focus on a woman university lecturer, it is suggested that she copes with her male colleagues by being flippant or frivolous; that 'she has to treat the situation of displaying her masculinity to men as a "game," as something not real, as a "joke"'(39). Irigaray (1977) also understood femininity in similar ways. She described the mimicry that she saw as constitutive of feminine subjectivity as a "masquerade of femininity" in which "the woman loses herself by playing on her femininity." The game of femininity is one which is imposed on women by male values and language. The sense of loss identified by Irigaray parallels an unease felt by many of my respondents. . . . In negotiating this alienation of identity, women are led into simulating appearances of femininity through masks and masquerade in an infinite regress.[28]

Women engage in the performance of stereotypical femininity to respond to men's expectations and to cope with their alienation in the male-dominated workplace, and they may even claim that any "masculine" behavior on their part is a "joke" or performance. McDowell concludes that the fact that women are caught in a performance of femininity under the norm of masculinity is "why so many women do not achieve the really powerful positions, and why some feel dismayed when they do."[29] Whether or not, in a highly male-dominated workplace, women workers should emulate masculinity, express femininity, or combine the two has long been debated. McDowell points out that even when it is not possible to avoid engaging with the norms of heterosexuality, there are different ways to express masculinity and femininity.[30] The answer about what women should emphasize depends on what it would take for a woman to reject the performance of femininity and what other options are available to her in the particular workplace.

In the case of Japanese companies, images of women being inadequate and relegated to assistant positions are pervasive because firms rely on gender-stereotypical customs and practices that continue to restrain women's power. Notions of women's incompetency, resulting from a very real lack of experience and professional training, are conflated with gender-essentialist characteristics of women and thus lead to stereotyping. The absence of women with power only reinforces management's distrust of and negativity toward women.

## Heroic Masculinity and Navigating Gendered Customs

Organizations usually embrace some type of "hero" images and narratives regarding their successful workers, often based on such "masculine" traits as entrepreneurialism, the ability to be visionary, leadership, competency, and risk taking.[31] Male workers legitimize gender biases by referring to their own or their firm's manhood narratives and masculine behaviors. In narratives of masculinity, workers imagine and embrace certain types of masculine behaviors that reinforce the view of women workers as having inferior judgment, being incapable of completing some tasks, and failing to meet the standards of the ideal worker.[32] Narratives of masculinity are embedded in such workplace practices as engaging in long hours of work, exhibiting loyalty to authority, demonstrating accomplishments and competitiveness, and navigating business networks. Men constantly measure their achievements comparatively, drawing boundaries between themselves and other men as well as between men and women in order to establish their competency.

Traditionally masculine characteristics of the business world, such as authoritarianism, paternalism, competition, informal networking, and workaholism or careerism, are known to be the central organizational practices that control men's power relations and exclusion of women.[33] David Collinson and Jeff Hearn write that in an authoritarian system, men may use aggressiveness, fear, power, and even bullying to assert their superiority over others.[34] In a paternalistic system, men perform polite and civilized manhood and softly relegate women to assistant positions. Men may perform competitiveness and efficiency, and develop informal networks as their own currency. Finally, Collinson and Hearn argue that workaholism is an important part of the ideal worker's "impression management." Importantly, workaholism and sacrificing oneself for a job and company have been distinct characteristics of Japan's postwar ideal of manhood, which has been promoted by the state and Japanese business.

In addition to these traditional characteristics of masculinity, researchers also note hypermasculine performance, especially in the global financial industry. McDowell characterizes the trading floor of a UK bank as having embraced macho men who exhibit hyperaggressiveness, excellence at math, speed, and "raw intelligence."[35] In McDowell's observation of trader masculinity, by enacting these traits, the men expect to earn high profits and command respect from others. The traders must be competitive but also team players, a characteristic that enhances male bonding and informal networking. McDowell finds that women are out of place in such a world; simply having a woman's body represents a lack of power in such a hypermasculine workplace.[36] Robin Leidner observed similar hypermasculine competition in insurance sales.[37] The insurance sales field can be viewed as traditionally feminine since it requires interpersonal skills, but it is also masculinized because of the emphasis on competition for clients and the attainment of sales goals. In the financial companies I looked at, men embraced hypermasculinity and showed indifference to women. This was most pronounced in the investment banking section of Mikado Bank. A couple of men at Shijo Asset Management also referred to the hypermasculine securities workers at the parent company, Shijo Investment Group, as model workers for the Japanese financial industry.

Sex segregation and the hypermasculine culture of investment banking and securities sales are distinctly Japanese but not limited to Japan. Eiji boasted of being the ideal worker by saying, "I would deserve a million-dollar salary if I worked on Wall Street." Eiji often referred to his American boss, who worked in a large bank in New York, and commented that elite Japanese workers like himself exhibit work habits and ethics similar to those of American bankers in their tendency to work long hours and engage in informal networking. Eiji started his career in corporate finance at Mikado Bank after graduating from college in 1992. As a new college graduate, he was assigned the earnings goal of $500 million. He said: "Other major Japanese banks assigned a new worker about $30 million, and we were aiming for a far bigger amount... . After three years of working for financing, I accomplished the goal of $1 billion. I never finished writing proposals before midnight. I thought I was just a slow writer. . . . Then the boss later told me that, among the four workers, I was the one who wrote over one hundred of the total number of two hundred proposals each year." Eiji had long envisioned himself as an eventual board member at the bank. In order to achieve this, he believed that he must become a *bucho* or general manager by the age of forty-five: "You must be a *todori* or board member after you have been a *bucho* for five years. If you just remain a *bucho* for over five years, that means you are useless as a manager."

After Mikado Bank underwent a financial crisis because of a large amount of bad debt in the late 1990s, Eiji would evaluate the bankrupted businesses and bad debts in order to refinance them. He said: "When I collected money from the failing businesses, I had to deal with some underground people, including yakuza." According to Eiji, only a man could handle this situation. He continued, "Women cannot go to property evaluations of such businesses as sex entertainment clubs and love hotels. . . . And some clients do not like women workers, while some clients might like to talk to women and give more information to them than to men." In his stories about his money collection and dealing with underground yakuza groups and governmental investigation agencies, his depiction of himself cleaning up the bad loans of the bank came across as a highly heroic drama of ideal manhood.

Long working hours had been a part of Eiji's daily life for years, and they continued even after he underwent surgery for a gastrointestinal problem. He would leave the workplace at 2 a.m. by taxi and come back to work at 8 every morning. "I pay two-thirds of all the taxi fees," he noted. Based on his experiences of working long hours with little sleep every day, prioritizing work over personal matters (including paying extra fees out of his own pocket for his early morning and late-night commutes between the firm and home), and dealing with various business clients, Eiji concluded that "it is impossible for women to work in investment banking." He repeated that women cannot work or are unwilling to work long hours and lack full dedication to their work. (Working long hours, a critically gendered tool, has long been a traditionally normalized assessment criterion to measure workers' ability in Japanese firms.)

Eiji believed that he embodies the characteristics of the ideal worker, such as deep dedication to work, devotion of long hours to it, comfort in navigating the male-dominated business culture, possession of skills to negotiate profitable business deals, and willingness to take risks for profit. Here is where the gender boundary is drawn. He asserted that very few women exhibit these behaviors, and thus they cannot meet the expectations demanded of good workers.

> It is difficult for women to go and get contracts in Shinjuku Ni-chōme [the red-light district of Tokyo]. . . . A woman usually cannot go to a *settai* [business negotiation over drinks] alone. A man can go alone. That means that the cost is half as much. Also, you have to pay from your own pocket all the time. It is wrong to think that you can negotiate business in your office. . . . Those who really contribute to the company always sacrifice themselves for the company in many ways. . . . I have not met such a woman who works like me or other dedicated male workers.

Men are also tactfully diplomatic yet profit driven in dealing with male clients.

> I go drinking with a client to finalize a business deal, say, to make him pay $2 million instead of $500,000. I have to prove to this person that I am worthy of that amount. Drinking with him until 4 in the morning, I must "grab a ball" to make him a business partner, so that we can

negotiate the amount and interest rate; by this I mean I grab the partner's weakness. Can a woman do that? Or I may settle on the offered
amount, but raise the interest rate. Initially, it was just a $500,000 job,
but I made my clients pay $2 million eventually. I have done this at least
two or three times. I am pretty good at it. . . . It is very difficult for men
to ask women to do this type of job.

In McDowell's study of trader masculinity, making clients feel special is seen
as an important skill, as are networking and developing personal contacts from
which women are excluded.[38] According to Eiji, a man can do more than a woman
because he can "grab a [man's] ball" or achieve a level of intimacy with business
clients in places such as the red-light district of Tokyo.

Many men whom I interviewed value the daily after-hours drinking and
socializing they are expected to do. The after-work activities vary from locker-
room-style bonding in hostess clubs to intra- or interfirm study groups and
business negotiations. Drinking is the major method of masculine performance
through which men deepen their bonds and solidarity.[39] Women's lack of access
to the men-only network and to behaviors based on men's bonding has long been
seen as an informal obstacle to their success.

Homosocial bonds, often bolstered by "locker-room" or adolescent behaviors
such as engaging in sexual banter and making jokes, provide men with a sense of
power, identity, competition, and solidarity.[40] Executive men in the highly male-
dominated advertising industry engage in such behaviors "with an attitude of
entitlement and enjoyment."[41] The woman worker is often excluded from these
practices, or encounters men's use of the double standard if she does try to participate.[42] Because the business culture itself is highly male centered and masculinized, not only do entertaining business clients and achieving homosocial
intimacy become labeled as men's duties, but excluding women from men's business clubs is normalized.

Male workers often proudly refer to their membership in the homosocial culture. Seiji, a forty-year-old male manager, talked about the age-based hierarchy
and solidarity among the men at his firm, saying, "Shijo Group values the hierarchy and order based on the year of starting jobs. Within the Shijo Group, we
call each other by the Japanese imperial year in which we joined the company."
Yoshio, a male business attorney, said, "Shijo Securities has a culture of training
men well. Some of the men there are practically legends. They have extensive
sales knowledge and multiple techniques and are able to convince clients well."

Many women not only lack an informal network of their own but also find it
difficult to access informal male networks. Misa, a twenty-four-year-old worker
at Daigo Life Insurance, said, "This company is very male dominated. It is a man's

world. It is like a male-only high school. It is hard for women to develop close connections with most of the workers." In looking back at the past, Rika, a thirty-seven-year-old female general manager at Shijo Asset Management, said it had long been the norm that upper managers have not included women in their meetings: "My boss would never include me in meetings and told me to go to the "women-only" meetings with the non-career-track women. This happened all the time. . . . In the last few years, the atmosphere has changed, mostly because a number of men who were in their fifties left the firm around the year 2000. It became very easy to work here after that." Networking ability may be seen as a more distinctively masculine skill in competitive financial jobs than in the manufacturing sector because men in the former field have a large number of corporate clients. But, according to information I learned in my interviews, informal male networks play an important role with regard to promotion in cosmetics companies, too. Yuko, a forty-two-year-old female general manager at Hanakage, noted that there is a close link between the informal network and future promotions: "Those who continue to get promoted in this firm have multiple networks and connections. You need to have powerful connections to rise high. In my case, those who have supported me quit one by one. Then things got difficult for me." She continued:

> The top board members like loyal "yes-sir" men. They avoid really excellent, smart, and capable workers. So those who actually have brains may end up staying somewhere else and not enter management. . . . Those guys want guys who are loyal and who just say yes and listen to their complaints over drinks. They can't do that with women. They can't develop those kinds of bonds with women. . . . I was a top runner one time, but I was not good at the politics. I explicitly revealed my opposition to some of the people. I could have gone up the ladder far more easily if I had not done that.

She saw herself as having difficulty in socializing with groups of men: "We used to go to China every month during the last few years. I do not go to karaoke [which often involves sex entertainment in China] or even go drinking after the meetings during the trip. But these guys often share common experiences; they talk about their preferences in women they meet at these places, and so on, like saying who is cute or who is their type." While she did not go to the nightclubs with male coworkers, she tried to listen to the men in order to smooth out her relations with them so that she can remain in the circle: "So I just lower my standards and listen to them. I sometimes have no idea what they are talking about, but I just act like I really enjoy the conversation."

At Daigo Life Insurance, an occasional woman who demonstrated a strong sales background, worked long hours, and participated in after-work drinking gatherings could successfully become "one of the boys." Tami, a thirty-eight-year-old manager, took part in after-work drinking sessions with her male bosses every day and played golf every weekend. She also attended hostess clubs with upper managers and their clients and considers these occasions enjoyable and valuable. As a single woman, she said she devoted 100 or 120 percent of her life to her current job, and networking over daily drinks and weekend golf with her male colleagues was a major part of her job.

Like Yuko and Tami, some women strive to gain access to the male network, as well as recognition from male colleagues that they are competent workers. Yet the network and customs remain highly gendered, and usually women must put forth a conscious and enormous effort to break through.

The lack of a network and close mentoring can work against women's chances of promotion. A thirty-five-year-old female manager was one of the very few career-track workers in the Tokyo office of Daigo Life Insurance. Nobody taught her what to do to get promoted, and to make things even more difficult, she never encountered female managers. When a workplace is highly male dominated, a woman may have no mentor—or only a male mentor, who may be reluctant to mentor a younger female worker because such professional relationships are uncommon in gender-divided workplaces in which women are mostly seen as assistants.

> I was a low-level manager in the investment section. Then one of my bosses said that I was far behind in my supposed promotion. He suggested what I should do and how to do the tasks. He said I should work much harder. He also suggested that I should aim for middle and upper management. . . . He was the only person who made those suggestions to me. Before that, I never knew how to improve myself or even the fact that I was behind other men in my promotion.

Regardless of some female managers' willingness to navigate the male networks and norms, masculine organizational customs reward more men than women and reinforce gender boundaries. As Kanter suggested, a very low number of token women in the workplace makes it far more difficult for competent women to combat the various stereotypes, gain access to informal networks and opportunities, and assimilate with or surpass competent men.

## Female Misogyny and Eroticized Bonding with Men

The tradition of the age-based hierarchy in Japan may make women's relationships with other women more hierarchical. Also, it may be the case that women's hostility or negativity toward other women is more pervasive in a less egalitarian society than it would be in a more egalitarian or gender-integrated society. Japan belongs to the former category: neither women nor men are accustomed to seeing women with power and authority in public places. In an organizational context, in highly competitive and male-dominated companies in which young women are concentrated in low-level jobs and lower management, they may adjust themselves to believe in male superiority and view their female managers negatively.

Some young women workers whom I interviewed, mostly in the cosmetics firms (in which the number of low-level women managers has been rapidly increasing), expressed significant negativity about women managers, describing them variously as mean, rude, emotional, irrational, and lacking professional attitudes. While the increase in women workers and women managers is often described as having a positive influence on young women workers because it offers them female role models, merely increasing the number of largely lower-level managers without changing traditional beliefs about gender does not alter the workers' gender bias.

The two cosmetics companies I studied are known as "women-friendly businesses," and all the women I spoke with in this industry could name quite a few lower-level female managers. Yet the rapid increase in women managers is seen as a source of some tension and problems. Seven of the fourteen workers whom I interviewed at Hanakage complained about female managers, and six expressed gender stereotypes during the interviews, while seven of the fifteen interviewed at Takane mentioned their relationships with senior female workers as a great concern. I heard these concerns about female managers only at cosmetics firms because they have a larger number of younger women and low- or midlevel female managers than the three financial firms. (However, the interviewees in the financial companies often mentioned tensions and conflicts among career-track women workers, non-career-track women workers, and temporary women workers, as well as discriminatory hiring divisions, as previously discussed.)

Young women workers in cosmetics companies contrasted female bosses' hysterical and emotional treatment of workers with male bosses' paternalistic and rational management style. Yuka, a twenty-nine-year-old worker in the marketing department at Hanakage, said that her current female-dominated section exhausts her because she expends much more energy trying not to offend senior women than she had to with senior men. "I think the organization functions in a healthier manner when it has more men. . . . The section loses integration without men," said Yuka. She views the women workers as more hierarchy oriented, based on age and years of employment, than the male workers and says that female managers are offended easily if they believe younger women workers do not show enough respect. She said, "Seniority is more intense among women than among men. For women, you pay far more attention to the *senpai-kohai* [elder-younger] relationships than with men. Women don't communicate with each other without men, either." Yuka and other young women's comments made me wonder why the older women care so much about getting enough respect from the younger women. Is this attributable to generational differences, because older women may have grown up with a stronger sense of seniority than younger women, who are more familiar with the idea of individual equality? (But if this is the main reason, why should it not apply equally to older men?) Yuka told me she thinks that the older women are unkind to the younger ones because they have little power and are insecure about their positions in the organization.

Yuka described some senior women at Hanakage as being too emotional, subjective, jealous, and desperate for the attention of their male superiors:

> Many women mix personal preferences and emotional matters with their work. . . . The women act really nice to people in front of their male bosses, but they become really mean to us when their bosses are not looking. . . . I have seen some women intentionally exclude one of the female subordinates from a meeting. Some women also get really jealous about my achievements in the section. . . . They just want attention from their male bosses.

Mariko, a twenty-eight-year-old worker in skin-care products at Hanakage, talked about having a hard time getting along with her female manager in her previous section.

> She never really listened to me. She yelled at me all the time: "Why can't you do this? Why can't you do that? I told you . . . ." But she never really told me anything about what to do or how to do it. Eventually, I got ill and lost hearing in my left ear. I never told anybody about her, but the people in human resources heard about my situation, and they transferred me to a different section. A man who worked for her also quit the company later because of her rude behavior. Another woman after me was also transferred to a different section. Can you believe this?

She recovered her health after she was transferred to the new section. But Mariko had a hard time separating her negative experience from her boss's gender. She said she never wanted to work for a female manager again. She said, "I can say anything to male managers. I know the other women workers in this firm feel the same way."

Because seniority determines pay and promotion in these firms, the organizational hierarchy based on age and years of employment certainly shapes a person's status and power within the firms. Ogasawara, in her ethnographic work on office ladies in a Japanese bank, described how non-career-track women's mutual relationships were divided based on their length of employment with the firm, their age, and their educational background; such divisions made it difficult for them to experience solidarity with other women and to improve their subordinate status.[43] As Yuka mentioned, it is likely that age-based hierarchy plays a more important role in women's relations than it does for the male workers, especially because women workers have fewer opportunities to gain upward mobility and power. If women have little chance to obtain power and authority, they may have a strong reason to claim their greater age as a legitimate source of power over the younger workers. Thus, it is likely that the senior women's "meanness" may simply reflect their scant opportunities to move up within the organization. Lack of mobility between companies or within the internal labor market under the Japanese management system (compared to the regular mobile labor market) may intensify competition on the internal promotion ladder.

It is also likely that women managers might be cast in a negative light by the heterosexually eroticized bonds between young women and senior men. Ogasawara notes that young, attractive women are explicitly valued by male workers in Japanese firms, and this situation could promote male workers' aversion to older female managers.[44] It is likely that these women managers are the target of "female misogyny," which occurs when women workers normalize or even eroticize positions in which they are subordinate to male managers or men with power, and "women find it difficult to deal with senior women" because the authority figures should, in their minds, be men.[45] So it might be that younger women project the heterosexual superior-subordinate relationship onto their view of female bosses and view female bosses negatively.

The senior men also participate in and promote female misogyny. Kaoru, a thirty-three-year-old worker in product development at Hanakage, said: "Senior men all like me, and I can say whatever I want to say to them. Senior women get jealous about that. The general manager constantly ignores and belittles my female boss, and each one only communicates with the other through me." However, the problem is not just young women's eroticization of male authority figures or senior men's eroticization of young females; it may be an organizational failure to identify women managers as figures who are just as powerful and responsible as the male managers.

Because the management structure is male dominated, Yuka speculated that female managers' "meanness" to younger women is a way for them to obtain affirmation of their authority. By treating the younger women as if they have some behavior worthy of punishment, the senior women may gain recognition and help from the senior men, much like a mother might try to gain some help from her husband for a problem with their children. Yuka said, "The top managers are all men. So the women managers want approval from those male managers. That is why those low female managers constantly try to show their power by being mean to us. . . . I don't think there would be any problem if all the workers were women like at my high school." Also, these young women's description of the female managers may have reflected their own misogyny.

The women managers were also judged by a double standard. They were often criticized for any display of traditional masculine behavior. In the interviews, many male workers noted the "male boss's yelling" and characterized it as being an aspect of "old-fashioned" organizational masculinity. However, women managers' yelling or expression of negative emotions was not seen as an enactment of corporate masculinity; instead, it was seen as a marker of deviant femininity. Kaoru said, "The managers sometimes yell at male workers. But I got this from a female manager, too. She even started gossiping about me and excluded me."

Workplace female misogyny is not uncommon. Phyllis Chesler writes, "The primary targets of women's aggression, hostility, violence, and cruelty are other women."[46] Judy Wajcman notes that women commonly undermine other women's authority in the workplace:

> Various constructions of femininity which women deploy in relating to men in power involve being flirtatious, admiring and generally supportive. In this way, women are actively reconstituting heterosexualized forms of dominance and subordination. They therefore can have trouble dealing with women in positions of power, because the strategies that they are accustomed to using with men are inappropriate for female bosses. Because women have internalized gender hierarchies, it seems almost proper for a male to be in a superior position. In the case of men, power is eroticized. This complex intertwining of power with sexuality means that powerful women provoke anxieties and ambivalence in women as well as in men.[47]

She writes that women who internalize sexism not only dislike or devalue each other but also unconsciously expect other women to "mother" them and thus attempt to fulfill unrealistic family or fantasy needs.[48] The women subordinates expect their female bosses to be more understanding, more nurturing, more giving, and more forgiving than men.[49] The female bosses are expected to emulate masculinity but at the same time may also feel pressure to act feminine,[50] because "women who fail to practice femininity according to feminine stereotypes that define women as subordinate lose approval and end up with even lower status."[51] That "successful women typically mix masculinity with feminine softeners" might be because of this double standard.[52]

It is not only the women managers' responsibility to improve workplace dynamics; the absence of women with authority in firms shapes women subordinates' view that superior women's authority is untrustworthy. For example, Kaoru at Hanakage said, "I don't care that they [the women managers] get mad at me. Because I look down on those women in this firm anyway." Such a comment demonstrates the subordinate young woman's misogyny and her view of women's power as illegitimate.

Comparing the junior women workers' identities in male-dominated law firms and gender-integrated law firms, Ely observed that the junior women in the male-dominated firms were more likely to criticize senior women as illegitimate and to view them less positively as role models than those in the sex-integrated firms.[53] Young women who rarely see women in positions of power are less likely to believe in the legitimacy of female managers. They tend to think that senior women do not deserve the power they have in the hierarchy or that they have obtained such positions of power because they were lucky or used some dubious means, not because they have talents and qualifications. In fact, many of the women and men I talked to in the five companies expressed the view that their companies had to promote unqualified women into managerial positions because of governmental and corporate pressure.

> A correlation between identity and hierarchical group membership, such that men tend to predominate in positions of authority while women tend to occupy more junior positions, may communicate to junior women that membership in their gender group is incompatible with membership in more powerful organizational groups. In these male-dominated organizations, senior women, as members of these two ostensibly incompatible groups, may represent a dilemma for junior women as they assess their own prospects for promotion. To make sense of a woman's rise to the top, junior women may come to view the possibility of success as available only to women who shed their feminine identity and are not truly women because they act like men or who have attained their positions of authority illegitimately.[54]

Ely's observation regarding young women's perception of managers as unfeminine may be slightly different than what I observed in the case of the cosmetics firms, but it still offers an interesting perspective on how women managers can be negatively judged by subordinates.

Similar to Ely's observation, the junior women in male-dominated firms did not see the senior women either as a source of emotional support or as models of authority whom they could respect. In the male-dominated organizations it is difficult for women workers to channel their feelings of envy and jealousy productively; the women's perception of their limited access to senior positions intensifies these negative feelings.[55] As we saw in the case of Hanakage, the women managers' apparently irrational negativity toward the younger women may reflect their lack of a productive way to channel their complaints and concerns about the work environment. It is likely that women's internalized sexism is more pronounced and even more accepted in a gender-unequal workplace.

Finally, Kanter argues that the "mean and bossy" stereotype of the female boss, characterized by jealousy, taking things too personally, and being too critical and demanding of others' attention, is not so much gendered as it is typical of individuals who are powerless.[56]

> People who feel vulnerable and unsure of themselves, who are plunged into jobs without sufficient training or experience, regardless of the official authority they are given, are more likely to first adopt authoritarian-controlling leadership styles. The behavior attributed to women supervisors is likely to be characteristic of new and insecure supervisors generally. . . . In a variety of ways, then, powerlessness stemming from organizational circumstance breeds a particular leadership style caricatured in the stereotype of the bossy woman.[57]

Kanter further argues that the powerless are those who do not have powerful alliances to help them manage the bureaucracy, including sponsors, peer connections, or promising subordinates.[58] Thus, even though Kanter says it is not a matter of gender, it is likely that the pathologization of women managers reflects the absence of adequate training and support in these firms. If the powerlessness of, or low confidence of, the female managers in a firm hinders workplace interactions among women as well as between men and women, it needs far more serious attention.

## Queen Bees and Negativity toward Women Subordinates

I have discussed young women's negativity toward women managers and the structural problems of gender that relate to this phenomenon. Managerial women may also employ gender stereotypes to criticize younger women, expressing reluctance to work with them or detaching themselves from the young women. On the part of female managers, such aversion to other women may derive from the high value they place on workplace masculinity. The women managers' enactment of their aversion to younger women may also be perceived by them as the best strategy for survival in a male-dominated workplace.

Most women managers I talked with opposed their firm's use of positive action. These women managers, much like male managers, viewed traditional masculine norms and customs as valuable and expressed the belief that hiring and promotions should be solely based on individual competency and hard work, not on gender.

There seem to be several factors that shape women managers' negativity toward younger women workers. First, these managers worked hard and achieved just like the male workers, and thus they value the male work norm. They believe that their firms should hire either men or women who are willing to work the way they did (or the way men do, at least according to the stereotype). One of the many options for surviving in a male-dominated workplace is becoming an "honorary man,"[59] and the senior women may expect the same levels of competency and hard work from the junior women. Young women may not always conform to this masculine work model. Second, there may be some generational differences between women managers and young employees in terms of how they approach work. Third, the women managers don't want to lose the "privileges" associated with being token females, and this may drive them to behave like "queen bees," especially when they feel threatened by the limited positions available to women in the male-dominated workplace. Finally, the female managers may detach themselves from younger women and avoid displays of femininity because they may view this as the best strategy for women to survive in a male-dominated workplace.

Female managers in the workplace are often expected to display both emulated masculinity and traditional femininity. In order to climb higher on the management ladder, where females are mostly invisible, women may find it necessary to emulate masculinity—being "tough" or even "thrusting" and "ruthless" to fit in.[60] Sacrificing femininity and expressing combativeness to join "the corporate crusade" are common strategies among female managers and professionals.[61] The career-track women workers in financial firms narrated the importance of displaying and conforming to the masculine aspects of their job performance, including working long hours and being competitive with others.

Some career-track women, such as Rika, a thirty-seven-year-old manager at Shijo Asset Management, were wary of the pressure to work, which included the necessity of staying at their offices until around midnight daily. "You are not given the job unless you work like a man. This hasn't changed for a long time in this firm, and it doesn't look like it will change anytime soon," she said. Meanwhile, other women whom I talked to described themselves as nonfeminine and thus just as suited to the work as their male colleagues. Maki, a thirty-nine-year-old deputy general manager in investment banking at Mikado Bank, said:

> I don't think about this place being a man's world, even though it is. . . .
> Many women I know just want to deal with clean, beautiful, and cute
> things. The job I have is the opposite of that. My job is not clean at

all, but they pay us better than they do for other jobs. . . . We call our customers and clients "debtors" when things get bad, and force them to pay money back to the bank. . . . When I go to meet the top managers at the bankrupted firms to collect debts, I have to deal with some men who belong to the yakuza or who are big-name business owners. . . . Some business owners bring all kinds of signed contracts and ask me to wait for their debt payment. Instead of asking for a deadline extension, they say things like, "I will kill myself right now here in front of you." I show little emotion to them. I am very dry and do not respond to those threats. I just need to get the job done.

Maki's male boss spoke positively to me about her, noting that she "works like a man."

Performing masculinity is not limited to a display of competitiveness and to fearless accomplishment of assigned jobs. It also includes a "willing[ness] to modify behaviour to become more like men or to be perceived as more male than men."[62] Tami, a thirty-eight-year-old manager at Daigo Life Insurance, spoke Japanese with three different accents, as she was in charge of three branches of the firm, in Tokyo, Nagoya, and Osaka. She started working at the firm as a non-career-track worker and only changed to a career-track position after ten years of service. When she was in charge of the local branch, she rarely left her office before midnight. At the same time, she achieved high sales in insurance, earning the company about $48 million almost every month. Her excellent sales record marked her as an ideal worker at the firm. Insurance sales skills can be viewed as traditionally feminine since they require interpersonal abilities, but they are also masculinized because of the emphasis on competition for clients and the attainment of sales goals.[63]

As one of the boys, Tami also valued her bonds with male colleagues and her participation in male networks, and she never missed the daily after-work drinking sessions and weekend golf. She said, "They [male colleagues and superiors] always teach me how to do the job. I really respect them. They are very supportive of me. I am just a token female manager. Those guys are far better workers than I am. I feel bad about being in the position of manager." While respecting and allying with masculinities, Tami looked down on, and distanced herself from, the other women at work.

I go out to eat with the men. There is one career-track woman in my section, but she does not go out with me; she goes out to eat with a temp worker. . . . I only go out with men for a drink, not with women. The women eat so slowly and eat very little. I can't stand that. I feel exhausted when I talk with women workers in the firm. . . . The women cry when they get scolded. That's unfair to the men. The women should be serious about their jobs. The men get into trouble if they are seen as the ones who make the women cry, and they no longer want to work with the women.

Tami expressed negativity toward women who display traditional femininity. She had a hard time seeing these women as serious about their jobs.

Tami also pointed out that some young career-track women's sense of entitlement gives them the idea that they do not have to work as much as other workers do. This is one reason why Tami opposed the firm's use of positive action in hiring and promotion of women.

> I disagree with this recent corporate obsession with hiring a larger number of career-track women. . . . Some women whine and complain too much, saying, "I don't want to do that job" or "I don't like to be treated like this". . . . I think women's consciousness needs to change first. They need to do everything that they are told to do because that's what being a career-track worker means. . . . There are not many women who work very hard or make sincere efforts. . . . I see some career-track women who want to take advantage of the firms' support of even those women who don't get their jobs done.

In referring to ideal workers who "make sincere efforts," Tami may have meant that women workers should be more collective goal oriented rather than individualistic and selfish. Such a collective goal orientation is one of the "masculine" characteristics of business leadership, which some experts argue that many women do not learn due to gender socialization.[64] Thus, Tami's criticisms of the young women workers derived from the values she absorbed regarding organizational masculinity. Tami and other senior women perceive younger women as more concerned about the timing of marriage, childbirth, and child-care leave and benefits than about their daily performance, and that they take advantage of management's "women-friendly" treatment.

Takako, a thirty-five-year-old manager at Daigo Life Insurance, shared Tami's negativity toward the younger generation of career-track women.

> The young women have such a sense of entitlement. Well, we can't do anything about the fact that they take long parental leaves. The bigger problem is their leaving work early. Some do work hard to get their jobs done, but others just leave without doing anything. They say they can't do it anyway. I was like, "You are paid for your work, so why don't you try to do some more?" I get complaints from the other workers, saying, "Why are these young mothers getting special treatment?"

Takako told me that the firm must be selective and hire "better" female workers in the first place, and that it might be hasty to hire a large number of women career-track workers. The complaints also may be due in part to the transition by Japanese companies toward hiring increased numbers of women workers with diverse backgrounds and lifestyles.

The women managers' negative view of young women as being inadequate workers might be partly due to the older women's successful assimilation to the male work norm and the sense of authority they possess because of their seniority. Young women may also detach themselves from women managers who do not demonstrate the ideal or caring femininity they might expect.

Sharon Mavin, citing Al Gini, argues that women managers internalize masculine imperatives regarding workplace customs and that this makes solidarity among women workers difficult.

> Women in senior management have not paved the way for other women. Thus, [they perpetuate] the incongruity between the managerial and the gender role without acknowledging the context in which senior women work. Gini argues that women are not very nice and this is why we do not like them. . . . The argument is that those few women who have broken through the glass ceiling have done so not by embracing feminism but by outperforming men on their own terms: classic careerists who happen to be women. . . . Known as the "only bra in the room syndrome," characteristics of these types of achievers [include] their lack of empathy and support of other working women, especially their subordinates. "Having achieved success by playing hardball and working hard, they expect the same from others . . . . Consequently, many women do not like to work for female bosses."[65]

Mavin argues that senior women's successful assimilation into the men's domain depends not on proving equal competency and skill but on outperforming them. Similarly, a study of a wide variety of jobs in the United States and United Kingdom by Elizabeth Gorman and Julie Kmec pointed out that women have to try harder than men even when men and women hold the same jobs, since employers impose higher performance standards on women than on men.[66] When women are expected to expend greater effort than men,[67] the senior women may ask the same from the younger women, making the senior women seem even more demanding.

In addition, the women managers' criticisms of the younger generation of women may reflect generational differences with regard to working conditions, given that combining job and family was not even an option for many women in the early 1990s. Yumiko, a forty-three-year-old manager at Shijo

Asset Management, expressed resentment about current and ongoing changes in women's employment. She remembered her past struggles to negotiate some leave with her boss after her first child was born in 1991 and having to deal with his complaints about her request to use early leave (in which a parent leaves the workplace an hour or two hours earlier than the formal leave time). "I feel very angry when I see the current parental leave law that pays all kinds of benefits and salaries to these women. I can't believe that," she said. Such generationally different experiences might be a common cause of tension among women. As can be seen in Tami's and Takako's criticism of the younger women's sense of entitlement with regard to having both family and work, the older generation was not given these options and sacrificed more than the younger generation, and this has caused them to have harsh feelings.

Williams summarizes this generational conflict among women (in the context of the United States):

> Older women, who entered the workplace when they had to conform to ideal-worker life patterns in order to survive, may see things very differently than younger women do. The latter expect to be able to both succeed at work and live up to the ideals of intensive motherhood that preclude them from outsourcing their children's lives. Women who played by the old rules, including those in my generation (I am fifty-seven), sometimes try to enforce those rules against younger women who seek to change them by taking maternity leave, working part-time, or interrupting their careers. The older women typically assert that these younger women "just don't understand" what it takes to be a doctor/ lawyer/banker/chief, to which the younger women typically respond, "We don't want your lives."[68]

Maki, a deputy manager at Mikado Bank, disagreed with her company's special efforts to hire or promote women because "women are different." She said, "I think it depends more on individuals than gender. I don't like too much emphasis on the division between men and women. Maybe I have just been privileged so I don't care about it. But I don't agree with affirmative action. I don't see it as a problem that the firm has a small number of women workers and managers. Women are different, not all the same." The women managers I talked with seemed, in general, highly skeptical of the younger workers' ambitions and lack of preparation. Tami strongly opposed Daigo Life Insurance's use of positive action because she did not see "many women who work very hard or make a sincere effort." Rika was ambivalent about Shijo Asset Management's effort to hire more women, because she views many women, including herself, as not willing to work like men: "The younger generations of women are sort of divided into two groups. One group of women takes child-care leave and leaves work early, and the other group works really hard, like men. But, overall, I don't think there are many ambitious women. Well, I am not. . . . The company wants to promote women. So I think I am given more points by the firm. " Rika was implying that she advanced in her job not because she was ambitious or worked particularly hard but because the firm simply wanted to move women along. Certainly, women are diverse in their approach to identity, work, and family. But emphasizing individual differences is an easy way to suppress workers' critical views of existing gender inequality and sex-segregated labor and employment conditions.

It is notable that many women managers mentioned that they have been treated far better than other women workers because of their elite college graduate status and the small number of career-track women. Yumiko, a forty-three-year-old manager at Shijo Asset Management, said she was treated so well because of having graduated from a top university: "I benefited from the brand of this university. . . . The company kept most graduates from this university in the headquarters. So they did not transfer me to the local branch. Working at a local branch is much harder." (Indeed, a few workers in all three financial firms pointed out that the career-track women in their firms were privileged, as the firms did not transfer them to a local branch and promoted them faster than men because of positive action.) Japanese feminist Chizuko Ueno argues that the women managers in Japanese firms are among those who explicitly profited from neoliberalism and the revision of the Equal Employment Opportunity Law (especially in contrast with the large number of temporary women workers who have barely any security in their economic lives).[69] The educational and bargaining privileges that they gained probably helped the female managers get to where they are.

Senior women's negativity toward younger women is sometimes described as "queen bee" behavior. This often takes the form of women emphasizing their own differences from other women and their own masculine characteristics.[70] Williams summarizes two possibilities for women's negativity toward other women:

> Queen bees tend to emerge in contexts of tokenism. "If you're used to being the one woman, and you've had to be that much smarter and that much better, then all of a sudden . . . it's almost like you can't work with other women because you're so used to being the only woman," said a woman science professor. This is one interpretation. Another is that a politically savvy woman gets the message that there is room for only one woman. The resulting struggles are not "cat fights." They are symptoms of a sexist environment.[71]

According to Williams, the token woman, who may be treated as one of the boys, may not like another woman colleague because she might feel that the amount of room for women at the top is very limited. Seen from another angle, if the number of women with power and authority increases, or if the paths to those positions are available to women in larger numbers (and in numbers equal to those of men), women's futile competition with each other can be lessened.

Mavin poses the question from a slightly different perspective, arguing that the term "queen bees" is itself problematic, as it implies solidarity among women or that women are "natural" allies, which, she argues, is a myth. However, she emphasizes the importance of examining workplace structures that shape tensions among women workers.

> Assumptions of solidarity behavior and constructions of Queen Bee result in another binary view of women, neglect within-group variations between women, and also polarize individual senior women as either "good," as a woman who is actively involved in supporting other women, or as "bad," as a woman who has achieved a senior management position by "selling out" other women. . . . Rather than recommending more senior women engage in solidarity behaviours through mentoring and as role models, whilst at the same time "blaming" them for being more male than men and not supporting other women, there is a need to focus future action on challenging and changing the overall gendered structures and systems in organizations.[72]

Indeed, as she suggests, Western media, in its portrayals of women in the workplace, often targets senior women for blame for being mean and rude and for harassing young, talented women.[73] Clearly, the ways in which women adapt to male-dominated organizations vary, and women should not be the focus of constant blame.

The other important argument about the queen bee phenomenon is that women managers detach themselves from younger women because of their perception that not allying with women is actually the best strategy in a male-dominated workplace. Belle Derks, Collette Van Laar, Naomi Ellemers, and Kim de Groot claim that "women's queen-bee behavior is an outcome of gender discrimination in the workplace."[74] They go on to argue that because "organizations that devalue women threaten the identity of female workers," women are reluctant to identify themselves with the group that has less organizational power (the women). They write: "When women come to perceive their gender as a liability, this may induce them to advance their career through queen-bee behavior: emphasizing their masculine characteristics, expressing gender-stereotypical views of other women, and denying the existence of gender bias."[75] The queen bee's detachment of herself from other women and denial of workplace gender inequality serve as the best strategy to differentiate herself from "the women." At the same time, queen bees "implicitly legitimize women's low organizational status and are unlikely to inspire their female subordinates as role models."[76] The women's lack of interest in other women and separation from them is the way to adapt to the male-dominated workplace and pursue their own ambitions and goals in climbing the career ladder.[77] Thus, it is a reflection of the shortage of powerful women in the workplace.

I have explained women managers' negativity toward younger women using various theories of gender-relational dynamics of organizations. A previous study explained Japanese women's difficulty in achieving solidarity because of their mutual tension over differences in age and education.[78] Similarly, senior women may act overbearing to their female subordinates because they associate age with power and because they perceive the young women as lacking in devotion, hard work, and a willingness to conform to masculine norms. It may also be partly because of the generation gap. But their detachment may also be a status-maintaining behavior, a rejection of the notion that they belong with other women—since being a woman or being feminine in a male-dominated firm means being inferior.

Women's negativity toward women can be a common organizational problem in workplaces in which women's power is mostly concentrated at the lower and middle levels of management. Women often are expected to outperform men in highly male-dominated workplaces. The combination of high sex segregation and high levels of competition may strain relations between the women managers, who are few in number, and the younger women employees. I am not interested in blaming women managers for conforming to the masculine norm or suggesting that they be more feminine, because their behaviors, ultimately, are a matter of their individual subjectivities.[79] However, that such behaviors are so commonplace should draw some attention to the gendered consequences of structural imbalance. Unless firms change this structural gender imbalance, women may continue to turn their backs on other women.

## Summary

I have described four processes by which gender stereotypes are reproduced and legitimized by both men and women workers in Japanese firms. First, male managers' negative images and distrust of women managers and workers relates to their adherence to essentialist beliefs. The dominance of workplace beliefs such as male primacy and separate spheres indicates that belief in the traditional male-breadwinner model and the Japanese employment system's long relegation of women workers to assistant positions continue to shape male managers' and workers' perceptions of women workers. The men's distrust of women is more pronounced in the financial firms than in the cosmetics firms because of the masculine characteristics of the tasks they are assigned and the small number of women in management. I found that even in the bank that is under US management, Japanese men's views of women workers are negative. Because even foreign-owned Japanese companies have not changed traditional gender patterns,[80] customs of sex segregation along with gendered employment and management patterns continue to persist in Japanese firms.

Second, as seen in the investment bankers' hegemonic masculinity, men legitimize existing gender biases by referring to their own hero behaviors or their firm's masculinity narratives. In narratives of masculinity, workers embrace particular masculine behaviors and legitimize their judgment of women workers as being inferior to men, incapable of doing some tasks that are mostly done by men, and unable to meet the standards of the ideal male worker. The women workers are outside of the men's informal network and their drama of hegemonic masculinity. As seen in the case discussed here, which concentrated on men in financial firms, hegemonic masculinity may be more pronounced in this type of firm than in a business such as a cosmetics firm because performance in the former is judged by aggression and competition, qualities that are seen as necessary to achieving high sales. Even though the hypermasculinity of particular jobs is not unique to Japan, the complete absence of women who do these traditionally masculine jobs, women's lack of access to them, and the absence of women who combat gender bias do characterize the Japanese management system.

Third, the young women workers whom I interviewed, mostly in the cosmetics firms, expressed negativity about female managers, describing them as mean, rude, and emotional. Young women workers' negativity toward low-ranking female managers in cosmetics firms may reflect organizational misogyny or the lack of adequate training for women managers, as both of these could promote gender bias against women managers. But, perhaps more significantly, the normalization of men in power in the workplace promotes young women's devaluation or dismissal of female authority figures. While the increase in women managers is sometimes interpreted as automatically beneficial to young women workers because the older women are seen as role models, it turns out that, without changing traditional gender beliefs, gender biases and sex-segregated customs persist.

Finally, in financial firms, most women managers expressed their opposition to positive action or their firm's increased hiring and promotion of women workers and managers. Some distanced themselves from the young women workers, expressing the opinion that the younger women did not work hard enough, were not ambitious enough, or were excessively individualistic. Such detachment of women managers from women subordinates also reinforces the existing norm of male dominance and the superiority of the masculine work norm.[81] The women managers' negativity toward other women can be explained by the concept of the queen bee; in other words, it might be related to the limited positions of power available to women, and thus it might constitute their strategy for survival in male-dominated workplaces. Either way, there seems to be a strong link between the absence of women with power in the workplace and women managers' denial of gender stratification.

In male-dominated workplaces such as many Japanese companies, do women workers who wish to climb the corporate ladder have any options beyond emulating masculine behaviors and working style? As I discussed, women managers are often under pressure to outperform men or feel they must try harder to gain recognition. McDowell points out that women's acting like men or emulating workplace masculinity may make male coworkers uneasy, but she acknowledges that this can be also a successful strategy in male-dominated institutions.[82] While McDowell warns that women's performance of femininity may hinder their success, Williams says that the most successful women seem to handle double standards, mixing masculinity with femininity.

Do women managers ever criticize the logic of masculinity, or can they choose other ways to get ahead of men? Can men and women remove themselves from or get beyond playing the gender game? According to some recent labor theorists and gender theorists such as Michael Burawoy and Judith Butler, the answer is no. Burawoy, employing Herbert Marcuse's definition of work and play, famously defines the game in the workplace as a consent-making process between management and worker in which "one cannot both play the game and at the same time question the rules."[83] While the workers play the "game" in order to compete with each other, often for self-expression and a sense of winning, the game has unintentional consequences, such as increasing individual output,[84] masking unequal labor conditions, and reproducing capitalist relations;[85] thus, it aids management in controlling the workers. "Two consequences of game-playing have so far been delineated: first, game playing obscures the relations of production in response to which the game is originally constructed; second, game-playing generates consent to the social relations in production that define the rules of the game."[86] The imperative of emulation of masculine work norms or aversion to femininity is similar to this concept of the "game." The individual gender play does not allow men and women to question the organizational and institutional logic of gender, and the deployment of gender (masculinity and femininity) serves to enhance workers' consent to the system of play.

Even though women's emulation of masculinity may be bound by this consensual process, the repetitive and excessive emulation of masculinity and femininity, as Butler argues about performativity, may at least make the existing gender norms and unequal system visible and could lead to destabilization of the normalized customs.[87] According to Butler, performance is the site where an individual both submits to social norms and reworks identity and resists the same norms. When increasing numbers of women conform to and accommodate masculinity and femininity, the ideology of male supremacy and of pathetic femininity may be increasingly challenged. Yet a change in gender norms still requires participation. In the context of Japanese companies, many Japanese women still quit their jobs when they marry or have children or exit the "game" to become housewives. Some Japanese feminists even promoted such an exit as the way to free a woman from the male work norm. However, avoiding subjection and exiting the game will not help to change the rules of the game. I am not suggesting that gender biases and inequality can be combated by the efforts of individual men and women. I argue, instead, that ending sex segregation in Japanese companies will clearly require institutional and organizational reforms beyond the individual, even though the consequences of the existing gender structure are highly personal.

# THWARTED AMBITIONS AND SYMPATHY

## Long Working Hours, Sex Segregation, and the Price of Masculinity

In the previous chapter, we saw that working long hours is one of the core characteristics of heroic masculinity in Japan, a practice that allows men to demonstrate their willingness to sacrifice for their jobs and companies and women to be judged as unwilling and inferior workers.

The custom of working long hours, which is strongly tied to workers' sense of discipline, identity, and feeling of belonging to a company, has been integral to the workplace throughout the history of the modern state of Japan. It played an important role in Japan's economic survival and its eventual parity with the West after World War II by saving Japanese firms huge labor costs. Working long hours has been considered mandatory by most employers in exchange for giving their workers lifelong employment. Japanese laws have also upheld firms' demands for overtime work.

In this chapter I examine how the custom of working long hours reinforces sex segregation by dichotomizing women workers' career prospects and opportunities. I illuminate the overwork culture in Japanese companies, which in turn will help us grasp the similar organizational culture that exists in the United States, especially in the financial and high-tech sectors.

Working long hours negatively influences women workers' career aspirations and even increases their motivation to opt out. It often polarizes women's choices because the ideology of separate spheres places most family responsibility on the woman. Cultural legitimization of the separate-sphere ideology, combined with corporate emphasis on overwork as a cost-saving measure, continues to reward those who spend long hours in the workplace. This reinforces vertical sex segregation, in the forms of remasculinization of management and reinforcing the gap between working mothers and working fathers. Working long hours, as a form of workplace masculinity, also harms the health and family life of male workers and hurts the firms for which they work.

## Origins of Long Work Hours in Japan

Japanese workers have historically worked longer hours than workers in many OECD countries.[1] In 1980, annual hours worked were about 1,813 in the United States, 1,767 in the United Kingdom, and 2,121 in Japan (table 6.1). Due to international pressure, Japan's annual working hours dropped to 1,821 by 2000 and 1,775—fewer than the 1,799 hours worked in the United States—by 2005. But even though these numbers make it seem as if the average work hours of employees in Japan have decreased dramatically, scholars are cautious about official statistics, as they do not reflect the reality for ordinary Japanese workers.[2] The statistics conceal a large amount of unpaid overtime "service," common in Japanese companies: this can reach up to 100 hours per month.[3] The overall average also fails to reflect the long hours of full-time workers, as the data include the hours worked by large numbers of part-time female workers.[4]

Whereas the average worker works fewer hours in Japan than in the United States, the number of employees who work long hours is higher in Japan. In 2012, the latest year for which there is available data, 22 percent of employed workers worked over 50 or more hours per week in Japan, while about 11 percent of employed workers worked over 50 or more hours per week in the United States (table 6.2). More specifically, statistics compiled by the Japan Institute for Labour Policy and Training show that about 39 percent of employed men and 18 percent of employed women in Japan worked more than 49 hours a week in 1995, and about 26 percent of men and 10 percent of women in the United

**TABLE 6.1**  Average annual hours actually worked per worker

|         | 1970  | 1980  | 1985  | 1990  | 1995  | 2000  | 2005  | 2010  | 2013  |
|---------|-------|-------|-------|-------|-------|-------|-------|-------|-------|
| Japan   | 2,243 | 2,121 | 2,093 | 2,031 | 1,884 | 1,821 | 1,775 | 1,733 | 1,735 |
| U.S.    | 1,902 | 1,813 | 1,836 | 1,831 | 1,844 | 1,836 | 1,799 | 1,777 | 1,788 |
| Germany | n/a   | n/a   | n/a   | n/a   | 1,529 | 1,471 | 1,431 | 1,405 | 1,388 |
| U.K.    | 1,937 | 1,767 | 1,760 | 1,765 | 1,731 | 1,700 | 1,673 | 1,652 | 1,669 |

*Source:* OECD, StatExtracts, "Average annual hours actually worked per worker."

*Note:* Per OECD, "For West Germany, data prior to 1991 have been revised by the Institut für Arbeitsmarkt- und Berufsforschung (IAB)," thus complete data for Germany prior to 1991 are not available.

**TABLE 6. 2**   Percentage of employees working fifty hours or more a week on average in 2012

|  | PERCENTAGE OF EMPLOYEES WORKING FIFTY HOURS OR MORE A WEEK |
|---|---|
| Japan | 22.3 |
| Korea | 18.7 |
| U.S. | 12.7 |
| U.K. | 11.3 |
| Germany | 5.2 |
| Sweden | 1.1 |

*Source:* OECD, Better Life Index, 2015.

States worked more than 49 hours a week in 1995.[5] The ratio of men and women working long hours in Japan did not change much from 1995 to 2011. About 39 percent of employed men and 20 percent of employed women in Japan worked more than 50 hours per week in 2011, while about 16 percent of employed men and 7 percent of employed women in the United States worked over 50 hours weekly that year.[6]

With the rise of the modern Japanese state in the nineteenth century, the custom of long working hours was instilled in the minds of the Japanese public as an aspect of nationalism. The Meiji state mandated long working hours, using slogans like "Catch up with and surpass the Western counterparts" and "Enrich the country, strengthen the military." Since the postwar period, a strong nationalist sentiment for economic development has dominated the Japanese public and private discourse of work. The chief of the Ministry of Health, Labour and Welfare expressed his ambivalence about an initiative to reduce work hours in 1992 by referring to Kinjiro Ninomiya, a national legend of the nineteenth century, whose hard work and "selfless servitude to the state" (*messhi houkou*) allowed him, formerly a poor peasant, to become a wealthy landowner.[7] An attitude of selflessness and devotion remains integral to the practice of overwork in Japan.

Before World War II, Japanese employees worked close to 3,300 hours a year;[8] it was only after 1947, when the United States forced the Labor Standards Act on the Japanese, that Japan's average went down to 2,000 hours a year.[9] Whereas the Labor Standards Act initially established a six-day, 48-hour work week, it was amended to a five-day, 40-hour week in 1987.[10] By 1998, the Labor Standards Act was also amended to enable the Minister of Health, Labour and Welfare to intervene to limit overtime hours to a maximum of 360 per year.[11]

Today, Japan's full-time work day is eight hours. Yet in 2006, over 60 percent of employees worked more than ten hours daily, and one in three male workers in their thirties and forties worked about twelve hours per day.[12] The same data also report that 40 percent of workers were not compensated for their overtime. In addition to their actual working hours, employed male workers reported a national average daily commute to work of one hour and ten minutes; employed women reported a commute of fifty minutes.[13] In 2004, while full-time workers in Japan were given 18 vacation days on average per year, they took off only 8.4 days.[14]

Some argue that the increase in the number of temporary workers since the mid-1980s might have contributed to the reduction in working hours of regular employees.[15] However, others point out that the average Japanese employee's work hours changed little from 1986 to 2006.[16] (And, in fact, another statistic backs up this claim: total sleeping hours have decreased by about four hours among men and three hours among women in the last thirty years.) This suggests that both men and women workers in Japan may face greater time pressures than ever before.

Regardless of the reduction in *legal* working hours in the 1990s, incidents of *karoshi* and *karo-jisatsu* remain common in Japan. *Karoshi* is death caused by cerebral or cardiac disease, and *karo-jisatsu* refers to a suicide or attempted suicide due to a mental disorder or depression caused by overwork.[17] Those who commit *karo-jisatsu* typically have been working extremely long hours with enormous responsibility, taking no holidays, managing a heavy workload, and enduring pressure to attain difficult goals.[18] It is estimated that more than ten thousand workers in Japan die annually as a result of cerebral or cardiac disease caused by work overload.[19] In the 1980s, the Ministry of Health, Labour and Welfare was initially reluctant to hold employers responsible for *karoshi* (rather, explaining it as an individual health problem), but eventually it changed, and the number of *karoshi* and *karo-jisatsu* cases approved by the ministry for payment under Workers' Accident Compensation soared between the late 1990s and 2006.[20] Between 2006 and 2010, the number of *karoshi* cases approved for payment decreased slightly, from 355 to 285 (with fewer than half of the submitted cases being approved), but the number of *karo-jisatsu* cases approved increased from 205 to 308 during the same period.[21]

## Overwork and Labor-Cost Adjustment

Working long hours in Japanese firms has been a cost-adjustment solution for employers and has also provided workers with the "security of tenure and flexibility of working conditions."[22] Under the flexicurity system, in exchange for lifelong economic security, employees are expected to work for lower-than-market wages in the early stages of their careers and to retire early when labor is in oversupply.[23] In a good economy, a firm can ask that existing workers work extra hours to avoid hiring new employees. But, during an economic downturn, firms cannot fire their workers and may also have to freeze new hires.

> Beginning with a series of cases in the 1950s, Japanese courts regulated the employment market to such an extent that it became practically impossible for most businesses, or at least large ones, to fire workers. As a consequence of the inability to dismiss workers legally, large Japanese firms hired a smaller number of workers than were necessary. Large employers rely on the working hours of this undersized cadre of workers, carefully screened to rule out the slothful, as a buffer. In bad times, the size of the work force makes dismissal unnecessary. In good times, workers are forced to work long hours. . . .[24]

Further,

> The law ensures security by vesting employees with a general right against unjust dismissal; it promotes flexibility by arming employers with the flexibility to alter working conditions, effect internal rotations and external transfers, build a casual workforce, and control working times.[25]

Japanese courts have also made it difficult for employers to lay off regular workers. The courts have ordered that a dismissal must have "reasonable grounds" and be acceptable "in light of social norms"; otherwise, the dismissal can be deemed an abuse of the worker's rights.[26] Even though the Labor Standards Act does not disapprove of dismissals, the Japanese courts have created norms that reinforce employers' avoidance of employee layoffs.[27] For example, the Osaka district court deemed the 1990s Sanyo Electric Company's dismissal of 1,200 regular workers invalid due to the company's insufficient efforts to avoid dismissal and it's not having made the option of voluntary resignation available.[28] At the same time, the courts have promoted the view that employees' overwork is an obligation. The Japanese Supreme Court's 1991 Hitachi decision "affirmed the validity of the dismissal of an employee who declined a request to work overtime" and "held that the overtime provision was a result of the management-labor bargain, and that the company thus was authorized to request overtime work."[29] The absence of government intervention has further perpetuated the unstated condition of overwork in exchange for employment security. It is not surprising, then, that the idea of working long hours has become the norm in Japanese workplaces, even for employees who do not work with a guarantee of lifelong economic security.

Even though firms currently are supposed to pay a rate of 125 percent of a worker's wages for extra working hours, they can avoid this extra labor cost by arranging a "discretionary work agreement" with the workers. Under a discretionary work schedule, workers and their employer reach an agreement in advance regarding the employees' work hours. Even when the actual work hours are high, they are calculated based on the execution of given duties and accomplishment of tasks.[30] Discretionary work hours can be applicable to a variety of tasks and positions, ranging from managerial planning to personnel, accounting, finances, sales, and production. The criteria for the adoption of discretionary work hours are broad enough to make it difficult to draw a line between jobs for which the discretionary scheme is applicable and jobs for which it is not. A firm can also avoid paying overtime to a worker when he or she carries an official management title.[31] The problem is that an employee might be promoted to a managerial position in name only so as to have to work long hours without overtime pay.[32]

Japanese firms have long attempted to adopt US-style white-collar exemptions, in which employees in particular positions—such as executive, administrative, professional, computer, and outside sales jobs—and who are paid at least $455 per week are exempt from earning overtime pay.[33] In Japan, the business community supports the adoption of the white-collar exemption for workers whose income exceeds $40,000 or so, but it faces opposition from labor unions.[34] There has been concern that the adoption of this custom would almost certainly "aggravate occupational health problems, including depression and suicide due to crushing workloads, yet make forced overwork more difficult to prove."[35]

When the law reduced work hours from 48 hours a week in 1987 to 40 hours a week (finalized in 1997), this increased employers' overwork payments. This cost increase for employers made them reluctant to hire new workers and contributed to further stagnation of the economy, with an increase in the unemployment rate and a deepening of the Japanese recession.[36] All evidence points to the advisability of Japanese firms not relying exclusively on employees' long work hours but, rather, exploring alternatives to getting work done, such as enhancing productivity or hiring more workers. The Japanese government and business community, however, are moving in the opposite direction, emulating the United States.

In April 2015, the Japanese Cabinet finalized a proposal to exempt those who earn over $100,000 (10,750,000 yen), including stock dealers and financial managers, from Japan's Labor Standards Act, which mandates that employers pay extra for work that exceeds 8 hours per day and 40 hours per week, as in the United States; such individuals won't be paid based on their work hours but instead by their completion of tasks.[37] The cabinet plans to start the new system in April 2016. The use of discretionary work without pay is currently limited to managers and planners in an office, but this new law will be expanded to sales and plant workers when they do quality control–related jobs. Unions have expressed concern that the new law will further worsen the overwork situation and increase the number of deaths by overwork, while the business community welcomes the change as critical to enhancing the flexibility and efficiency of the workforce. The chief of the Ministry of Health, Labour and Welfare stressed that the change will enhance business productivity as well as workers' motivation and creativity, which, he claims, are necessary in Japan because of the globalization of the economy. But long work hours continue to perpetuate the system of self-sacrificing corporate masculinity, which contributes to men's health problems and worsens sex segregation and the gender divide in Japanese companies.

## Changes in the Culture of Overwork

The workers I talked with mentioned that, before 2000, they worked every day until midnight or even later but that such extreme overwork had become less common. However, regardless of these large firms' recent official reductions in long work hours, the overwork norm remained dominant in all five firms.

Many workers I talked to, both male and female, stayed at work until 8, 9, or 10 p.m. daily. They said leaving the workplace earlier is not often an option, either because of the large amount of work they have to do or because of workplace pressure not to leave before 8 p.m. Some managers also worked extra hours at home every day. The recent policy changes regarding reductions in work hours are not substantial enough to encourage workers or managers to actually spend more time with their families.

A couple of years before my interviews in 2007, two firms that I studied started forcing workers to leave work at 9 or 10 p.m. by shutting down their computers and closing the office buildings. Two of the other firms also explicitly counseled workers to avoid excessive overwork. But it made little difference, at least to the career-track workers and managers who, in the financial firms, stayed until the buildings were closed and thus still worked excessively long hours. (The non-career-track workers and temp workers usually left work by 6, and some workers who were mothers left work around 4.)

At Daigo Life Insurance in 2002, the firm started shutting down workers' computers and closing buildings at 10 p.m. and then, in 2005, changed the shutdown time to an hour earlier. Also, many workers in the firm had begun work around 6 or 7 a.m. in the past, but the firm disabled workers' use of the computers until 8 a.m. in order to discourage them from working extra hours in the morning. The men and women career-track workers at Daigo Life Insurance whom I interviewed, therefore, usually arrived at work around 8 in the morning and stayed until 9 p.m.—still a thirteen-hour work day, on average.

Takashi, a thirty-seven-year-old manager in the financial investment section at Daigo Life Insurance, started his work day at 7:30 a.m. and left around 9 p.m.

"I used to work on Sunday and Saturday until a year ago," he said. Since spending long hours at work is an important part of a man's identity, the work-hour reduction might seem to threaten men's sense of belonging to the firm. In fact, a few male workers did comment negatively about the firm's overwork regulations. Takashi said, "You know, I and even young men in my section are sacrificing our private and family lives for our company. I feel that I cannot be without this company. . . . That's why this work-hour reduction thing is extremely frustrating. . . . It is just very constraining to us. I feel like I cannot work whenever I want to." Another manager, this one forty-two years old, also complained: "I don't know why they are reducing the work hours. When I started working at this company in 1989, we used to sleep at our desks."

Conversely, there were some men who welcomed the work-hour reduction because they found themselves spending more time with their families at home. A forty-one-year-old manager told me it was such a big change to leave the workplace at 9; until six years before our interview, he never left work before 10. And he commuted between the office and home for a total of about three hours every day.

> I would never leave work at 10 in the past, you know. I would arrive at home around 11:30 or midnight. I would go to bed and wake up at 6 every day. I worked every weekend. Never missed a day, every weekday and every weekend day. Working long hours was seen as a great thing. Staying late was seen as a sign of effort and commitment. . . . Now, I leave here at 7 p.m. and arrive at home at 8:30. I go home to see my daughter. I cannot see my daughter if I can't make it home until 9 in the evening. So I leave work no later than 7.

He was the only person, among all the career-track workers at Daigo Life Insurance whom I interviewed, who left the workplace at 7 p.m., since the normal quitting time was between 8 and 9. The fact that he was an established longtime middle manager might have made his leaving early relatively more acceptable. Few men told me that they left the office before 8, but some men did say that they made a far more conscious effort to spend time with their family than in the past. A forty-two-year-old male manager said, "On Saturday, I often have to golf with our clients. If I don't have to, I try to spend all day with my daughter in the park and pool so that my wife can take a short break from child rearing. . . . I usually golf all day on Sunday, though." Many managerial men whom I talked with, across all the firms, still spent some of their time on weekends finishing work or attending work-related events; they spoke about their few hours of family time as extremely valuable and something they never had in the past. A thirty-seven-year-old manager proudly described his effort to be an available father:

I am very different from my father, who was a very busy salaryman. I don't remember anything about playing with my father. There was always only my mother at home. It seems like my father was just absent in my childhood. . . . But I am different. I spend much more time with my kids. . . . When we drink, we compete with other guys over the competence and smartness of our kids. This one guy's five-year-old kid is just so smart. He said his kid can associate national flags with the capitals of the countries that they are from. He is teaching this to his kid when he gives him baths. I've got to do something to win.

Meanwhile, many younger workers at Daigo Life Insurance said it was hard for them to leave the workplace before 8 or 9 p.m. A twenty-seven-year-old female area-career-track worker said, "Even when I finish my job before 9, it is difficult to leave early because many others still stay. I try not to pay too much attention to it and just go home. Or I try to help those who haven't finished." A twenty-four-year-old career-track worker said. "I have to come up with some excuse even when I leave at 7. It has to be at least 8, for some reason. The company still values our working long hours. There is no way you can just leave at 5."

In addition, the career-track women and men at Daigo Life Insurance continue to be expected to spend no more than fifteen minutes eating lunch. A twenty-seven-year-old female area-career-track worker said:

> Career-track men and women go to lunch and take only fifteen minutes to eat. That is considered a virtue in this company. . . . Since our office has no cubicles, I can see what is going on with other people. . . . One time, all four men in one section went to lunch together in the cafeteria. The boss in that section was not able to find any of them when he needed some help with data analysis, and he was furious that he had no subordinates around. After fifteen minutes, they all came back from lunch. The boss yelled at them, "I told you over and over not to go to lunch together!" These four guys just kept apologizing to their boss. They were not even allowed to ask why their boss needed them so urgently or how important the data was.

The long-held negativity toward workers who leave early continues to be dominant at Daigo Life Insurance. Takako, a thirty-five-year-old female manager, found that her evaluations got worse after she left work early for a year due to her mother's illness: "My father's business went into bankruptcy. My mother was severely ill and depressed. I had to take care of them. I had to go home early, around 5:30 or 6. I know everybody thought it was too early. But I had to do this for a year or so. I talked with my boss, and I thought he approved it and that it was OK. But it wasn't OK. My evaluation during that time went down. I thought they understood my situation." Also, even though some of the workers whom I interviewed in the Tokyo office of Daigo Life Insurance may have left around 8 or 9, the managers in the local branches left their workplaces closer to midnight because of the different types of tasks that they had to perform, involving more face-to-face interactions with individual clients.

Like other firms I studied, Daigo Life Insurance had started encouraging workers to request partial overtime pay. However, such requests are understood by the workers to be acceptable only rarely. A twenty-nine-year-old worker said, "Well, nobody actually really requests overtime pay. Even if we stay until 10, we request only one hour or, at most, two hours. That's what everybody does . . . especially when you are still new to the job, learning or getting training to do the job, you just feel bad about requesting overtime when it is part of your training. . . . The MHLW does check overtime pay, so the company encourages workers to request it. We get paid about 3,000 yen per hour." At Daigo Life Insurance, only the workers in their twenties, whose years of service do not exceed eight, are allowed to request overtime payments. A forty-two-year-old manager explained it to me: "It is like a white-collar exemption. In our ninth year, we come to be regarded as *jisyu kanrisou,* or "self-management"–type workers, and just work until 9 o'clock with no extra pay all the time. We cannot get any extra pay for overwork. Some of us also work on weekends with no such pay, of course." Many workers at Daigo Life Insurance may leave the workplace earlier than before, but they also said they have off-site drinking meetings about three times or more a week, so they do not return home until around midnight on those days.

The workers I talked with at Daigo Life Insurance also took very few vacation days. One twenty-seven-year-old non-career-track worker said she was explicitly told by her boss not to take any days off. She said the non-career-track female workers also overwork, even though they do fewer hours than career-track workers. She said, "I work from 8:30 to 6 every day. Even though you can leave with the bosses' approval after 4:50, I always leave at 6. We do overtime sometimes until 7. But if you are a non-career-track worker, you can't request overtime payments beyond fifty hours in three months."

Hanakage Cosmetics initiated a curfew announcement and security check in the buildings after 9 or 10 p.m., and at that time the workers are warned to leave for home. The workers at Hanakage also reported that their leaving by 9, instead of midnight or 1 a.m., has been a huge change that took place just a couple of years before my interviews. A twenty-eight-year-old woman laughed and said, "I leave work around 9 p.m., much earlier than before. I used to go home by taxi around 1 a.m. every day . . . but still, I am usually away in China and Hong Kong at least two weeks every month. My life just has a way-too-irregular schedule."

Much like those at Daigo Life Insurance, the employees at Hanakage could ask for some pay for overtime work. A twenty-nine-year-old female worker in marketing at Hanakage said:

> When I started my job in this company, I used to work past midnight, often until 1 a.m., every day until February 2006. No Saturdays and Sundays. It was just normal in the marketing section. Now, it is so much better as I can leave at 9. . . . For overtime pay, I can't ask for more than 120 hours in three months. That means two hours every day or 40 hours monthly. They pay 2,000 yen per hour. That is about 80,000 yen every month. I guess it is better than nothing.

The workers at Takane Cosmetics similarly mentioned 40 hours per month (or 120 hours in three months) as the maximum number they could request for overwork pay. A thirty-nine-year-old male researcher at Takane said the managers are not happy to see the increased overtime pay requests: "I don't know about the other sections or branches of Takane, as I am talking about only my research section. . . . I work from 8 a.m. to 8 or 9 p.m. daily. I request about 30 hours of overtime every month. We get noticed if we request more than 40 hours of overtime pay per month."

The workers at Hanakage thought that overtime hours had been reduced but argued that a shorter stay at work does not necessarily mean shorter work hours. A thirty-nine-year-old male manager at Hanakage said, "Nowadays, those who work overtime are more likely to be seen as incompetent or as unable to manage their time. The last two years, we have been expected to leave here at 10 o'clock. But the amount of work remains the same or even greater. I also have at least two to three business trips every month. I seem to be doing more work either at home or somewhere else, even though I leave the workplace earlier than before." The idea of getting work done in a shorter time also means workers taking fewer vacations days. He continued, "I have to tell people not to take vacation time; otherwise their overtime work may increase. My boss complains if he sees that I am letting those who do overtime work also take vacation time. He may think that such people are not doing their jobs efficiently. . . . I feel bad when I have to tell those who work overtime to cut more hours and not to take days off." In the past, workers were allowed to spend as much time as they wanted to in order to get their work done, but now they are pressured to achieve the same outcome in a shorter amount of time.

At Takane, the work-hour norm varied depending on the employee's division or section. Researchers at Takane said they usually work from 8 in the morning until 8 or 9 in the evening. Some requested thirty hours' overtime pay per month, as they would be warned if they report over forty hours. Others in the consumer product section said the workers in that section leave around 6, much earlier than those in other sections, since many in that section are mothers.

Most workers I talked with stayed at the workplace for long hours because of heavy workloads, peer pressure, and a sense of obligation to get the work done so that they would not delay coworkers' completion of tasks. Yuri, a twenty-nine-year-old who works in marketing at Hanakage, said, "We can take a maximum of twenty days off per year. But I never take more than a few days off. I don't like to get behind. I just cannot ask other people because I feel very bad missing a day. In my section, I cannot ignore or belittle my relationships with other workers. We feel *such* an obligation to each other. This sense of obligation and responsibility are at the center of our work relationships." It appears that some group-oriented or teamwork-oriented aspects of organizational culture might make it even more difficult for workers to leave early or take time off. But, for the most part, it is the longstanding expectation and tradition of long work hours that makes it hard for workers to leave early, while still offering many workers, particularly male workers, a sense of identity and belonging to the firm.

## Long Work Hours and Vertical Sex Segregation

Looking at research on the US workplace, Youngjoo Cha concluded that overwork (fifty or more hours of work per week) is a cause of occupational segregation and workplace gender inequality, because women in a workplace that values overwork are more likely to be evaluated poorly, less likely to receive opportunities for promotion, and more likely to leave their jobs than men.[38] The women, especially those who are mothers, suffer from a "penalty for deviating from the norm."[39] She points out two ways in which the overwork norm reinforces occupational sex segregation in the US workplace: (1) the anticipation of overwork discourages women from entering into male-dominated jobs; and (2) the time demands at work intensify work-family conflicts.[40] The overwork norm reinforces gender biases against women and mothers as being less committed to work and inferior to men (even though single women can be exempt from such biases), reifies the unequal power dynamics in the office, and legitimizes employers' discriminatory hiring and promotion customs. The combination of the overwork custom and gender biases makes it hard for women to attain positions, power, and recognition similar to those of male workers. Also, as Cha noted, women's anticipation of overwork not only discourages them from entering male-dominated occupations but also leads them to stay in less-demanding positions. Indeed, Naomi Cassirer and Barbara Reskin argue that men's longer working hours exacerbate the gender gap in men's and women's promotion aspirations.[41] Men's longer hours may derive from the greater rewards men get from work or the workplace culture that rewards overwork, but it may also be that long working hours lowers women's aspirations and increase their pessimism about their career opportunities.

The custom of working long hours also serves as a corporate surveillance system that reinforces inequalities and insecurities among managers.[42] Engaging in overtime work is not a voluntary behavior on the part of the individual but a "stated policy" of the leadership that serves as a major means of control and assessment of workers.[43] Many organizations are deeply wedded to the ideology of separate spheres, reinforcing "the gendered divide between paid work and unpaid family reproductive work, consigning the latter, and women, to a subordinated and devalued position."[44] This assumption about the separate spheres promotes men's acting on their machismo or heroic identity to gain recognition that is valuable to their survival at work and encourages women toward following traditional femininity.[45]

In Japanese firms, the managers continue to work long hours. David Collinson and Margaret Collinson write that the imperative of long working hours may lead to a "remasculinization of management in which women managers at all hierarchical levels will only survive if they follow the example of most of their male counterparts and subordinate home and family to company and career."[46] Remasculinization of management occurs when the workplace incorporates women who work hours that are equal to those of men, or even longer. Under the explicit demands of the long-work-hour norm, women are expected to endure pressure from two sources: (1) the pressure to emulate the male work norm, and (2) the pressure to remain fully responsible for the home and family. It is probably inevitable that the women in such a workplace culture will resort to one of two distinctly different strategies: either following the male overwork model or choosing the less-demanding option of leaving work.

A workplace is masculinized when the workers engage in overwork and reinforce gender biases against those who don't work long hours. The men in management positions may reaffirm the importance of long work hours by engaging in "boundary-heightening" behavior,[47] in which workers identify overwork as a sign of commitment and power. Williams argues that denying oneself sleep, regardless of how it may contribute to lowered productivity, becomes a test of physical endurance and thus a way to prove masculine superiority.[48]

With the remasculinization of management, the workplace that values overwork often holds up the image of the ideal worker as an example, one that is not reconcilable with the image of the caretaker. Workers who are mothers thus can be seen as the opposite of the ideal worker. A woman who wishes to combine the caretaker role with her role as a worker may face a "motherhood penalty," or negative stereotyping for being less than competent and not suitably committed to paid work.[49] In one study of civil engineers it was noted that a pregnant woman was removed from a decision-making position and faced a promotion penalty.[50] For a working mother, family-oriented attitudes can be interpreted as "explicit withdrawal from the competition for power";[51] in contrast, men's career opportunities are not constrained by fatherhood.[52] Those women who take parental leave are mostly nonmanagerial women, not upper-level managers.[53] In order to avoid the sanctions associated with motherhood and to stay on a masculine career path, young women often choose to postpone maternity.[54] One study concluded that, for women managers in a bank, "motherhood would spell the end of their career," and promotions were synonymous with childlessness.[55]

Women managers' childlessness is so common that family-friendly or work-life balance policies have not been effective in reversing the trend.[56] Williams writes:

> Women who perform as ideal workers often have paid a higher price than men for doing so: most either gave up having children or struggled with the dual demands of work and motherhood, facing daily challenges and abiding fears that they were being "bad mothers." . . . Many of these women have a lot invested in the view that being an ideal worker is what the job takes: otherwise, why did they sacrifice having children or having time with them?[57]

Yet women who make it to the top by emulating masculinity face other negative stereotypes, such as having "lost their femininity" or being "cutthroat, thrusting and ruthless."[58] As neither balancing two roles nor committing to the ideal worker role is easy in the overwork-driven workplace, overwork customs may promote women's taking a less demanding position or opting out, choosing the caretaker role over the ideal worker role. In a study of professional women who quit their jobs to become homemakers, Pamela Stone writes, "That work and family were incompatible was the overwhelming message [women] took from their experiences."[59] Also, among dual-earner professional couples, spousal overwork increases a woman's likelihood of quitting her job.[60] If she wants to keep the caretaker role, has few financial concerns, and sees more gender obstacles in the workplace, she may see her effort to balance work and family as not worthwhile and become convinced that opting out is a more reasonable choice.

## Men and Women in Middle Management

Men and women in various positions—including managers, career-track workers, non-career-track female workers, young women workers, and working mothers—have differently accommodated the custom of working long hours, and accommodations by women managers have differed from those of men and disadvantaged women, thus perpetuating vertical sex segregation at work. Overwork becomes a benchmark for women's attainment, even though the ways in which women experience the resulting pressures and sanctions differ depending on their positions in the hierarchy as well as on their parental status. In the 1990s, most middle-level managers, who are normally in their mid- to late thirties, worked overtime on a daily basis, often until midnight. They held the view that working long hours was necessary for completing their given tasks and also an indicator of their commitment. Whereas the large Japanese firms implemented informal rules regarding overwork reduction after the 1990s, managers at the upper levels continued to work long hours, which they viewed as necessary to bolstering their formal and informal power, status, and recognition. This masculinized management custom has also been followed by women managers.

Most male managers I talked to had wives who took full responsibility for the family, and therefore they stayed at work until 9 or 10 p.m. daily and often worked on the weekends. Koji, a forty-six-year-old middle manager at Takane, said, "There is really no work-life balance for me. . . . I arrive at work at 8:30 a.m. and stay until 10 or 11 p.m. . . . I go to the office and do work on Saturdays to prepare for meetings on Mondays." Takashi, a thirty-seven-year-old middle manager at Hanakage, said, "On average, I work from 8:30 a.m. to 9 p.m. daily. I used to leave about midnight or later by taxi until early 2000. This was because in the late 1990s and early 2000s, my firm froze new hires, and the amount of work just surged. . . . The bosses keep giving us job after job. It was not until last year that I could start going home around 8 or 9 p.m." Takashi also saw himself as having no life outside of work: "Work takes quite a large part of my life. I am not separating my private life from work very well. My life is actually all about the work, and I feel like I am only taking short breaks between work. . . . I think I am kind of old-school Japanese, as I feel I live for the company, I mean for the consumers and products." Men's overwork and their idea of self-sacrifice is strongly tied to their sense of belonging to the company; in the 1980s such men were referred to as "corporate warriors" in Japan. Many middle-management men, even today, still have this sense of themselves. Workers' emotional ties to the firm, through this sense of belonging or even subordination to the firm, make the overtime custom very difficult to change.

The notion of corporate warriors may be outdated, but many Japanese workers continue to see their firm as more than an employer: it is an entity that offers them a sense of community and belonging. A thirty-eight-year-old male general manager at Mikado Bank said, ambivalently, "My generation is in transition. Some still devote their lives to the company. . . . I am not working for the money. I am working for what I want to do. I am having fun, so it is more for myself, for self-realization." Many men I talked to continue to legitimize their overwork as an aspect of their loyalty and commitment to the job itself, to the firm, or as a path to a higher self. In this light, overwork takes the form of a heroic sacrifice, and there is a certain religiosity in the compulsive adherence and commitment that workers have to it.[61]

Engaging in overwork is a method of displaying masculine identity; a man can demonstrate his competence through physical and mental endurance. Eiji, a thirty-eight-year-old general manager in mergers and acquisitions at Mikado Bank, leaves work after midnight and arrives home by taxi around 2 a.m. Like other men, he complained about his firm's new policy of shutting down the building to force workers to leave, even though he himself has not been influenced by this as he turns in paperwork to his boss for permission to stay late. He pays two-thirds of his taxi fees between work and home out of his own pocket because he has to miss the last commuter train. He said:

> Recently, the company has been forced to close the building early. I think this is silly. I often hear stupid comments such as, "I can work more efficiently when I leave early." This is ridiculous. If you work efficiently during the day, you can also do so in the evening. . . . I know some guys who are forced to leave the building, but they go to a karaoke room and work there. . . . There is nobody who goes home at 6 in my section. Are you kidding me? Stupid. What kind of work did you do today if you can leave that early? . . . If the baseball player Ichiro says, "I don't practice after 5," that would be stupid. It is the same in our situation.

Equating himself with the baseball player Ichiro, a masculine hero whom he imagines to be stoically committed to his profession with no life outside, Eiji emphasized overwork as an imperative of professionals. He proudly described his extremely short sleeping hours and extremely long working hours as a necessary sacrifice for the ideal investment banker to make: "For me, full time doesn't mean from 9 to 5, but from 9 to midnight. . . . I haven't slept much the last two to three years. I arrive home between 12 and 2 a.m., go to bed by 4 a.m. at the latest, and get up at 7 to go to work. . . . I think a man can function when he sleeps three hours." Working long hours also includes maneuvering in the informal business culture for the profit of the firm after regular working hours. Eiji's working hours extend to very late in the evening because he goes out with his clients: "You have to go to drink, paying from your own pocket all the time. It is wrong to assume that you can convince clients in the office. . . . Those who really contribute to the company need to sacrifice themselves in certain ways." Going out with clients after work is a custom of the male-centered business culture, where informal business events and deals frequently take place through the mediation of alcohol, food, and sexual entertainment late into the evening.

Many male managers attended drinking meetings at least a couple of times per week as an extension of their regular work to engage in business networking or in some cases just to hang out casually with colleagues. Many men and women viewed their attendance at these drinking meetings as critically important to their future promotions, recognition, and even survival at work. Yet, compared to the women I interviewed, the men attended these events more often and valued them more highly. Drinking in Japanese companies not only enhances workers' bonds but serves as a lubricant for easing social constraints among workers in the rigid status hierarchy that exists in society and in business. In other words, drinking allows one to be "oneself" after hours.

A thirty-seven-year-old attorney and manager at Shijo Asset Management told me he worked daily from 8 a.m. to 2 a.m. and at least one day on the weekend. He expressed confidence that he would soon be promoted, as he is successful in his career. He said he has "been pretty much in the center of everything at Shijo Asset Management." He says his overwork is necessary to "motivate his colleagues and subordinates. Among all the financial firms in Japan, Shijo is the most demanding firm. It is very difficult to survive here. You have to be fun and entertain the team all the time. If you can't do that for them, they won't like you. So I always take my subordinates to drink after work. We end up staying at the bar until 4 a.m. I need to cheer up my group and keep my section positive."

The middle-level male managers in Japanese firms described their daily overwork as a necessary sacrifice, an obligation to the larger organization, a test of physical and mental endurance, a realization of their masculine selves, and an opportunity for recognition and leadership. By bolstering their power and prestige in this way, the managers reinforce the culture of masculinity both in management and in the workplace culture overall.[62]

How do women managers respond to or accommodate this overwork custom? As Collinson and Collinson point out, "remasculinization of management" signifies that women can break into the organizational hierarchy or managerial positions only when they emulate their male counterparts by subordinating their family and private lives to their work lives;[63] thus, the middle-level women managers I interviewed were often unmarried and childless. Eight out of twelve women managers in the five firms did not have children, and five were not married. Some single women managers were reluctant to marry. Only a couple of women managers with children had managed to curtail their overwork after the births of their children.

Most female middle-level managers, except for those who were mothers, viewed long work hours as inevitable and necessary for getting their scheduled work done. Some were explicit about the difficulty of having both a family and work, or they mentioned the necessity of subordinating private life to work. A thirty-eight-year-old manager, Tami, at Daigo Life Insurance said:

> I think it is stupid that the media sells the image of this company as woman friendly. . . . I can devote 100 to 120 percent to the company because I am single. I would not have been able to do what I do now if I were married. . . . I don't really care about work-family balance. Balancing work and family is not possible. You can't work as a branch manager and have a family. . . . When I was the branch manager in a local office, I would stay until 12 or 1 a.m. We saw taking clients out, who were usually the presidents of midsize firms, as very important. We needed to go out drinking, playing golf, and all that. Then, as a branch manager, you deal with the sales staff, and they wanted to talk with me after work. I needed to be there for them. I never left at 5.

Tami's work schedule as a branch manager reminds us of what the male manager at Mikado Bank said about the true meaning of full-time work: from 9 to midnight, not 9 to 5. If the workers are expected to work a 9 to midnight schedule, Tami's view of the impossibility of having a family makes absolute sense:

> Women can do some desk or computer work easily. No problem. But not be a branch manager who is required to deal with clients and salespeople. . . . If I married and had children, I would ask for only 60 or 70 percent of my salary. Because married women are different and can't do the same work. . . . It is ridiculous that they only do 60 percent of what we do and they want to get paid the same salary. I believe that women really feel entitled or take advantage of a company that tries to be known as "woman friendly."

Tami attained a superb sales record, earned about $50 million every month for her firm as a branch manager, moved to the Tokyo office, and managed nine subordinates as a middle manager. She went out for drinks with her bosses and colleagues every night. She loved hanging out with them, as she respected them, even though she was the only woman among them. "I wish I had a housewife. I really want someone to wash my clothes and cook food for me!" she said. She was busy on weekends playing golf with her colleagues. In our interview, she repeated several times that it is impossible for someone to have both a job and family and do it perfectly. She was one of the few women managers I spoke to who devoted so much of herself to her work.

Some woman managers were concerned that their busy work life would not be reconcilable with marital life. Shizuka, a thirty-eight-year-old female manager of the securities section at Mikado Bank, had lived with her parents all her life. "I used to work until 1 or 2, sometimes 3 in the morning," she reported. "Once the stock market opens in other countries, and it is almost midnight here in Tokyo, it is just hard to leave work." She had postponed marriage to her boyfriend of over ten years who was also a corporate worker. She expressed ambivalence about "balancing" her job and marriage. She said, "I want to marry and have a baby. . . . But I am not sure if I will be able to maintain a marriage with this job."

Although most women managers whom I interviewed in the five firms did not have children, a few did. Two of the women with children had given birth in their late thirties. It was not uncommon for a woman to choose family over work because of exhaustion over masculine competition. Maki, a thirty-eight-year-old female manager at Mikado Bank, said she had never thought about having a baby. She used to work every day until midnight, but her health deteriorated until she requested a transfer from Tokyo to another branch where she could finish her job two or three hours earlier than in Tokyo. When she eventually came back to headquarters in Tokyo, she said, she decided to have a baby at the age of thirty-five: "I felt I had reached the limitations of my career. It was just that I felt I could not compete with younger, talented men any more. This drove me in the direction of wanting to have a child and a family. . . . After the birth of my baby, I made a huge effort to get things done by 5." For her, the exhaustion and sense of resignation at work drove her to curtail her long working hours and start a family. She said, "Since I got the title of deputy general manager, I can assign tasks to others. I just call people in other sections and ask them to do the work. . . . I have very little pressure. I just check outcomes." Her comments indicate that a woman might be able to prioritize her family over her job, but only when she remains in a management position so that she can leave early with little pressure.

Despite her promotion to middle manager and the birth of her child, Keiko, a thirty-seven-year-old employee at Shijo Asset Management, continued working long hours. She said most workers in her section—the human resources office—worked over one hundred extra hours every month. She said, "You are not given this job unless you work like a man." Keiko normally worked until 10 or 11 p.m. daily. She managed her dual roles of manager and mother by arranging to leave early (at 8 o'clock) twice a week to pick up her child from day care. When the firm became extremely busy in the spring, she could not leave the workplace at 8, even twice a week, so she often asked her mother to stay at her home to take care of her child. Keiko's mother's stays with Keiko and her family sometimes for more than three months. Without her, Keiko would have no way to keep working long hours (as late as midnight) every day.

Keiko's husband came home as late as she did but had agreed to pick up their child once a week. Keiko commented that she needed a child-care facility that stayed open until midnight so that she could work overtime easily: "I never left the company early when I was pregnant. It was hard. . . . I did seventy hours of overtime every month during my pregnancy. . . . I had never seen any woman at work who had a child before. So I thought I should just keep pushing myself and work as much as I could. . . . I was not able to even stand up on weekends during my pregnancy. I should have taken more rest." She was often warned by her doctor about the high risk of premature birth. When she took her year of parental leave, a couple of male managers expressed their disapproval by ignoring her e-mails and phone calls. She said, "I took a year off after childbirth. . . . There was only one woman who took parental leave before me. Those men in their fifties acted like they were 'kindly offering' it to me and that they didn't need to be nice to a woman like me." Keiko mentioned that such overt hostility had greatly diminished by the time of our interviews, since an increasing number of women in the workplace were taking parental leave. As Kimoto found in men's hostile comments about women in her study of a general merchandise store (such as, "If you want to be accepted like the men in this company, then work like a dog"),[64] whether one works long hours or not demarcates gender boundaries and stereotypes. Working long hours seems to be more important than working efficiently and being productive in a given time. Keiko said, "My boss knows that I work hard. But he says he cannot ask certain tasks of me because I leave early." Some scholars point out that employers should pay more attention to workers' hourly productivity than to their daily productivity in evaluating them, since this could lead to a reduction in gender bias against women and working mothers.[65] Yet how can one measure productivity in such managerial tasks as dealing with stock, going out with clients, and informal networking after business hours? This will require further discussion.

A small number of women managers are incorporated into Japanese firms, but only when they successfully prioritize their jobs over their personal and family lives. Many remain childless, and some remain single, so that they can devote as much time to their work as men. Some women in their late thirties decide to have children after deciding to informally resign from the promotion race or when they decide they can manage a child with their parents' help. The ideology of separate spheres, in which women are expected to take full responsibility for the family and men only have to worry about their jobs, remains stable in Japan and is little questioned. Under the remasculinization of management, women are often the targets of suspicion and questions when they enter into a man's world; the culture of long working hours only intensifies such suspicion and continues to serve as a physical and mental test for those women who consider challenging the boundary between the sexes that exists in the Japanese workplace.

## Long Work Hours and Young Women's Aspirations

Cassirer and Reskin argue that men's longer working hours exacerbates the gender gap in men's and women's promotion aspirations.[66] This may be because the culture of overwork enhances men's aspirations as it rewards them for working long hours, yet lowers women's aspirations by increasing their awareness of family-work conflict. These "depressed aspirations" that many women experience are a response to their blocked opportunities. It is also known that women's blocked opportunities lead them to choose marriage and domesticity over work.[67] Thus, it is likely that women's low aspirations, resulting from anticipation and experiences of overwork, push them toward opting out. The overwork custom may therefore drive men and women further into the separate spheres of work and family.

Career-track hiring in Japanese firms, relegating many women to dead-end clerical positions with few opportunities for promotion, is known to be a major cause of sex segregation. This hiring system limits women's career paths by legitimizing "blocked opportunities" and women's "depressed aspirations."[68]

At Daigo Life Insurance, most non-career-track women I interviewed were elite college graduates with qualifications that were not inferior to those of the women who were career-track workers. Regardless of their educational backgrounds, none of these women wanted to change to career-track positions because of career-track workers' long working hours and daily after-work drinking. Many non-career-track women left the workplace between 5 and 7, while most career-track workers left for home around 8 or 9. A twenty-seven-year-old non-career-track worker at Daigo Life Insurance said, "I never want to change to a career-track position in this firm. The career-track workers seem pretty ambitious. . . . The women have to go drinking and play golf. . . . Non-career-track women never have to do any of those after-work events. . . . But, even though I know this is contradictory, I also want to do more difficult and responsible work." Another twenty-six-year-old non-career-track worker at Daigo Life Insurance said, "I know that non-career-track women are just assistants. . . . Why did I want a non-career-track position? I had worked at a publisher, and I saw that many women who constantly overwork eventually became ill there. I didn't want that. I don't want to force myself to work too hard." While some non-career-track women with four-year college degrees reacted negatively to the level of work given to assistants and to their lower salaries, they did not want to risk their health by going for the career track. But many of these women, especially in the cosmetics companies, also seemed uncertain about their own career and professional goals in these firms. Many of them seemed to have a hard time envisioning themselves being successful or established in their firms.

A few of the non-career-track women I interviewed were either married or lived with their parents. In addition to being averse to overwork, having someone else they could rely on financially may have contributed to their having low levels of ambition. Also, the requirements for changing career track, such as taking exams and accumulating sales experience, seemed to discourage many women from making a track change.

At Shijo Asset Management, some area-career-track women who worked long hours wished to leave their jobs when they married. Saki, a thirty-one-year-old regional-career-track employee in sales, had a hard time feeling hopeful about her career. During our interview she mentioned that her most viable option was quitting work and getting married. Saki made daily trips to branches of the parent firm, Shijo Securities, all over the country. Although she worked past 10 p.m. nearly every day, and often until after midnight, she was paid only the equivalent of twenty dollars for each trip, with no overtime payment: "Right now, I sleep at most about five hours a day. I try to sleep on trains. On weekends, I just sleep and play games in my room. There is no time left to do or think about anything else. . . . I want to change to be a career-track worker, because I want to say things to management and get involved in changing the rules, but once you become a career-track worker, you work even longer and have more work to do." Even though she mentioned wanting to change to a better position, Saki had come to see marriage as the only solution to getting away from her low-paying job and all the overtime she was expected to do. At Shijo Asset Management, the three other area-career-track women I talked with left the workplace between 6 and 8 p.m. daily, earlier than Saki; none of them mentioned wanting to quit their jobs. Because area-career-track positions and non-career-track positions normally allow shorter work hours (although this was not the case with Saki), women who see overwork as a concern for their personal and emotional health may take such positions.

The custom of long work hours can also be a major opportunity-blocking factor for women who have concerns about the conflict between work and family plans. The two cosmetics companies where I conducted interviews are known as women-friendly workplaces, and most of the women whom I interviewed at these firms worked in career-track positions. Married women and women with children were visible. However, five out of ten of the single women workers whom I interviewed at the cosmetics firms foresaw that their careers would be incompatible with their future family plans. None of the young women at Hanakage believed they could continue to work in their current departments after marriage and childbirth. For example, a twenty-nine-year-old worker, Yuri, who worked in the marketing department at Hanakage, usually stayed at work until 9 or 10 p.m. every day. She went out drinking after work three times a week. She had had stomach pains because of her lack of sleep. Living with her parents made it easier for her to focus on her job. Still, she found it difficult to go out with friends after work: "We have meetings all the time after 5:30. But I never tell my friends this. I cannot say to them that I work until after 10 p.m. I just tell them I am busy, that I am about to do things with my parents or something. If I told them the truth, they would think I was just too career oriented and unfriendly. My male friends would think I was not very womanly." Yuri was adamant about quitting her job if she marries: "I don't mind quitting the company. I am not career oriented. I want to take care of my family. I may do some part-time work after marriage." She attributed her desire to leave her job to a lack of interest in a career and a strong belief in traditional femininity, and she referred to the custom of working long hours as a masculine behavior that she should not be bound by. Working long hours daily made her concerned about differing from the typical woman, and it also convinced her that working would not be compatible with her image of having a family.

Asked about the lenient policy regarding parental leave and the increasing number of lower-level women managers at Hanakage, a thirty-two-year-old woman, Satomi, who usually worked from 8:30 a.m. to 9 or 10 p.m. in one of the marketing sections, said, "For me, I don't know what to do about my future marriage and children. . . . This section is very busy. If you want to work like these lower-level managers, you need huge support from your own mother or mother-in-law." Yuri went on: "There are some women with children who get promoted, but they almost always live with their parents, who take care of their children. . . . Even if you are single, if you are a woman, you have to work really hard to get promoted, and there will be no time for family and children. I do not want that."

I should note that long work hours are not the sole factor that pushes employed women out of their jobs. In my interviews, the women also expressed great dissatisfaction with, among other things, the traditional seniority pay system, which does not reflect young workers' long hours of labor and their achievement. Yuri, a twenty-nine-year-old female worker in the marketing department at Hanakage, said, "Because promotions occur based on seniority . . . even if you work really hard and get excellent evaluations, it does not make much difference. I have received excellent evaluations, but my bonus only increased about five dollars or something. I would say the maximum is only about ten dollars. If I don't work hard, I may get bad evaluations, but the payment is still the same. I suppose I could be transferred to a different section." Under the seniority system in Japanese firms, the workers usually start receiving a high salary and promotions at the end of their thirties. Seniority pay that disregards individual achievement makes hard-working women feel that their talents are being wasted and affects their ambitions and aspirations. Yuri continued, "Young women like us just get used by the firm. Even after we reach the age of thirty, it is the men who get promoted more." Megumi, a thirty-three-year-old worker at Hanakage, also commented on the problem of promotions: "I see many senior men who don't do much work getting promoted. . . . I think promotions should be based solely on performance." The traditional seniority pay starts to increase and promotions become more likely at exactly the time of life when many women want to start a family. Therefore, many women see the system as unfairly disadvantageous to young women.

Interestingly, there are some small exceptions to the seniority-promotion system. Yuri commented that her three single female colleagues received exceptionally high evaluations and were paid larger salaries and bonuses because they were having affairs with their bosses. "In Japan, sexual affairs rarely lead to divorce; the men instead give promotions to the women with whom they have affairs," she said.

In any case, Yuri's current goal is to marry a man and leave her job, and she thinks her career change to housewife largely depends on her future husband's salary. "At my age, the man should make at least $80,000 per year, with much potential for future promotions," she said. Megumi is also considering quitting her job and marrying her long-term boyfriend, another corporate worker who is soon to be transferred to the West Coast in the United States. She said, "I am OK with being a housewife, decorating our house beautifully and buying lots of Laura Ashley stuff. My boyfriend says it is up to me." Thus, it is also obvious that these women's visions to opt out depend on whether Japanese firms will continue to be able to pay fat salaries to male breadwinners in their late twenties and thirties.

When I asked the women at Hanakage and Takane if they felt their options were limited, they responded that men's options are far more limited, so they should not complain; in fact, they felt sorry for the male workers. "Men do not have any option but to work long hours every day for the rest of their lives. Men's lives are much harder," said Megumi, referring to the strong cultural belief in the male-breadwinner role. Quite a few of the female employees said that they appreciate having the option, however limiting, to "quit working upon marriage or childbirth"—an option not given to men. The female employees seemed to accept the fact that women hold less power in the corporate structure because of men's larger responsibilities and obligations, including working long hours. There seems to be a general consensus that the masculine work norm harms male workers by depriving them of personal and family time, as well as damaging their health.

It is not just the non-career-track system per se that makes women want to quit their jobs but also that having worked long hours lowers their aspirations and dims their future prospects. The ideology of separate spheres also emerges as a justification for women's low status and their tendency to opt out, and obscures the institutional mechanisms of sex segregation by diminishing women workers' complaints against unfair organizational and cultural customs and leaving them with a sense of sympathy toward male workers.

## Workers Who Are Parents

The custom of working long hours builds on the ideology of separate spheres, which normalizes men's disassociation from the private sphere and women's unpaid devotion to it. In my interviews, expectations regarding long working hours intensified the time constraints on mothers in the workplace. All of them had husbands who also worked for large corporations and were hardly ever available to help fill the caretaker role at home. Working mothers often arranged for their parents to help with child care and brought their work home instead of staying late at the workplace. Few of these women had high hopes for future promotions, and they also had concerns about being asked to move to different sections. Meanwhile, working fathers continued to work long hours; most of them were indifferent to the subject of parental leave since most of them had wives at home.

Although long parental leave provides an incentive for women's continuous employment and does help to attract many women workers, workers who become mothers, in contrast with those who become fathers, have a much harder time arranging for child care, enduring salary reductions and potential moves, and dealing with other workers' negative images of them.

Most of the men I interviewed expressed indifference to their firm's long parental leave, as they mostly had wives who were homemakers. They typically worked long hours with few days of vacation. They often responded that they did not even think of parental leave as a man's concern. Shigeo, a forty-one-year-old male worker at Hanakage, said, "It may be common for a man to take a parental leave at Procter & Gamble, but not here. I have never heard of a man taking parental leave. I don't even know how that works. I don't understand why a man would need to take it, either. The men won't take such a leave even in the future." While he asserted that early quitting time is something that mothers may need, he did admit that he had also benefitted from it. He liked the fact that he could leave the workplace early and spend more time with his family at home: "I used to leave my company around 9, until recently. Now I arrive home at 9 so that I can talk with my kids about thirty minutes before they go to bed. I think I can go home more easily and earlier than men in other sections because there are more women who are mothers in my section." In his section, which included ten workers, there were eight women, most of whom were married with children, and only two men. He viewed the section meetings as being an outlet for the mothers to gossip or chitchat rather than a place for professional exchanges of opinion. He did not like working in this section because he thought it was too "women dominated." But he did enjoy the increased time with his family.

A forty-year-old worker in research and development at Takane was one of the few men in my interviews whose wife also worked full time. They had one son who was four years old. His wife took a year and half of parental leave and also left work early to pick up their son, while the husband helped little. He said, "I don't want to take parental leave. I know one man in this firm who has taken it, though. I just can't be with a child all the time. . . . My wife does all the pickups and does everything for him. . . . I take him to the park or shopping on weekends. . . . She goes to work on weekends, too. . . . I don't see her much at home lately." He laughed and emphasized his inability to take care of a child. Like him, many men in Japanese firms see caring for children and family tasks as work that is optional for them to participate in, whereas women see this work as their full responsibility. Thus, even though I heard frequent comments from men about how they were spending more time with their wives and children and working fewer hours in recent years, that rarely meant that they were taking a greater interest in doing more work related to the family and household. At Takane, which offers two weeks of paid leave to both fathers and mothers, about thirteen hundred workers took parental leave in 2011, but only fifteen of them were men.

Among those whom I interviewed, only one man had taken parental leave. Masao, a twenty-nine-year-old male worker at Daigo Life Insurance, was the first man in the company to take parental leave. However, it was not his voluntary act as a parent but a masculine "sacrifice" for the company so that it could get governmental approval as a family-friendly company.

> If one man takes parental leave in a firm, the Japanese government approves the firm as being family friendly and adds it to the list of family-friendly companies. The company needed one man. I had to sacrifice myself. . . . I really didn't want to take such a leave. . . . It was just for the image of the firm. It might be better for the profits of the firm. . . . No man wants to take such a leave. When you take parental leave, you get a 3.3 percent reduction in your salary.

Masao concluded, "I think the leave is useless for men." The male workers I talked to did not believe that their firms encouraged men to share in child care, especially as parental leave involves a salary reduction. Interestingly, some large multinational firms such as Sony and Sharp show a high rate of fathers taking parental leave,[69] but this may be because of pressure from foreign stockholders or the non-Japanese management's emphasis on emulating the Western business model. In Japanese firms, the only way to change, even a little, men's consciousness regarding child care and family responsibilities may be to enforce the emulation of this business model. And, needless to say, changing men's consciousness also requires changing firms' sex-segregated customs such as extremely long work hours.

The workers I interviewed who were mothers in the two cosmetics firms had commonly taken long parental leaves of between one and two years. Some took two to three years total for two different children. One worker in Takane had taken a total of five years for three children. The women often commented that they chose to work for their firms because of the "woman-friendly" or "mother-friendly" images. In addition to doing their regular cooking and cleaning at home, the married women with children picked up their children from nursery school, made dinner boxes for their children's evening cram schools (where they study for entrance exams), prepared their children for their entrance exams for elementary and middle school, and attended weekend school meetings.

All the women with children whom I interviewed had corporate husbands who typically came home after midnight daily, and they were not able to rely on their husbands for help at home. Some women relied on their own or their husbands' parents for help. Mari, a thirty-eight-year-old mother of two children who worked at Takane, lived separately from her husband after his firm transferred him to Nagoya. She and her husband had remodeled their home so that her parents could live with her and help her take care of her children. She said, "My husband lives in Nagoya during weekdays and comes home to Tokyo on weekends. I can do some work on weekends when he is around the house with our kids." Mari's parents would usually pick her children up at kindergarten and take care of her house, but it was her job to leave her workplace at 5:15 to make boxed dinners for her children, who attended evening cram schools.

Whereas Mari received help from her own parents who lived with her, Saeko, a forty-two-year-old mother of three children who worked at Takane, found it hard living with her husband's parents.

> My husband has been very busy. I never saw him at home on weekends until just recently. He comes home around midnight. . . . My first child became really ill and was hospitalized. I had also an early birth with the second child, and I was hospitalized for six months. So we lived with his parents. . . . I felt I was married to my husband's parents. I couldn't complain about their help, but I wasn't able to stay at home because his parents were at home all the time. I never felt relaxed.

Some workers who did not have their parents' help with children had to arrange multiple babysitting shifts. A thirty-nine-year-old woman at Hanakage had taken one year of parental leave for her first child and another one-and-a-half years for her second child. She left work early (around 6) every day but had to hire two or three different babysitters so that she could stay at her workplace to do overtime work about six days a month.

Many mothers revealed that they found it difficult to leave the workplace at 5 p.m. When they left at 5, they said they felt they were not doing adequate work because most people stayed until 8 p.m. or later. In addition to the pressure to work long hours, the penalty of a salary reduction that comes with an early quitting time increased their sense of inadequacy. Kaoru, a thirty-one-year-old worker at Takane, accepted a salary reduction in order to be able to leave at 4:30 p.m. Kaoru felt guilty toward her coworkers, who needed to shoulder what work she did not finish: "I felt really bad about leaving at 4:30. To catch up with work, I ended up working at home. But I still got a salary reduction. I didn't like it at all. So, I try not to take it now. I leave work around 6 now." Saeko, a forty-two-year-old worker, also took a few years of early departure with a salary reduction also after her parental leave: "I used to leave early, around 4:30 or so, and they reduced my salary. When I started this job, my salary was under $1,000 every month, and most of the money went to the nursery school. So I questioned the meaning of my work. Why am I doing this? I thought about quitting the job. . . . But women who quit their job at my age will never be employed full time again." Kaoru decided not to take early leave (two hours every day) because of the salary reduction and a mediocre evaluation. She said, "My boss evaluated me as neither good nor bad when I took early leave. I worked so hard during that time. But he didn't see it that way. I didn't get 'excellent' because I left early." Kaoru saw the salary reduction and the boss's indifferent evaluation as "costs" or "penalties" for not working longer hours. Whereas many large Japanese firms have initiated their own "family-friendly" policies and generous parental leave, this often puts mothers at a disadvantage while not pressuring fathers to take any action. Therefore, the long parental leaves sends a message about who should be the sole caretaker and thus reinforces the belief that it must always be the woman.

It is not uncommon for companies to remain "non-responsible for reproduction," in Joan Acker's words.[70] She writes: "Non-responsibility consigns caring needs to areas outside the organization's interests and, thus, helps to maintain the image of the ideal, even adequate, employee as someone without such obligations. Thus, organizational policies and practices continue to encode this gendered notion of the employee." Japanese firms have supported the male-breadwinner role by offering extra family benefits to male workers. But they provide no benefits to support working mothers in their dual roles.

In my interviews, both mothers and women who were not mothers praised their firm's lenient parental leave policy. But the costs associated with having children are high, including arranging extra help for child care, dealing with guilt over unfinished work, feeling pressure to stay at work late or bring work home, and being forced to accept salary reductions and negative evaluations in return for permission to leave early.

Furthermore, as many previous studies have pointed out, the "motherhood penalty" includes negative stereotyping of mothers in the workplace and their reduced promotion opportunities.[71] Most mothers with whom I talked viewed their chances to move further up in the hierarchy as slim, particularly since they would not be able to work in the sections where long work hours were the norm. If employees want to be considered as potential managers, they are expected to accumulate experience in various departments of a company, including departments that normalize overtime work. Mothers are often seen as inflexible and as more likely to make special requests to have their working hours shortened. A thirty-eight-year-old female worker noted that the sections that welcome mothers are limited, and said:

> I have no interest in promotion. I won't be able to move to other parts of Japan, either. . . . It is also difficult to work in sections where there are some single women, such as product development or marketing. They don't accept women with children. My current section is just so special, and I think people here are really nice and accepting of me. I know that the women who are mothers in product development have to leave work really quietly.

Saeko agreed with this: "Most women in management are either single or married with no children. . . . I don't think I can go much higher than my current position."

Misa, a twenty-six-year-old worker in human resources at Takane who is in charge of training selected candidates for low and middle management, said that those women who get promotions, even at the lowest levels of management, tend to be unmarried. She offered specifics:

> This year, we have only four women out of fifteen selected candidates for lower-level managers. Three out of the four women are single, and all the men are married. For middle-level managers, we have only about three women out of fourteen total. All three women are single, but only two of the men are single. So, I definitely get the impression that if you are a woman and want to be promoted, you have to work really hard. You won't be able to marry and have children.

At Takane, a "woman-friendly" or "family-friendly" Japanese cosmetics firm, regardless of the large number of mothers who continue to work after childbirth and who praise the company for its lenient leave policy and for its large number of workers who are mothers, the deeply ingrained culture of separate spheres continues to shape fathers' attitudes toward work and family. The overall absence of men at home because of their long hours of work continues to impose a heavy burden on mothers, who must assume the full caretaker role, making it impossible for them to do daily overtime without the extra help of family members or babysitters. The firm may be friendly to mothers in the sense that it provides them with long leaves, but its explicit and continuing valuing of men who overwork further intensifies the segregation between men and women.

## How Heroic Masculinity Harms Men

Social and cultural norms allow men little room for deviating from the model of the ideal worker or masculine breadwinner. Robin Ely and Irene Padavic remind us that workplace masculinity is not just about power but also about costs and constraints when they point out that "men have less latitude than women in their gender identity enactments."[72]

The sociologist and *New York Times* columnist Stephanie Coontz points out that men and boys in the United States endure harsher social and cultural expectations than women and girls, because women are not expected to compete for power and success to the same degree that men are.[73] She writes about the masculinity pressure that men and boys are under:

> Most of the problems men are experiencing today stem from the flip side of the 20th-century feminine mystique—a pervasive masculine mystique that pressures boys and men to conform to a gender stereotype and prevents them from exploring the full range of their individual capabilities. The masculine mystique promises men success, power and admiration from others if they embrace their supposedly natural competitive drives and reject all forms of dependence. Just as the feminine mystique made women ashamed when they harbored feelings or desires that were supposedly "masculine," the masculine mystique makes men ashamed to admit to any feelings or desires that are thought to be "feminine." . . . Girls had such leeway precisely because they were never expected to compete for public success or to wield power over others. . . . Boys are held to higher standards of stoicism than girls and receive harsher treatment when they do not compete successfully. Throughout their lives men face constant pressure to demonstrate their masculinity to others.[74]

She describes the masculine mystique as a social and cultural pressure that drives men to seek success, power, and admiration throughout their lives, from early childhood and adolescence onward, but her discussion is also applicable to the masculine pressures that shape men's workplace behaviors and beliefs.

In my interviews, some women workers in cosmetics firms noted that men are not given any other option besides working long hours until they retire, while women have the choice to quit their jobs to stay home with their families. These women viewed men's choices of career paths or workplace behaviors as far more limited than their own. If men were expected, or at least allowed, to opt out in order to take care of their family, would more men take a caretaker role? Does a man still gain respect and recognition when he does not work like a "typical man"? Would it be possible to change the cultural expectations of masculinity, transforming the image of the ideal man of work to the image of the ideal man of work and family?

As the cultural norm of masculinity pressures men to conform to particular behaviors and beliefs, this conformity can have serious negative consequences. Robin Ely and Debra Meyerson point out that men's engagement in traditional masculine behaviors can result in workers' poor-quality or compromised decisions; ineffective training of recruits; marginalization of women workers; violations of civil/human rights; and alienation of men with regard to their health, emotions, and relationships with others.[75]

Enactment of masculinity can cost human lives. It is well known that, leading up to the Space Shuttle Challenger accident, there were "masculinity contests" between engineers who insisted on technical proficiency and managers who insisted on risk-taking actions, and there was little discussion of the human consequences of these contests.[76] James Messerschmidt argues that risk-taking actions are often seen by managers as synonymous with corporate goals and corporate loyalty;[77] these attitudes are often associated with such positive masculine traits as drive and competency and suppression of emotionality, fear, and uncertainty.[78] Conversely, engineers are not interested in pursuing risk-taking behaviors; a technical failure threatens their masculinity. In the case of the Challenger, these different occupational masculinities mutually contested within the hierarchy of power, and it was the manager masculinities that prevailed over the engineer masculinities.[79]

Though my interviewees did not suggest that men's risk-taking behaviors had resulted in any tragic incidents, some of the white-collar crimes that have occurred in Japanese firms could have been enactments of traditional masculinity. An example is when board members at one Japanese company, Olympus, covered up large financial losses over ten years—insisting that they hid the loss of the money purely for the sake of the company, not to protect themselves.

In my interviews, some individuals mentioned fraternity-like male rituals involving binge drinking that were common when they were new workers. Takashi, a thirty-seven-year-old male section chief at Daigo Life Insurance, likened his first month's training to military experience: "I was so scared. I was expecting men to throw ashtrays at each other. You get up at 4 in the morning and run a marathon. The senior men train you how to bow over and over. So much drinking at night." Takashi was also in charge of 550 women sales workers in a local branch. He said, laughing: "There was sexual harassment everywhere. I had to dance with many women. These women would kiss me and touch me all over. I was totally an *otoko geisha* [a male worker who is forced to entertain male bosses or clients by engaging in degrading performances in drinking settings]." Men-only rituals as a means to indoctrinate *gaman* [fighting spirit, hierarchal relationships, obedience to authority, group cooperation, and especially respect for tradition],[80] a critical component of masculinity in Japan, continue to exist in many firms.

Working long hours costs men their mental and physical health and family lives. The physical and mental exhaustion of workers can also result in unexpected costs to the firms. Overwork is considered a common cause of workers' depression and suicide. In 2010 over 70 percent of suicides in Japan occurred among men, and men in their thirties, forties, fifties, and sixties—the prime working years—are the most vulnerable. If employers lose men who are highly skilled and highly trained, they have to replace them; this represents an obvious cost. And if there are too many incidents of this kind associated with a particular company, it can hurt the firm's brand and name and make it harder to acquire skilled workers.

In my interviews, four male managers who worked long hours in their thirties and forties in financial companies reported experiences of long-term medical treatment for health problems, including severe depression. Eiji, the thirty-eight-year-old worker at Mikado Bank interviewed above, asserted that his illness was evidence of his being a good banker. He claimed that his recent gastrointestinal surgery was not a big deal and said, "This level of illness is common. All the people I know who work as investment bankers have been hospitalized at least once by the age of forty." He described himself as not being a typical "athlete type" worker in the financial industry; by this, he meant "a man who doesn't cry, doesn't give in to any kind of pressure, and works hard twenty-four hours." But he said his ambition mirrored that of such men. "I chose to work for this bank because I wanted money and fame—more money than fame." Similar to other men I spoke with, he rarely saw his son on weekdays. His homemaker wife tutored their son so that they could send him to an elite private middle school and eventually the elite college that Eiji and his brother had attended. He said, "It might be OK to see someone else's kids in the nursery, but not my son. [He went to a private kindergarten.] I don't think such places provide the highest level of education and produce the smartest children. . . . I want my son to be someone who can contribute so much to society." Even though his overworking cost him his family life, Eiji showed little concern, because this was how he grew up in relation to his own father, an engineer who also worked in a large Japanese firm.

There are many examples of men's overworking costing them their health and sometimes even their jobs. Two managers at Shijo Asset Management suffered from long-term clinical depression and physical ailments that had forced them to resign their previous positions. They shared similar stories; they both used to work long hours daily, under constant pressure to attain profit goals, and received little help or support; they also both dealt with authoritarian bosses who were constantly resentful of them and hostile to them.

Ryo, a forty-year-old marketing manager, moved from a large securities firm to Shijo Asset Management two years prior to our interview. While working in his previous workplace, he had undergone surgeries for a severe gastrointestinal problem, from which he had not quite recovered when I spoke with him. His wife had repeatedly asked him to quit his job. In his previous workplace, Ryo had worked until after midnight every day, along with two more twelve-hour workdays on Saturdays and Sundays. At Shijo Asset Management, he only worked weekdays until 9 or 10, which he described as "much easier." He said, "I was working just too much there [at his previous job]. Too many responsibilities and risks. . . . Every day, I did all the work myself, an amount of work that probably should have taken about ten to twenty workers to complete. . . . I did all the work on investments, which the fund manager was supposed to do." Because his excessive daily workload started to affect his health, Ryo kept asking his bosses if they could hire or assign someone to help him, but they never did. He worked too many hours with too little sleep, and it finally compromised his health. When the Ministry of Finance started investigating a case in which Ryo mistakenly sold a client's stocks on a date when he was not supposed to sell them, his boss forced him to write and sign a letter from the firm, claiming responsibility for the mistake and absolving the firm and other employees of blame. This situation caused him to realize, finally, that the company had not treated him fairly for all the sacrifices he had made and the devotion he had exhibited. "My boss and the company were never on my side," he said. Ryo collapsed at work and was hospitalized for over a month. "I worked so hard for this company. But this is what I got. I was not able to stop crying in the hospital. I didn't want this. I didn't want to die like this. I sacrificed myself too much. I felt I could have been killed by the company . . . it was terrible." When he was released from the hospital and went back to his job, he found all his unfinished work just piled up on his desk. He quit the job and moved to Shijo Asset Management. However, when I interviewed him, he was far from recovered from his severe depression.

During our interview, Ryo criticized the normalized custom of overwork: "Even in this section, four of us work daily until 9 or 10 p.m." He wished that he could spend more time at home with his wife, with whom he had begun infertility treatments.

Satoru, a forty-five-year-old manager, used to do sales in a large securities firm in Japan before he moved to Shijo Asset Management. In the previous securities firm, he was assigned a high sales goal, as much as $1 million every week. "You must go everywhere to reach that amount. It was crazy. But everybody has to do it," he said. He never went home before midnight and often stayed at hotels to get some sleep. After several years selling securities, he was promoted to a position in which he was in charge of hundreds of sales stores in the asset management firm of the same group. He described his work pressures: "I always felt I was running a hundred-meter dash with someone pulling on my neck with a rope. . . . I was running so hard, but I felt like I lost where I was and why I was even running." Around the same time, he found himself spending very little time at home and being angry and authoritarian with his two sons.

> I felt bad. I never committed to my children. . . . Whatever I said to them was not convincing because I was never around. . . . When I was at home, I would just say to them, "Study hard" or "Work more." I was really harsh to them. Because I didn't have much time at home, I wanted to give them effective discipline. I yelled at them to force them to work hard. My children were very fearful of me, and I thought it was a good thing. I was always angry at them, like my boss, who was always yelling at me and complaining about my work. I was kind of the same way with my kids.

He found his older son had repeatedly stolen money from his wife and had also shoplifted. "My wife took care of everything with the children. I blamed my wife, telling her it was her fault that our kids had become deviant," he said. Around the same time, he collapsed in the workplace with a severe headache and depression. The symptoms were so bad that he quit his job and stayed at home for over a year. He started going to a therapist. Instead of blaming his wife and children, he decided to spend more time with them.

Satoru started a new job at Shijo Asset Management four years before our interview, but he still struggled with headaches and depression, which forced him to take another half-year leave recently. Another manager in his late thirties at Daigo Life Insurance said he had to take a month leave from his work due to illness. Similar to Satoru's, his illness changed his priorities, and he decided he needed to focus less on his work and more on his health and family. He said, "I was really pushing myself, working too long. . . . If others get promotions faster than I do, I have to accept it. If I really have to choose either my work or my family, I would choose my family, my kids, over work." In my interviews, three men out of four who had serious illnesses reported that, after the illness, they changed the main priority of their life from their job to their personal health and family lives.

Ryo described himself as being "killed by the company," and Satoru felt that he was forced to run a hundred-meter dash with a rope around his neck; both men described their experiences of daily overwork in securities firms as forced labor, a situation requiring absolute obedience that gave them few options. Yet most of the men I spoke to did not explicitly criticize the overwork custom. This may be because they viewed their overwork as being a legally and culturally legitimized custom and also a fair trade in exchange for lifelong or at least long-term economic security.

Workers' subordination to authority, passivity, and displays of loyalty and sacrifice to the company or to their jobs are considered important qualities of the ideal masculine worker in Japan. Tetsuro Kato explains that the Japanese workplace mandates an attitude of conformity and subordination to authority in which "workers rarely express their own opinions or exhibit any originality in their work," and "workers who are reluctant to follow the company's recommendation may be considered not to be in harmony with the objectives of the company."[81] Subordination and passivity may seem antithetical to the notion of masculinity, but active conformity to authority or active inaction are "goal driven and instrumental" actions for the sake of success and institutional recognition,[82] and thus they are heroic acts of self-control and submission to identification with a higher authority.

During my interviews, one man at Mikado Bank said that his two bosses had committed suicide in the late 1990s when the bank's bad debts were found to be massive. "These guys killed themselves in order to prevent the information from being revealed to the government and public," he said. Committing suicide in Japan can be an extreme form of enacting masculinity—a display of one's absolute subordination to the firm.

An organization's normalization of its workers' sacrifice, loyalty, and subordination to authority may, however, cost the firm. As we have seen, these values may promote inhumane work practices, such as extremely long working hours, as the norm and may cause those who do not subordinate themselves, such as outsiders who may criticize and compete with the firm, to be shunned—thus reinforcing the insider-based culture and sustaining organizational inertia.

A recent white-collar crime in Japan, Olympus's cover-up of its investment losses, revealed in 2011, has been seen as a good example of the absence of checks and balances in the country and an indication that an outside independent director who could rigorously check firms' financial transactions might be needed.[83] The case of Olympus also reveals the unchanging nature of the Japanese insider-oriented culture and its strong emphasis on passivity and obedience. Seven people at Olympus—including the former chairman, the executive vice president, the former company auditor, and an outside investment adviser on the board—were arrested for secretly moving over $1.7 billion of investment losses off the books over a period of thirteen years. The former president and chief executive, Michael Woodford, who is British, was fired as a foreigner who did not fit in to Japanese culture when he brought a question to the chairman regarding a series of payments made by the company. The company's biggest domestic shareholders also sided against him, another indication of "Japan's resistance to outsiders and change."[84] Regarding the idea of adding an outside director to allow for tighter checking, Keidanren, the Japanese business organization, argued that there had already been sufficient external scrutiny and thus further monitoring was not necessary.

The absence of public and corporate criticism and the lack of pressure from the shareholders in the Olympus case could be because of the firm's strong ties to the large Japanese banks. According to the *Economist*, "Olympus's shares lost about 80% of their value, yet its institutional shareholders uttered not 'one word' of criticism against the company's board."[85] And the fact that the company's domestic shareholders also sided against Woodford confirms foreign investors' fears regarding Japan's strong resistance to outsiders and change.[86] Eventually, a former director of Sumitomo Mitsui Bank was appointed as chairman of the firm, while a former executive of the Bank of Tokyo Mitsubishi UFJ was nominated as a director; Sumitomo Mitsui Bank and Mitsubishi UFJ are large lenders to Olympus.[87] Foreign investors have been concerned that the appointment of the bank-affiliated chairman may signify that the bank will retain control over the firm.[88] There has been much scholarly discussion of the topic, yet the Olympus scandal illustrates how closed, and how bank centered, the Japanese business culture remains.

The Olympus scandal also illuminates the culture of subordination, inaction, and conformity in Japanese firms. Apparently, Olympus management handled the firm's losses by using a *tobashi* scheme, in which a company hides losses of assets by selling debts to other companies, often dummies.[89] *Tobashi* schemes were commonly used by Yamaichi Securities, which collapsed in 1997. Yamaichi had a corporate culture in which the board members would not criticize the firm or even raise questions outside their area of specialization; thus, they did nothing about the losses even though they might have known about them.[90] In this climate, outside criticisms and concerns are ignored. Such an insider-oriented culture, bolstered by an atmosphere of subordination, passivity, and inaction, seems to have greatly contributed to the long years of cover-ups of investment losses.

Masculinity in the workplace has costs for both individual men and the firms they work for. Ely and Meyerson, in their study of offshore firms in which men's engagement with patterns of dominant masculinity could result in safety issues, asks "how these organizations, where the work is deemed masculine and the workforce is mostly men, [might] reorient male workers away from proving their masculinity."[91] Their study shows that the organizational will to address this problem at the collective level was often present, and that workers, managers, and contractors took part in wide initiatives to make safety their highest priority.[92] The question of whether Japanese firms are willing to institute these kinds of initiatives to change the masculine customs that are a part of workplace culture, including long work hours, insider orientation, and an emphasis on the virtues of subordination, passivity, and sacrifice, needs further research. The costs of manhood are an important issue for the future labor force in Japan, since the long-work-hour custom and its negative repercussions will affect men's decisions in the labor market. The custom not only leads to men's physical and mental illness but may alienate younger men looking to enter the corporate world, potentially leading them to choose an alternative path as temp workers rather than going down the road of lifelong employment. (About one third of college graduates are reportedly quitting their first jobs within three years.[93]) The traditional emphasis on sacrifice and its sustenance via long work hours is central to Japanese manhood; thus, changes in the customs may require dramatic alterations in corporate culture and governance of Japanese firms. The current Japanese state and business community further enforce these customs because they minimize labor costs—regardless of the criticisms and harmful consequences that arise from them.

We have seen how the informal processes by which the custom of long work hours has become ingrained in the workplace culture of Japanese firms has intensified vertical sex segregation. Working long hours has been legitimized as a critical labor condition of workers' lifelong employment in Japan. The overwork custom is a solution that firms use to save labor costs, one that has been legally and culturally supported for a long time. However, overwork can mean high wages and higher costs for employers, and it may also discourage employers from hiring new workers. The custom of overwork can lower the likelihood of new hires and make younger workers' economic situation worse. Also, continuing the overwork practice discourages firms' efforts to find ways to enhance productivity.

The middle-level male managers I interviewed saw their daily overwork as a necessary sacrifice; an obligation to the larger organization; a custom of physical and mental endurance; a tool to fully realize their masculine selves; and an opportunity for visibility, recognition, and leadership. A small number of women managers are incorporated into the firms, but only when they successfully prioritize their jobs over their personal and family lives. The female managers often remain childless and sometimes single so that they can devote themselves to their work to the same degree as men. The custom of long work hours also keeps non-career-track workers' aspirations low and thus preserves their marginal status. The combination of career-track hiring and the custom of working long hours is an effective corporate tool to legitimize the low status and pay of the majority of women. Long working hours, particularly when they are not well compensated, lower women's aspirations and encourage them to opt out by hampering their ability to balance work and family. Although workers who are mothers were visible in the cosmetics firms where I conducted interviews, these women often struggled to balance work and family, having to resort to hiring extra help, taking salary reductions, and giving up mobility. A company may be considered "women friendly" because it provides mothers with long leaves after childbirth, but if it continues to explicitly value men who overwork, this intensifies the division between men and women. At the same time, for some men, overworking costs them their mental and physical health and family time. Following and engaging in masculinity norms and emphasizing the virtue of manhood in organizational culture can harm not just individual workers but also organizations, exacerbating organizational inertia in Japan.

Working long hours has been a critical part of traditional Japanese management and a driving force behind Japan's modernization. The custom is interwoven with the nationalist sentiment of the Japanese people and the workplace values and ethics of Japanese companies. The value of working long hours also has ties to the system of lifelong employment and has allowed Japanese firms that have normalized the custom to avoid cuts by hiring fewer employees. The gendered costs of long working hours in Japanese companies will not disappear as long as management sees the custom as its best cost-saving tactic and employers are unable to come up with other options in the rigid and traditional Japanese labor market.

# OBLIGATORY FEMININITY AND SEXUAL HARASSMENT

In previous chapters I focused on how Japan's business community, through its institutional and organizational practices, promotes sex segregation in the areas of salary, promotion, gender bias, and working hours. In this chapter I will show how sex segregation and women's low status in Japanese companies contribute to patterns of workplace sexual interaction. Some argue that group orientation in Japanese firms feeds sexual harassment,[1] and others point out that the compulsory norms of femininity that young women are expected to perform (such as obedience, cuteness, and weakness) promote sexual harassment at work.[2] As the term, and the concept of, "sexual harassment" did not exist until 1989, and it was 1999 before a policy against it was enforced in Japan—an amendment to the Law for Equal Employment Opportunity—little is known about workplace sexual behaviors and sexual harassment in Japanese companies.[3]

The gender imperatives of the five Japanese firms I looked at normalize and foster sexual interactions and obscure harassing behaviors in their organizations' workplace culture. Sexual harassment policy and law differs in Japan and Germany, France, and the United States. In contrast with the United States, which defines sexual harassment as a form of gender "discrimination," Japan has taken a stance closer to that of the European Union, which approaches sexual harassment as a violation of "individual dignity." This definition may allow for a wider range of applications than the US definition in which a victim has to prove adverse working conditions as a result of sexual harassment.

Women in the five firms described "obligatory" workplace sexual interactions: (1) taking clients to hostess clubs, which women workers often see as "a part of their job"; (2) playing the hostess role at after-work drinking meetings, where a certain amount of touching and groping by men is seen as "joking around" or simply as behavior that is to be expected from men; and (3) repetitive or threatening sexual advances occurring during normal working hours, which are seen as harassment and frequently cause women to take corrective action. Even though women's interpretations of sexual behaviors can vary from positive to very negative depending on the context, I argue that Japanese organizational culture, through its normalization of male dominance and female subordination, fosters and obscures harmful behaviors.

## Sexual Harassment and Workplace Culture

Given that Japan is one of the least gender-equal countries in the world,[4] it is not surprising that the term "sexual harassment" first gained the Japanese public's attention only in the 1990s, much later than in the United States. In fact, around this time, sexual harassment in Japanese companies drew considerable attention in the United States because of some sexual harassment lawsuits against Japanese transplants in the United States. In 1996, the United States Equal Employment Opportunity Commission filed a class action against Mitsubishi Motor Manufacturing of America for engaging in sexual harassment, and the company eventually agreed to pay $34 million to all eligible claimants.[5] In another case, brought against Toyota Motor North America in 2006, a secretary filed a $190 million lawsuit against the company's president for his unwanted sexual advances.[6] The plaintiff argued that the president's sexual advances strongly reflected corporate culture in Japan, where a workplace culture of sexism remains rampant.[7] Extending previous studies of how women draw boundary lines regarding workplace sexual behaviors,[8] I further investigate the impact of cultural organizational practices on women's interpretations of these behaviors in Japanese firms.

Researchers have argued that sexual harassment occurs because of women's subordination in a patriarchal system,[9] their low status in labor markets and in the occupational structure,[10] and the combination of their lack of power with men's dominant sexuality in organizations.[11] Power imbalances based on gender shape workplace culture, providing a set of informal rules that determine sexual interactions and behaviors.[12] For example, women in low-status jobs or feminized forms of employment, such as temporary work, often experience sexual objectification.[13] At the same time, women's entrance into male-dominated jobs or jobs not traditionally held by women increases the likelihood and extent of sexual harassment.[14]

Not all sexual interactions are harmful or should be deemed harassment, and workers experience sexual behaviors and interactions differently. Some may take certain interactions as enjoyable or fun, while others may view the same interactions in a negative light. As Christine Williams, Patti Giuffre, and Kirsten Dellinger argue, "sexual harassment and sexual consent are not polar opposites, in contrast to the assumption of much legal theory"; rather, how workers identify sexual harassment and draw boundary lines depends on workplace contexts.[15]

For example, women who work as waitresses may see sexual interactions as a part of the job, even an enjoyable part, especially when they are interactions with potential intimate partners. Yet they may categorize very similar encounters as harassment when they involve sexual advances from someone in a more powerful position, such as a manager, or someone of a different race or sexual orientation.[16] When a workplace is highly sexualized, women workers are sometimes expected to participate in sexual banter and accept the sexualized aspects of the job.[17] Women's interpretation of sexual interactions can be ambiguous because women may see sexualized actions as "normal" in a "man's world" and thus something that should not bother them.[18] Women's reluctance to label harmful behaviors as harassment may be part of a strategy for survival in a male-dominated workplace.[19]

## Sexual Harassment in Japanese Firms

In contrast with the Western management style, Japanese firms are characterized by a seniority-based hierarchy that emphasizes group uniformity over individualism, meaning that workers are expected to strictly obey their seniors in the firm in exchange for lifelong employment.[20] Japanese feminists have argued that the emphasis on group conformity has made women more vulnerable to sexual harassment and less likely to fight it.[21] Also, cultural expectations regarding women's behavior in the workplace—for example, that they should speak less frequently and more indirectly than men—have also promoted sexual harassment of women.[22] Some studies found that reported harassers in Japan tend to be supervisors, while reported harassers in the United States are often coworkers or subordinates.[23] Japanese feminists argue that sexual harassment in Japan often follows one (or more) patterns: (1) a man imposes the wife role on a woman worker; (2) a man deludes himself into believing that a woman worker feels personal affection toward him; (3) a man feels envy and resentment toward a woman who has superior talent or who rejects taking roles subordinate to him; or (4) a man takes revenge against a woman who does not accept his sexual desire for her.[24]

A number of court cases illustrate the common pattern of sexual harassment in which the harasser is a male supervisor. In 2002 a woman worker who was sexually assaulted by a top manager in Oita tried to avoid his repeated sexual advances; the manager responded by firing her for excessive absences and having a poor work attitude.[25] In 2008 the Ministry of Health, Labour and Welfare mediated a case in which a woman worker had suffered from continual sexual harassment by the top manager of her company. After refusing his advances, the worker was fired by the manager for her "bad work attitude." This manager insisted that he did not realize his behaviors could be considered sexual harassment and maintained that he fired her because she lacked "cooperative attitudes" with regard to the other workers.[26] Both cases resulted in the court's ordering the firms to pay compensation to the female workers.

In Japanese firms, sexual behavior among workers often occurs at after-work drinking meetings. After-work drinking in restaurants, bars, and hostess clubs has long been a critical part of Japanese organizational culture. Kazue Muta argues that drinking-based organizational events—such as outings, banquets, and overnight trips that Japanese companies often arrange for the purpose of developing "group harmony" in the workforce—promote foolish, even outlandish, behavior among male workers, including sexual harassment.[27]

In addition, male workers' use of hostess clubs has long been a popular business custom in Japan. Anne Allison, in her study of Japanese hostess clubs, discusses men's use of these clubs as a way of enhancing male homosocial bonds and displaying their power over women.[28] Japanese women in hostess clubs are expected to please male customers by "servicing the cigarettes and drinks of customers, servicing male egos with compliments and flattery, and servicing male authority by never contradicting what the man says."[29] They essentially take care of the men almost as motherly figures. Hostess women "accept, reflect, and augment" the men to enhance their self-images,[30] and the men focus on themselves and their male relations by depersonalizing the women.[31] Male workers' use of the sex entertainment industry, including strip clubs and sex workers, is also common. In 1996, the *New York Times* reported, "[In Japan], clients might be taken to a 'soapland,' an establishment in which a naked woman bathes a male customer. In New York, the Japanese businessman belonged to a members-only club, 30 to 40 percent of whose members were Japanese, that featured a sauna, swimming pool and prostitutes."[32]

As Allison describes, the unique gender dynamic that exists in hostess clubs dictates that sexual interactions between men and women will operate based on a hegemonic script of male camaraderie, empowerment, and entertainment, in which the women are expected to cater to the men's pleasure and mediate the men's relationships with other men. Allison describes the sexually "masturbatory" dynamic:

> The women may use a sexually flirtatious style, but what is produced has less to do with a heterosexual relationship than with a man's relationship with himself or other men. In this sense, the sexuality is masturbatory; the erotic object is not the woman but the man, and the female is just a device to enhance the male's self-image.[33]

> [. . .]

> That a hostess is expected to empty herself in a sense—strip herself of a personal identity and subjectivity to become the image and construct of woman desired by men in hostess clubs—is common knowledge.[34]

The male worker–hostess woman script has long been used to maintain organizational order and group integration in Japanese companies. This does not mean that Japanese women workers always suffer in drinking places; in fact, both women and men may enjoy interacting casually with other workers. But the gendered script often forces women workers into a position of "emphasized femininity,"[35] mirroring the gender inequality and sex segregation in Japanese organizations as well as the cultural images of subordinate femininity so commonplace there.

## Sexual Harassment Laws and Policies in Japan

Due to the openness of its legal system and its tradition of individual rights, the United States has taken the leading role in the regulation of sexual harassment.[36] In the United States, sexual harassment is defined as a form of gender discrimination, prohibited under Title VII of the 1964 Civil Rights Act. The EEOC has the authority to investigate discrimination complaints and file lawsuits against employers.

Internationally, the legal definition and the use of the term "sexual harassment" varies from country to country. In France, sexual harassment is covered under the penal code and is defined as a form of sexual violence, a category that also includes rape, sexual assault, and exhibitionism, whereas employment retaliation linked to sexual harassment is addressed under the labor code.[37] Punishment for sexual harassment under the French penal code is harsh, as it involves a one-year prison term. In Germany, labor law views sexual harassment as the failure of employers to protect individuals from harassment; thus, it is defined as a violation of the work contract.[38] Different from its characterization in the United States, sexual harassment in Germany is considered an unfair workplace practice that is often seen as a type of conflict among coworkers, or between superiors and employees. Thus, it is seen as a collective problem rather than as an individual or personal matter.[39] The European Commission defines sexual harassment as a "violation of dignity," which draws on the Continent's tradition of workers' rights and the international discourse of human rights.[40]

In Japan, provisions on sexual harassment first appeared in 1997, when the revised Equal Employment Opportunity Law defined two types: quid pro quo and hostile work environment. Sexual harassment in Japan is illegal under the tort law of the Civil Code, as it violates women's "personality rights" or "rights to the dignity of [their] personality regarding sexuality" or "personal interest"— terms that derive from German law.[41] Here, a "right" means a "legally protected interest" or "interest that is considered to need protection under tort law."[42] When a supervisor demands sexual favors from a plaintiff, such conduct can be seen as an infringement of the plaintiff's personal rights, personal dignity, or sexual freedom, and whether the behavior is illegal or not is determined "in light of the totality of the circumstances."[43]

In its emphasis on the personal right to dignity and workers' rights, the legal interpretation of sexual harassment in Japan appears to be close to the European definition. Similar to the European Union's "individual dignity" approach, Japan's personal rights approach may have wider applicability than the US sex-discrimination approach, especially "in cases where courts cannot find that working conditions were adversely altered by sexual harassment or that the harassing conduct was carried out because of gender."[44]

While the development of legal regulations in Japan has been important in terms of protecting workers', and particularly women workers', personal rights, the Equal Employment Opportunity Law lacks mechanisms for effective legal enforcement.[45] The 1997 EEOL only required employers to make an effort in good faith to prevent sexual harassment,[46] and while the 2007 revision included a maximum penalty, it only involved publicizing a firm's name when it failed to comply with the law.[47] Consolation money to be paid to the victims is not substantial, with the maximum being about $25,000.[48] And individuals cannot sue employers under the EEOL itself;[49] a worker can only bring a case to a local branch of the Ministry of Health, Labour and Welfare, which provides mediation services. Penalties for harassers in Japanese firms can include salary reduction, demotion, transfer to a different section, suspension, and termination of employment.

Some US firms prohibit intimate relationships among employees in order to legally protect the firms;[50] in Japan, however, firms' monitoring of workers' intimate involvement as an official policy is uncommon. Still, a small number of firms, including IBM Japan, have officially prohibited intimate relationships between supervisors and subordinate workers as inappropriate.[51]

# Sexualized Workplace Culture and Women's Obligations

How do women view and define sexual interactions in different workplace contexts? I examine three common interpretations of sexual behaviors in Japanese firms. First, women workers viewed sexual interactions as a part of their jobs when taking clients to hostess clubs, although this responses differed depending on work status. Second, women saw men's touching or groping as "joking around" when such actions occurred in an after-work drinking setting. Third, when sexual interactions took place during regular working hours, women defined the behaviors as sexual harassment.

## Taking Clients to Hostess Clubs

Laurie Morgan and Karin Martin reported that US saleswomen who attended strip clubs with male workers expressed varying responses, from viewing the occasions as opportunities for networking to feeling left out or alienated.[52] Among the Japanese workers I interviewed, a couple of women had accompanied male coworkers to such venues, although a majority of the women had not but knew that men attended hostess clubs and sex entertainment clubs. The women's responses to such customs varied from annoyed to envious, and sometimes a combination of both. Kaoru, a thirty-three-year-old at a cosmetics firm, talked about her boyfriend who worked at a trading company: "I don't want him to go to such places . . . but he has to," she said. "They are all paid for by his company. They go to *fuzoku* [sex entertainment clubs], too. When his friend in the same company made business trips to Thailand and Vietnam, his boss would tell this guy to pick a woman at the dinner place." These women at the dinner table were sex workers.

Tami, a thirty-eight-year-old manager, worked in Daigo Life Insurance. She and her boss often took the CEOs of client companies to hostess clubs. "It is a part of the sales job," she said. She claimed that she mingled really well with hostess women in the clubs: "I would just join these hostess women and act like them, joking with my bosses, pouring alcohol for the clients, and chatting with clients and these women. The clients usually like it. They would remember me really well, because they had never seen a female branch manager before." Tami found it enjoyable and beneficial to align herself with the hostesses and play up her femininity; it gave her an opportunity to network and also gave her access to organizational power.

Calling herself *oyaji* (the term applied to a middle-aged Japanese salary-man bound to the company) and viewing herself as "one of the boys," Tami attended daily drinking sessions with her bosses, coworkers, and clients, and played golf every weekend. She said, "I don't care if some of these men hold my shoulder or touch me jokingly. If they did more than just touching, I would tell them to stop it in a nice way." She established boundaries by viewing this type of "joking" touching by clients as acceptable. Tami also never went to hostess clubs alone with her clients; she always went with others, usually her bosses.

Naomi, a twenty-seven-year-old who formerly worked as an MR (medical representative) at a pharmaceutical company, offered a contrast to Tami. Naomi described her previous workplace as full of sexism and misogyny. She said that a large number of women were hired as MRs solely to entertain the medical doctors. Naomi revealed that she spent so much time at these clubs that she sometimes went straight there from home in the morning rather than going to the office first.

Naomi's workplace consisted mostly of men and was highly male dominated. The women sales workers in the company were explicitly valued for their young appearance and obedience, and were seen as disposable by the time they reached the age of thirty. Naomi said:

> Only young women can do sales because the client doctors are mostly men and they like young women. . . . These doctors hate older women who would say things to them. Most women in this company were concerned and terrified when they come close to the age of thirty, and they usually quit working then. . . . These doctors would tell me, "Don't become that kind of woman who cannot marry and just has to work in this company after she passes the age of thirty." How miserable that is! Their wives would always tell me to find a good man to marry soon.

Naomi would take her clients to hostess clubs or sex entertainment clubs daily, "because they want to go to those places," but she was usually told to wait for them outside in the car or at a coffee shop: "These doctors want to go to mostly *kyabakura* [hostess clubs], and sometimes *fuzoku* [sex entertainment clubs]. They would not allow me to go in with them. I was told to wait outside in the car or go home. All the time. I could only enter new half clubs [gay clubs]. . . . I tried to view taking them to these places positively. I mean, they would at least tell me honestly they wanted to go to such places, like they would tell men."

Naomi did not enjoy the routine of waiting outside clubs to make sure that the clients were entertained. What she described to me was a highly misogynistic workplace in which women were constantly criticized or bullied and only valued for their youth and their ability to play subordinate roles. Naomi did try to make the best of things, interpreting going to the *kyabakura* positively because she could be seen as being "understanding" of the workplace culture, just like male workers. But she had few options apart from tolerating these organizational practices, and she eventually left her MR job "to find a more humane workplace."

Unlike Tami, Naomi viewed taking clients to the hostess clubs and sex entertainment clubs as sexist and "not humane." Women workers may enjoy taking clients to hostess clubs if they see it as a marker of organizational privilege, and because access to them is usually denied to women, but they may also view it as a sexist custom when their sole obligation is to please male clients, and when their performance of that obligation directly affects their job evaluation and chances of promotion.

In the United States, corporations have been cautious about business use of strip clubs because of the risk of sex-discrimination lawsuits. When women workers are excluded from such events, they lose clients and miss information and thus risk losing promotional opportunities. In 1996, more than twenty women at Smith Barney claimed sex discrimination and sexual harassment as a result of male workers' fraternity-like "boom-boom room" practices. Morgan Stanley instituted a no-strip-clubs policy in 2002, and it also paid out $54 billion in 2004 in a case in which a saleswoman was excluded from a trip to a strip club and other client events.[53] But while some industries and specific firms may have strict regulations, others continue to use strip clubs for the purpose of networking and the exchange of professional information.[54]

In my interviews with workers in Japan, only a couple of women managers mentioned that they lack access to the men's network and that not attending hostess club meetings and sexually oriented activities might affect their promotion chances. The revised EEOL, enacted in 2007, prohibits sexual harassment of both women and men. Since then, the Japanese media often talks about the common practice of men forcing other men to visit hostess clubs and sex entertainment clubs after work, and speculates that this could represent sexual harassment against men.[55] But there has never been a discussion of whether conducting meetings in such places could harm women workers or the work environment.

## Playing the Hostess at Drinking Meetings

Earlier studies have indicated that women are reluctant to label and report coworkers' sexual advances as sexual harassment because they see sexual interactions as a part of the job.[56] Or, to put it another way, women try to accommodate or grow accustomed to invasive sexual interactions because they are a custom of the "man's world" and women feel they need to fit in.[57] Women workers may interpret sexual advances from supervisors or someone in power as "harassment," but they are reluctant to see sexual interactions with "potential partners" as harassing.[58] Sexual interactions in the workplace can also affirm women workers' belief in their attractiveness and femininity in highly sexualized work contexts.[59] In short, the boundaries between acceptable behavior and harassing behavior can be ambiguous, especially when workplace culture normalizes this type of behavior.

In after-work drinking meetings in Japan, which take place from dinnertime to midnight in restaurants or bars, workers interact informally, chat, perform karaoke, and do stunts such as singing company songs, doing magic tricks, or chugging a bottle of beer or other alcohol. New or young workers are often forced to engage in these stunts, a type of hazing. Women workers are commonly expected to sit next to their male managers or bosses. Also, the women or the youngest workers are expected to "pour alcohol" for the senior workers. Workers and managers in a section or floor may call for these meetings as often as three or four times a week. The traditional aim of such meetings is the enhancement of group solidarity. As Japanese firms emphasize solidarity and conformity, willingness to attend these events can affect bosses' informal evaluations.

Women workers commonly drew boundary lines between the sexual conduct that occurs in drinking settings and during regular work hours. However, in the legal sense, invasive and harmful sexual behaviors at these after-hours meetings have been treated the same as similar behaviors during working hours. In 1998, an Osaka court ordered a male worker and his employer to pay compensation because the man forced a female worker down on a sofa, kissed her hands, and put his hands under her skirt at an after-work drinking meeting. The court claimed that the male worker took advantage of his superior position at work, and thus his behavior related to his job. The man's behavior was described as a violation of the woman's personal rights.[60] However, in 1998, a Tokyo district court denied a woman's claim that she suffered from being forced to attend drinking meetings after work, arguing that forcing workers to attend drinking meetings might be inappropriate but it is not illegal.[61]

Most of the workers I interviewed saw after-work drinking as an important custom of their company. Many of the women reported having been touched, grabbed, and groped by men at such events. Some women said they genuinely enjoyed drinking meetings, even though there were almost always some forced activities. Yuka, the twenty-nine-year-old woman who worked at Hanakage in marketing, would go drinking after work, usually at nine or ten at night, about three times a week. She said, "They often force younger workers to perform some stunts and sing a company's song. The women pour alcohol for the men. I enjoy it. It's fun. . . . I knew one woman who didn't like such events, and she eventually quit the company."

Rika, a thirty-seven-year-old manager at Shijo Asset Management, remembered the older male workers saying, "*Ne-chan*" [Hey, girl] to her, as if she were an employee in a club. She said, "These senior men would see us the same as some girls in the clubs. I saw so many non-career-track women who were touched and groped by their bosses who called such behaviors "massage." That was just so normal in the past. . . . I am a career-track worker, so nobody has touched me." The boundary line was drawn in accord with women's job status, whereby women on the lower rungs were viewed as more acceptable to touch in a sexual way. Rika thought that men avoided sexual interactions with the few career-track women workers.

Similar to women profiled in Amy Denissen's study of tradeswomen who regarded workplace sexual interactions as something they had to get used to in a "man's world,"[62] the women workers I interviewed also saw men's touching in drinking settings as "joking around," or as a behavior that is common in a male-dominated workplace and not something to take personally. Emi, a thirty-eight-year-old worker at Takane, described sexual interactions in drinking meetings in exactly this way. She said, "I think sexual harassment is a matter of whether you take it seriously or not. I don't take things seriously." Saki, a thirty-one-year-old non-career-track worker at Shijo Asset Management, had moved there from a securities company that was a parent firm of her current company. At the securities company, she was often touched and groped by male workers of her age in drinking settings: "It happened all the time. Some men would grab my chest from behind. . . . I would respond by twisting their arms when they extended over my body. I always tried to sit far from particular men who would do those things. . . . I try not to take things seriously." She tried to make jokes out of men's behaviors so as not to offend the men. She said, "One time I was sick, and this guy came up to me and teased me about being pregnant. . . . I was furious, but I laughed and said, 'Oh well, it's because you never use protection.' This guy was surprised and left."

Young workers, and those who were new to a company, considered it especially important to attend drinking meetings and gain recognition from other workers. Some thought that both sexual and nonsexual interactions at such events could facilitate mutual acceptance, recognition, and understanding among workers. But some women I interviewed felt ambivalent about their sexualized roles in these situations. Misa, a twenty-four-year-old, worked at Daigo Life Insurance as a career-track worker and attended the after-work drinking sessions three or four times a week. While she enjoyed the drinking meetings, she was frustrated by the hostess role she was expected to play, which included enduring touching and even men laying their heads in her lap:

> The men usually ask me to sit next to them. I don't mind doing that . . . but then, I feel like I am a hostess in a club. They want me to listen to them. I have to constantly say, "Wow, that's great" or "I understand," and nod to whatever they say. Then they touch my knees. I try to remove their hands from my body without offending them. Those who are in their forties and fifties are usually the ones who touch me, hold my shoulder, and put their faces on my knees. . . . Nobody helps me.

Misa added, "I am usually not allowed to sit next to women workers. I can't talk with other women. The men are having fun. I don't share in the fun with these men. I just sit there and smile. I think that's just part of my job." Despite being a career-track worker and having an educational background similar to that of the men, she had to put extra effort into being a good listener and not challenging the men. She said she responded to the sexually invasive jokes and touching as if she didn't mind them.

Some women explicitly described men's physical touching in drinking settings as being harmful, but they also expressed concern about the potential repercussions from taking action against these men. Kaoru, thirty-three, had repeated experiences of being touched, grabbed, and hugged at drinking clubs: "When I go to drinking clubs, guys will come up to me and say, 'Hey, you work hard,' and put their hands on my neck and shoulders. When I go to the bathroom, guys will follow me and start touching me." Kaoru tried to avoid attending these sessions after repeated physical touching by men. Because she had worked at her job a long time, she hoped that not attending might not negatively affect her. But she noted that younger workers seemed to be in a more vulnerable position, as they could be targets of exclusion and bullying if they refused to take part: "While drinking or performing karaoke, they [male superiors or elders of the sections] would force us to perform some stunts. When you say no, or say something against them, they tend to exclude you at work, too. It happened in my third and fourth year."

Some women resented the cultural imperatives of gender in drinking settings, which relegate women to the hostess role. Like hostess women, women workers are also expected to make drinks and serve food to male workers. Mariko, a twenty-eight-year-old worker at Hanakage, did not enjoy drinking meetings:

> When we go drinking, some men totally believe making drinks is a woman's job. I don't mind making some drinks for them, but I hate that they think it is a woman's job. This guy who sits next to me once asked

me why I didn't put salad on his plate, while I was still making drinks for him. Even Mama-san [the female owner of the bar] said, "I should put all the food in front of this girl [so that Mariko could serve all the food to the men]." I was really angry. My hands were trembling.

Demeaning women at a drinking establishment often turns out to be a man's outlet for humiliating women workers and gaining a sense of power over them. Akiko, a thirty-year-old worker in Shijo Asset Management, was appalled when her boss started evaluating the physical appearances of women workers during after-work drinking: "He said to my female boss in her forties, 'You are old. You don't even have a period anymore, do you?' Then he told another woman that she had too many lumps and marks on her face and she needed to cover them better. Then he said to me, 'You look like you would be more suitable as a mistress than for marrying and being a wife.' I just couldn't believe him."

She said that all the women sat silently and just smiled back at their boss. "I think the women in this company are more mature than the men, so they just kept quiet and smiled," said Akiko. A man's humiliation of women workers follows the hegemonic script of gender in the Japanese workplace, wherein women workers are expected to tolerate man's rude behaviors by saying nothing.

Similar to the tradeswomen's informal "coping" responses in the United States,[63] many of the women I interviewed tried to ignore sexual interactions that took place during informal drinking settings or viewed them as a "joking" type of interaction to be expected in the male-dominated workplace culture. In 1997, a Japanese court (in *Kono v. Shimizu Construction Co.*) denied a woman's claim of sexual harassment because of her failure to counterattack or take action.[64] While the court eventually overturned the case in favor of the woman, Japanese feminists criticized the court's gender-biased decision.[65] The findings in this section confirm that women's tolerance of men's actions should not be interpreted as their giving consent.[66]

## Taking Action against Sexual Harassment

Among the thirty-nine women I interviewed, only one had reported an instance of sexual harassment to her company. Earlier studies indicated that women report incidents of sexual harassment when violence or the threat of violence is involved,[67] when the offensive conduct escalates or persists, or when a third party supports the woman's view of an incident having crossed the line.[68] Confronting a harasser directly or having a third person mediate her request to change a harasser's behavior may be risky for a woman because it may result in counter-accusations against her.[69]

Kaoru, thirty-three, experienced repeated touching and grabbing by men. When she talked with her boss at Takane in a conference room, he would start touching her. When she went on an overseas trip, another boss of hers sat next to her on a train and touched and kissed her. Though such incidents continued for a couple of months, she was reluctant to report them to the company: "I just didn't want to make a big deal out of these things. I just tried to leave in such situations, saying, 'Sorry, I need to go' or 'I have to meet this person now.' I think I have been pretty good about it." Kaoru asked her manager to allow her to go on an overseas trip alone and tried to avoid intimate interactions with male workers in general.

Denissen has discussed US tradeswomen's informal responses to troubling situations of sexual harassment in terms of four strategies that women might employ: (1) ignoring the actions, (2) changing their own appearance and/or actions, (3) withdrawing from the situation or avoiding the offender, and (4) quitting their job.[70] The women in her study resorted to these informal relief measures because of the potential costs of formally reporting the behaviors. Similarly, Kaoru was concerned about being seen negatively by coworkers if she made "a big deal out of the incidents," and therefore she chose to respond by avoiding the harassers.

As most individuals in Japanese firms stay on until they retire, women workers, who are concerned about being seen as a problem, are unlikely to report harassers to their employers. Furthermore, since Japanese laws did not penalize companies until recently for their failure to have counseling services, training, and prevention programs on sexual harassment, many women may have deemed it useless to report incidents to management. Finally, as a sense of shame and embarrassment operates much more strongly in Japanese companies as a means to control workers than it does in US companies,[71] women workers might see reporting offensive sexual behaviors as shameful and embarrassing, and might thus avoid doing so.

Kanako, a twenty-seven-year-old worker at Takane, did report two incidents of sexual harassment to the management over a three-year period. The first incident involved repeated sexual touching by a male coworker. Kanako called the second situation (discussed below) a combination of sexual harassment and power harassment. In both cases, the men were immediately moved to different sections within the company.

Many workers in Kanako's company want to work at the headquarters in Tokyo, so the selection process to fill positions there was highly competitive. A couple of years prior to our interview, Kanako was ordered by one manager in Tokyo to move from the local branch to work under him. As soon as she started working for him, the manager asked her to assist him on all his trips and to go to lunch and dinner with him every day. He often indicated that he liked her, and he soon started demanding that she call and e-mail him every day after work. Kanako said, "He really liked me. . . . If I went to lunch with other workers, he would be mad at me. I had to call him and e-mail him every day and just tell him what happened at work or to me. If I didn't e-mail him back, he would be so angry the next day. So I would return his e-mails. . . . These people don't understand what sexual harassment is at all."

Kanako's boss would also occasionally make her a target of his bullying. In Japanese companies in which the workers' sense of shame and embarrassment often serves as a means to maintain their compliance,[72] managers commonly exert and confirm their authority over subordinates by publicly shaming them. Kanako said:

> He wrote about all of my problems, like . . . the way I talk, the way I do presentations, the way I instruct training . . . probably about twenty problems about not just what I do, but also about who I am. Then he made me read the list out loud in front of all the workers. . . . Nobody could tell him anything. I was crying all the time. It was not just one time. He would not stop his anger until I cried. He never really suggested how to improve. Then, whenever I cried, he would come to me and say really kind words to me. It was very strange.

His aberrant behaviors of scolding and consoling, and his demands to e-mail him daily and accompany him on his trips and out to lunch and dinner, lasted about six months. One time, Kanako directly confronted him. "I complained to him that this was 'power harassment,'" she said. "Then it got worse. He got defensive." Kanako eventually went to the company's counseling room and also told the section's general manager about what she had endured. Her boss, the harasser, was transferred to a different section, with a demotion.

There may be a few factors that explain Kanako's report to the firm. Uggen and Shinohara found that women in their twenties are the most likely among all age groups to report harassment.[73] Legal changes and sanctions against sexual harassment seem to have had the greatest impact on younger women workers' attitudes. Moreover, the cosmetics firm for which Kanako worked has been known as one of the most woman-friendly firms in Japan because of its efforts to increase its number of female managers, to retain women workers with children, and to provide parental leave benefits. The firm has also long emphasized its commitment to combating sexual harassment. Finally, coworkers had witnessed the boss bullying Kanako in the meeting, and such public evidence might have made Kanako more confident about making a formal report to the management.

This chapter extends on previous research to show that where women draw boundary lines between consensual sexual interactions and harmful ones depends on the workplace context.[74] Organizational customs not only shape sexual behaviors, they also shape women workers' responses and thus the meanings of sexual harassment. Many customs and practices discussed here center on enhancing men's camaraderie and their display of hegemonic masculinity, with the expectation that women workers will engage in subordinate roles in a display of traditional femininity.

At hostess clubs, some women workers put extra effort into informally accommodating men's sexual behaviors and interactions. Tami, a female manager, even claimed to enjoy the events, while Naomi viewed her job as inhumane and eventually quit. Most of the women I interviewed did not take seriously men's sexual advances occurring during after-hours drinking, instead interpreting them as organizational customs or simply ignoring them. But some of the women considered men's personal touching, groping, or rude remarks about women's appearances harmful. The workers' informal sexual interactions in after-work drinking meetings often follow a hegemonic gendered script wherein men enjoy camaraderie and women engage in serving roles; such a gendered script can foster men's sexual advances and harassing of female workers, although harassing and harmful conduct are often obscured by the discourse of "joking around." Kanako confronted her harasser and eventually consulted with her firm's counseling room and general manager. Her assertiveness in taking public action might have been influenced by several factors, such as her having witnesses in the workplace, her belonging to the postlaw generation and thus being well-informed about her legal rights, and the firm's public efforts to eradicate sexual harassment.

Because these findings are based on a very small sample, they cannot be assumed to reflect the situation of all Japanese workers. Further large-scale studies of organizational cultures and practices that legitimize certain sexual interactions and behaviors will be necessary. A study of men's experiences of organizational sexuality would also further illuminate gender inequality in sexual interactions in Japanese firms. The findings do suggest that research on sexual harassment in Japan should take into account that the male-dominant organizational culture, and women's lack of power in the workplace, normalizes or supports sexual interactions that some women consider harmful. As Giuffre and Williams found, many women are active participants in the sexualized culture of the workplace, but the hegemonic script about gender legitimizes certain sexual interactions and makes sexual harassment hard to identify and eradicate.[75]

In the context of the United States, Morgan and Martin suggest enforcing policies that prohibit entertaining clients in settings that restrict women's access, including strip clubs and golf courses, and reevaluating the appropriateness of offsite entertainment.[76] These suggestions should also inform Japanese firms' use of hostess clubs and the sex industry. At the same time, I argue that the absence of women in middle and upper management in the organizational hierarchy contributes to the maintenance of misogynistic organizational practices in Japanese firms. In addition to policy enforcement to regulate business practices, desegregation of the labor market and the employment structure, as well as equalizing the gender hierarchy in organizations, is necessary.

# Conclusion

Even though the rise of educated women in Japan enhances women's aspirations for economic independence and inculcates gender-egalitarian attitudes,[1] it is likely that Japanese companies will continue to block women's advancement into middle and upper management positions. A set of long-established management and employment customs in Japanese companies, including seniority pay and promotion and track hiring of women, counteracts gender equality and women's upward mobility. Because of the traditional absence of women leaders in the Japanese business community, organizational gender biases and stereotypes remain strong. The practice of having long work hours has also legitimized vertical sex segregation and normalized men's physical and psychological suffering. And a lack of labor mobility and an exclusive emphasis on in-firm skills in the marketplace constrain employees' options when it comes to changing jobs.

The exclusion of a large part of the workforce from positions of authority and their relegation to a low status has led to savings on labor costs, an increase in management control, tight control of the labor market, and the stabilization of business-state relations. A vertically sex-segregated employment pattern has sustained male lifetime economic security, the male-breadwinner family structure, stable state-bank-led management, and a conformity and insider-based workplace culture with little pressure from outside shareholders. Because vertical sex segregation in Japanese companies has played a critical role in Japanese business and in the sustenance of Japan's system of coordinated capitalism (including the male-breadwinner family and the welfare regime as well as management that is state-bank led and male-protection oriented), Japanese management is unlikely to let go of its dependence on cheap female labor by making the status and pay of women equal to that of men. Unless the Japanese state and business community come up with better cost-saving options, the current sex-segregated customs of pay and promotion and dual hiring will continue to keep down the number of women in leadership positions.

Large Japanese companies uphold the logic of using economical female labor not just in terms of hiring large numbers of temporary female workers but also in terms of seniority pay and promotions, track hiring, household-benefit payments, and the restraint of labor market mobility. Japanese companies' confinement of workers under their own terms and conditions, with no labor mobility, hampers women's chances to go up the corporate ladder. I do not mean that Japanese companies should remove employment protection from workers so that they are free to move to different jobs at the expense of their economic security. But I do argue that equalizing the employment protections that exist for lifelong-employed men and for women is necessary, and that it is also important to increase the choices of jobs and opportunities for promotion and higher salaries (based on a worker's skill set) beyond the current narrow range.

Just as Japanese management has long taken advantage of women workers' cheap labor, other institutions, including the family, state, banks, and courts, have upheld and benefited from Japanese companies' sex segregation. Sex segregation is sustained by corporate management and state policymakers who continue to rely on the traditional employment system and have little interest in rights or equality. As Mari Miura notes, the Liberal Democratic Party and Japanese conservative elites have been hostile to the idea of human rights and have historically resisted the institution of policies based on these rights in Japan.[2] It is apparent that gender inequality has been functional and beneficial to the Japanese state and business community, which continue to prioritize Japan's economic development as a national goal at the cost of the development of Japan as a civil society.

The major reason why there has been little change in Japanese management, the labor market, and state/business-led institutional dependence in Japan is the Japanese business culture's style of conformity management, characterized by a reluctance to implement necessary innovations and liberal reforms or to diversify and mobilize the labor market. Japanese management places too much emphasis on conformity, and the elderly dominate Japan's decision making, which makes change extremely difficult. The elderly top executives of Toshiba resigned in 2015 after demanding that their subordinates attain an unrealistically high profit goal, which led those subordinates to engage in many years of systemic accounting fraud and cover-up. The Japanese media reported that the main cause of this fraud and accompanying cover-up was the authoritarian and conformity-driven culture, in which no subordinate can say anything against top management.[3] Lifelong employment and seniority further sustain these vested interests and ensure the continuation of male dominance. Women's low status will continue to be blocked by this institutional and organizational inertia.

Can Japanese companies catch up with Western companies in terms of gender equality and the betterment of employed women's status? The Japanese government has proclaimed a national goal of increasing women in leadership positions, and Japanese companies often seem to achieve this by using positive action to increase, by a small amount, the number of women managers while continuing to relegate a large number of women to lower positions. But adding token women in business and politics does not equate with structural improvements leading to gender equality.

The implementation of gender-equal programs in Japanese firms has not been dealt with as an organizational and management issue (or, needless to say, as an issue of individual rights, equality, and justice) that requires changes to traditional customs and informal rules as well as to formal policies. The Japanese government is unwilling to pressure Japanese companies to change their approach to management. As a result, the emphasis has often been placed on women needing to adapt themselves to the traditional system. Yet, as Robin Ely and Debra Meyerson famously have written, the "fix the women" approach is limited.[4] When women are the sole targets of organizational intervention, they are given training programs, leadership courses, and networking workshops to develop their skills; this approach leaves male standards intact, blames only the women for being in the lower positions than the men, and can even generate a backlash among men who see the programs as providing unfair advantages to women. Ely and Meyerson also argue that even the most common policy approaches to creating equal opportunities, such as initiating affirmative action programs, establishing transparent promotion policies to ensure fairness, instituting formal mentoring programs for women to have access to informal networks, and introducing work-family programs, are not adequate, as they do not "fundamentally challenge the sources of power or the social interactions that reinforce and maintain the status quo."[5] Indeed, Japan's current approach to increasing the number of female managers and employees without addressing organizational and structural problems is far from the solution that is needed to change most of the gender-biased customs I have discussed in this book.

Obviously, Prime Minister Abe's approach to the issue of women's status is inadequate. It puts little pressure on the Japanese business community to make any further structural reforms that would affect women and asks for nothing more than minimal voluntary changes. The government's initial motive for addressing the issue of gender equality and work-life balance was its wish to raise the country's birthrate.[6] However, Japan's low birth rate is itself possibly exacerbated by the sex-segregated employment structure and traditional gender-bound family in Japan,[7] and the government has no option but to consider shifting the norm of the typical Japanese family from the male-breadwinner type to a more egalitarian structure. It needs to come up with better policies and programs, perhaps among them providing firms with monetary incentives to move toward gender equality, imposing harsher penalties on firms that continue to employ discriminatory customs, and promoting a shift from an emphasis on the male-breadwinner family regime to a more egalitarian work-family structure. It should also address the problem of the weak role of Japanese laws and courts in advancing gender equality and their tendency to conform to the wishes of the state and business community.

Although lenient paid parental leave may result in increased numbers of working women and working mothers, it does almost nothing to change the distinct pattern of vertical segregation in Japanese business. Because generous parental leave policies for mothers promote gender bias, these policies may exacerbate employers' overall gender biases and reinforce sex segregation so that the majority of women, especially mothers, remain on the lowest rungs of the ladder.[8] Again, government-led reforms will be effective only if they are combined with significant changes in Japanese management customs.

The Japanese business community should eliminate customs that equate women with cost savings for firms and should find alternative methods of saving on labor costs. As I have stressed throughout this book, the adoption of mid-career hires, performance-based pay, and globalized standards of business skills would not only move Japan's business system and capitalism forward but would also enhance women's chances to move up. A performance-based promotion system would allow the attainment of rewards to advance women in their careers at a much earlier stage of their lives and would make it more likely that women could sustain positions of authority or climb the career ladder, regardless of their having children or other career interruptions.

Kuniko Ishiguro, in her study of female managers in three companies, found high rates of female managers and highly egalitarian practices in a company that used performance-based evaluation rather than seniority promotion.[9] She pointed out that this egalitarian Japanese firm also had a history of hiring a large number of women college graduates because they were not able to hire men with the same education (as there was a shortage of men in the growing economy). Her study indicates that gender-equal hiring and performance-based promotion, even under the lifelong-employment system, could reduce vertical sex segregation. Further study of such examples of reforms of Japanese management and sex segregation will be necessary. It is likely that with a large number of retirees looming in Japan, Japanese companies could increasingly replace retired lifelong employees with temporary workers to save money. Yet, such short-term cutting of labor costs may lead to decreased economic security for employees and a lowering of workers' skills and motivation. Increasing the number of temporary workers also exacerbates women's overall low status in Japanese companies, as many temp workers are women.

In conducting my interviews for this book, I found strong gender stereotypes among Japanese workers, both male and female. Judging and sorting women based on gender essentialism (as emotional, irrational, and unprofessional), the ideology of separate spheres (that a woman's place is in the home), and gender hierarchy (that women should be men's assistants) is pervasive in Japanese firms. To address this, first, the number of women in leadership and authority positions does need to increase; if the population of women workers becomes far more diverse, workers and managers will realize that their imposition of monolithic traits and essentialist images on women does not reflect the reality of women workers. Second, voluntary positive action in promotion and hiring at the firm level is not sufficient to reduce gender inequality in Japanese firms; institutions of higher education must also provide better educational and training programs in the process of socialization regarding the value of gender equality and other types of equality and diversity. The government and women's and feminist groups all need to aid in social and cultural consciousness raising regarding the equality of women. In short, transforming traditional concepts of masculinity and femininity in Japanese companies will require both organizational changes and individual consciousness raising.

Even though the Japanese government emphasizes the idea of increasing women's employment as an engine of economic growth, a more systematic and structurally convincing approach is needed to make the reform truly happen—beyond asking employers to hire more women. In order to increase the number of women leaders, Japanese companies and related institutions must revise management, labor, and employment practices from the mode of state-led economic survival with an exclusive emphasis on male protection to one of global competition, self-expression, and individual skills.

The Japanese business community and the Japanese state are not willing to undertake a major transformation of management customs unless they feel serious pressure from global competition—pressure in the form of decreased profits.[10] In general, of course, vested interests are unlikely to change existing corporate customs as such changes might jeopardize their own economic security.[11] Indeed, changing customs such as seniority pay and promotion would not be easy in Japan, as these customs interact with companies' profit goals, their relationships with banks and other companies, and labor practices. Reforming or changing one part of Japanese management and corporate governance will reveal the necessity of further reforms to the entire system and will have a great impact on institutional equilibrium.

If a company decides to change the seniority system and starts rewarding workers based on individual performance regardless of age, this will distort the traditional system of seniority pay and promotion; thus, the company would no longer be able to save on labor costs through seniority pay. Also, those who are promoted in the early stages of their careers may leave the company for a better deal at another company, especially if more and more Japanese companies are open to changing the pay and promotion system. In addition, firms' hiring of increasing numbers of women under the current traditional system of Japanese management could eventually expose the gender bias in existing customs, and this would generate further pressure for firms to make changes. Of course, such pressure may not arise as long as senior men dominate and control the existing customs.

One possibility is that implementing gender egalitarianism in Japanese companies, combined with further intensification of global competition, may force changes in traditional Japanese management. If the labor market in Japan diversifies and the current system of lifelong employment loses legitimacy, Japanese companies will change (as will their relationships with banks and other financial institutions), as they will be unable to sustain long-term management while pursuing short-term profits. This may also weaken the long-term strength of the main banking system and the close state-business ties in Japan. Changes to the lifelong-employment system would make it difficult for Japanese firms to save on labor costs through customs such as long working hours and low pay for young workers, not to mention the hiring of many women at the assistant level.

Changes to, or the decline of, existing lifelong-employment and seniority-pay customs could make the maintenance of insider-only privilege and control of Japanese management difficult. Further pressure for transparency, openness, and fairness in management may arise. Consensus-based decision making, which has been maintained by the insiders and the old boys' clubs, will lose popularity if increasing numbers of men and women newly hired in mid-career obtain positions of power within companies. Because lifelong employment was the basis of loyalty and commitment to the community firm, the decline of lifelong employment may lead to the decline of loyalty-based, monolithic, paternal management. In contrast with such a possible future scenario, many Japanese companies and the Japanese business community may continue to resist changes.

# Feminism in Japan and the United States

Feminist movements, feminist discourses, and the cultural ideology of each country have influenced women's strides in employment and desegregation patterns in the United States and Japan. In the United States, attainment of the American dream or material success is regarded as important, and education is the tool used to climb the ladder. Likewise, women's economic and educational advances have also been critical goals of US feminist movements. Paula England writes that liberal individualism and gender egalitarianism in the United States have played critical roles in promoting the belief in individual achievement, equal opportunity, and access to education and self-chosen careers.[12] This emphasis on self-advancement and equal opportunity has led a large number of middle-class educated women who aspire to upward mobility to enter traditionally male-dominated jobs because most traditionally female jobs do not lead to the higher salaries and status of traditionally male jobs. A large number of women taking these traditionally male jobs has reduced sex segregation and increased women's visible advancement in the United States.

The US public increasingly views gender egalitarianism as critical to the evolution of their society. Feminist criticism and gender egalitarianism are also well integrated into educational institutions. High school and college students learn in the classroom that the masculine and feminine traits some might believe are innate characteristics are actually constructed socially and culturally, that men and women are more alike than different, and that traits some might perceive as gendered are often produced by gender inequality in society.[13] For example, many "masculine" and "feminine" traits and related emotions—such as tenderness, ambition, nurturing, and competence—are human qualities that both men and women share and should have equal access to.[14] Men's demasculinization and the degendering of everyone's life have been important goals of American feminist discourse. Achievement of gender equality in the United States is also about individual rights and civil responsibility. The absence of material resources, such as well-paid jobs and property for women, has traditionally made women financially vulnerable, and this is another issue that has been at the forefront of feminist discourse.[15] Additionally, women are now able to fulfill the civil obligation of fighting in the military.[16] Essentially, the idea that women should have the same economic and social rights as men is the basis of liberal feminism in the United States.

Joan Williams writes, "Assimilationist feminism is very strong in the United States. . . . The United States is probably the best industrialized country in the world for tomboys."[17] Williams points out that this popular belief has, at the same time, alienated some women who value traditional femininity.[18] She cites some feminist writers' negative views of housewives, depicting them as dressing like children and inhabiting a "private world of laundry and kissing boo-boos" or serving their families as "unpaid servants."[19] In a country like Japan, where the woman's economic dependence on the man was normalized under the male-breadwinner family regime, the idea of women's assimilation into a man's world may itself be seen as "different" and unacceptable.

Decoupling gender from existing customs and norms is one of the important ideas in American feminism. The existing models of manhood and masculinity are criticized not just for the harm they do to women but also for the damage they do to men and men's lives. Similar to Michael Kimmel, Williams writes that it is important to "decouple gender from the key habits and conventions that impoverish too many men and women—and brutalize others who cannot fit within the simple masculine-feminine dichotomy."[20] She elaborates:

> Healthy living does not consign men to a life of strategic self-seeking at the expense of the women who selflessly support them. Nor does it consign men to a life of endless work, outsourcing their children's childhoods to women and abandoning any hope of nonstrategic social connections. Feminists need to return to the early feminist insight that our current gender system impoverishes the lives of men as well as women. . . . We need to deconstruct gender, in order to allow men more room for caring, connection, and community and to allow women more room for an entitled sense of self-development, assertiveness and competition.[21]

For a healthy life, individuals, regardless of gender, should be able to earn a living and have equal access to economic, social, and cultural opportunities. But such degendering, as well as gender desegregation in both the public and private spheres, might not be easy to apply to Japanese men and women given that they have long been taught to live gendered lives in separate spheres of work and family.

In contrast, Japanese feminists have traditionally expressed suspicion and negativity toward American feminists' emphasis on women's assimilation into a man's world. Unlike the radical US feminists who see mothering as a site of women's oppression, past Japanese feminists have seen motherhood as empowering and revolutionary for women, even though the idea is limited since it is complicit with the Japanese state ideology of gender and traditional femininity, which have long confined women to the private sphere. Setsu Shigematsu notes the different line taken by Japanese feminist activists in the 1970s who "critiqued the state-sanctioned concept of motherhood" and were interested in women's control over their own reproduction.[22] They insisted on "decouple[ing] the legitimacy of giving birth from the marriage system and emphasized the need [for the Japanese state] to create the socioeconomic and cultural conditions under which women could freely determine whether or not to give birth." Meanwhile, Japanese feminists overall distanced themselves from women's economic achievement and the possibility of women's assimilation into a man's economic world. Shigematsu cites the notion held by the famous Japanese feminist Yayori Matsui, who stated, "I am suspicious about the American model of empowerment, which means the right to grasp for power just as men do."[23] Japanese feminists have viewed American feminists' strategy of attaining power in the same manner as powerful men as deceptive and inappropriate in light of the goal of achieving women's liberation. Japanese women's negativity toward US feminism might partly reflect the relationship of the two countries, particularly Japan's subordinate relationship to the United States in the postwar period. It might also reflect Japanese women's subordination to and dependence on the male-breadwinner ideology, given that Japanese women in the past were much more constrained in their economic and job options than American women of the same time period.

A famous feminist in the fields of literary criticism and sociology at the University of Tokyo, Chizuko Ueno, once explained that Japanese feminists, having focused on obtaining pleasure from the experience of motherhood, hoped they could maternalize society so that its members could build warm, caring relationships based on close bonds like those within families or between mother and child.[24] Ueno viewed this goal as a cultural product of Japan's group-oriented (rather than individualistic) values. She also pointed out that Japanese feminists' adherence to such maternal themes has legitimized male dominance and relegated women to the sphere of family.[25] However, it is not clear whether such idealization of motherhood or femininity remains dominant in Japan in the present day. Also, if so many Japanese women see mothering as such a liberating and empowering site, why is the birthrate steadily declining?

Japanese feminists have distanced themselves from promoting women's assimilation into a man's world, mostly because they view it as not helping but as exacerbating the exploitative and inhumane labor conditions in Japan, especially the extremely long working hours that men have no choice but to endure.[26] These feminists have viewed Japanese women's pursuit of power by working like men as futile for bringing about ideological change; instead, living "as humans" is what they suggest as a solution.[27] They see women's equality with men as not desirable if it means women too will work themselves to death in devotion to their companies. Suggesting that women withdraw from the world of work, however, simply reifies the Japanese state and corporate emphasis on separate-sphere ideology in which women do not need to work and Japanese men must put up with the long work hours. Also, with regard to claiming motherhood as a strategy for criticizing dominant masculinity, such a "value the feminine" approach—emphasizing the importance of traditionally feminine skills such as listening, collaborating, nurturing, and behind-the-scenes peacemaking—does little more than reinforce gender stereotypes and show women's appropriateness for "performing housekeeping duties of management."[28] Yet Japanese feminists have been reluctant to see the applicability of the American or Western feminist movement to the case of Japan.[29]

After the 1990s, Japanese feminism also became far more postmodern and further distanced itself from a commitment to social and policy changes. Ayako Kano, citing Aiko Okoshi's criticism of Japanese feminism's inadequate engagement with the human rights perspective and general discrimination issues, asserts that "Japanese postmodernism" targets the masses with an emphasis on consumerism and nullifies the modern concepts of independence and equality.[30] She also points out that Japanese postmodern feminism never questions the self or individual autonomy. A lack of questioning about the importance of women's economic and social independence may imply that women's lives continue to be deeply buried in the sphere of the home and family. Feminist scholars are, however, now increasingly addressing policy changes regarding women's employment status because of the surge in the number of female temporary workers with little economic security. Mari Osawa at the University of Tokyo draws on feminist and Marxist political economy in criticizing Japan's corporate centrism and male-breadwinner orientation and arguing that they shape gender stratification and lead to gaps between men and women in income, employment, and benefits.

Japanese feminists could learn from American feminists in many ways. With the intensifying demands of the global economy, Japanese firms no longer enjoy the economic growth and prosperity that they did in the 1980s. When fewer and fewer young men have lifelong economic security or earn an income that is adequate to support an entire family, women—who are increasingly educated—may need to work and become breadwinners. As is the case in the United States, when men's wages go down, women are more likely to be seen as an important source of family income. Thus, relegating themselves to the home sphere is no longer an option for many women. Also, with the rise of divorce and the decline of the birthrate in Japan, women's employment and economic independence are becoming increasingly important.

The Japanese people have long been subjugated by the state-led gender ideology of separate spheres in which women take care of the family and men devote themselves to their companies. Yet Japanese men and women need to learn to find individual happiness beyond their assigned roles in these separate gendered spheres. American feminists see men as the group whose consciousness needs to be raised, as they have also subjugated themselves to the ideology of gender. Japanese women and men should also learn to decouple their economic responsibility and social and familial obligations from gendered traits, and the organization and business culture should evolve to adjust more to individual needs.

As long as government and businesses continue to protect the gender-polarized family over the dual-earner family, they discourage educated women from assimilating into the world of men and they block women's aspirations and upward mobility. Also, the government's privileging housewives and women who depend entirely on their husbands explicitly weakens many women's economic independence and wastes women as an important labor resource in Japan.

In this book I have touched on how women workers sometimes express negativity about other women in the workplace, and I argue that this is due to the women's differing employment statuses and positions, ages, education levels, and degree of internalization of sexism and male superiority, as well as being a result of workplace misogyny and a male-dominant organizational culture. With this in mind, is women's solidarity at all possible in Japan? In the context of the United States, Williams claims that women's solidarity can be difficult because women have different interests and agendas. Some want assimilation into the man's world, but others embrace traditional femininity. She writes, "The assumption that women will join in automatic sisterhood reflects an unwarranted premise: the women are inevitably bound together by their experience of womanhood. . . . If feminists are to mold a coalition of women, we need to carefully tap into what different groups of women care about passionately. Women do not all agree just because they are women."[31] As Williams says, women are certainly different; yet the various groups of women in the United States still share a long history of shared understandings, beliefs, and images of "sisterhood" as a political and strategic tool for social change, and as an individual tool for connecting with other women in different communities. The shared goals of feminism and a belief in the value of gender equality are strong among women from various backgrounds. In Japan, it seems that feminism, or strategic "sisterhood," has not been as successful as it has been in the United States. To make matters worse, perhaps, Japanese feminists have embraced individualism or isolationism rather than collective activism.[32] Susan Holloway, in her research on Japanese mothers, argues that because of the lack of a powerful feminist movement and collective remedial resources in Japan, Japanese women feel more comfortable in searching for individualistic solutions than in pursuing collective means of resistance; she notes that such limited individual change, while being safe and nonthreatening to the Japanese "iron triangle"—corporations, government bureaucrats, and politicians—is inadequate and reinforces gendered lives in Japan.[33] In order to truly change women's status in Japanese society, Japan's mode of economy and production will have to change so that women and men can be more equal in their productivity and more alive in both the public and the private spheres. Educational institutions and employment training should do more to address this—even offering remedial programs to raise awareness of gender and diversity—and to help individuals close the gap between men and women in competence, competitiveness, network-formation ability, and leadership skills.[34] Increasing the number and power of women leaders in Japanese firms should be taken seriously as a goal by both the government and corporate management because increasing the number of women in positions of authority in Japanese firms and other major institutions will require seriously reforming the postwar gender regime and upsetting the equilibrium of Japan's coordinated capitalism. Japanese feminists' theoretical and policy interventions with regard to the empowerment of women, as well as their ability to dialogue with global feminism, are becoming more important than ever. They should take charge of not only supporting formal and informal policy changes but also of promoting educated Japanese women's economic independence and leadership roles in Japan.

# Notes

**CHAPTER 1**

1. Keidanren, *Action Plan for Women, 2014*, https://www.keidanren.or.jp/policy/2014/029_honbun.pdf (accessed October 1, 2014).

2. Maria Charles and David B. Grusky, *Occupational Ghettos: The Worldwide Segregation of Women and Men* (Stanford: Stanford University Press, 2004).

3. Mary C. Brinton, *Women and the Economic Miracle: Gender and Work in Postwar Japan* (Berkeley: University of California Press, 1993), 60.

4. Mary C. Brinton and Hang-Yue Ngo, "Age and Sex in the Occupational Structure: A United States–Japan Comparison," *Sociological Forum* 8, no. 1 (1993): 94, 106.

5. Charles and Grusky, *Occupational Ghettos*, 180–85.

6. Heidi Gottfried and Laura Reese, "Gender, Policy, Politics, and Work: Feminist Comparative and Transnational Research," *Review of Policy Research* 20, no. 1 (2003): 5.

7. Ibid., 4.

8. Cecilia L. Ridgeway, "Interaction and the Conservation of Gender Inequality: Considering Employment," *American Sociological Review* 62 (1997).

9. Charles and Grusky, *Occupational Ghettos*, 21.

10. Gøsta Esping-Andersen, *The Incomplete Revolution: Adapting to Women's New Roles* (Cambridge, UK: Polity Press, 2009), 20–23.

11. Paula England, Janet Gornick, and Emily F. Shafer, "Women's Employment, Education, and the Gender Gap in 17 Countries," *Monthly Labor Review* 3 (2013).

12. Ibid., 12.

13. Maria Charles, "A World of Difference: International Trends in Women's Economic Status," *Annual Review of Sociology* 37 (2011): 366.

14. Mizuho Aoki, "Japan's Poor Gender Gap Worsening, WEF Survey Finds," *Japan Times*, October 25, 2013.

15. Kazutaka Ito, "Report: Japan Ranks 101st in the World in Gender Equality," *Asahi Shimbun*, October 25, 2012.

16. Gender Equality Bureau Cabinet Office, "Toward Gender Equal Society, 2012," http://www.gender.go.jp/pamphlet/pamphlet-main/index.html (accessed October 1, 2014).

17. Gender Equality Bureau Cabinet Office, "White Paper on Gender Equal Society, 2014," http://www.gender.go.jp/about_danjo/whitepaper/h26/gaiyou/html/honpen/b1_s05.html (accessed October 1, 2014).

18. Mari Osawa, *Making Gender Equal Society* (Tokyo: NHK Books, 2004); Heidi Gottfried and Nagisa Hayashi-Kato, "Gendering Work: Deconstructing the Narrative of the Japanese Economic Miracle," *Work, Employment and Society* 12, no. 1 (1998).

19. Kimiko Kimoto, *Gender and Japanese Management*, trans. Teresa Castelvetere (Melbourne, Australia: Trans Pacific Press, 2005); Yuko Ogasawara, *Office Ladies and Salaried Men: Power, Gender, and Work in Japanese Companies* (Berkeley: University of California Press, 1998); Karen A. Shire, "Gendered Organization and Workplace Culture in Japanese Customer Services," *Social Science Japan Journal* 3, no. 1 (2000); Heidi Gottfried, "Temp(t)ing Bodies: Shaping Bodies at Work in Japan," *Sociology* 37, no. 2 (2003).

20. John Benson, Masae Yuasa, and Philippe Debroux, "The Prospect for Gender Diversity in Japanese Employment," *International Journal of Human Resource*

*Management* 18, no. 5 (2007); Brinton, *Women and the Economic Miracle*; Wei-hsin Yu, *Gendered Trajectories: Women, Work, and Social Change in Japan and Taiwan* (Stanford: Stanford University Press, 2009).

21. Takeshi Inagami and D. Hugh Whittaker, *The New Community Firm: Employment, Governance and Management Reform in Japan* (Cambridge: Cambridge University Press, 2005): Sven Steinmo, *The Evolution of Modern States: Sweden, Japan, and the United States* (Cambridge, UK: Cambridge University Press, 2010).

22. Mari Miura, *Welfare through Work: Conservative Ideas, Partisan Dynamics, and Social Protection in Japan* (Ithaca: Cornell University Press, 2012).

23. Herbert J. Gans, "The Positive Functions of Poverty," *American Journal of Sociology* 78, no. 2 (1972).

24. Herbert J. Gans, "The Uses of Poverty: The Poor Pay All," *Social Policy* 2 (1971): 24.

25. Peter A. Hall and David Soskice, "An Introduction to Varieties of Capitalism," in *Varieties of Capitalism: The Institutional Foundations of Comparative Advantage*, ed. Peter A. Hall and David Soskice, 1–68 (Oxford: Oxford University Press, 2001).

26. Michael A. Witt, "Japan: Coordinated Capitalism between Institutional Change and Structural Inertia," in *Oxford Handbook of Asian Business Systems,* ed. Michael A Witt and Gordon Redding, 100–122 (Oxford: Oxford University Press, 2014).

27. Hall and Soskice, "Introduction."

28. Edward J. Lincoln, *Arthritic Japan: The Slow Pace of Economic Reform* (Washington, DC: Brookings Institution Press, 2001).

29. Ibid., 134.

30. Ibid., 146.

31. Michael A. Witt, *Changing Japanese Capitalism: Societal Coordination and Institutional Adjustment* (Cambridge, UK: Cambridge University Press, 2006); Lincoln, *Arthritic Japan.*

32. Witt, *Changing Japanese Capitalism.*

33. Lincoln, *Arthritic Japan*; 134; Steinmo, *Evolution of Modern States*, 131.

34. Steven K. Vogel, *Japan Remodeled: How Government and Industry Are Reforming Japanese Capitalism* (Ithaca: Cornell University Press, 2006), 14.

35. Masahiko Aoki, *Corporations in Evolving Diversity: Cognition, Governance, and Institutions* (Oxford: Oxford University Press, 2010), 89–90.

36. Vogel, *Japan Remodeled*, 206, 212.

37. Ibid., 203.

38. George Olcott, *Conflict and Change: Foreign Ownership and the Japanese Firm* (Cambridge, UK: Cambridge University Press, 2009).

39. Ibid.

40. Aoki, *Corporations*; Olcott, *Conflict and Change.*

41. Steinmo, *Evolution of Modern States*, 126.

42. Lincoln, *Arthritic Japan.*

43. Witt, "Japan."

44. Michael A. Witt and Gordon Redding, "Culture, Meaning and Institutions: Executive Rationale in Germany and Japan," *Journal of International Business Studies* 40 (2009): 874.

45. Ibid., 876.

46. Inagami and Whittaker, *New Community Firm*, 20.

47. Steinmo, *Evolution of Modern States*, 231.

48. Richard Katz, cited in Steinmo, *Evolution of Modern States*, 130; Lincoln, *Arthritic Japan*, 136.

49. Inagami and Whittaker, *New Community Firm.*

50. Lincoln, *Arthritic Japan*, 188. About sixty thousand were laid off at IBM in 1993 and forty thousand at AT&T.

51. Arjan B. Keizer, "Non-Regular Employment in Japan: Continued and Renewed Dualities," *Work, Employment and Society* 22, no. 3 (2008).

52. Ibid.

53. Miura, *Welfare through Work*.

54. Brinton, *Women and the Economic Miracle*.

55. Yu, *Gendered Trajectories*.

56. Benson, Yuasa, and Debroux, "Prospect for Gender Diversity."

57. Ogasawara, *Office Ladies*; Karen A. Shire, "Stability and Change in Japanese Employment Institutions: The Case of Temporary Work," ASIEN 84 (2002).

58. Shire, "Gendered Organization," 49.

59. Ogasawara, *Office Ladies*, 65, 12, 5.

60. Kimoto, *Gender and Japanese Management*.

61. Alice C. Lam, *Women and Japanese Management: Discrimination and Reform* (New York: Routledge, 1992).

62. Ibid., 66.

63. Gottfried, "Temp(t)ing Bodies," 268.

64. Ibid., 266.

65. Margarita Estevez-Abe, "Gender Bias in Skills and Social Policies: The Varieties of Capitalism Perspective on Sex Segregation," *Social Politics* 12, no. 2 (2005); Margarita Estevez-Abe, "Gendering the Varieties of Capitalism: A Study of Occupational Segregation by Sex in Advanced Industrial Societies," *World Politics* 59 (2006).

66. Estevez-Abe, "Gendering Varieties of Capitalism," 195.

67. Mary C. Brinton, "Christmas Cakes and Wedding Cakes: The Social Organization of Japanese Women's Life Course," in *Japanese Social Organization*, ed. Takie Sugiyama Lebra, 79–107 (Honolulu: University of Hawaii Press, 1992).

68. Mary C. Brinton, *Lost in Transition: Youth, Work, and Instability in Postindustrial Japan* (New York: Cambridge University Press, 2011).

69. Ronald Inglehart and Christian Welzel, *Modernization, Cultural Change, and Democracy: The Human Development Sequence* (New York: Cambridge University Press, 2005), 282–84.

70. Ronald Inglehart, Pippa Norris, and Christian Welzel, "Gender Equality and Democracy," *Comparative Sociology* 1, no. 3/4 (2002).

71. Ronald Inglehart and Christian Welzel, "Changing Mass Priorities: The Link between Modernization and Democracy," *Perspectives on Politics* 8, no. 2 (2010): 553.

72. Inglehart, Norris, and Welzel, "Gender Equality."

73. Christian Welzel and Ronald Inglehart, "The Role of Ordinary People in Democratization," *Journal of Democracy* 19, no. 1 (2008): 132–35.

74. Lincoln, *Arthritic Japan*; Steinmo, *Evolution of Modern States*; Witt, *Changing Japanese Capitalism*.

75. Mary Alice Haddad, *Building Democracy in Japan* (New York: Cambridge University Press, 2012), 17.

76. Gøsta Esping-Andersen, "Hybrid or Unique? The Japanese Welfare State between Europe and America," *Journal of European Social Policy* 7, no. 3 (1997).

77. Ibid., 186.

78. Haddad, *Building Democracy*.

79. Francis Fukuyama, "Confucianism and Democracy," *Journal of Democracy* 6, no. 2 (1995).

80. Thomas P. Rohlen, "Order in Japanese Society: Attachment, Authority, and Routine," *Journal of Japanese Studies* 15, no. 1 (1989): 36.

81. Inagami and Whittaker, *New Community Firm*.

82. Frank J. Schwartz and Susan J. Pharr, eds. *The State of Civil Society in Japan* (Cambridge, UK: Cambridge University Press, 2003), 4.

83. Andrew E. Barshay, "Capitalism and Civil Society in Postwar Japan: Perspectives from Intellectual History," in *The State of Civil Society in Japan,* ed. Frank Schwartz and Susan Pharr (Cambridge: Cambridge University Press, 2003), 76–77; Kiyoaki Hirata, ed., *Gendai shimin shakai to kigyo kokka* [Contemporary Civil Society and the Enterprise State] (Tokyo: Ochanomizu Shobo, 1994), 41–43; Toshio Yamada, "Kigyo shakai to shin shakai" [Corporate Society and Civil Society], in *Gendai shimin shakai to kigyo kokka* [Comtemporary Civil Society and the Enterprise State], ed. Hirata Kiyoaki, Yamada Toshio, Kato Tetsuro, Kurosawa Nobuyuki, and Ito Masazumi, 47–74 (Tokyo: Ochanomizu Shobo, 1994).

84. Barshay, "Capitalism and Civil Society," 77; Tetsuro Kato, "Karoshi to sabisu zangyo no seiji keizaigaku" [Political Economy of Overwork Death and Service Overtime], in *Gendai shimin shakai to kigyo kokka* [Comtemporary Civil Society and the Enterprise State], ed. Hirata Kiyoaki, Yamada Toshio, Kato Tetsuro, Kurosawa Nobuyuki, and Ito Masazumi, 75–126 (Tokyo: Ochanomizu Shobo, 1994).

85. Barshay, "Capitalism and Civil Society," 78.

86. Rikki Kersten, *Democracy in Postwar Japan: Maruyama Masao and the Search for Autonomy* (London: Routledge, 1996).

87. Inglehart and Welzel, *Modernization,* 282–84.

88. Steinmo, *Evolution of Modern States,* 231.

89. Paula England, "The Gender Revolution: Uneven and Stalled," *Gender & Society* 24, no. 2 (2010).

90. Hiroshi Segi, *Zetsubo no saibansyo* [Hopeless court of justice] (Tokyo: Kodansya Gendai Shinsyo, 2014).

91. Frank Dobbin and Erin L. Kelly, "How to Stop Harassment: The Professional Construction of Legal Compliance in Organizations," *American Journal of Sociology* 112, no. 4 (2007): 1203–43.

92. Paula England and Nancy Folbre, "Gender and Economic Sociology," in *Handbook of Economic Sociology,* ed. Neil Smelser and Richard Swedberg, 627–49 (Princeton: Princeton University Press, 2005).

93. Estevez-Abe, "Gendering Varieties of Capitalism," 144.

94. Barbara F. Reskin, "Including Mechanisms in Our Model of Ascriptive Inequality," *American Sociological Review* 68 (2003).

95. Joan Acker, "Hierarchies, Jobs, Bodies: A Theory of Gendered Organizations," *Gender & Society* 4, (1990); Joan Acker, "Inequality Regimes: Gender, Class, and Race in Organizations, *Gender & Society* 20 (2006); Britton, "The Epistemology of the Gendered Organization," *Gender & Society* 14, no. 3 (2000); Christine L. Williams, *Still a Man's World: Men Who Do 'Women's' Work* (Berkeley: University of California Press, 1995).

96. Dana Britton and Laura Logan, "Gendered Organizations: Progress and Prospects," *Sociology Compass* 2, no. 1 (2008): 118.

97. Acker, "Hierarchies, Jobs, Bodies," 146.

98. Joan Acker, "The Future of 'Gender and Organizations': Connection and Boundaries," *Gender, Work & Organizations* 5, no. 4 (1998): 197.

99. Ibid.

100. Acker, "Inequality Regimes"; Deborah Kerfoot and David Knights, "Managing Masculinity in Contemporary Organizational Life: A 'Managerial Project,'" *Organization* 5, no. 1 (1998).

101. Kirsten Dellinger, "Masculinities in 'Safe' and 'Embattled' Organizations: Accounting for Pornographic and Feminist Magazines," *Gender & Society* 18 (2004): 563.

102. Dana Britton, "The Epistemology of the Gendered Organization," *Gender & Society* 14, no. 3 (2000): 429.

103. Britton and Logan, "Gendered Organizations," 115.

104. Christine L. Williams, Chandra Muller, and Kristine Kilanski, "Gendered Organizations in the New Economy," *Gender & Society* 26 (2012): 549.

105. Robin J. Ely and Debra E. Meyerson, "Theories of Gender in Organizations: A New Approach to Organizational Analysis and Change," *Research in Organizational Behavior* 22 (2000): 104–5.

106. Robin J. Ely, Herminia Ibarra, and Deborah Kolb, "Taking Gender into Account: Theory and Design for Women's Leadership Development Programs," *Academy of Management Learning & Education* 10, no. 3 (2011): 475.

107. Ely and Meyerson, "Theories of Gender," 107–8.

108. Ibid., 115.

109. Frank Dobbin, Soohan Kim, and Alexandra Kalev, "You Can't Always Get What You Need: Organizational Determinants of Diversity Programs," *American Sociological Review* 76, no. 3 (2011).

110. Barbara F. Reskin and Debra B. McBrier, "Why Not Ascription? Organizations' Employment of Male and Female Managers," *American Sociological Review* 65, no. 2 (2000): 211–12.

111. Kevin Stainback, Donald Tomaskovic-Devey, and Sheryl Skaggs, "Organizational Approaches to Inequality: Inertia, Relative Power, and Environments," *The Annual Review of Sociology* 36 (2010): 226, 230.

112. Donald Tomaskovic-Devey and Sheryl Skaggs, "An Establishment-Level Test of the Statistical Discrimination Hypothesis," *Work and Occupations* 26, no. 2 (1999): 426.

113. Paula England, *Comparable Worth: Theories and Evidence* (New York: Aldine de Gruyter, 1992); Tomaskovic-Devey and Skaggs, "Establishment-Level Test," 426.

114. Tomaskovic-Devey and Skaggs, "Establishment-Level Test," 441.

115. Elizabeth H. Gorman and Julie A. Kmec, "Hierarchical Rank and Women's Organizational Mobility: Glass Ceilings in Corporate Law Firms," *American Journal of Sociology* 114, no. 5 (2009): 1465.

116. Gorman, "Work Uncertainty," 879.

117. Elizabeth H. Gorman and Julie A. Kmec, "We (Have to) Try Harder: Gender and Required Work Effort in Britain and the United States," *Gender & Society* 21, no. 6 (2007): 844–45.

118. Ibid., 845.

119. Christine Beckman and Damon Phillips, "Interorganizational Determinants of Promotion: Client Leadership and the Attainment of Women Attorneys," *American Sociological Review* 70 (2005); Elizabeth H. Gorman, "Gender Stereotypes, Same-Gender Preferences, and Organizational Variation in the Hiring of Women: Evidence from Law Firms," *American Sociological Review* 70 (2005); Elizabeth H. Gorman, "Work Uncertainty and the Promotion of Professional Women: The Case of Law Firm Partnership," *Social Forces* 85, no. 2 (2006); Gorman and Kmec, "Hierarchical Rank," 1433.

120. Reskin and McBrier, "Why Not Ascription?," 212.

121. Barbara F. Reskin and Patricia A. Roos, *Job Queues, Gender Queues: Explaining Women's Inroads into Male Occupations* (Philadelphia: Temple University Press, 1990).

122. David Purcell, Kelly R. MacArthur, and Sarah Samblanet, "Gender and the Glass Ceiling at Work," *Sociology Compass* 4, no. 9 (2010): 711.

123. Gorman, "Gender Stereotypes."

124. Purcell, MacArthur, and Samblanet, "Glass Ceiling at Work," 714; Phillip N. Cohen and Matt L. Huffman, "Working for the Woman? Female Managers and the Gender Wage Gap," *American Sociological Review* 72 (2007): 681–704; Heather A. Havemen, Joseph P. Broshcak and Lisa E. Cohen, "Good Times, Bad Times: The Effects of Organizational Dynamics on the Careers of Male and Female Managers," *Research in the Sociology of*

*Work* 18 (2009): 119–48; Jeffrey W. Lucas. "Status Processes and the Institutionalization of Women as Leaders," *American Sociological Review* 68, no. 3 (2003): 464–80.

125. James N. Baron, Brian S. Mittman, and Andrew E. Newman, "Targets of Opportunity: Organizational and Environmental Determinants of Gender Integration within the California Civil Service, 1979–1985," American Journal of Sociology 96, no. 6 (1991): 1362–401; Matt Huffman, Phillip Cohen, and Jessica Pearlman, "Engendering Change: Organizational Dynamics and Workplace Gender Segregation: 1975–2005," *Administrative Science Quarterly* 55, no. 2 (2010): 255–77; all cited in Kevin Stainback, Donald Tomaskovic-Devey, and Sheryl Skaggs, "Organizational Approaches to Inequality: Inertia, Relative Power, and Environments," *The Annual Review of Sociology* 36 (2010): 235.

126. Phillip N. Cohen and Matt L. Huffman, "Working for the Woman? Female Managers and the Gender Wage Gap," *American Sociological Review* 72 (2007): 681–704; Mia Hultin and Ryszard Szulkin, "Mechanisms of Inequality: Unequal Access to Organizational Power and the Gender Wage Gap," *European Sociological Review* 19 (2003):143–59; Mia Hultin and Ryszard Szulkin, "Wages and Unequal Access to Organizational Power: An Empirical Test of Gender Discrimination," Administrative Science Quarterly 44 (1999): 453–72; all cited in Stainback, Tomaskovic-Devey, Skaggs, "Organizational Approaches," 235.

127. Dobbin, Kim, and Kalev, "Organizational Determinants of Diversity Programs."

128. Kevin Stainback and Soyoung Kwon, "Female Leaders, Organizational Power and Sex Segregation," *Annals of the American Academy of Political and Social Science* 639, no. 1 (2012), 220; Gorman, "Gender Stereotypes"; Gorman, "Work Uncertainty"; Robin J. Ely, "The Effects of Organizational Demographics and Social Identity on Relationships among Professional Women," *Administrative Science Quarterly* 39 (1994); Daniel J. Brass, "Men and Women's Networks: A Study of Interaction Patterns and Influence in an Organization," *Academy of Management Journal* 28, no. 2 (1985): 327–43; Hermenia Ibarra, "Personal Networks of Women and Minorities in Management: A Conceptual Framework," *Academy of Management Review* 18, no. 1 (1993): 56–87; Alison M. Konrad, Vicki Kramer, and Sumru Erkut, "Critical Mass: The Impact of Three or More Women on Corporate Boards," *Organizational Dynamics* 37 (2008): 145–64.

129. Stainback and Kwon, "Female Leaders," 231.

130. Robin J. Ely, "The Power in Demography: Women's Social Constructions of Gender Identity at Work," *Academy of Management Journal* 38 (1995).

131. Ibid., 618.

132. Belle Derks, Colette Van Larr, Naomi Ellemers, and Kim de Groot, "Gender-Bias Primes Elicit Queen-Bee Responses among Senior Policewomen," *Psychological Science* 22 (2011); Belle Derks, Naomi Ellemers, Colette Van Laar, and Kim de Groot, "Do Sexist Organizational Cultures Create the Queen Bee?" *British Journal of Social Psychology* 50 (2011).

## CHAPTER 2

1. Aoki, "Corporations," 166.

2. Miura, *Welfare through Work*, 71.

3. E.g., Brinton, *Women and the Economic Miracle*.

4. Leon Wolff, "The Death of Lifelong Employment in Japan?," in *Corporate Governance in the 21st Century: Japan's Gradual Transformation*, ed. Luke Nottage, Leon Wolff, and Kent Anderson (Cheltenham, UK: Edward Elgar, 2008), 63; Hiroshi Ono, "Lifetime Employment in Japan: Concepts and Measurements," *Journal of the Japanese and International Economies* 24 (2009): 2.

5. Brinton, *Women and the Economic Miracle*, 126, 131.

6. Ibid., 79.

7. Ono, "Lifetime Employment," 23.

8. Brinton, *Women and the Economic Miracle*, 126.

9. Ibid.; Masahiko Aoki, Gregory Jackson, and Hideaki Miyajima, *Corporate Governance in Japan: Institutional Change and Organizational Diversity* (New York: Oxford University Press, 2008), 1.

10. Ronald Dore, *Innovation for Whom? Institute for Technology, Enterprise and Competitiveness*, Research Paper 04–01 (Kyoto, Japan: Doshisha University, 2004), 15.

11. Brinton, *Women and the Economic Miracle*, 46.

12. Ibid., 66–67.

13. Dore, *Innovation for Whom?*, 208.

14. Ronald Dore, "Will Global Capitalism Be Anglo-Saxon Capitalism? *New Left Review* 6 (2000): 107.

15. Dore, *Innovation for Whom?*, 209.

16. Ton Wilthagen and F. H. Tros, "The Concept of Flexicurity: A New Approach to Regulating Employment and Labour Markets," *Transfer: European Review of Labour and Research* 10, no. 2 (2004); cited in Wolff, "Death of Lifelong Employment."

17. Wolf, "Death of Lifelong Employment," 65.

18. Witt, *Changing Japanese Capitalism*; Witt and Redding, "Culture, Meaning and Institutions; Aoki, *Corporations*.

19. Christina Ahmadjian and Gregory E. Robbins, "A Clash of Capitalisms: Foreign Shareholders and Corporate Restructuring in 1990s Japan," *American Sociological Review* 70 (2005); Aoki, Jackson, and Miyajima, *Corporate Governance*, 3; Wolff, "Death of Lifelong Employment," 64.

20. Wolff, "Death of Lifelong Employment," 64.

21. Aoki, Jackson, and Miyajima, *Corporate Governance*, 8.

22. Dan W. Puchiniak, "Perverse Rescue in the Lost Decade: Main Banks in the Post-Bubble Era," in Nottage, Wolff, and Anderson, *Corporate Governance*, 86.

23. Jennifer A. Amyx, *Japan's Financial Crisis: Institutional Rigidity and Reluctant Change* (Princeton: Princeton University Press, 2006), 122.

24. Ibid., 120–23.

25. Ibid.

26. Aoki, Jackson, and Miyajima, *Corporate Governance*, 8.

27. Ahmadjian and Robbins, "Clash of Capitalisms," 452.

28. Aoki, Jackson, and Miyajima, *Corporate Governance*, 18.

29. Ahmadjian and Robbins, "Clash of Capitalisms," 456.

30. Aoki, Jackson and Miyajima, *Corporate Governance,* 10.

31. Ahmadjian and Robbins, "Clash of Capitalisms," 458.

32. Ibid., 467.

33. Aoki, Jackson, and Miyajima, *Corporate Governance*, 25.

34. Naohito Abe and Satoshi Shimizutani, "Employment Policy and Corporate Governance: An Empirical Comparison of the Stakeholder and the Profit-Maximization Model," *Journal of Comparative Economics* 35 (2007): 363.

35. Gregory Jackson, "Employment Adjustment and Distributional Conflict in Japanese Firms," in *Corporate Governance in Japan: Institutional Change and Organizational Diversity*, ed. Masahiko Aoki, Gregory Jackson, and Hideaki Miyajima (New York: Oxford University Press, 2008), 298.

36. E.g., Hyung Je Jo and Jong-Sung You, "Transferring Production Systems: An Institutionalist Account of Hyundai Motor Company in the United States," *Journal of East Asian Studies* 11 (2011); Pardi Tommaso, "Where Did It Go Wrong? Hybridization and Crisis of Toyota Motor Manufacturing UK, 1989–2001," *International Sociology* 20 (2005);

Hiromichi Shibata, "Productivity and Skill at a Japanese Transplant and Its Parent Company," *Work and Occupation* 28 (2001).

37. Shire, "Stability and Change," 27–28.

38. Kimiko Kimoto, *Empirical Research on Women Laborers and Organizations*, Grant-in-Aid Research Report (Melbourne: Japan Ministry of Education, Culture, Sports, Science and Technology, 2008), 27, 28, 30.

39. Japan Institute for Labour Policy and Training, "Research on Workers' Motivation and Management, 2004," http://www.jil.go.jp/kokunai/statistics/doko/h1607/index.html (accessed October 1, 2012).

40. Arjan B. Keizer, "Transformations in- and outside the Internal Labour Market: Institutional Change and Continuity in Japanese Employment Practices," *International Journal of Human Resource Management* 20, no. 7 (2009).

41. Vogel, *Japan Remodeled*, 123.

42. Brinton, *Women and the Economic Miracle*, 131.

43. Shire, "Stability and Change," 25.

44. Keizer, "Non-Regular Employment."

45. Ibid., 420.

46. Gender Equality Bureau Cabinet Office, "White Paper on Gender Equal Society, 2011," http://www.gender.go.jp/whitepaper/h23/zentai/html/zuhyo/zuhyo01–02–06.html (accessed October 1, 2012).

47. Shire, "Stability and Change," 26–27.

48. Karen A. Shire and Jun Imai, "Flexible Equality: Men and Women in Employment in Japan," Duisburg Working Papers on East Asian Studies, 2000, 1. http://www.uni-due.de/in-east/fileadmin/publications/ gruen/paper30.pdf (accessed March 7, 2012).

49. Heidi Gottfried, "Comment: Stability and Change: Typifying 'Atypical' Employment in Japan," *ASIEN* 84 (2002): 32.

50. Chizuko Ueno, "Gender Equality and Multiculturalism under Japanese New-Liberalist Reform in the Era of Globalization," in *Gender Equality in Multicultural Societies: Gender, Diversity, and Conviviality in the Age of Globalization,* ed. Miyoko Tsujimura and Mari Osawa (Sendai, Japan: Tohoku University Press, 2010), 32.

51. Ibid.

52. Keizer, "Non-Regular Employment"; Keizer, "Transformations."

53. Keizer, "Transformations," 1532.

54. Leon Wolff, "Lifelong Employment, Labor Law and the Lost Decade: The End of a Job for Life in Japan?," in *Innovation and Change in Japanese Management,* ed. Parissa Hghirian (Basingstoke, UK: Palgrave Macmillan, 2010), 91.

55. Ronald Dore, "Shareholder Capitalism Comes to Japan." The Other Canon Foundation and Tallinn University of Technology Working Papers in Technology Governance and Economic Dynamics, TUT Institute of Public Administration (2007), 213.

56. Kazuo Yamaguchi and Yoshio Higuchi, *Ronso: Work-Life Balance in Japan* [*Nihon no waku raifu baransu*] (Tokyo: Nihon Keizai Shimbunsha, 2008), 23.

57. Ibid., 25.

58. Ibid., 29.

59. Lincoln, *Arthritic Japan,* 102.

60. Aoki, *Corporations.*

61. Olcott, *Conflict and Change.*

62. Witt, "Japan."

63. Witt, *Changing Japanese Capitalism*, 16.

64. Steinmo, *Evolution of Modern States*, 212, 126, 132, 134.

65. Lincoln, *Arthritic Japan,* 134.

66. Dore, "Global Capitalism," 117.

67. Gottfried and Hayashi-Kato, "Gendering Work," 37; Leonard Schoppa, *Race for the Exits: The Unraveling of Japan's System of Social Protection* (Ithaca: Cornell University Press, 2006), 58.

68. Schoppa, *Race for the Exits,* 59.

69. Osawa, *Making Gender Equal Society,* 136.

70. Osawa, *Governance* 147, 144.

71. Ibid.

72. Osawa, *Making Gender Equal Society,* 81.

73. Mari Osawa, "Women's Resistance" [Jyosei no teiko ga sekai o jizoku kanou ni suru], in *Feminism in Japan,* ed. Syoko Amano, Kimiko Ito, Ruri Ito, Teruko Inoue, Chizuko Ueno, Yumiko Ehara, Mari Osawa, and Mikiyo Kano (Tokyo: Iwanami Syoten, 2009), 13.

74. Osawa, *Making Gender Equal Society,* 71.

75. Sakiko Shiota, "Japanese Feminism and Current Japanese Social Policy: 1970–1990" [Gendai feminizumu to nihon no syakaiseisaku] in Amano et al., *Feminism in Japan,* 128.

76. Ibid., 125.

77. Ibid., 134.

78. "The Wife's Pension Exemption: Seventy Percent of Those Who Are Exempted Earn More Than 9 Million Yen," *Asahi Shinbun,* February 4, 2012, http://www.asahi.com/national/update/0203/TKY201202030704.html (accessed October 1, 2012).

79. Mari Osawa, *Seikatsu hosho no gabanansu* [Governance of Livelihood Security] (Tokyo: Yuhikaku, 2013), 321.

80. Gottfried and Hayashi-Kato, "Gendering Work," 38.

81. Ibid., 39, 41.

82. Osawa, *Making Gender Equal Society,* 139.

83. Ibid., 146.

84. Ibid., Ayako Kano, "Backlash, Fight Back, and Back Pedaling: Responses to State Feminism in Contemporary Japan," *International Journal of Asian Studies* 8, no. 1 (2011): 45–46.

85. Osawa, "Women's Resistance," 29.

86. Shire and Imai, "Flexible Equality," 3.

87. Jennifer Chan-Tiberghien, *Gender and Human Rights Politics in Japan: Global Norms and Domestic Networks* (Stanford: Stanford University Press, 2004), 119.

88. Glenda Roberts, "Balancing Work and Life: Whose Work? Whose Life? Whose Balance?" *Asian Perspective* 29, no. 1 (2005); Glenda Roberts, "Similar Outcomes, Different Paths: The Cross-National Transfer of Gendered Regulations of Employment," in *Gendering the Knowledge Economy: Comparative Perspectives,* ed. Sylvia Walby, Heidi Gottfried, Karin Gottschall, and Mari Osawa, 140–60 (Basingstoke, U.K.: Palgrave Macmillan, 2007).

89. Roberts, "Similar Outcomes," 146.

90. Roberts, "Balancing Work and Life," 181–82.

91. Roberts, "Similar Outcomes," 158.

92. Roberts, "Balancing Work and Life," 207.

93. Ministry of Health, Labour and Welfare, "Current Situation on Employed Women, 2009," http://www.mhlw.go.jp/bunya/koyoukintou/josei-jitsujo/09.html (accessed March 8, 2012).

94. Gender Equality Bureau Cabinet Office, "White Paper on Gender Equal Society, 2010," http://www.gender.go.jp/ whitepaper/h22/gaiyou/html/honpen/b1_s08.html (accessed October 1, 2012).

95. Roberts, "Balancing Work and Life," 193.

96. Reskin and Roos, *Job Queues,* 154–62.

97. Brinton, *Women and the Economic Miracle*; Charles and Grusky, *Occupational Ghettos*.

98. Brinton and Ngo, "Age and Sex,"109.

99. Gender Equality Bureau Cabinet Office, "White Paper on Gender Equal Society, 2011."

100. Gender Equality Bureau Cabinet Office, "Toward Gender Equal Society, 2012."

101. Ministry of Health, Labour and Welfare, "Basic Survey on Women's Employment, 2007," http://www.mhlw.go.jp/houdou/2007/08/h0809–1/02.html (accessed October 1, 2012).

102. Mary C. Brinton, "Gender Stratification in Contemporary Urban Japan," *American Sociological Review* 54, no. 4 (1989); Brinton and Ngo, "Age and Sex"; Ogasawara, *Office Ladies*; Shire, "Gendered Organization."

103. Ministry of Health, Labour and Welfare, "Career-Track Hiring, 2015."

104. Ibid.

105. Shire, "Gendered Organization," 49.

106. Reskin and Roos, *Job Queues*; Shire, "Gendered Organization," 38.

107. Shire, "Gendered Organization," 39.

108. Ogasawara, *Office Ladies*, 12.

109. Ibid., 60, 68.

110. Lam, *Women and Japanese Management*, 63.

111. Ibid.; Kimoto, *Gender and Japanese Management*.

112. Ibid., 82.

113. Ibid., 88.

114. Toshiaki Tachibanaki, *Current Issues surrounding Women at Work and in the Family: Proposals Going Beyond This Age of Decreasing Population* (Tokyo: Minerva Shobou, 2005), 2.

115. Lam, *Women and Japanese Management*, 204, Kimoto, *Gender and Japanese Management,* 105.

116. Gender Equality Bureau Cabinet Office, "White Paper on Gender Equal Society, 2011."

117. Ministry of Health, Labour and Welfare, "Current Situation on Employed Women, 2013," http://www.mhlw.go.jp/bunya/koyoukintou/josei-jitsujo/13.html (accessed October 1, 2014).

118. Schoppa, *Race for the Exits*, 74.

119. Ueno, "Gender Equality," 32.

120. Heidi Gottfried and Jacqueline O'Reilly, "Institutionally Embedded Gender Models: Re- Regulating Breadwinner Models in Germany and Japan," in *Equity in the Workplace: Gendering Workplace Policy Analysis*, ed. Heidi Gottfried and Laura A. Reese (Lanham, MD: Lexington Books, 2004), 104.

121. Kimoto, "Empirical Research," 78.

122. Schoppa, *Race for the Exits*, 73.

123. National Institute of Population and Social Security Research, "Trends in Marriage and Fertility in Japan" [*Dai juyon- kai shusho doko kihon chosa*], 2011, http://www.ipss.go.jp/ps-doukou/j/doukou14_s/chapter3.html#32a (accessed October 1, 2012).

124. Yoshio Higuchi, "Support for the Women's Continual Work and the Consequences— Logic and Economy of Childcare Leave," in *Working/Women Work*, vol. 7, ed. Emiko Takeishi (Tokyo: Minerva Shobo, 2009); Kazuma Sato and XinXin Ma, "Influence of the Childcare Leave Revision on the Women's Continual Employment" [Ikujikyugyoho no kaiseiga jyosei no keizoku syugyo ni oyobosu eikyo] in *Japanese Household Behavior Dynamism IV: Institutional Policy Changes and Employment Behaviors,* ed. Yoshio Higuchi, Miki Seko, and the CEO program at Keio University, 119–39 (Tokyo: Keio University Press, 2008).

125. Shingou Ikeda and Tomohiro Takami, "Employment Plan during Childbirth and Childcare" [Syussan ikujikino syugyo keizoku], Japan Institute for Labour Policy and Training 136 (2011): 1–165.

126. Ibid., 10.

127. Ibid., 31.

128. Ibid.

129. Mari Okutsu and Masaharu Kuniyoshi, "Kekkon Syussan Ikujikino taisyoku to saisyusyoku" [Resignation and Reemployment during the Period of Marriage, Childbirth and Child Rearing: Women's Career Development and Issues], Japan Institute for Labour Policy and Training 105 (2009).

130. Ikeda and Takami, "Employment Plan."

131. Gender Equality Bureau Cabinet Office, "White Paper on Gender Equal Society, 2009," http://www.gender.go.jp/ whitepaper/h20/zentai/html/zuhyo/zuhyo1_03_09.html (accessed October 1, 2014).

132. Ueno, "Gender Equality," 25–42.

133. Johanna Brenner, "Transnational Feminism and the Struggle for Global Justice," *New Politics* 9, no. 2 (2003).

134. Bina Agarwal, "Are We Not Peasants Too? Land Rights and Women's Claims in India," *Seeds,* November 21, 2002; Bina Agarwal, "'Bargaining' and Gender Relations: Within and beyond the Household," *Feminist Economics* 3, no. 1 (1997).

135. Frances Raday, "CEDAW's Substantive Equality and Its Ideological Challengers," in *Equality as a Social Right: Towards a Concept of Substantive Equality in Comparative and International Law* (coordinated by Judy Fudge), Onati International Institute for the Sociology of Law, 2006, http://www.iisj.net/antBuspre.asp?cod=3657&nombre=3657&prt=1.

136. Osawa, *Making Gender Equal Society*; Kano, "Backlash"; Nüket Kardam, "The Emerging Global Gender Equality Regime from Neoliberal and Constructivist Perspectives in International Relations," *International Feminist Journal of Politics* 6, no. 1 (2004).

137. Joyce Gelb, *Gender Policies in Japan and the United States: Comparing Women's Movements, Rights, and Politics* (New York: Palgrave Macmillan, 2003), 50.

138. Ibid., 54.

139. Kristina Geraghty, "Taming the Paper Tiger: A Comparative Approach to Reforming Japanese Gender Equality Laws," *Cornell International Law Journal* 41, no. 2 (2008): 508.

140. Ibid., 510; Ryuichi Yamakawa, "We've Only Just Begun: The Law of Sexual Harassment in Japan," *Hastings International and Comparative Law Review* 22, no. 3 (1999).

141. Yuko Ogasawara, "Women's Solidarity: Company Policies and Japanese Office Ladies," in *Women's Working Lives in East Asia*, ed. Mary Brinton, 151–79 (Stanford: Stanford University Press, 2001).

142. Geraghty, "Paper Tiger," 515.

143. Ibid., 516; Shire and Imai, "Flexible Equality," 13.

144. Shire, "Stability and Change."

145. Geraghty, "Paper Tiger," 516–17.

146. Starich, "Comment," 560.

147. Starich, "Comment"; Geraghty, "Paper Tiger," 517.

148. Starich, "Comment," 560.

149. Ibid., 563.

150. Geraghty, "Paper Tiger," 521.

151. Starich, "Comment," 563.

152. Geraghty, "Paper Tiger," 523.

153. Ibid.

154. Starich, "Comment," 570.

155. Ibid., 567.

156. Osawa, *Making Gender Equal Society*.

157. Geraghty, "Paper Tiger," 527.

158. Shire and Imai, "Flexible Equality," 3.

159. Geraghty, "Paper Tiger," 541–42.

160. Ibid., 521–22.

161. Roberts, "Balancing Work and Life."

162. *Nihon Keizai Shinbun,* "Syusyo ikujikyugyo sannen hyoumei" [The Prime Minister Announced the Three-Year Childcare Leave Extension] April 18, 2013, http://www.nikkei.com/article/DGXNASFS1804W_Y3A410C1EA1000/ (accessed December 4, 2015).

163. Nihon Keizai Dantai Rengoukai, "Industrial and Business Views of Declining Birthrate in Japan, 2006" [Sangyoukai kigyo ni okeru syoshikataisaku no torikumi nitsuite], https://www.keidanren.or.jp/japanese/policy/2006/028/index.html (accessed October 1, 2012).

164. Ministry of Health, Labour and Welfare, "Basic Survey on Equal Employment, 2008," http://www.mhlw.go.jp/houdou/2008/08/h0808-1.html (accessed March 8, 2012). According to the Ministry of Health, Labour and Welfare, "Gender Equality Employment, 2010," of those women who took leave for child care in 2010, 32% took ten to twelve months and 25% took twelve to eighteen months. Also, according to the Ministry of Internal Affairs and Communications (Statistical Topics No. 30), 2008, married women in dual-earner couples spent about three hours on housework and five hours on their jobs each day, while married men spent only about twenty-five minutes on housework and eight hours on their jobs each day.

165. Ministry of Health, Labour and Welfare, "Gender Equality Employment, 2010."

166. I have selected for discussion recent court cases that involved Japanese feminists and the women's movement and that drew public attention in the Japanese media.

167. Geraghty, "Paper Tiger," 506.

168. Starich, "Comment," 554.

169. Ibid., 554.

170. Syouetsu Matsumoto, "Logic of Equal Employment Opportunity Law and Court Cases," *Cyukyo Hougaku* 27 (1992): 20–22.

171. Geraghty, "Paper Tiger," 507–8.

172. Ibid., 508; Bureau of Industrial and Labor Affairs, "Working Women and Labor Law 2011," Tokyo, Japan: Tokyo Metropolitan Government, 202.

173. Starich, "Comment," 555–56.

174. Ibid., 555.

175. Showa Shell Co. Labor Union, http://homepage3.nifty.com/showashelllaborunion/.

176. Yasuko Yunoki, "From the Court: Showa Shell Co. Wage Discrimination Case," *Bulletin of the Society for the Study of Working Women* [*Jyosei rodo kenkyuu zashi*] 54 (2010): 160–62.

177. Geraghty, "Paper Tiger," 519.

178. Miyoko Tsujimura, "Employment, Social Security, and Gender" [Koyo Syakai Hosyo to Jenda Byodou] in *Employment, Social Security, and Gender,* ed. Sayaka Dake and Shigeto Tanaka (Sendai, Japan: Tohoku University Press, 2007), 115.

179. Working Women's Network, "Sumitomo kagaku sabetsu jiken wakai ni tsuiteno bengodan kankai" [Report on Sumitomo Chemical].

180. Mutsuko Asakura, *Labor Laws and Gender* (Tokyo, Japan: Keiso Syobou, 2004), 175.

181. Ibid., 184.

182. Ibid., 186.

183. Ibid.

184. Tsujimura, "Employment, Social Security, Gender," 114.

185. Mitsuko Miyaji, "On the Sumitomo Electric Industries Case" [Sumitomo denko danjyo chingin sabetsu sosyo], Kanagawa University Departmental Bulletin Paper no. 22, 2004.

186. Ibid.

187. Hideki Ushikubo and Takeshi Murakami, *Nihon no rodou o sekai ni tou* [Examining Japanese Labor Standards: Learning ILO Treaty] (Tokyo: Iwanami Syoten, 2014), 24–25.

188. Tomoko Sasanuma, "On Indirect Discrimination," *Bulletin of the Society for the Study of Working Women* [*Jyosei rodo kenkyuu zashi*] 49 (2006); Bureau of Industrial and Labor Affairs, *Working Women*, 201.

189. Asia-Japan Women's Resource Center, "Kanematsu Sex Discrimination Case" [Syosya kanematsu jiken towa], 2012, http://ajwrc.org/jp/modules/bulletin/index.php?page=article&storyid=390 (accessed November 1, 2013).

190. Working Women's Network, *WWN Report to the United Nations Committee on Economic, Social and Cultural Rights* for the Pre-sessional Working Group 49th Session Japan, Osaka, Japan, March 2012.

191. Mitsuko Miyaji, *Women and Labor*, paper Presented at the Symposium on Women Joint Law Offices, Osaka, Japan, March 17, 2012.

192. Ibid.

193. Working Women's Network, *WWN Report to the United Nations Committee on Economic, Social and Cultural Rights.*

194. E.g., Masumi Mori and Mutsuko Asakura, *Doitsu kachi rodo doitsu chingin gensoku no jisshi sisutemu* [*Practicing the Principle of Equal Pay for Equal Work and Work of Equal Value*] (Tokyo: Yuhikaku, 2010).

195. Working Women's Network, *WWN Report to the United Nations Committee on Economic, Social and Cultural Rights.*

196. Mitsuko Miyaji, The Chugoku Electric Power Co. Case, presented at the WWN symposium on the Chugoku Electric Power Co. Case, Meiji University, Tokyo, Japan, December 23, 2013.

197. Ibid.

198. Working Women's Network, Request to the Supreme Court: The Chugoku Electric Power Co. no. 1908, case 2327, the WWN symposium on the Chugoku Electric Power Co. Case, Meiji University, Tokyo, Japan, December 23, 2013.

199. Miyaji, WWN symposium, December 23, 2013.

200. Supreme Court General Secretariat, Japan, "Summary of the Meetings of Labor, Civil, and Administrative Judges, July 10, 2001," *Roudo houritsu jyunpou* [Labor law journal] 1524 (2002).

201. Working Women's Network, Newsletter no. 76, July 31, 2014, 13.

202. "Summary of the Meetings among Labor, Civil, and Administrative Judges," July 10, 2010, 1.

203. Ibid., 4.

204. Working Women's Network, Newsletter no. 79, April 28, 2015, 10.

205. Daniel H. Foote, *Nameless Faceless Justice* (Tokyo: NTT Press, 2007), 136–37.

206. Segi, *Zetsubo no saibansyo*, 113.

207. Ibid., 141.

208. Dobbin and Kelly, "How to Stop Harassment"; Frank Dobbin, *Inventing Equal Opportunity* (Princeton: Princeton University Press, 2009).

209. Marjorie A. Stockford, *The Bellwomen: The Story of the Landmark AT&T Sex Discrimination Case* (New Brunswick, NJ: Rutgers University Press, 2004).

210. CNN, "Mitsubishi Settles for $34M," June 11, 1998, http://money.cnn.com/1998/06/11/companies/mitsubishi/ (accessed January 1, 2010).

211. Dawn.com, "US Court Okays Bank of America's $39m Gender Bias Deal," December 29, 2013, http://www.dawn.com/news/1077013/us-court-okays-bank-of-americas-39m-gender-bias-deal (accessed October 1, 2014).

212. Patrick McGeehan, "Morgan Stanley Settles Bias Suit with $54 Million," *New York Times,* July 13, 2004.

213. Jayne O'Donnell, "Should Business Execs Meet at Strip Clubs?" *USA Today*, March 22, 2006, http://www.usatoday.com/money/companies/management/2006-03-22-strip-clubs-usat_x.htm (accessed October 1, 2014).

214. Swissinfo, "Novartis to Pay Millions for Sex Discrimination," May 19, 2010, http://www.swissinfo.ch/eng/novartis-to-pay-millions-for-sex-discrimination/8903518 (accessed November 1, 2014).

215. Carl F. Goodman, *The Rule of Law in Japan: A Comparative Analysis,* 3rd ed. (The Hague, The Netherlands: Kluwar Law Intl., 2012).

216. Noriko Iki, "Jyosei rodo seisaku no tenkai" [*The Progress of the Women Labor Policy: From the Point of Justice, Utilization, and Welfare*], Labour Policy Report 9 (Tokyo: Japan Institute for Labour Policy and Training, 2011), 116.

217. Naoko Suzuki, "On the Companies' Support of Childrearing: Current Status and Issues," *Reference* 54 (2004): 8.

218. Iki, Jyosei rodo seisaku [*Women Labor Policy*], 116–17.

219. Chen-Tiberghien, *Gender and Human Rights,* 122.

220. David Sadler and Stuart Lloyd, "Neo-Liberalising Corporate Social Responsibility: A Political Economy of Corporate Citizenship," *Geoforum* 40 (2009): 618.

221. Peter Utting, "Corporate Responsibility and the Movement of Business," *Development in Practice* 15 (2005): 383.

222. Peter Utting, "The Struggle for Corporate Accountability," *Development and Change* 39, no. 6 (2008): 964.

223. Sadler and Lloyd, "Neo-Liberalizing Corporate Social Responsibility," 621.

224. Ibid.

225. Masatsugu Takeda, "Human Resource Management under the Era of Declining Population in Japan" [Syousikajidai no jinji roumu kanrinitsuite], *Ritsumeikan keieigaku* [Ritsumeikan Management] 44, no. 5 (2006): 21.

226. Keidanren, Management Labor Policy Committee Report 2005 [Keieiroudou Seisaku Iinkai Houkoku], in Junko Nakagawa, "Danjo kyodo sankaku syakai to jenda" [Gender Equal Society and Gender]," *Ritsumeikan sangyo syakaironnsyu* [*Ritsumeikan Industrial sociology*] 42, no. 1 (2006): 55.

227. Ibid.

228. E.g., Akira Kawaguchi, *Gender Inequality in Economic Status* (Tokyo: Keiso Syobo, 2008).

229. Stephanie Assmann, "The Long Path toward Gender Equality in Japan: The Revision of the Equal Employment Opportunity Law and Its Implementation," in *Innovation and Change in Japanese Management*, ed. Parissa Haghirian (London: Palgrave Macmillan, 2010), 152.

230. Leon Wolff, "The Corporate Regulation of Gender Harassment in Japan," in *Employment, Social Security and Gender,* ed. Sayaka Dake and Shigeto Tanaka, 71–92 (Sendai, Japan: Tohoku University Press, 2007).

231. Chan-Tiberghien, *Gender and Human Rights,* 14.

232. Dobbin, *Inventing Equal Opportunity*, 3–4.

233. Ibid., 13.

234. Ibid., 221–22.

235. Ibid., 6.

236. Kano, "Backlash," 51–53; Kuniko Funabashi, "Gender Equal Policy and Backlash," in *Wako University Annual Report, 2007*, 18–29 (Tokyo: Wako University, 2007).

237. Yayo Okano, "Politics of Gender," in *Gender Free Trouble*, ed. Ryoko Kimura, 55–74 (Tokyo: Hakutakusya, 2005).

238. Shire and Imai, "Flexible Equality," 3.

239. Mutsuko Asakura, "Danjyo kyoudou sankaku sisaku no houteki kadai" [Legal Problems of Basic Law for the Gender Equal Society], *Ohara syakai mondai kenkyujyo zasshi* [*Ohara Journal of Social Issues*] 546, no. 5 (2004): 2.

## CHAPTER 3

1. Olcott, *Conflict and Change.*

2. Acker, "Future of 'Gender and Organizations.'"

3. Aoki, *Corporations*, 166.

4. Ibid., 153.

5. Ibid., 153–55.

6. Ibid., 155.

7. Ödül Bozkurt, "Foreign Employers as Relief Routes: Women, Multinational Corporations and Managerial Careers in Japan," *Gender, Work & Organization* 19, no. 3 (2012).

8. Olcott, *Conflict and Change*, 45.

9. Ibid., 261.

10. George Olcott and Nick Oliver, "The Impact of Foreign Ownership and Gender and Employment Relations in Large Japanese Companies," *Work Employment & Society* 28, no. 2 (2014).

11. Thomas Cargill, "What Caused Japan's Banking Crisis?," in *Crisis and Change in the Japanese Financial System*, ed. Takeo Hoshi and Hugh Patrick, 37–58 (Boston: Kluwer Academic Publishers, 2000); Takeo Hoshi, "What Happened to Japanese Banks?" *Monetary and Economic Studies* 19, no. 1 (2001).

12. Hoshi, "What Happened to Japanese Banks?," 4.

13. Ibid.

14. Olcott, *Conflict and Change.*

15. Geoffrey Jones, *Beauty Imagined: A History of the Global Beauty Industry* (New York: Oxford University Press, 2010).

16. Ibid., 186.

17. Ibid., 314.

18. Ibid., 315.

19. Ibid., 120.

20. Ibid., 315.

## CHAPTER 4

1. Vicki Smith, *Managing in the Corporate Interest: Control and Resistance in an American Bank* (Berkeley: University of California Press, 1990), 190–91.

2. Brinton, *Women and the Economic Miracle,* 66–67.

3. Ibid.

4. On the seniority-based career ladder, workers accumulate in-firm human capital through gaining experience in different sections, and they are rotated to different divisions every few years. Workers have little control over this process, and it often takes fifteen years before a worker is promoted to management.

5. The exchange rate was calculated based on $1 equals 100 yen.

6. Alexandra Kalev, "Cracking the Glass Cages? Restructuring and Ascriptive Inequality at Work," *American Journal of Sociology* 114, no. 6 (2009).

7. Steinmo, *Evolution of Modern States*, 98.

8. Ibid.

9. Mary C. Brinton, "The Social-Institutional Bases of Gender Stratification: Japan as an Illustrative Case," *American Journal of Sociology* 94, no. 2 (1988): 313–14.

10. Brinton and Takehiko Kariya, "Institutional Embeddedness in Japanese Labor Markets," in *The New Institutionalism in Sociology*, ed. Mary C. Brinton and Victor Nee, 181–207 (New York: Russell Sage Foundation, 1998).

11. Ibid., 197–201.

12. Vogel, *Japan Remodeled*, 215.

13. Rosabeth M. Kanter, *Men and Women of the Corporation* (New York: Basic Books, 1977), 140.

14. Ibid., 163.

15. W. E. Lambert, R. C. Hodgson, R. Gardner, and S. J. Fillenbaum, "Evaluative Reactions to Spoken Languages," *Journal of Abnormal and Social Psychology* 60 (1960); Henri Tajfel, *Human Groups and Social Categories* (Cambridge: Cambridge University Press, 1981); both cited in Ely, " Effects of Organizational Demographics."

16. Vicki Smith, *Crossing the Great Divide: Worker Risk and Opportunity in the New Economy* (Ithaca: Cornell University Press, 2001), 103.

17. Ibid., 112.

18. Ibid., 115.

19. Laura M. Crothers, John Lipinski, and Marcel Minutolo, "Cliques, Rumors and Gossip by the Water Cooler: Female Bullying in the Workplace," *Psychologist-Manager Journal* 12 (2009): 101.

20. Ibid., 103.

21. Ibid.

22. Ogasawara, *Office Ladies*.

23. Brinton, *Lost in Transition*.

24. Anne H. Litwin and Lynne O'Brien Hallstein, "Shadows and Silences: How Women's Positioning and Unspoken Friendship Rules in Organizational Settings Cultivate Difficulties among Some Women at Work," *Women's Studies in Communication* 30, no. 1 (2007): 127.

25. Kimoto, *Gender and Japanese Management*, 82.

26. Ely, "Effects of Organizational Demographics," 224.

27. Ibid., 225, 226.

28. Kazuo Yamaguchi, "Howaito karaa saisyain no kanrisyokuwariai no danjyo kakusano ketteiyouin" [White-Collar Regular Employees, Managers, and Gender Gap], *Rieti Discussion Paper Series* 13-J-069 (2013).

**CHAPTER 5**

1. Yamada, *Kigyo Shakai,* cited in Barshay, "Capitalism and Civil Society," 76.

2. Barshay, "Capitalism and Civil Society," 63.

3. Ibid.

4. Robert W. Connell, *Gender and Power: Society, the Person, and Sexual Politics* (Stanford: Stanford University Press, 1987).

5. James W. Messerschmidt, *Masculinities and Crime: Critique and Reconceptualization of Theory* (Lanham, MD: Rowman & Littlefield, 1993), 83.

6. Kerfoot and Knights, "'Managing Masculinity.'"

7. Kanter, *Men and Women*, 22.

8. David Collinson and Jeff Hearn, "Naming Men as Men: Implications for Work, Organization and Management," *Gender, Work & Organization* 1, no. 1 (1994).

9. Patricia Y. Martin, "Mobilizing Masculinities: Women's Experiences of Men at Work," *Organization* 8, no. 4 (2001).

10. Michael S. Kimmel, *The Gendered Society* (New York: Oxford University Press, 2000), 11.

11. Robert Connell quoted in Kimmel, *Gendered Society*, 11.

12. Romit Dasgupta, "The Lost Decade of the 1990s and Shifting Masculinities in Japan," *Culture, Society & Masculinity* 1 (2009).

13. James E. Roberson and Nobue Suzuki, eds., *Men and Masculinities in Contemporary Japan: Dislocating the Salaryman Doxa* (London: Routledge Curzon, 2003), 5.

14. James E. Roberson, "Japanese Working-Class Masculinities: Marginalized Complicity," in Roberson and Suzuki, *Men and Masculinities*, 127.

15. Robin M. LeBlanc, *The Art of the Gut: Manhood, Power, and Ethics in Japanese Politics* (Berkeley: University of California Press, 2010).

16. Gordon Mathews, "Can 'a Real Man' Live for His Family? Ikigai and Masculinity in Today's Japan," in Roberson and Suzuki, *Men and Masculinities*, 109–25.

17. Mathews, "Can 'a Real Man.'"

18. Paul A. Christensen, *Japan, Alcoholism and Masculinity: Suffering Sobriety in Tokyo* (London: Lexington Books, 2015), 23.

19. Justin Charlebois, "Herbivore Masculinity as an Oppositional Form of Masculinity," *Culture, Society, and Masculinities* 5 (2013).

20. Ibid., 91.

21. LeBLanc, *Art of the Gut,* 168–69.

22. Kanter, *Men and Women*; Ely, "Effects of Organizational Demographics"; Ely, "Power in Demography."

23. Kanter, *Men and Women*, 230.

24. Ely, "Effects of Organizational Demographics"; Ely, "Power in Demography."

25. Acker, "Future of 'Gender and Organizations.'"

26. Kanter, *Men and Women*.

27. Joan C. Williams, *Reshaping the Work-Family Debate: Why Men and Class Matter* (Cambridge: Harvard University Press, 2010), 100.

28. Linda McDowell, *Capital Culture: Gender at Work in the City* (Oxford: Blackwell, 1997), 206.

29. Ibid., 207.

30. Ibid.

31. Ely and Meyerson, "Theories of Gender," 116.

32. Ibid.

33. Collinson and Hearn, "Naming Men as Men."

34. Ibid.

35. McDowell, *Capital Culture*.

36. Ibid., 159.

37. Robin Leidner, "Selling Hamburgers and Selling Insurance: Gender, Work, and Interactive Service Jobs," *Gender & Society* 4, no. 2 (1991); Robin Leidner, *Fast Food, Fast Talk: Service Work and the Routinization of Everyday Life* (Berkeley: University of California Press, 1993).

38. McDowell, *Capital Culture*.

39. Christensen, *Japan, Alcoholism*.

40. Michele R. "Gregory, "Inside the Locker Room: Male Homosocialibility in the Advertising Industry," *Gender, Work and Organizations* 16, no. 3 (2009).

41. Ibid., 343.

42. Ibid.

43. Ogasawara, *Office Ladies*, 48.

44. Ibid., 56.

45. Sharon Mavin, "Venus Envy: Problematizing Solidarity Behaviour and Queen Bees," *Women in Management Review* 21, no. 4 (2006): 272–74.

46. Chesler, *Woman's Inhumanity to Woman*, 36.

47. Wajcman, *Managing Like a Man*, 165.

48. Chesler, *Woman's Inhumanity to Woman*, 349.

49. Virginia O'Leary and Maureen M. Ryan, "Women Bosses: Counting the Changes That Count," in *Women in Management: A Developing Presence*, ed. Morgan Tanton (London: Routledge, 1994), 72, cited in Sharon Mavin, "Queen Bees, Wannabees and Afraid to Bees: No More 'Best Enemies' for Women in Management?," *British Journal of Management* 19 (2008).

50. Mavin, "Venus Envy."

51. Patricia Y. Martin, "'Said and Done' versus 'Saying and Doing': Gendering Practices, Practicing Gender at Work," *Gender & Society* 17, no. 3 (2003): 360.

52. Williams, *Reshaping the Work-Family Debate*, 123.

53. Ely, "Effects of Organizational Demographics"; Ely, "Power in Demography."

54. Ely, "Effects of Organizational Demographics," 207.

55. Ibid., 225.

56. Kanter, *Men and Women*, 202.

57. Ibid., 204–5.

58. Ibid., 188.

59. McDowell, *Capital Culture*, 159.

60. Sonia Liff and Kate Ward, "Distorted Views through the Glass Ceiling: The Construction of Women's Understandings of Promotion and Senior Management Positions," *Gender, Work & Organization* 8, no. 1 (2001): 25–27.

61. G. Coates, "Integration or Separation: Women and Appliances of Organizational Culture," *Women in Management in Review* 13, no. 3 (1998): 122.

62. Judy Wajcman, *Managing Like a Man: Men and Woman in Corporate Management* (University Park: Pennsylvania State University Press, 1998), 7–8.

63. Leidner, "Selling Hamburgers."

64. Ely, Herminia, and Kolb, "Taking Gender into Account," 476.

65. Al Gini, *My Job, My Self: Work and the Creation of the Modern Individual* (London: Routledge, 2001), 99, 100, cited in Mavin, "Venus Envy," 268–69.

66. Gorman and Kmec, "We (Have to) Try Harder," 844–45.

67. Ibid.

68. Williams, *Reshaping the Work-Family Debate*, 101.

69. Ueno, "Neo-Liberal Reform," 32.

70. Derks, Van Laar, Ellemers, and de Groot, "Gender-Bias," 1243.

71. Williams, *Reshaping the Work-Family Debate*, 101.

72. Mavin, "Queen Bees," 82–83.

73. Peggy Drexler, "The Tyranny of the Queen Bee," *Wall Street Journal*, March 6, 2013, http://online.wsj.com/article/SB10001424127887323884304578328271526080496.html?mod=wsj_valettop_email (accessed November 1, 2012).

74. Derks, Van Laar, Ellemers, and de Groot, "Gender-Bias," 1244.

75. Ibid.

76. Ibid., 1247.

77. Derks, Ellemers, Van Laar, and de Groot, "Sexist Organizational Cultures," 530.

78. Ogasawara, *Office Ladies*.

79. See Mavin, "Queen Bees," 77.

80. Olcott and Oliver, "Impact of Foreign Ownership."

81. Derks, Van Laar, Ellemers, and de Groot, "Gender-Bias"; Derks, Ellemers, Van Laar, and de Groot, "Sexist Organizational Cultures."

82. McDowell, *Capital Culture*, 159.

83. Michael Burawoy, *Manufacturing Consent: Changes in the Labor Process under Monopoly Capitalism* (Chicago: University of Chicago Press, 1979), 81.

84. Ibid., 86.

85. Ibid., 81–82.

86. Ibid., 82.

87. Judith Butler, *Bodies That Matter: On the Discursive Limits of Sex* (London: Routledge, 1993).

## CHAPTER 6

1. Tetsuro Kato, "The Political Economy of Japanese Karoshi (Death from Overwork)," *Hitotsubashi Journal of Social Studies* 26, no. 2 (1994); Yuko Kawanishi, "On Karo-Jisatsu (Suicide by Overwork): Why Do Japanese Workers Work Themselves to Death? *International Journal of Mental Health* 37, no. 1 (2008); Mark West, "Employment Market Institutions and Japanese Working Hours, paper #03-016, December 12, 2003, John M. Olin Center For Law & Economics, University of Michigan Law School, http://law.bepress.com/umichlwps/olin/art22/ (accessed March 8, 2012).

2. Kato, "Political Economy."

3. Kato, "Political Economy"; Tetsuro Kato, *Contemporary Civil Society and the Corporate State* (Tokyo: Ochaynomizu-Shobou Press, 1994); Kawanishi, "On Karo-Jisatsu."

4. Kato, "Political Economy."

5. Japan Institute for Labour Policy and Training (JILPT), "Data Book International Labor Statistics, 2014," 202.

6. Ibid.

7. Kato, "Political Economy."

8. West, "Employment Market Institutions," 6.

9. Kato, *Contemporary Civil Society.*

10. West, "Employment Market Institutions," 17.

11. Ibid.

12. Research Institute for Advancement of Living Standards, Rengou Souken Survey, November 2006, http:// rengo-soken.or.jp/report_db/pub/detail.php?uid=39 (accessed March 8, 2012).

13. Ministry of Internal Affairs and Communications, Statistics Bureau, "Basic Survey on Social Life, 2006," http://www.stat.go.jp/data/shakai/2006/pdf/gaiyou2.pdf (accessed March 8, 2012).

14. Ministry of Health, Labour and Welfare, "Research on Working Conditions, 2006," http://www.mhlw.go.jp/toukei/itiran/roudou/jikan/syurou/06/kekka1.html (accessed March 8, 2012).

15. West, "Employment Market Institutions," 27.

16. Sachiko Kuroda, "How Long Do Japanese Work? A Comparison before and after the Shorter Work Week," RIETI Policy Discussion Paper Series 10-P-002 (2010).

17. Atsuko Kanai, "Karoshi (Work to Death)' in Japan," *Journal of Business Ethics* 84, no. 2 (2009): 1.

18. Kawanishi, "On Karo-Jisatsu."

19. Hiroshi Kawahito, *Suicide by Overwork* (Tokyo: Iwanami Shoten, 1998).

20. Kanai, "Karoshi," 2.

21. Ministry of Health, Labour and Welfare, "On Workers' Accident Compensation, 2012," http://www.mhlw.go.jp/stf/houdou/2r9852000001f1k7.html (accessed November 1, 2012).

22. Wilthagen and Tros, "Flexicurity," 2004, cited in Wolff, "Death of Lifelong Employment," 65.

23. Wolff, "Death of Lifelong Employment," 65.

24. West, "Employment Market Institutions," 4.

25. Wolff, "Death of Lifelong Employment," 75.

26. Ibid., 11.

27. Daniel H. Foote, "Judicial Creation of Norms in Japanese Labor Law: Activism in the Service of Stability?," *UCLA Law Review* 43 (1996); West, "Employment Market Institutions," 12–13.

28. West, "Employment Market Institutions," 12.

29. Ibid., 14.

30. E.g., Yoichi Shimada, "Working Hour Schemes for White-Collar Employees in Japan," *Japan Labor Review* 1, no. 4 (2004).

31. See, e.g., Scott North and Charles Weathers, "The End of Overtime Pay: More Production or Just More Work for Japan's White Collar Workers?," *Asia-Pacific Journal,* 2006. http://www.japanfocus.org/-S-North/2320 (accessed November 1, 2013).

32. Sachiko Kuroda and Isamu Yamamoto, "How Are Hours Worked and Wages Affected by Labor Regulations? The White-Collar Exemption and 'Name-Only Managers' in Japan," RIETI Discussion Paper series 09-E-032 (2009).

33. United States Department of Labor, Wage and Hour Division (WHD), 2011, http://www.dol.gov/whd/regs/compliance/fairpay/fs17a_overview.htm (accessed November 1, 2013).

34. The minimum salary necessary to exempt workers from overtime compensation in the United States in 2004 was only about $23,660 per year. North and Weathers, "End of Overtime Pay."

35. North and Weathers, "End of Overtime Pay."

36. Daiji Kawaguchi, Hisahiro Naito, and Izumi Yokoyama, "Labor Market Responses to Legal Work Hour Reduction: Evidence from Japan," Cabinet Office, Economic and Social Research Institute (ESRI) Discussion Paper Series no. 202 (2008).

37. Huffington Post Japan, "The Cabinet Decide the Proposal on Zero Pay for Overwork," April 3, 2015, http://www.huffingtonpost.jp/2015/04/03/angyodai-zero-kakugi_n_6998224.html (accessed June 1, 2015).

38. Youngjoo Cha, "Overwork and the Persistence of Gender Segregation in Occupations," *Gender & Society* 27, 2 (2013): 2.

39. Ibid., 6.

40. Ibid., 3.

41. Naomi Cassirer and Barbara Reskin, "High Hopes: Organizational Position, Employment Experiences, and Women's and Men's Promotion Aspirations," *Work and Occupations* 27, no. 4 (2000): 458.

42. David L. Collinson and Margaret Collinson, "The Power of Time: Leadership, Management and Gender," in *Fighting for Time: Shifting Boundaries of Work and Social Life*, ed. Cynthia F. Epstein and Arne L. Kalleberg (New York: Russell Sage Foundation, 2004), 239.

43. Ibid., 230, 237, 240.

44. Acker, "Future of 'Gender and Organizations,'" 197.

45. Williams, *Reshaping the Work-Family Debate*, 86; Collinson and Collinson, "Power of Time," 230–31.

46. Ibid., 240.

47. Kanter, *Men and Women*, 221.

48. Williams, *Reshaping the Work-Family Debate*, 87.

49. Shelley J., Correll, Stephen Bernard, and In Paik, "Getting a Job: Is There a Motherhood Penalty?," *American Journal of Sociology* 112, no. 5 (2007): 1297–338.

50. Jacqueline Watts, "'Allowed into a Man's World' Meanings of Work-Life Balance: Perspectives of Women Civil Engineers as 'Minority' Workers in Construction," *Gender, Work & Organization* 16, no. 1 (2009): 49.

51. Ibid.

52. Arlie R. Hochschild, *The Time Bind: When Work Becomes Home and Home Becomes Work* (New York: Metropolitan Books, 1997); Dawn Lyon and Alison E. Woodward, "Gender and Time at the Top," *European Journal Women's Studies* 11, no. 2 (2008); Watts, "'Allowed into a Man's World.'"

53. Mindy Fried, *Taking Time: Parental Leave Policy and Corporate Culture* (Philadelphia: Temple University Press, 1998), 41.

54. Cecile Guillaume and Sophie Pochic, "What Would You Sacrifice? Access to Top Management and the Work-Life Balance," *Gender, Work & Organization* 16, no.1 (2009): 29.

55. Liff and Ward, "Distorted Views through the Glass Ceiling," 26–27.

56. Glenice J. Wood and Janice Newton, "Childlessness and Women Managers: 'Choice,' Context and Discourses," *Gender, Work & Organization* 13, no. 4 (2006): 339.

57. Williams, *Reshaping the Work-Family Debate*, 90.

58. Liff and Ward, "Distorted Views through the Glass Ceiling," 25–26.

59. Pamela Stone, "The Rhetoric and Reality of 'Opting Out,'" *Contexts* 6, no.4 (2007): 18.

60. Youngjoo Cha, "Reinforcing Separate Spheres: The Effect of Spousal Overwork on Men's and Women's Employment in Dual-Earner Households," *American Sociological Review* 75, no. 2 (2010).

61. Joan C. Williams, "Creating Workplace Gender Equality." Paper presented at the Annual Meeting of the American Sociological Association, Denver, CO, August 2012.

62. Collinson and Collinson, "Power of Time," 240.

63. Ibid.

64. Kimiko Kimoto, *Gender and Japanese Management*, trans. Teresa Castelvetere (Melbourne, Aust.: Trans Pacific Press, 2005), 199.

65. E.g., Kazuo Yamaguchi, "Women's Employment and Dysfunction of Japanese Firms," RIETI Policy Discussion Paper Series 13-P-002 (2013), 18.

66. Cassirer and Reskin, "High Hopes," 458.

67. Kathleen Gerson, *Hard Choices: How Women Decide about Work, Career, and Motherhood* (Berkeley: University of California Press, 1985).

68. Kanter, *Men and Women*.

69. Yoshihiro Kishimoto, "Company Ranking 100 in Childcare Takers [Ikujisyutokusyasuu ranking top 100]," January 4, 2012, Toyo Keizai Online, http://toyokeizai.net/articles/-/8366/ (accessed November 1, 2013).

70. Acker, "Future of 'Gender and Organizations,'" 200.

71. Correll, Bernard, and Paik, "Getting a Job"; Liff and Ward, "Distorted Views through the Glass Ceiling"; Watts, "'Allowed into a Man's World.'"

72. Connell, *Gender and Power*, quoted in Robin J. Ely and Irene Padavic, "A Feminist Analysis of Organizational Research on Sex Differences," *Academy of Management Review* 32, no. 4 (2007): 1135.

73. Stephanie Coontz, "Yes, I've Folded Up My Masculine Mystique, Honey," February 24, 2013, *London Times*, http://www.thesundaytimes.co.uk/sto/newsreview/article1219753.ece.

74. Ibid.

75. Robin J. Ely and Debra E. Meyerson, "An Organizational Approach to Undoing Gender: The Unlikely Case of Offshore Oil Platforms," *Research in Organizational Behavior* 30 (2010): 4.

76. Messerschmidt, "Managing to Kill."

77. Ibid., 41–42.

78. Ibid., 43.

79. Ibid.

80. Eric Larson, "An Institutional Hazing System," *Japan Times,* February 14, 2007, http://search.japantimes.co.jp/cgi-bin/rc20070214a2.html (accessed October 1, 2010).

81. Kato, "Political Economy," 50.

82. Kerfoot and Knights, "Managing Masculinity."

83. *Economist,* "Back to the Drawing Board," November 3, 2012, http://www.economist.com/news/business/21565660-after-olympus-scandal-japan-inc-wants-less-scrutiny-back-drawing-board (accessed November 1, 2013).

84. Hiroko Tabuchi, "Arrests in Olympus Scandal Point to Widening Inquiry into a Cover-Up," *New York Times,* February 16, 2012, http://www.nytimes.com/2012/02/17/business/global/7-arrested-in-olympus-accounting-cover-up.html?_r=0 (accessed November 1, 2013).

85. *Economist,* "Back to the Drawing Board."

86. Tabuchi, "Arrests in Olympus Scandal."

87. Michiyo Nakamoto, "Foreign Investors Urge Olympus to Rethink," *Financial Times,* March 21, 2012, http://www.ft.com/cms/s/0/ff458e86-7354-11e1-aab3-00144feab49a.html#axzz2RjDWQqZW (accessed November 1, 2013).

88. Ibid.

89. Tabuchi, "Arrests in Olympus Scandal."

90. Chiaki Kitazawa, "Organizational Culture of Ignoring the Problems: The Case of Olympus," *Nihon Keizai Shinbun,* November 19, 2011, http://www.nikkei.com/article/DGXNASFK1703Z_Y1A111C1000000/ (accessed November 20, 2011).

91. Ely and Meyerson, "Organizational Approach," 5.

92. Ibid., 15.

93. Ministry of Health, Labour and Welfare, "Rate of New Graduates Leaving Their Jobs, 2015," http://www.mhlw.go.jp/topics/2010/01/tp0127-2/dl/24-18.pdf (accessed May 20, 2015).

## CHAPTER 7

1. Kazue Muta, "The Making of *Sekuhara*: Sexual Harassment in Japanese Culture," in *East Asian Sexualities: Modernity, Gender and New Sexual Cultures,* ed. Stevi Jackson, Liu Jieyu, and Woo Juhyun, 52–68 (London: Macmillan, 2008).

2. Kumiko Akita, "A Female Teacher and Sexual Harassment in a Japanese Women's Junior College: A Case Study," *Women and Language* 25, no. 1 (2002).

3. Muta, "Making of *Sekuhara*," 54–56.

4. Aoki, "Japan's Poor Gender Gap."

5. CNN, "Mitsubishi Settles for $34M," CNNMoney, June 11, 1998, http://money.cnn.com/1998/06/11/companies/mitsubishi/ (accessed January 1, 2010).

6. Hannah Clark, "Toyota's Otaka Sued for Sexual Harassment," *Forbes,* February 6, 2006, http://www.forbes.com/2006/05/02/toyota-otaka-harassment-cx_hc_0502autofacescan07.html (accessed January 1, 2010).

7. Michael Orey, "Trouble at Toyota," *Businessweek,* May 22, 2006, http://www.businessweek.com/magazine/content/06_21/b3985078.htm (accessed June 1, 2010).

8. Kirsten Dellinger and Christine L. Williams, "The Locker Room and the Dorm Room: Workplace Norms and the Boundaries of Sexual Harassment in Magazine Editing," *Social Problems* 49, no. 2 (2002); Amy M. Denissen, "Crossing the Line: How Women in the Building Trades Interpret and Respond to Sexual Conduct at Work," *Journal of*

*Contemporary Ethnography* 39, no. 3 (2010); Patti A. Giuffre and Christine L. Williams, "Labeling Sexual Harassment in Restaurants," *Gender & Society* 8, no. 3 (1994); Christine L. Williams, Patti A. Giuffre, and Kirsten Dellinger, "Sexuality in the Workplace: Organizational Control, Sexual Harassment, and the Pursuit of Pleasure," *Annual Review of Sociology* 25 (1999).

9. Catharine A. MacKinnon, *Sexual Harassment of Working Women: A Case of Sex Discrimination* (New Haven: Yale University Press, 1979).

10. Nathalie Hadjifotiou, *Women and Harassment at Work* (London: Pluto Press, 1983); Michele A. Paludi and Richard B. Barickman, *Academic and Workplace Sexual Harassment: A Resource Manual* (Albany: State University of New York Press, 1991).

11. David L. Collinson and Margaret Collinson, "Sexuality in the Workplace: The Domination of Men's Sexuality," in *The Sexuality of Organization*, ed. J. Hearn, D. L. Sheppard, P. Trancred-Sherif, and G. Burrell, 91–109 (London: Sage, 1989).

12. Fiona Wilson and Paul Thomson, "Sexual Harassment as an Exercise of Power," *Gender, Work, and Organization* 8, no. 1 (2001): 67.

13. Jackie K. Rogers and Kevin D. Henson, "Hey, Why Don't You Wear a Shorter Skirt: Structural Vulnerability and the Organization of Sexual Harassment in Temporary Clerical Employment," *Gender & Society* 11, no. 2 (1997): 234.

14. Margaret Collinson and David L. Collinson, "'It's Only Dick': The Sexual Harassment of Women Managers in Insurance Sales," *Work, Employment & Society* 10, no. 1 (1996).

15. Williams, Giuffre, and Dellinger, "Sexuality in the Workplace," 77; Dellinger and Williams, "Locker Room and Dorm Room"; Giuffre and Williams, "Labeling Sexual Harassment."

16. Giuffre and Williams, "Labeling Sexual Harassment."

17. Dellinger and Williams, "Locker Room and Dorm Room."

18. Denissen, "Crossing the Line."

19. Jacqueline Watts, "Porn, Pride and Pessimism: Experiences of Women Working in Professional Construction Roles," *Work, Employment & Society* 21, no. 2 (2007).

20. Kato, "Political Economy."

21. Muta, "Making of *Sekuhara*," 57.

22. Akita, "Female Teacher and Sexual Harassment," 10.

23. Christopher Uggen and Chika Shinohara, "Sexual Harassment Comes of Age: A Comparative Analysis of the United States and Japan," *Sociological Quarterly* 50 (2009): 206.

24. Yumi Suzuki, "Sexual Harassment Prevention Handbook," 1994, http://www5f.biglobe.ne.jp/~constanze/nomarin267.html (accessed June 1. 2010).

25. Ministry of Health, Labour and Welfare, "Major Court Cases on Women and Labor, 2004," http://www.mhlw.go.jp/shingi/2004/10/s1007-6a.html.

26. Ibid.

27. Muta, "Making of *Sekuhara*," 57–58.

28. Anne Allison, *Nightwork: Sexuality, Pleasure, and Masculinity in a Tokyo Hostess Club* (Chicago: University of Chicago Press, 1994).

29. Ibid., 177.

30. Ibid.

31. Ibid., 186.

32. Andrew Pollak, "It's See No Evil, No Harassment in Japan," *New York Times*, May 7, 1996, http://www.nytimes.com/1996/05/07/business/it-s-see-no-evil-have-no-harassment-in-japan.html (accessed June 1, 2010).

33. Allison, *Nightwork*, 182.

34. Ibid., 185.

35. Kimmel, *Gendered Society*.

36. Kathrin S. Zippel, *The Politics of Sexual Harassment: A Comparative Study of the United States, the European Union, and Germany* (Cambridge, UK: Cambridge University Press, 2006).

37. Abigail C. Saguy, "Employment Discrimination or Sexual Violence? Defining Sexual Harassment in American and French Law," *Law and Society Review* 34, no. 4 (2000).

38. Kathrin S. Zippel, "Practices of Implementation of Sexual Harassment Policies: Individual versus Collective Strategies," *Review of Policy Research* 20, no. 1 (2003).

39. Ibid., 188.

40. Ibid., 114.

41. Yamakawa, "We've Only Just Begun," 537.

42. Ibid., 533.

43. Ibid., 538.

44. Ibid., 558.

45. Geraghty, "Taming the Paper Tiger."

46. Yamakawa, "We've Only Just Begun,"

47. Geraghty, "Taming the Paper Tiger"; Megan Starich, "Comment: The 2006 Revisions to Japan's Equal Opportunity Employment Law—A Narrow Approach to a Pervasive Problem," *Pacific Rim Law & Policy Journal* 16 (2007); Yamakawa, "We've Only Just Begun."

48. Yamakawa, "We've Only Just Begun."

49. Starich, "Comment."

50. Williams, Giuffre, and Dellinger, "Sexuality in the Workplace," 83.

51. Japan IBM, 2010, http://www-06.ibm.com/jp/ibm/bcg/03.shtml#3.3 (accessed June 1, 2010).

52. Laurie A. Morgan and Karin A. Martin, "Taking Women Professionals Out of the Office: The Case of Women in Sales," *Gender & Society* 20, no. 1 (2006).

53. O'Donnell, "Should Execs Meet at Strip Clubs?"

54. Morgan and Martin, "Out of the Office," 116–17.

55. Naoko Omika, "Sexual Harassment Can Occur among Men," Allabout.co.jp, April 12, 2007, http://allabout.co.jp/health/stressmanage/closeup/CU20070412A/ (accessed June 1, 2010).

56. Giuffre and Williams, "Labeling Sexual Harassment."

57. Dellinger and Williams, "Locker Room and Dorm Room"; Denissen, "Crossing the Line."

58. Giuffre and Williams, "Labeling Sexual Harassment."

59. Meika Loe, "Working for Men: At the Intersection of Power, Gender, and Sexuality," *Sociological Inquiry* 66, no. 4 (1996).

60. Japan Institute for Labour Policy and Training, "Sexual Harassment, 2009," http://www.jil.go.jp/hanrei/conts/092.htm (accessed June 1, 2010).

61. Ibid.

62. Denissen, "Crossing the Line."

63. Ibid.

64. Curtis J. Milhaupt, J. Mark Ramseyer, and Mark D. West, *The Japanese Legal System: Cases, Codes, and Commentary* (New York: Foundation Press, 2006), 600–14.

65. Tamie Kainou, "Judicial Remedies for Sexual Harassment and Its Limit," *F-GENS Journal* 7 (2007).

66. Denissen, "Crossing the Line"; Louise F. Fitzgerald, Suzanne Swan, and Karla Fischer, "Why Didn't She Just Report Him?," *Journal of Social Issues* 51 (1995).

67. Giuffre and Williams, "Labeling Sexual Harassment," 396–97.

68. Denissen, "Crossing the Line."

69. Ibid.

70. Ibid.

71. Emiko Kobayashi and Harold Grasmick, "Workers' Decisions to Comply: A Comparison of the Perceived Threats of Managerial Sanctions, Embarrassment, and Shame in Japan and the United States," *Journal of Language, Culture and Communication* 4 (2002).

72. Ibid.

73. Uggen and Shinohara, "Sexual Harassment."

74. Williams, Giuffre, and Dellinger, "Sexuality in the Workplace"; Giuffre and Williams, "Labeling Sexual Harassment."

75. Giuffre and Williams, "Labeling Sexual Harassment."

76. Morgan and Martin, "Out of the Office."

## CONCLUSION

1. England, Gornick, and Shafer, "Women's Employment."

2. Miura, *Welfare through Work*, 5.

3. *Nihon Keizai Shinbun,* "Custom of Not Saying No to the Boss," July 20, 2015, http://www.nikkei.com/article/DGXLASFK20H2H_Q5A720C1000000/ (accessed August 1, 2015).

4. Ely and Meyerson, "Theories of Gender," 107–8.

5. Ibid., 112.

6. Roberts, "Similar Outcomes, Different Paths."

7. E. g., Kumiko Nemoto, "Postponed Marriage: Exploring Women's Views of Matrimony and Work in Japan," *Gender & Society* 22, no. 2 (2008).

8. Estevez-Abe, "Gender Bias."

9. Kuniko Ishiguro, "Career Formation of Women Managers: Case Studies," *GEMC Journal* 7 (2012).

10. In 2014, Hitachi announced the abolition of the seniority pay system for managers.

11. Lincoln, *Arthritic Japan.*

12. England, "Gender Revolution," 158.

13. Kimmel, *Gendered Society*, 280–90.

14. Ibid., 291.

15. Judith Lorber, "Dismantling Noah's Ark," *Sex Roles* 14, no. 11/12 (1986).

16. Ibid.

17. Williams, *Reshaping the Work-Family Debate*, 126.

18. Ibid.

19. Linda Hirschman, quoted in Williams, *Reshaping the Work-Family Debate*, 124; Leslie Bennetts, quoted in Williams, *Reshaping the Work-Family Debate*, 125.

20. Williams, *Reshaping the Work-Family Debate*, 106.

21. Ibid., 107.

22. Setsu Shigematsu, *Scream from the Shadows: The Women's Liberation Movement in Japan* (Minneapolis: University of Minnesota Press, 2012), 20–21.

23. Ibid., 176.

24. Chizuko Ueno, *Onnatoiu kairaku* [The pleasure of being a woman] (Tokyo: Keiso Syobou, 1991), 126.

25. Ueno, *Onna toiu kairaku*, 125–28.

26. Mackie, *Feminism in Modern Japan: Citizenship, Embodiment and Sexuality* (Cambridge, UK: Cambridge University Press, 2003), 183.

27. Shigematsu, *Scream from the Shadows*, 115.

28. Ely and Meyerson, "Theories of Gender," 109.

29. Ueno criticized the concept of human rights as representing traditionally Western and male rights; thus, it cannot be applicable to Japan or Japanese women. See Chizuko Ueno, *Ikinobiru Tameno Shiso* [Ideas for survival] (Tokyo: Iwanami Shoten, 2006).

30. Ayako Kano, "Japanese Feminist Debates in the Twentieth Century," in *Feminism*, ed. Yumiko Ehara and Yoshiko Kanai (Tokyo: Shinyosya, 1997), 213–14.

31. Ibid., 107.

32. Ibid., 127.

33. Susan D. Holloway, *Women and Family in Contemporary Japan* (New York: Cambridge University Press, 2010).

34. Ely, Ibarra, and Kolb, "Taking Gender into Account," 475. Ely, Ibarra, and Kolb argue that "women have not been socialized to compete successfully in the world of men, and so they must be taught the skills their male counterparts have acquired as a matter of course."

# Bibliography

Abe, Naohito, and Satoshi Shimizutani. "Employment Policy and Corporate Governance: An Empirical Comparison of the Stakeholder and the Profit-Maximization Model." *Journal of Comparative Economics* 35 (2007): 346–68.

Acker, Joan. "The Future of 'Gender and Organizations': Connection and Boundaries." *Gender, Work & Organizations* 5, no. 4 (1998): 195–206.

——. "Hierarchies, Jobs, Bodies: A Theory of Gendered Organizations." *Gender & Society* 4, (1990): 139–58.

——. "Inequality Regimes: Gender, Class, and Race in Organizations. *Gender & Society* 20 (2006): 441–64.

Agarwal, Bina. "Are We Not Peasants Too? Land Rights and Women's Claims in India." *Seeds.* November 21, 2002.

——. "'Bargaining' and Gender Relations: Within and beyond the Household." *Feminist Economics* 3, no. 1 (1997): 1–51.

Ahmadjian, Christina, and Gregory E. Robbins. "A Clash of Capitalisms: Foreign Shareholders and Corporate Restructuring in 1990s Japan." *American Sociological Review* 70 (2005): 451–71.

Akita, Kumiko. "A Female Teacher and Sexual Harassment in a Japanese Women's Junior College: A Case Study." *Women and Language* 25, no. 1 (2002): 8–13.

Allison, Anne. *Nightwork: Sexuality, Pleasure, and Masculinity in a Tokyo Hostess Club.* Chicago: University of Chicago Press, 1994.

Amyx, Jennifer A. *Japan's Financial Crisis: Institutional Rigidity and Reluctant Change.* Princeton: Princeton University Press, 2004.

Aoki, Masahiko. *Corporations in Evolving Diversity: Cognition, Governance, and Institutions,* Oxford: Oxford University Press, 2010.

Aoki, Masahiko, Gregory Jackson, and Hideaki Miyajima. *Corporate Governance in Japan: Institutional Change and Organizational Diversity.* New York: Oxford University Press, 2008.

Aoki, Mizuho. "Japan's Poor Gender Gap Worsening, WEF Survey Finds." *Japan Times.* October 25, 2013. http://www.japantimes.co.jp/news/2013/10/25/national/japans-poor-gender-gap-worsening-wef-survey-finds/#.VF2RXoe6epx (accessed September 10, 2014).

Asakura, Mutsuko. *Labor Laws and Gender.* Tokyo, Japan: Keiso Syobou, 2004.

——. "Legal Problems of Basic Law for the Gender Equal Society." *Ohara syakai mondai kenkyujyo zasshi* [Ohara Journal of Social Issues] 546, no. 5 (2004): 1–10.

Asia-Japan Women's Resource Center. "Kanematsu Sex Discrimination Case" [Syosya Kanematsu Jiken towa]. 2012. http://ajwrc.org/jp/modules/bulletin/index.php?page=article&storyid=390 (accessed November 1, 2013).

Assmann, Stephanie. "The Long Path toward Gender Equality in Japan: The Revision of the Equal Employment Opportunity Law and Its Implementation." In *Innovation and Change in Japanese Management.* Edited by Parissa Haghirian, 139–56. London: Palgrave Macmillan, 2010.

Baron, James N., Brian S. Mittman, and Andrew E. Newman. "Targets of Opportunity: Organizational and Environmental Determinants of Gender Integration within the California Civil Service, 1979–1985." *American Journal of Sociology* 96, no. 6 (1991): 1362–1401.

Barshay, Andrew E. "Capitalism and Civil Society in Postwar Japan: Perspectives from Intellectual History,." In *The State of Civil Society in Japan*. Edited by Frank Schwartz and Susan Pharr, 63–82. Cambridge: Cambridge University Press, 2003.

Beckman, Christine, and Damon Phillips. "Interorganizational Determinants of Promotion: Client Leadership and the Attainment of Women Attorneys." *American Sociological Review* 70 (2005): 678 701.

Benson, John, Masae Yuasa, and Philippe Debroux. "The Prospect for Gender Diversity in Japanese Employment." *International Journal of Human Resource Management* 18, no. 5 (2007): 890–907.

Bozkurt, Ödül. "Foreign Employers as Relief Routes: Women, Multinational Corporations and Managerial Careers in Japan." *Gender, Work & Organization* 19, no. 3 (2012): 225–53.

Brass, Daniel J. "Men's and Women's Networks: A Study of Interaction Patterns and Influence in an Organization." *Academy of Management Journal* 28, no. 2 (1985): 327–43.

Brenner, Johanna. "Transnational Feminism and the Struggle for Global Justice." *New Politics* 9, no. 2 (2003): 78–87.

Brinton, Mary C. "Christmas Cakes and Wedding Cakes: The Social Organization of Japanese Women's Life Course." In *Japanese Social Organization*. Edited by Takie Sugiyama Lebra, 79–107. Honolulu: University of Hawaii Press, 1992.

——. "Gender Stratification in Contemporary Urban Japan." *American Sociological Review* 54, no. 4 (1989): 549–64.

——. *Lost in Transition: Youth, Work, and Instability in Postindustrial Japan*. New York: Cambridge University Press, 2011.

——. "The Social-Institutional Bases of Gender Stratification: Japan as an Illustrative Case." *American Journal of Sociology* 94, no. 2 (1988): 300–34.

——. *Women and the Economic Miracle: Gender and Work in Postwar Japan*. Berkeley: University of California Press, 1993.

Brinton, Mary C., and Takehiko Kariya. "Institutional Embeddedness in Japanese Labor Markets." In *The New Institutionalism in Sociology*. Edited by Mary C. Brinton and Victor Nee, 181–207. New York: Russell Sage Foundation, 1998.

Brinton, Mary C., and Hang-Yue Ngo. "Age and Sex in the Occupational Structure: A United States–Japan Comparison." *Sociological Forum* 8, no. 1 (1993): 93–111.

Britton, Dana. "The Epistemology of the Gendered Organization." *Gender & Society* 14, no. 3 (2000): 418–34.

Britton, Dana, and Laura Logan. "Gendered Organizations: Progress and Prospects." *Sociology Compass* 2, no. 1 (2008): 107–21.

Burawoy, Michael. *Manufacturing Consent: Changes in the Labor Process under Monopoly Capitalism*. Chicago: University of Chicago Press, 1979.

Bureau of Industrial and Labor Affairs. *Working Women and Labor Law*. Tokyo: Tokyo Metropolitan Government, 2011.

Butler, Judith. *Bodies That Matter: On the Discursive Limits of Sex*. London: Routledge, 1993.

Cargill, Thomas. "What Caused Japan's Banking Crisis?" In *Crisis and Change in the Japanese Financial System*. Edited by Takeo Hoshi and Hugh Patrick, 37–58. Boston: Kluwer Academic Publishers, 2000.

Cassirer, Naomi, and Barbara Reskin. "High Hopes: Organizational Position, Employment Experiences, and Women's and Men's Promotion Aspirations." *Work and Occupations* 27, no. 4 (2000): 438–63.

Cha, Youngjoo. "Overwork and the Persistence of Gender Segregation in Occupations." *Gender & Society* 27, no. 2 (2013): 158–84.

———. "Reinforcing Separate Spheres: The Effect of Spousal Overwork on Men's and Women's Employment in Dual-Earner Households." *American Sociological Review* 75, no. 2 (2010): 303–29.

Chan-Tiberghien, Jennifer. *Gender and Human Rights Politics in Japan: Global Norms and Domestic Networks*. Stanford: Stanford University Press, 2004.

Charles, Maria. "A World of Difference: International Trends in Women's Economic Status." *Annual Review of Sociology* 37 (2011): 355–71.

Charles, Maria, and David B. Grusky. *Occupational Ghettos: The Worldwide Segregation of Women and Men*. Stanford: Stanford University Press, 2004.

Charlebois, Justin. "Herbivore Masculinity as an Oppositional Form of Masculinity." *Culture, Society, and Masculinities* 5, no. 1 (2013): 89–104.

Chesler, Phyllis. *Woman's Inhumanity to Woman*. New York: Nation Books, 2001.

Christensen, Paul A. *Japan, Alcoholism and Masculinity: Suffering Sobriety in Tokyo*. London, UK: Lexington Books, 2015.

Clark, Hannah. "Toyota's Otaka Sued for Sexual Harassment." *Forbes*. February 6, 2006. http://www.forbes.com/2006/05/02/toyota-otaka-harassment-cx_hc_0502autofacescan07.html (accessed January 1, 2010).

CNN. "Mitsubishi Settles for $34M." CNNMoney. June 11, 1998. http://money.cnn.com/1998/06/11/companies/mitsubishi/ (accessed January 1, 2010).

Coates, G. "Integration or Separation: Women and Appliances of Organizational Culture." *Women in Management in Review* 13, no. 3 (1998): 114–24.

Cohen, Phillip N., and Matt L. Huffman. "Working for the Woman? Female Managers and the Gender Wage Gap." *American Sociological Review* 72 (2007): 681–704.

Collinson, David. L., and Margaret Collinson. "The Power of Time: Leadership, Management and Gender." In *Fighting for Time: Shifting Boundaries of Work and Social Life*. Edited by Cynthia F. Epstein and Arne L. Kalleberg, 219–46. New York: Russell Sage Foundation, 2004.

———. "Sexuality in the Workplace: The Domination of Men's Sexuality." In *The Sexuality of Organization*. Edited by J. Hearn, D. L. Sheppard, P. Trancred-Sherif, and G. Burrell, 91–109. London: Sage, 1989.

Collinson, David, and Jeff Hearn. "Naming Men as Men: Implications for Work, Organization and Management." *Gender, Work & Organization* 1, no. 1 (1994): 2–22.

Collinson, Margaret, and David L. Collinson. "'It's Only Dick': The Sexual Harassment of Women Managers in Insurance Sales." *Work, Employment & Society* 10, no. 1 (1996): 29–56.

Connell, Robert W. *Gender and Power: Society, the Person, and Sexual Politics*. Stanford: Stanford University Press, 1987.

Coontz, Stephanie. "Yes, I've Folded Up My Masculine Mystique, Honey." February 24, 2013. *The London Times*. http://www.thesundaytimes.co.uk/sto/newsreview/article1219753.ece.

Correll, Shelley J., Stephen Bernard, and In Paik. "Getting a Job: Is There a Motherhood Penalty? *American Journal of Sociology* 112, no. 5 (2007): 1297–338.

Crothers, Laura M., John Lipinski, and Marcel C. Minutolo. "Cliques, Rumors and Gossip by the Water Cooler: Female Bullying in the Workplace." *Psychologist-Manager Journal* 12 (2009): 97–110.

Dasgupta, Romit. "'The Lost Decade' of the 1990s and Shifting Masculinities in Japan." *Culture, Society & Masculinity* 1 (2009): 79–95.

Dawn.com. "US Court Okays Bank of America's $39m Gender Bias Deal." December 29, 2013. http://www.dawn.com/news/1077013/us-court-okays-bank-of-americas-39m-gender-bias-deal (accessed October 1, 2014).

Dellinger, Kirsten. "Masculinities in 'Safe' and 'Embattled' Organizations: Accounting for Pornographic and Feminist Magazines." *Gender & Society* 18 (2004): 545–66.

Dellinger, Kirsten, and Christine L. Williams. "The Locker Room and the Dorm Room: Workplace Norms and the Boundaries of Sexual Harassment in Magazine Editing." *Social Problems* 49, no. 2 (2002): 242–57.

Denissen, Amy M. "Crossing the Line: How Women in the Building Trades Interpret and Respond to Sexual Conduct at Work." *Journal of Contemporary Ethnography* 39, no. 3 (2010): 297–327.

Derks, Belle, Naomi Ellemers, Colette Van Laar, and Kim de Groot. "Do Sexist Organizational Cultures Create the Queen Bee?" *British Journal of Social Psychology* 50 (2011): 5129–535.

Derks, Belle, Colette Van Laar, Naomi Ellemers, and Kim de Groot. "Gender-Bias Primes Elicit Queen-Bee Responses among Senior Policewomen." *Psychological Science* 22 (2011): 1243–49.

Dobbin, Frank. *Inventing Equal Opportunity*. Princeton: Princeton University Press, 2009.

Dobbin, Frank, and Erin L. Kelly. "How to Stop Harassment: The Professional Construction of Legal Compliance in Organizations." *American Journal of Sociology* 112, no. 4 (2007):1203–43.

Dobbin, Frank, Soohan Kim, and Alexandra Kalav. "You Can't Always Get What You Need: Organizational Determinants of Diversity Programs." *American Sociological Review* 76, no. 3 (2011): 386–411.

Dore, Ronald. *Innovation for Whom? Institute for Technology, Enterprise and Competitiveness*. Research Paper 04–01. Kyoto, Japan: Doshisha University, 2004.

———. "Shareholder Capitalism Comes to Japan." The Other Canon Foundation and Tallinn University of Technology Working Papers in Technology Governance and Economic Dynamics. TUT Institute of Public Administration (2007): 207–14.

———. "Will Global Capitalism Be Anglo-Saxon Capitalism?" *New Left Review* 6 (2000): 101–19.

Drexler, Peggy. "The Tyranny of the Queen Bee." *Wall Street Journal*. March 6, 2013. http://online.wsj.com/article/SB1000142412788732388430457832827152608049 6.html?mod=wsj_valettop_email (accessed November 1, 2012).

*Economist*. "Back to The Drawing Board." November 3, 2012. http://www.economist.com/news/business/21565660-after-olympus-scandal-japan-inc-wants-less-scrutiny-back-drawing-board (accessed November 1, 2013).

Ely, Robin J. "The Effects of Organizational Demographics and Social Identity on Relationships among Professional Women." *Administrative Science Quarterly* 39 (1994): 203–38.

———. "The Power in Demography: Women's Social Constructions of Gender Identity at Work." *Academy of Management Journal* 38 (1995): 589–634.

Ely, Robin J., Herminia Ibarra, and Deborah Kolb. "Taking Gender into Account: Theory and Design for Women's Leadership Development Programs." *Academy of Management Learning & Education* 10, no. 3 (2011): 373–493.

Ely, Robin J., and Debra E. Meyerson. "An Organizational Approach to Undoing Gender: The Unlikely Case of Offshore Oil Platforms." *Research in Organizational Behavior* 30 (2010): 3–34.

——. "Theories of Gender in Organizations: A New Approach to Organizational Analysis and Change." *Research in Organizational Behavior* 22 (2000): 103–51.

Ely, Robin J., and Irene Padavic. "A Feminist Analysis of Organizational Research on Sex Differences." *Academy of Management Review* 32, no. 4 (2007): 1121–43.

England, Paula. *Comparable Worth: Theories and Evidence.* New York: Aldine de Gruyter, 1992.

England, Paula. "The Gender Revolution: Uneven and Stalled." *Gender & Society* 24, no. 2 (2010): 149–66.

England, Paula, and Nancy Folbre. "Gender and Economic Sociology." In *Handbook of Economic Sociology.* Edited by Neil Smelser and Richard Swedberg, 627–49. Princeton: Princeton University Press, 2005.

England, Paula, Janet Gornick, and Emily F. Shafer. "Women's Employment, Education, and the Gender Gap in 17 Countries." *Monthly Labor Review* 3 (2013): 3–12.

Esping-Andersen, Gøsta. "Hybrid or Unique? The Japanese Welfare State between Europe and America." *Journal of European Social Policy* 7, no. 3 (1997): 179–89.

——. *The Incomplete Revolution: Adapting to Women's New Roles.* Cambridge, UK: Polity Press, 2009.

Estevez-Abe, Margarita. "Gender Bias in Skills and Social Policies: The Varieties of Capitalism Perspective on Sex Segregation." *Social Politics* 12, no. 2 (2005): 180–215.

——. "Gendering the Varieties of Capitalism: A Study of Occupational Segregation by Sex in Advanced Industrial Societies." *World Politics* 59 (2006): 142–75.

Fitzgerald, Louise F., Suzanne Swan, and Karla Fischer. "Why Didn't She Just Report Him?" *Journal of Social Issues* 51 (1995): 117–38.

Foote, Daniel H. "Judicial Creation of Norms in Japanese Labor Law: Activism in the Service of Stability?" *UCLA Law Review* 43 (1996): 635–709.

——. *Nameless Faceless Justice.* Tokyo: NTT Press, 2007.

Fried, Mindy. *Taking Time: Parental Leave Policy and Corporate Culture.* Philadelphia: Temple University Press, 1998.

Fukuyama, Francis. "Confucianism and Democracy." *Journal of Democracy* 6, no. 2 (1995): 20–33.

Funabashi, Kuniko. "Gender Equal Policy and Backlash" [Jenda byoudo seisaku to bakkurassyu no haikei]. *Wako University Annual Report, 2007*, 18–29.

Gambles, Richenda, Susan Lewis, and Rhona Rapoport. *The Myth of Work-Life Balance: The Challenge of Our Time for Men, Women and Societies.* Chichester, UK: Wiley, 2006.

Gans, Herbert J. "The Uses of Poverty: The Poor Pay All." *Social Policy* 2 (1971): 21–24.

——. "The Positive Functions of Poverty." *American Journal of Sociology* 78, no. 2. (1972): 275–89.

Geiger, Daniel, and Elena Antonacopoulou. "Narratives and Organizational Dynamics: Exploring Blind Spots and Organizational Inertia." *Journal of Applied Behavioral Science* 45, no. 3 (2009): 411–36.

Gelb, Joyce. *Gender Policies in Japan and the United States: Comparing Women's Movements, Rights, and Politics.* Palgrave Macmillan, 2003.

Gender Equality Bureau Cabinet Office. "Toward Active Participation of Women as the Core of Growth Strategies, White Paper on Gender Equality, 2013." http://www.gender.go.jp/english_contents/about_danjo/whitepaper/pdf/2013-01.pdf.

——. "Toward Gender Equal Society, 2012." http:// www.gender.go.jp/pamphlet/ pamphlet-main/index.html.

——. "White Paper on Gender Equal Society, 2009." http://www.gender.go.jp/ whitepaper/h20/zentai/html/zuhyo/zuhyo1_03_09.html.

——. "White Paper on Gender Equal Society, 2010." http://www.gender.go.jp/ whitepaper/h22/gaiyou/html/honpen/b1_s08.html.

——. "White Paper on Gender Equal Society, 2011." ttp://www.gender.go.jp/whitepaper/h23/zentai/html/zuhyo/zuhyo01–02–06.html.

——. "White Paper on Gender Equal Society, 2013." http://www.gender.go.jp/about_danjo/whitepaper/h25/zentai/.

——. "White Paper on Gender Equal Society, 2014." http://www.gender.go.jp/about_danjo/whitepaper/h26/gaiyou/html/honpen/b1_s05.html.

Geraghty, Kristina. "Taming the Paper Tiger: A Comparative Approach to Reforming Japanese Gender Equality Laws." *Cornell International Law Journal* 41, no. 2 (2008): 503–4.

Gerson, Kathleen. *Hard Choices: How Women Decide about Work, Career, and Motherhood.* Berkeley: University of California Press, 1985.

Gini, Al. *My Job, My Self: Work and the Creation of the Modern Individual.* London: Routledge, 2001.

Giuffre, Patti A., and Christine L. Williams. "Labeling Sexual Harassment in Restaurants." *Gender & Society* 8, no. 3 (1994): 378–401.

Goodman, Carl F. *The Rule of Law in Japan: A Comparative Analysis.* 3rd ed. The Hague, The Netherlands: Kluwar Law Intl., 2012.

Gorman, Elizabeth H. "Gender Stereotypes, Same-Gender Preferences, and Organizational Variation in the Hiring of Women: Evidence from Law Firms." *American Sociological Review* 70 (2005): 702–28.

——. "Work Uncertainty and the Promotion of Professional Women: The Case of Law Firm Partnership." *Social Forces* 85, no. 2 (2006): 865–90.

Gorman, Elizabeth H., and Julie A. Kmec. "Hierarchical Rank and Women's Organizational Mobility: Glass Ceilings in Corporate Law Firms." *American Journal of Sociology* 114, no. 5 (2009): 1428–74.

——. "We (Have to) Try Harder: Gender and Required Work Effort in Britain and the United States." *Gender & Society* 21, no. 6 (2007): 828–56.

Gottfried, Heidi. "Comment: Stability and Change: Typifying 'Atypical' Employment in Japan." *ASIEN* 84 (2002): 31–33.

——. "Temp(t)ing Bodies: Shaping Bodies at Work in Japan." *Sociology* 37, no. 2 (2003): 257–76.

Gottfried, Heidi, and Nagisa Hayashi-Kato. "Gendering Work: Deconstructing the Narrative of the Japanese Economic Miracle." *Work, Employment and Society* 12, no. 1 (1998): 25–46.

Gottfried, Heidi, and Jacqueline O'Reilly. "Institutionally Embedded Gender Models: Re- Regulating Breadwinner Models in Germany and Japan." In *Equity in the Workplace: Gendering Workplace Policy Analysis.* Edited by Heidi Gottfried and Laura A. Reese, 103–30. Lanham, MD: Lexington Books, 2004.

Gottfried, Heidi, and Laura Reese. "Gender, Policy, Politics, and Work: Feminist Comparative and Transnational Research." *Review of Policy Research* 20, no. 1 (2003): 3–20.

Gregory, Michele R. "Inside the Locker Room: Male Homosocialibility in the Advertising Industry." *Gender, Work and Organizations* 16, no. 3 (2009): 323–47.

Guillaume, Cecile, and Sophie Pochic. "What Would You Sacrifice? Access to Top Management and the Work-Life Balance. *Gender, Work & Organization* 16, no.1 (2009): 14–36.

Haddad, Mary Alice. *Building Democracy in Japan*. New York: Cambridge University Press, 2012.

Hadjifotiou, Nathalie. *Women and Harassment at Work*. London: Pluto Press, 1983.

Hall, Peter A., and David Soskice. "An Introduction to Varieties of Capitalism." In *Varieties of Capitalism: The Institutional foundations of Comparative Advantage*. Edited by Peter A. Hall and David Soskice, 1–68. Oxford: Oxford University Press, 2001.

Havemen, Heather A., Joseph P. Broshcak, and Lisa E. Cohen. "Good Times, Bad Times: The Effects of Organizational Dynamics on the Careers of Male and Female Managers." *Research in the Sociology of Work* 18 (2009): 119–48.

Higuchi, Yoshio. "Support for the Women's Continual Work and the Consequences— Logic and Economy of Childcare Leave." In *Working/Women Work*, vol. 7. Edited by Emiko Takeishi, 106–30. Tokyo: Mineruva Shobo, 2009.

Hirata, Kiyoaki ed. *Gendai shimin shakai to kigyo kokka* [Comtemporary Civil Society and the Enterprise State]. Tokyo, Japan: Ochanomizu Shobo, 1994.

Hultin, Mia, and Ryszard Szulkin. "Mechanisms of Inequality: Unequal Access to Organizational Power and the Gender Wage Gap." *European Sociological Review* 19 (2003): 143–59.

——. "Wages and Unequal Access to Organizational Power: An Empirical Test of Gender Discrimination." Administrative Science Quarterly 44 (1999): 453–72.

Hochschild, Arlie R. *The Time Bind: When Work Becomes Home and Home Becomes Work*. New York: Metropolitan Books, 1997.

Holloway, Susan D. *Women and Family in Contemporary Japan*. New York: Cambridge University Press, 2010.

Hoshi, Takeo. "What Happened to Japanese Banks?" *Monetary and Economic Studies* 19, no. 1 (2001): 1–29.

Huffington Post Japan. "The Cabinet Decides the Proposal on Zero Pay for Overwork." April 3, 2015. http://www.huffingtonpost.jp/2015/04/03/angyodai-zero-kakugi_n_6998224.html (accessed June 1, 2015).

Huffman, Matt, Phillip Cohen, and Jessica Pearlman. "Engendering Change: Organizational Dynamics and Workplace Gender Segregation: 1975–2005." *Administrative Science Quarterly* 55, no. 2 (2010): 255–77.

Ibarra, Hermenia. "Personal Networks of Women and Minorities in Management: A Conceptual Frame Work." *Academy of Management Review* 18, no. 1 (1993): 56–87.

Iki, Noriko. "Jyosei rodo seisaku no tenkai" [The Progress of the Women Labor Policy: From the Point of Justice, Utilization, and Welfare]. Labour Policy Report 9. Tokyo: Japan Institute for Labour Policy and Training, 2011.

Inagami, Takeshi, and D. Hugh Whittaker, *The New Community Firm: Employment, Governance and Management Reform in Japan.* Cambridge: Cambridge University Press, 2005.

Inglehart, Ronald, Pippa Norris, and Christian Welzel. "Gender Equality and Democracy." *Comparative Sociology* 1, no. 3/4 (2002): 321–46.

Inglehart, Ronald, and Christian Welzel. *Modernization, Cultural Change, and Democracy: The Human Development Sequence.* New York: Cambridge University Press, 2005.

——. "Changing Mass Priorities: The Link between Modernization and Democracy." *Perspectives on Politics* 8, no. 2 (2010): 551–67.

Irigaray, Luce. *Ce Sexe qui n'en est pas un.* Paris: Les Editions de Minuit, 1977.

Ishiguro, Kuniko. "Career Formation of Women Managers: Case Studies" [Josei Kanrishoku no Kyaria Keisei: Jirei Karano K satsu]. *GEMC Journal* 7 (2012): 104–28.

Ito, Kazutaka. "Report: Japan Ranks 101st in the World in Gender Equality." *Asahi Shimbun*. October 25, 2012. http://ajw.asahi.com/article/behind_news/social_affairs/AJ201210250065 (accessed September 10, 2014).

Jackson, Gregory. "Employment Adjustment and Distributional Conflict in Japanese Firms." In *Corporate Governance in Japan: Institutional Change and Organizational Diversity*. Edited by Masahiko Aoki, Gregory Jackson, and Hideaki Miyajima, 282–309. New York: Oxford University Press, 2008.

Japan IBM. 2010. http://www-06.ibm.com/jp/ibm/bcg/03.shtml#3.3 (accessed June 1, 2010).

Japan Institute for Labour Policy and Training (JILPT). "Data Book International Labor Statistics, 2014."

——. "Research on Workers' Motivation and Management, 2004." http://www.jil.go.jp/kokunai/statistics/doko/h1607/index.html (accessed November 1, 2012).

——. "Sexual Harassment, 2009." http://www.jil.go.jp/hanrei/conts/092.htm (accessed November 1, 2012).

Jo, Hyung Je, and Jong-Sung You. "Transferring Production Systems: An institutionalist Account of Hyundai Motor Company in the United States." *Journal of East Asian Studies* 11 (2011): 41–73.

Jones, Geoffrey. *Beauty Imagined: A History of the Global Beauty Industry.* New York: Oxford University Press, 2010.

Kainou, Tamie. "Judicial Remedies for Sexual Harassment and Its Limit." *F-GENS Journal* 7 (2007): 214–22.

Kalev, Alexandra. "Cracking the Glass Cages? Restructuring and Ascriptive Inequality at Work." *American Journal of Sociology* 114, no. 6 (2009): 1591–643.

Kanai, Atsuko. "'Karoshi (Work to Death)' in Japan." *Journal of Business Ethics* 84, no. 2 (2009): 209–16.

Kano, Ayako. "Backlash, Fight Back, and Back Pedaling: Responses to State Feminism in Contemporary Japan." *International Journal of Asian Studies* 8, no. 1 (2011): 41–62.

——. "Japanese Feminist Debates in the Twentieth Century." In *Feminism*. Edited by Yumiko Ehara and Yoshiko Kanai, 196–244. Tokyo: Shinyosya, 1997.

Kanter, Rosabeth M. *Men and Women of the Corporation*. New York: Basic Books, 1977.

Kardam, Nüket. "The Emerging Global Gender Equality Regime from Neoliberal and Constructivist Perspectives in International Relations." *International Feminist Journal of Politics* 6, no. 1 (2004): 85–109.

Kato, Tetsuro. "Karoshi to sabisu zangyou no seijikeizaigaku" [Political Economy of Death by Overwork and Service Overtime]. In *Gendai shimin shakai to kigyo kokka* [Comtemporary Civil Society and the Enterprise State]. Edited by Hirata Kiyoaki, Yamada Toshio, Kato Tetsuro, Kurosawa Nobuyuki, and Ito Masazumi, 75–126. Tokyo, Japan: Ochanomizu Shobo, 1994.

——. "The Political Economy of Japanese Karoshi (Death from Overwork)." *Hitotsubashi Journal of Social Studies* 26, no. 2 (1994): 41–54.

Kawaguchi, Akira. "Corporate Governance by Investors and the Role of Women." *Japan Labor Review* 6, no. 1 (2009): 72–90.

——. *Gender Inequality in Economic Status.* Tokyo: Keiso Syobo, 2008.

Kawaguchi, Daiji, Hisahiro Naito, and Izumi Yokoyama. "Labor Market Responses to Legal Work Hour Reduction: Evidence from Japan." Cabinet Office, Economic and Social Research Institute (ESRI). Discussion Paper Series no. 202 (2008): 1–31.

Kawahito, Hiroshi. *Suicide by Overwork*. Tokyo: Iwanami Shoten, 1998.

Kawanishi, Yuko. "On Karo-Jisatsu (Suicide by Overwork): Why Do Japanese Workers Work Themselves to Death?" *International Journal of Mental Health* 37, no. 1 (2008): 61–74.

Keidanren (Japan Business Federation). *Action Plan for Women.* April 15, 2014. https://www.keidanren.or.jp/policy/2014/029_honbun.pdf (accessed October 1, 2014).

Keizer, Arjan B. "Non-Regular Employment in Japan: Continued and Renewed Dualities." *Work, Employment and Society* 22, no. 3 (2008): 407–25.

———. "Transformations in- and outside the Internal Labour Market: Institutional Change and Continuity in Japanese Employment Practices." *International Journal of Human Resource Management* 20, no. 7 (2009): 1521–35.

Kerfoot, Deborah, and David Knights. "Managing Masculinity in Contemporary Organizational Life: A 'Managerial Project.'" *Organization* 5, no. 1 (1998): 7–26.

Kersten, Rikki. *Democracy in Postwar Japan: Maruyama Masao and the Search for Autonomy.* London: Routledge, 1996.

Kimmel, Michael S. *The Gendered Society.* New York: Oxford University Press, 2000.

Kimoto, Kimiko. *Empirical Research on Women Laborers and Organizations.* Grant-in-Aid Research Report. Melbourne, Aust.: Japan Ministry of Education, Culture, Sports, Science and Technology, 2008.

———. *Gender and Japanese Management.* Translated by Teresa Castelvetere. Melbourne, Aust.: Trans Pacific Press, 2005.

Kishimoto, Yoshihiro. "Company Ranking 100 in Childcare Takers" [Ikujisyutokusya-suu ranking top 100]. January 4, 2012. Toyo Keizai Online. http://toyokeizai.net/articles/-/8366/ (accessed November 1, 2013).

Kitazawa, Chiaki. "Organizational Culture of Ignoring the Problems: The Case of Olympus." *Nihon Keizai Shinbun.* November 19, 2011. http://www.nikkei.com/article/DGXNASFK1703Z_Y1A111C1000000/ (accessed November 20, 2011).

Kobayashi, Emiko, and Harold Grasmick. "Workers' Decisions to Comply: A Comparison of the Perceived Threats of Managerial Sanctions, Embarrassment, and Shame in Japan and the United States." *Journal of Language, Culture and Communication* 4 (2002): 1–12.

Konrad, Alison M., Vicki Kramer, and Sumru Erkut. "Critical Mass: The Impact of Three or More Women on Corporate Boards." *Organizational Dynamics* 37 (2008):145–64.

Kuroda, Sachiko. "How Long Do Japanese Work? A Comparison before and after the Shorter Work Week." RIETI Policy Discussion Paper Series 10-P-002 (2010): 1–17.

Kuroda, Sachiko, and Isamu Yamamoto. "How Are Hours Worked and Wages Affected by Labor Regulations? The White-Collar Exemption and 'Name-Only Managers' in Japan." RIETI Discussion Paper Series 09-E-032 (June 2009): 1–27.

Lam, Alice C. *Women and Japanese Management: Discrimination and Reform.* New York: Routledge, 1992.

Lambert, Wallace E., Richard C. Hodgson, Robert C. Gardner, and Samuel Fillenbaum. "Evaluative Reactions to Spoken Languages." *Journal of Abnormal and Social Psychology* 60 (1960): 44–51.

Larson, Eric. "An Institutional Hazing System." *Japan Times.* February 14, 2007. http://search.japantimes.co.jp/cgi-bin/rc20070214a2.html (accessed October 1, 2010).

LeBlanc, Robin M. *The Art of the Gut: Manhood, Power, and Ethics in Japanese Politics.* Berkeley, University of California Press, 2010.

Leidner, Robin. *Fast Food, Fast Talk: Service Work and the Routinization of Everyday Life.* Berkeley: University of California Press, 1993.

———. "Selling Hamburgers and Selling Insurance: Gender, Work, and Interactive Service Jobs." *Gender & Society* 4, no. 2 (1991): 154–77.

Liff, Sonia, and Kate Ward. "Distorted Views through the Glass Ceiling: The Construction of Women's Understandings of Promotion and Senior Management Positions." *Gender, Work & Organization* 8, no. 1 (2001): 19–36.

Lincoln, Edward J. *Arthritic Japan: The Slow Pace of Economic Reform*. Washington, DC: Brookings Institution Press, 2001.

Litwin, Anne H., and Lynne O'Brien Hallstein. "Shadows and Silences: How Women's Positioning and Unspoken Friendship Rules in Organizational Settings Cultivate Difficulties among Some Women at Work." *Women's Studies in Communication* 30, no. 1 (2007): 111–42.

Loe, Meika. "Working for Men: At the Intersection of Power, Gender, and Sexuality." *Sociological Inquiry* 66, no. 4 (1996): 399–421.

Lorber, Judith. "Dismantling Noah's Ark." *Sex Roles* 14, no. 11/12 (1986): 567–80.

Lucas, Jeffrey W. "Status Processes and the Institutionalization of Women as Leaders." *American Sociological Review* 68, no. 3 (2003): 464–80.

Lyon, Dawn, and Alison E. Woodward. "Gender and Time at the Top." *European Journal Women's Studies* 11, no. 2 (2008): 205–21.

Mackie, Vera. *Feminism in Modern Japan: Citizenship, Embodiment and Sexuality*. Cambridge, UK: Cambridge University Press, 2003.

MacKinnon, Catharine A. *Sexual Harassment of Working Women: A Case of Sex Discrimination*. New Haven: Yale University Press, 1979.

Martin, Patricia Y. "Mobilizing Masculinities: Women's Experiences of Men at Work." *Organization* 8, no. 4 (2001): 587–618.

——. "'Said and Done' versus 'Saying and Doing': Gendering Practices, Practicing Gender at Work." *Gender & Society* 17, no. 3 (2003): 342–66.

Mathews, Gordon. "Can 'a Real Man' Live for His Family? Ikigai and Masculinity in Today's Japan." In *Men and Masculinities in Contemporary Japan: Dislocating the Salaryman Dox*a. Edited by James E. Roberson and Nobue Suzuki, 109–25. London: RoutledgeCurzon, 2003.

Matsumoto, Syouetsu. "Danjyo kikai kinto houri to hanrei riron" [Logic of Equal Employment Opportunity Law and Court Cases]. *Cyukyo Hougaku* 27, no. 3/4 (1992): 1–44.

Mavin, Sharon. "Queen Bees, Wannabees and Afraid to Bees: No More 'Best Enemies' for Women in Management?" *British Journal of Management* 19 (2008): 75–84.

——. "Venus Envy: Problematizing Solidarity Behaviour and Queen Bees." *Women in Management Review* 21, no. 4 (2006): 264–76.

McDowell, Linda. *Capital Culture: Gender at Work in the City*. Oxford: Blackwell, 1997.

McGeehan, Patrick. "Morgan Stanley Settles Bias Suit with $54 Million." *New York Times*. July 13, 2004.

Messerschmidt, James W. *Masculinities and Crime: Critique and Reconceptualization of Theory*. Lanham, MD: Rowman & Littlefield, 1993.

Messerschmidt, James. "Managing to Kill: Masculinities and the Space Shuttle Challenger Explosion." In *Masculinities in Organizations*. Edited by Clifford Cheng, 29–53. Thousand Oaks, CA: Sage, 1996.

Milhaupt, Curtis J., J. Mark Ramseyer, and Mark D. West. *The Japanese Legal System: Cases, Codes, and Commentary*. New York: Foundation Press, 2006.

Ministry of Health, Labour and Welfare. Basic Survey on Equal Employment, 2008, http://www.mhlw.go.jp/houdou/2008/08/h0808-1.html (accessed October 1, 2012).

——. "Basic Survey on Women's Employment, 2007." http://www.mhlw.go.jp/houdou/2007/08/h0809–1/02.html (accessed October 1, 2012).

——. "Career Track Hiring, 2015." http://www.mhlw.go.jp/stf/houdou/0000089473. html.

——. "Current Situation on Employed Women, 2009." http://www.mhlw.go.jp/bunya/ koyoukintou/josei-jitsujo/09.html (accessed March 8, 2012).

——. "Current Situation on Employed Women, 2013." http://www.mhlw.go.jp/bunya/ koyoukintou/josei-jitsujo/13.html (accessed October 1, 2014.

——. "Data on Career-Track Hiring and Positive Action, 2013." http://www.mhlw. go.jp/stf/shingi/2r98520000036fum-att/2r98520000036fy2.pdf (accessed June 1, 2015).

——. "Gender Equality Employment, 2010." http://www.mhlw.go.jp/stf/ houdou/2r9852000001ihm5-att/2r9852000001ihnm.pdf.

——. "Major Court Cases on Women and Labor, 2004." http://www.mhlw.go.jp/ shingi/2004/10/s1007-6a.html (accessed January 8, 2011).

——. "On Workers' Accident Compensation, 2012." http://www.mhlw.go.jp/stf/ houdou/2r9852000001f1k7.html.

——. "Rate of New Graduates Leaving Their Jobs, 2015." http://www.mhlw.go.jp/ topics/2010/01/tp0127-2/dl/24-18.pdf (accessed May 20, 2015).

——. "Research on Working Conditions, 2006." http://www.mhlw.go.jp/toukei/itiran/ roudou/jikan/syurou/06/kekka1.html (accessed March 8, 2012).

Ministry of Internal Affairs and Communications. Statistics Bureau. "Basic Survey on Social Life, 2006." http://www.stat.go.jp/data/shakai/2006/pdf/gaiyou2.pdf (accessed March 8, 2012).

——. "Statistical Topics No. 30.", 2008." http://www.stat.go.jp/data/shakai/topics/ topi30.htm (accessed March 8, 2012).

Miura, Mari. *Welfare through Work: Conservative Ideas, Partisan Dynamics, and Social Protection in Japan*. Ithaca: Cornell University Press, 2012.

Miyaji, Mitsuko. "On Sumitomo Electric Industries Case" [Sumitomo denko danjyo chingin sabetsu sosyo]. Kanagawa University Departmental Bulletin Paper 22, 2004: 140–34.

——. *Women and Labor*. Paper Presented at the Symposium on Women Joint Law Offices in March 17, 2012. Osaka, Japan.

——. *The Chugoku Electric Power Co. Case*. Presented at the WWN Symposium on the Chugoku Electric Power Co. Case, on December 23, 2013. Meiji University, Tokyo, Japan.

Morgan, Laurie A., and Karin A. Martin. "Taking Women Professionals out of the Office: The Case of Women in Sales." *Gender & Society* 20, no. 1 (2006): 108–28.

Mori, Masumi, and Mutsuko Asakura. *Doitsu kachi rodo doitsu chingin gensoku no jisshi sisutemu* [Practicing the Principle of Equal Pay for Equal Work and Work of Equal Value]. Tokyo: Yuhikaku, 2010.

Muta, Kazue. "The Making of *Sekuhara*: Sexual Harassment in Japanese Culture." In *East Asian Sexualities: Modernity, Gender and New Sexual Cultures*. Edited by Stevi Jackson, Liu Jieyu, and Woo Juhyun, 52–68. London: Macmillan, 2008.

Nakagawa, Junko. "Gender Equal Society and Gender" [Danjo kyodo sankaku syakai to jenda]. *Ritsumeikan sangyo syakaironnsyu* 42, no. 1 (2006): 53–63.

Nakamoto, Michiyo. "Foreign Investors Urge Olympus to Rethink." *Financial Times*. March 21, 2012. http://www.ft.com/cms/s/0/ff458e86-7354-11e1-aab3-00144feab49a.html#axzz2RjDWQqZW (accessed November 1, 2013).

National Institute of Population and Social Security Research. "Trends in Marriage and Fertility in Japan" [*Dai juyon- kai shusho doko kihon chosa*]. 2011. http:// www.ipss.go.jp/ps-doukou/j/doukou14_s/chapter3.html#32a (accessed October 1, 2012).

Nemoto, Kumiko. "Long Work Hours and the Corporate Gender Divide in Japan." *Gender, Work & Organization* 20, no. 5 (September 2013): 512–27.

——. "Postponed Marriage: Exploring Women's Views of Matrimony and Work in Japan." *Gender & Society* 22, no. 2 (2008): 219–37.

——. "Sexual Harassment and Gendered Organizational Culture in Japanese Firms." In *Gender and Sexuality in the Workplace* (Research in the Sociology of Work 20). Edited by Christine Williams and Kirsten Dellinger, 203–25. Bingley, UK: Emerald Group Publishing Ltd., 2010.

Nihon Keizai Dantai Rengoukai. "Industrial and Business Views of Declining Birthrate in Japan, 2006" [Sangyoukai kigyo ni okeru syoshikataisaku no torikumi nitsuite]. https://www.keidanren.or.jp/japanese/policy/2006/028/index.html.

*Nihon Keizai Shinbun*. "Custom of Not Saying No to the Boss" [Jyoushi ni sakaraenai kigyou huudo ga sonzaiJuly]. July 20, 2015. http://www.nikkei.com/article/DGXLASFK20H2H_Q5A720C1000000/ (accessed August 1, 2015).

*Nihon Keizai Shinbun*. "Syusyo ikujikyugyo sannen hyoumei" [The Prime Minister Announced the Three-Year Childcare Leave Extension]. April 18, 2013. http://www.nikkei.com/article/DGXNASFS1804W_Y3A410C1EA1000/ (accessed December 4, 2015).

North, Scott, and Charles Weathers. "The End of Overtime Pay: More Production or Just More Work for Japan's White Collar Workers?" *Asia-Pacific Journal: Japan Focus*. January 9, 2007. http://www.japanfocus.org/-S-North/2320 (accessed November 1, 2013).

O'Donnell, Jayne. "Should Business Execs Meet at Strip Clubs?" *USA Today*. March 22, 2006. http://www.usatoday.com/money/companies/management/2006-03-22-strip-clubs-usat_x.htm (accessed June 1, 2010).

OECD. Better Life Index. http://www.oecdbetterlifeindex.org/topics/work-life-balance/ (accessed May 31, 2015).

——. StatExtracts. "Average Annual Hours Actually Worked per Worker." https://stats.oecd.org/Index.aspx?DataSetCode=ANHRS# (accessed May 31, 2015).

Ogasawara, Yuko. *Office Ladies and Salaried Men: Power, Gender, and Work in Japanese Companies*. Berkeley: University of California Press, 1998.

——. "Women's Solidarity: Company Policies and Japanese Office Ladies. In *Women's Working Lives in East Asia*. Edited by Mary Brinton, 151–79. Stanford: Stanford University Press, 2001.

Okano, Yayo. "Jenda no seiji [Politics of Gender]." In *Gender Free Trouble*. Edited by Ryoko Kimura, 55–74. Tokyo: Hakutakusya, 2005.

Okutsu, Mari, and Masaharu Kuniyoshi. "Kekkon Syussan Ikujikino taisyoku to saisyusyoku" [Resignation and Reemployment during the Period of Marriage, Childbirth, and Child Rearing: Women's Career Development and Issues]. Japan Institute for Labour Policy and Training 105 (2009): 1–213.

Olcott, George. *Conflict and Change: Foreign Ownership and the Japanese Firm*. Cambridge, UK: Cambridge University Press, 2009.

Olcott, George, and Nick Oliver, "The Impact of Foreign Ownership and Gender and Employment Relations in Large Japanese Companies." *Work Employment & Society* 28, no. 2 (2014): 206–24.

O'Leary, Virginia, and M. M. Ryan. "Women Bosses: Counting the Changes or Changes That Count." In *Women in Management: A Developing Presenc*. Edited by M. Tanton. London: Routledge, 1994.

Omika, Naoko. "Sexual Harassment Can Occur among Men." Allabout.co.jp. April 12, 2007. http://allabout.co.jp/health/stressmanage/closeup/CU20070412A/ (accessed June 1, 2010).

Ono, Hiroshi. "Lifetime Employment in Japan: Concepts and Measurements." *Journal of the Japanese and International Economies* 24 (2009): 1–27.

Orey, Michael. "Trouble at Toyota." *Businessweek*. May 22, 2006. http://www.businessweek.com/magazine/content/06_21/b3985078.htm (accessed June 1, 2010).

Osawa, Mari. *Governance of Livelihood Security* [Seikatsu hosho no gabanansu]. Tokyo: Yuhikaku, 2013.

——. *Making Gender Equal Society*. Tokyo: NHK Books, 2004.

——. "Women's Resistance" [Jyosei no teiko ga sekai o jizoku kanou ni suru]. In *Feminism in Japan*. Edited by Syoko Amano, Kimiko Ito, Ruri Ito, Teruko Inoue, Chizuko Ueno, Yumiko Ehara, Mari Osawa, and Mikiyo Kano, 1–39. Tokyo: Iwanami Syoten, 2009.

Paludi, Michele A., and Richard B. Barickman. *Academic and Workplace Sexual Harassment: A Resource Manual*. Albany: State University of New York Press, 1991.

Pardi, Tommaso. "Where Did It Go Wrong? Hybridization and Crisis of Toyota Motor Manufacturing UK, 1989–2001." *International Sociology* 20, no. 1 (2005): 93–118.

Pollak, Andrew. "It's See No Evil, No Harassment in Japan." *New York Times*. May 7, 1996. http://www.nytimes.com/1996/05/07/business/it-s-see-no-evil-have-no-harassment-in-japan.html (accessed June 1, 2010).

Puchiniak, Dan W. "Perverse Rescue in the Lost Decade: Main Banks in the Post-Bubble Era." In *Corporate Governance in the 21st Century*. Edited by Luke Nottage, Leon Wolff, and Kent Anderson, 81–107. Cheltenham, UK: Edward Elgar, 2008.

Purcell, David, Kelly R. MacArthur, and Sarah Samblanet. "Gender and the Glass Ceiling at Work." *Sociology Compass* 4, no. 9. (2010): 705–17.

Raday, Frances. "CEDAW's Substantive Equality and Its Ideological Challengers." In *Equality as a Social Right: Towards a Concept of Substantive Equality in Comparative and International Law* (coordinated by Judy Fudge). Oñati International Institute for the Sociology of Law, 2006. http://www.iisj.net/antBuspre.asp?cod=3657&nombre=3657&prt=1 (accessed November 1, 2012).

Ramseyer, J. Mark, and Eric Rasmusen. *Measuring Judicial Independence: The Political Economy of Judging in Japan*. Chicago: University of Chicago Press, 2003.

Research Institute for Advancement of Living Standards. Rengou Souken Survey. November 2006. http:// rengo-soken.or.jp/report_db/pub/detail.php?uid=39 (accessed March 8, 2012).

Reskin, Barbara F. "Including Mechanisms in Our Model of Ascriptive Inequality." *American Sociological Review* 68 (2003): 1–21.

Reskin, Barbara F., and Debra B. McBrier. "Why Not Ascription? Organizations' Employment of Male and Female Managers." *American Sociological Review* 65, no. 2 (2000): 210–33.

Reskin, Barbara F., and Patricia A. Roos. *Job Queues, Gender Queues: Explaining Women's Inroads into Male Occupations*. Philadelphia: Temple University Press, 1990.

Ridgeway, Cecilia L. "Interaction and the Conservation of Gender Inequality: Considering Employment." *American Sociological Review* 62 (1997): 218–35.

Riviere, Joan. "Womanliness as a Masquerade." In *Formations of Fantasy*. Edited by Victor Burgin, James Donald, and Cora Kaplan, 35–44. London: Methuen, 1986.

Roberson, James E. "Japanese Working-Class Masculinities: Marginalized Complicity." In *Men and Masculinities in Contemporary Japan: Dislocating the Salaryman Doxa*. Edited by James E. Roberson and Nobue Suzuki, 126–43, London: RoutledgeCurzon, 2003.

Roberson, James E., and Nobue Suzuki. *Men and Masculinities in Contemporary Japan: Dislocating the Salaryman Doxa*. London: RoutledgeCurzon, 2003.

Roberts, Glenda. "Balancing Work and Life: Whose Work? Whose Life? Whose Balance?" *Asian Perspective* 29, no. 1 (2005): 175–211.

——. "Similar Outcomes, Different Paths: The Cross-National Transfer of Gendered Regulations of Employment." In *Gendering the Knowledge Economy: Comparative Perspectives*. Edited by Sylvia Walby, Heidi Gottfried, Karin Gottschall, and Mari Osawa. Basingstoke: Palgrave Macmillan, 2007.

Rogers, Jackie K., and Kevin D. Henson. "Hey, Why Don't You Wear a Shorter Skirt: Structural Vulnerability and the Organization of Sexual Harassment in Temporary Clerical Employment." *Gender & Society* 11, no. 2 (1997): 215–27.

Rohlen, Thomas P. "Order in Japanese Society: Attachment, Authority, and Routine." *Journal of Japanese Studies* 15, no. 1 (1989): 5–40.

Sadler, David, and Stuart Lloyd. "Neo-Liberalising Corporate Social Responsibility: A Political Economy of Corporate Citizenship." *Geoforum* 40 (2009): 613–22.

Saguy, Abigail C. "Employment Discrimination or Sexual Violence? Defining Sexual Harassment in American and French Law." *Law and Society Review* 34, no. 4 (2000): 1091–1128.

Sasanuma, Tomoko. "On Indirect Discrimination." *Bulletin of the Society for the Study of Working Women* [*Jyosei rodo kenkyuu zashi*] 49 (2006): 19–32.

Sato, Kazuma, and XinXin Ma, "Ikujikyugyoho no kaiseiga jyosei no keizoku syugyo ni oyobosu eikyo" [Influence of the Childcare Leave Revision on the Women's Continual Employment]. In *Japanese Household Behavior Dynamism IV: Institutional Policy Changes and Employment Behaviors,* 119–39. Tokyo: Keio University Press, 2008.

Schoppa, Leonard. *Race for the Exits: The Unraveling of Japan's System of Social Protection*. Ithaca: Cornell University Press, 2006.

Schwartz, Frank J., and Susan J. Pharr, eds. *The State of Civil Society in Japan.* Cambridge, UK: Cambridge University Press, 2003.

Segi, Hiroshi. *Zetsubo no saibansyo* [Hopeless Court of Justice]. Tokyo: Kodansya Gendai Shinsyo, 2014.

Shibata, Hiromichi. "Productivity and Skill at a Japanese Transplant and Its Parent Company." *Work and Occupation* 28, no. 2 (2001): 234–60.

Shigematsu, Setsu. *Scream from the Shadows: The Women's Liberation Movement in Japan*. Minneapolis: University of Minnesota Press, 2012.

Shimada, Yoichi. "Working Hour Schemes for White-Collar Employees in Japan." *Japan Labor Review* 1, no. 4 (2004): 48–67.

Shiota, Sakiko. "Japanese Feminism and Current Japanese Social Policy: 1970–1990" [Gendai feminizumu to nihon no syakaiseisaku]. In *Feminism in Japan*. Edited by Syoko Amano, Kimiko Ito, Ruri Ito, Teruko Inoue, Chizuko Ueno, Yumiko Ehara, Mari Osawa, and Mikiyo Kano, 119–39. Tokyo: Iwanami Syoten, 2009.

Shire, Karen A. "Gendered Organization and Workplace Culture in Japanese Customer Services." *Social Science Japan Journal* 3, no. 1 (2000): 37–58.

——. "Stability and Change in Japanese Employment Institutions: The Case of Temporary Work." *ASIEN* 84 (2002): 21–30.

Shire, Karen A., and Jun Imai. "Flexible Equality: Men and Women in Employment in Japan." Duisburg Working Papers on East Asian Studies 30/2000. Institute for East Asian Studies. March 2000. http://www.uni-due.de/in-east/fileadmin/publications/ gruen/paper30.pdf (accessed March 7, 2012).

Showa Shell Co. Labor Union Home Page, 2012. http://homepage3.nifty.com/showashelllaborunion/ (accessed November 1, 2012).

Smith, Vicki. *Crossing the Great Divide: Worker Risk and Opportunity in the New Economy.* Ithaca: Cornell University Press, 2001.

——. *Managing in the Corporate Interest: Control and Resistance in an American Bank.* Berkeley: University of California Press, 1990.

Stainback, Kevin, and Soyoung Kwon. "Female Leaders, Organizational Power and Sex Segregation." *Annals of the American Academy of Political and Social Science* 639, no. 1 (2012): 217–35.

Stainback, Kevin, Donald Tomaskovic-Devey, and Sheryl Skaggs. "Organizational Approaches to Inequality: Inertia, Relative Power and Environments." *Annual Review of Sociology* 36 (2010): 225–47.

Starich, Megan. "Comment: The 2006 Revisions to Japan's Equal Opportunity Employment Law—A Narrow Approach to a Pervasive Problem." *Pacific Rim Law & Policy Journal* 16 (2007): 551–78.

Steinmo, Sven. *The Evolution of Modern States: Sweden Japan and the United States,* Cambridge, UK: Cambridge University Press, 2010.

Stockford, Marjorie A. *The Bellwomen: The Story of the Landmark AT&T Sex Discrimination Case.* New Brunswick, NJ: Rutgers University Press, 2004.

Stone, Pamela. "The Rhetoric and Reality of 'Opting Out.'" *Contexts* 6, no. 4 (2007): 14–19.

Supreme Court General Secretariat, Japan. "Summary of the Meetings of Labor, Civil, and Administrative Judges, July 10, 2001." *Roudo houritsu jyunpou* [Labor Law Journal] 1524 (2002): 14–23.

Suzuki, Naoko. "Kigyo no kosodate shien o megutte: genjyo to kadai" [Japanese Companies' Support of Childrearing: Current Status and Issues]. *Reference* 54, no. 8 (2004): 7–30.

Suzuki, Yumi. "Sexual Harassment Prevention Handbook." 1994. http://www5f.biglobe. ne.jp/~constanze/nomarin267.html (accessed June 1, 2010).

Swissinfo. "Novartis to Pay Millions for Sex Discrimination." May 19, 2010. http:// www.swissinfo.ch/eng/novartis-to-pay-millions-for-sex-discrimination/8903518 (accessed November 1, 2014).

Tabuchi, Hiroko. "Arrests in Olympus Scandal Point to Widening Inquiry into a Cover-Up." *New York Times.* February 16, 2012. http://www.nytimes.com/ 2012/02/17/business/global/7-arrested-in-olympus-accounting-cover-up. html?_r=0 (accessed November 1, 2013).

Tachibanaki, Toshiaki. *Current Issues surrounding Women at Work and in the Family: Proposals Going beyond This Age of Decreasing Population.* Tokyo: Minerva Shobou, 2005.

Tajfel, Henri. *Human Groups and Social Categories.* Cambridge: Cambridge University Press, 1981.

Takeda, Masatsugu. "Human Resource Management under the Era of Declining Population in Japan" [Syousikajidai no jinji roumu kanrinitsuite]. *Ritsumeikan keieigaku* [Ritsumeikan Management] 44, no. 5 (2006): 19–44.

Tomaskovic-Devey, Donald, and Sheryl Skaggs. "An Establishment-Level Test of the Statistical Discrimination Hypothesis." *Work and Occupations* 26, no. 2 (1999): 422–45.

Tsujimura, Miyoko. "Employment, Social Security, and Gender." In *Employment, Social Security, and Gender.* Edited by Sayaka Dake and Shigeto Tanaka, 93–120. Sendai, Japan: Tohoku University Press, 2007.

Ueno, Chizuko. "Gender Equality and Multiculturalism under Japanese New-Liberalist Reform in the Era of Globalization." In *Gender Equality in Multicultural Societies: Gender, Diversity, and Conviviality in the Age of Globalization.* Edited by

Miyoko Tsujimura and Mari Osawa, 25–42. Sendai, Japan: Tohoku University Press, 2010.

——. *Ikinobiru Tameno Shiso* [Ideas for Survival]. Tokyo: Iwanami Shoten, 2006.

——. *Onna toiu kairaku* [The Pleasure of Being a Woman]. Tokyo: Keiso Syobou, 1991.

Uggen, Christopher, and Chika Shinohara. "Sexual Harassment Comes of Age: A Comparative Analysis of the United States and Japan." *Sociological Quarterly* 50 (2009): 201–34.

United States Department of Labor. Wage and Hour Division (WHD), 2011. http://www.dol.gov/whd/regs/compliance/fairpay/fs17a_overview.htm (accessed November 1, 2013).

Ushikubo, Hideki, and Takeshi Murakami. *Nihon no rodou o sekai ni tou* [Examining Japanese Labor Standards: Learning ILO Treaty]. Tokyo: Iwanami Syoten, 2014.

Utting, Peter. "Corporate Responsibility and the Movement of Business." *Development in Practice* 15 (2005): 375–88.

——. "The Struggle for Corporate Accountability." *Development and Change* 39, no. 6 (2008): 959–75.

Vogel, Steven K. *Japan Remodeled: How Government and Industry Are Reforming Japanese Capitalism*. Ithaca: Cornell University Press, 2006.

Wajcman, Judy. *Managing Like a Man: Men and Woman in Corporate Management*. University Park: Pennsylvania State University Press, , 1998.

Watts, Jacqueline. "'Allowed into a Man's World' Meanings of Work–Life Balance: Perspectives of Women Civil Engineers as 'Minority' Workers in Construction." *Gender, Work & Organization* 16, no. 1 (2009): 37–59.

——. "Porn, Pride and Pessimism: Experiences of Women Working in Professional Construction Roles." *Work, Employment & Society* 21, no. 2 (2007): 299–316.

Welzel, Christian, and Ronald Inglehart. "The Role of Ordinary People in Democratization." *Journal of Democracy* 19, no. 1 (2008): 126–40.

West, Mark. "Employment Market Institutions and Japanese Working Hours." 2003. University of Michigan. *Law & Economics Working Papers Archive: 2003–2009*. Paper 22. http://repository.law.umich.edu/law_econ_archive/art22 (accessed March 8, 2012).

Williams, Christine L. *Still a Man's World: Men Who Do 'Women's' Work*. Berkeley: University of California Press, 1995.

Williams, Christine L., Patti A. Giuffre, and Kirsten Dellinger. "Sexuality in the Workplace: Organizational Control, Sexual Harassment, and the Pursuit of Pleasure." *Annual Review of Sociology* 25 (1999): 73–93.

Williams, Christine L., Chandra Muller, and Kristine Kilanski. "Gendered Organizations in the New Economy." *Gender & Society* 26 (2012): 549–73.

Williams, Joan C. "Creating Workplace Gender Equality." Paper presented at the Annual Meeting of the American Sociological Association. Denver, CO. August 2012.

——. *Reshaping the Work-Family Debate: Why Men and Class Matter*. Cambridge: Harvard University Press, 2010.

Wilson, Fiona, and Paul Thompson. "Sexual Harassment as an Exercise of Power." *Gender, Work, and Organization* 8, no. 1 (2001): 61–83.

Wilthagen, Ton, and F. H. Tros. "The Concept of Flexicurity: A New Approach to Regulating Employment and Labour Markets." *Transfer: European Review of Labour and Research* 10, no. 2 (2004): 166–86.

Witt, Michael A. *Changing Japanese Capitalism: Societal Coordination and Institutional Adjustment*. Cambridge, UK: Cambridge University Press, 2006.

——. "Japan: Coordinated Capitalism between Institutional Change and Structural Inertia." In *Oxford Handbook of Asian Business Systems.* Edited by Michael A Witt and Gordon Redding, 100–122. Oxford: Oxford University Press, 2014.

Witt, Michael A., and Gordon Redding. "Culture, Meaning and Institutions: Executive Rationale in Germany and Japan." *Journal of International Business Studies* 40 (2009): 859–85.

Wolff, Leon. "The Corporate Regulation of Gender Harassment in Japan." In *Employment, Social Security and Gender.* Edited by Sayaka Dake and Shigeto Tanaka, 71–92. Sendai, Japan: Tohoku University Press, 2007.

——. "The Death of Lifelong Employment in Japan?" In *Corporate Governance in the 21st Century: Japan's Gradual Transformation.* Edited by Luke Nottage, Leon Wolff, and Kent Anderson, 53–80. Cheltenham, UK: Edward Elgar, 2008.

——. "Lifelong Employment, Labor Law and the Lost Decade: The End of a Job for Life in Japan?" In *Innovation and Change in Japanese Management.* Edited by Parissa Hghirian, 77–138. London: Palgrave Macmillan, 2010.

Wood, Glenice J., and Janice Newton. "Childlessness and Women Managers: 'Choice,' Context and Discourses." *Gender, Work & Organization* 13, no. 4 (2006): 338–58.

Working Women's Network. Newsletter 76. July 31, 2014.

——. Newsletter 79. April 28, 2015.

——. "Sumitomo kagaku sabetsu jiken wkai ni tsuiteno bengodan kankai" [Report on Sumitomo Chemical]. June 29, 2004. wwn-net.org/wp-content/themes/WWN/pdf/02.pdf (accessed October 1, 2012).

——. *WWN Report to the United Nations Committee on Economic, Social and Cultural Rights,* for the Presessional Working Group 49th Session Japan. Osaka, Japan. March, 2012.

——. Request to the Supreme Court: The Chugoku Electric Power Co. no. 1908, case 2327. December 24, 2013. WWN symposium on the Chugoku Electric Power Co. Case, December 23, 2013. Meiji University, Tokyo, Japan.

Yamada, Toshio. "Kigyo shakai to shin shakai" [Corporate Society and Civil Society]. In *Gendai shimin shakai to kigyo kokka* [Contemporary Civil Society and the Enterprise State]. Edited by Hirata Kiyoaki, Yamada Toshio, Kato Tetsuro, Kurosawa Nobuyuki, and Ito Masazumi, 47–74. Tokyo, Japan: Ochanomizu Shobo, 1994.

Yamaguchi, Kazuo. "Howaito karaa saisyain no kanrisyokuwariai no danjyo kakusano ketteiyouin" [White-Collar Regular Employees Managers and Gender Gap]. *Rieti Discussion Paper Series* 13-J-069 (2013).

——. "Women's Employment and Dysfunction of Japanese Firms." RIETI Policy Discussion Paper Series 13-P-002 (January 2013): 1–64.

Yamaguchi, Kazuo, and Yoshio Higuchi. *Ronso: Work-Life Balance in Japan* [*Nihon no waku raifu baransu*]. Tokyo: Nihon Keizai Shimbunsha, 2008.

Yamakawa, Ryuichi. "We've Only Just Begun: The Law of Sexual Harassment in Japan." *Hastings International and Comparative Law Review* 22, no. 3 (1999): 523–66.

Yu, Wei-hsin. *Gendered Trajectories: Women, Work, and Social Change in Japan and Taiwan.* Stanford: Stanford University Press, 2009.

Yunoki, Yasuko. "From the Court: Showa Shell Co. Wage Discrimination Case." In *Bulletin of the Society for the Study of Working Women* [Jyosei rodo kenkyuu zashi] 54, 160–62. Tokyo: Aoki Syoten, 2010.

Zippel, Kathrin S. *The Politics of Sexual Harassment: A Comparative Study of the United States, the European Union, and Germany.* Cambridge, UK: Cambridge University Press, 2006.

——. "Practices of Implementation of Sexual Harassment Policies: Individual versus Collective Strategies." *Review of Policy Research* 20, no. 1 (2003): 175–98.

# Index

Page numbers followed by the letter *t* indicate tables.